Connecticut
Revolutionary Pensioners

Connecticut
Revolutionary Pensioners

Compiled by

**The Connecticut Daughters
of the American Revolution**

Baltimore
GENEALOGICAL PUBLISHING CO., INC.
1982

Originally published as Appendix A of the
Twenty-First Report of the National Society
of the Daughters of the American Revolution,
March 1, 1917, to March 1, 1918 (Washington, D.C., 1919).
Reprinted, by arrangement with the NSDAR, by
Genealogical Publishing Co., Inc.
Baltimore, 1982.
Library of Congress Catalogue Card Number 82-81255
International Standard Book Number 0-8063-0986-5
Made in the United States of America

PENSION RECORDS OF THE REVOLUTIONARY SOLDIERS FROM CONNECTICUT.

FOREWORD.

The copying of the pension records of the Revolutionary soldiers from Connecticut, which are herein published, was due primarily to the initiative and efforts of the Connecticut Daughters of the American Revolution. In 1913 it was brought to their attention that the original records on file in the Pension Office in Washington, D. C., were in danger of destruction by fire, exposure, and careless handling, and that copies should be made before it was too late. Accordingly, at their State conference in March, 1914, it was voted to petition the Connecticut Legislature of 1915 to make an appropriation for this purpose. To carry out this vote the State regent, Mrs. John Laidlaw Buel, appointed a committee, known as the Pension Records Committee, Connecticut Daughters of the American Revolution, with Mrs. George Maynard Minor, vice president general, National Society Daughters of the American Revolution, from Connecticut, as chairman.

Mrs. Minor's committee drew up a bill for presentation to the legislature and enlisted the organized effort of all the chapters of the Daughters of the American Revolution in Connecticut in its behalf by urging them to approach their local representatives and to attend the hearing on the bill before the appropriations committee. The interest and cooperation of Mr. George S. Godard, librarian of the Connecticut State library, was also secured by the committee.

The result was an appropriation by the legislature of $1,000, the expenditure of which was placed in the hands of Mr. Godard, who requested that the Connecticut Daughters of the American Revolution Pension Records Committee remain in existence as an advisory committee to him in the work to be undertaken.

It was under the able and enthusiastic direction of Mr. Godard that the work of copying these invaluable records was instituted and brought to a successful conclusion. The copies are safely housed in the Connecticut State library at Hartford, to which institution we are indebted for the photostat copies from which this publication is made.

[Revolutionary pensioners who served from Connecticut and whose applications are on file in the Pension Office, Washington, D. C. Copied by Mrs. Amos G. Draper, formerly registrar general, D. A. R. Volume I: A–I. Hartford Connecticut State Library, 1918.]

NOTE.

Cont. (Conn.) means that a man was paid by the United States Government but enlisted from the State of Connecticut.

Cont. and Conn. means that he served in the Continental, also in the State regiments.

Rejected widows' claims.—Where there is nothing after the name that means that either the soldier did not apply or was rejected. In list beginning " E " notice is made where soldier was pensioned and the widow alone was rejected.

The service for which a man was pensioned is not necessarily all of the service that he actually performed. Often, from old age, a man neglected to

1

mention part of his service; and again he might be unable after the lapse of years to prove it.

S means survivor's file; W, widow's file; and R, rejected file. Often a man was pensioned and the widow's claim rejected for technical reasons, she may not have been married before 1794, or not have been a widow at the time of the passage of the act, etc. The case is marked by the last action, so that most of the cases marked R are really proven claims as far as the soldier is concerned.

BLWt. means bounty land warrant. Those issued before 1804 are marked first with the number of the warrant; then with the number of the acres granted. Those issued later are marked first with the number of the warrant, second with the number of acres, third with 55, indicating that the act under which the warrant was issued was passed in 1855. This act allowed children as well as pensioners to obtain land.

REVOLUTIONARY PENSIONERS WHO SERVED FROM CONNECTICUT, AS SHOWN BY THE PAPERS IN THE OFFICE OF THE COMMISSIONER OF PENSIONS, WASHINGTON, D. C.

There are 776 drawers in the files, 12 of which are filled with other material or are vacant, leaving 764 drawers. These are divided as follows:

Letter.	Number of drawers.	Number of cases from Connecticut.	Average.	Letter.	Number of drawers.	Number of cases from Connecticut.	Average.
A	23	400	17	N	12½	166	13
B	83	1,451	17½	O	7	111	16
C	67	1,030	15	P	43	732	17
D	39	466	12	Q	1	7	7
E	13½	183	13	R	35	507	14½
F	26½	424	16	S	77	1,106	14½
G	36	545	15	T	30	456	15¼
H	66	1,018	15	U	1	19	19
I	2½	35	14½	V	9	21	2½
J	15½	271	17	W	60	923	15¼
K	17	222	13	X [1]	...	...	...
L	34	414	12	Y	4	25	6¼
M	60½	617	10½	Z	1	1	1

[1] No pensioner from any State.

The greatest percentage to a drawer is in those whose names begin with the letter "B."
The smallest in those whose names begin with the letter "Z."
The total number of names from Connecticut are 11,150.
According to drawers the letters are graded as follows: B, S, C, H, M, W, P, D, G, R, L, T, F, A, K, J, E, N, V, O, Y, I, U, Q, Z, the last three being equal.
According to number of pensioners from Connecticut, B, S, C, H, W, P, M, G, R, D, T, F, L, A, J, K, E, N, O, I, Y, V, U, Q, Z.

Revolutionary pensioners who served from Connecticut as found in the Pension Office, Washington, D. C.

A.

ABBE, ABBEE, ABBEY or ABBY.
    Eleazer.. BLWt. 267–100
    George.. S 11931
    Hezekiah, Conn. & Conn. Sea service................................ S 21034
    James or Joseph James.. R 1
    Jeduthan (Qr. Mr. Serg't. 1818).................................... W 12225
        Lucretia Roberts, former wid. of.
    Joseph James. (See James.)
    Nathaniel.. W 26215
        Nancy Little, former wid. of.
    Richard, wid. Lydia... W 17197
    Samuel, BLWt. 101726–160–55....................................... W 5150
        Margaret Mitchell, former wid. of.
    Thomas, Cont. (Conn.)... S 38105
        (Pensioner, 1818).
    William Conn. & Cont. wid. Lydia................................... W 20556
        (N. Y. in 1818)

ABBAT, ABBATT, ABBOT or ABBOTT.
Aaron (Conn. 1818; 82 in 1840, New Canaan.).. S 38101
Asa, wid. Elizabeth... W 20558
Benjamin, Conn. & N. Y... S 11933
James (Fairfield Co. in 1832).. S 17229
John.. W 22434
    Temperance Tarbox, former wid. of.
Joseph, wid. Nancy... W 20553
Stephen (Fairfield Co. in 1832).. S 17231
ABEL or ABELL. Abel (Pensioner in 1818; Middlesex Co. in 1832; 77 in 1840, Chatham.)...... S 11930
David, Conn. & Cont.. S 10314
Elijah.. S 17805
John.. S 4257
Simon, wid. Betsy.. R 7
William, wid. Lois.. W 20559
ABORN. Samuel (Conn. in 1818)... S 38103
ABRO. Benajah (Conn. in 1818)... S 38104
ACHMET. Hamet (81 in 1840, Middletown).. S 38107
ACHOR, ACOR or ACRE... S 39144
Jacob... BLWt. 1145-100
ACKELEY, ACKLEY, AKELEY or AKELY.
Ahira, wid. Miriam... W 4872
Champion, wid. Abigail... W 5197
Edward... S 11935
Elihu.. S 44544
Isaac (Chalker)... S 17232
    (Middlesex Co. 1832; 80 in 1840, East Haddam, known in later life as Chalker, according
    to his grandson.)
Ithamer.. S 28614
Nathaniel.. R 20
Simeon... S 18680
Stephen. wid. Mehitable.. W 17198
    (Middlesex Co. 1832.)
Thomas (Conn. in 1818).. S 38106
ACOR or ACRE. (See ACHOR.)
ADAMS, ADDAMS or ADDOMS.
Abijah, Conn. & R. I.. R 24
Abraham (Fairfield Co. in 1832)... S 14914
Benjamin, Conn. & Cont., wid. Susan.. W 20570
David (Serj't. in N. Y. in 1818)... S 45171
David, BLWt. 30-400, Surgeon was issued Jan. 28, 1790. No papers.
Deliverance, Conn. & Penna... S 45170
    (Penna. in 1818).
Ebenezer, Conn. & Cont... S 37647
    (Conn. in 1818)
Elijah, wid. Sarah.. W 21604
Elijah, Conn. & Mass... S 2494
Elijah, Conn. & N. Y., wid. Sarah... R 46
    BLWt. 34592-160-55
Elisha.. R 28
Gideon, Conn. & Cont., wid. Rhoda.. W 23395
    (N. Y. in 1818).
Hitty, former wid. of Asa Hoskins.. W 25366
James.. S 11937
Jedediah, Conn. & Cont... S 49293
    (Penna. 1818).
John.. S 11947
John (Orleans Co., Vt.)... S 15728
Joseph (Windham Co. in 1832) Wid. Rebecca....................................... R 45
Joshua (Fairfield Co. in 1832), BLWt. 13201-160-55 wid. Sarah..................... W 25337
Levi, Conn. & Vt... S 11941
Luke (Conn. in 1818)... S 37652
Mary former wid. of John Hutchinson... W 20571
Moses (Ohio in 1818)... S 45174
Reuben, wid. Abigail... W 23399
Reuben, wid. Lydia... W 20568
Roswell, Conn. & Privateer, wid. Eunice.. W 23411
Samuel (Vt. in 1818)... S 38483
    Vt. res. & Agency... BLWt. 955-100
Samuel C. (Windham Co. in 1832; 76 in 1840, Canterbury)......................... S 11948
Shubael.. S 28615
Silas... S 12905
Timothy, wid. Susannah.. W 21600
    (Soldier in Windham Co. in 1832; wid. 98 in 1840, Canterbury.)
Titus... R 50
William (N. Y. in 1832).. S 11946
William (Lisbon, New London Co., in 1832; 87 in 1840, Lisbon)..................... S 45173
ADDEE or ADYE, Caleb... S 6465
John.. S 21595
ADKINS, David (80 in 1840, Plymouth)... S 12012
Isaiah (Corp. N. Y. in 1818).. S 49292
    BLWt. 649-100.
Jabez... S 33248
Luther, wid. Azubah (Mass. in 1818).. W 23400
    (See also ATKINS.)
ADYE. (See ADDEE.)
AERY. (See AVERY.)

3

AGARD, Hezekiah.. S 23092
    John... R 62
    Joseph, Conn. & N. Y... S 45179
    Noah, Conn. & N. Y... S 45180
AGGLESTON. (See EGGLESTON.)
AIKEN, AKIN, or AKINS, James, wid. Amy, Conn. & N. Y. service...................... W 1349
    Seth, wid. Sally... W 25341
    Thomas.. S 4258
    Thomas.. S 16595
AINSWORTH, Edward, wid. Polly... R 67
AKELEY. (See ACKELEY.)
AKEN or AKINS. (See AIKEN.)
ALCOCK, ALLCOCKS, ALCOX, or ALLCOX.
    Asa, Conn. & Cont. (N. Y. in 1818)... S 23513
    David (as Alcox in N. Y. in 1818, as Serj't)...................................... S 45186
    John Blakesley, wid. Lois.. W 17209
    Samuel, wid. Lydia... W 17211
ALDEN, Judah, Cont. (Conn.)... BLWt. 1150–300
    Roger, wid. Elizabeth... W 4113
ALDERMAN, Ephraim.. S 45185
    Gad, Cont. & Conn... S 32639
    Timothy, wid. Ruth... R 77
ALDRICH or ALDRICK, John, Conn. & Navy... S 21601
ALEXANDER, Benjamin, Conn. & Cont., wid. Elizabeth.............................. R 84
    James (N. Y. in 1818)... S 38490
    James, Conn. & R. I... S 16599
      (Voluntown, Windham Co. in 1832.)
ALFORD or ALVORD.
    Alexander, Conn. & Green Mt. Boys... W 20600
      (Vt. in 1818.) Wid. Elizabeth or Eliza.
    Benedict, Conn., Mass. & Vt.. S 8016
    Eber (Hartford Co. in 1832; 79 in 1840, Canton, as Aber)..................... S 11966
    John (N. Y. in 1818)... S 39932
    John (90 in 1840, Fairfield).. S 15314
    Phineas.. S 18295
    Seth (Middlesex Co. in 1832).. S 11959
ALGER or ALGIER.
    Asa, Conn. & Mass., wid. Sarah.. R 94
    Elijah.. S 11962
    Nathaniel, wid. Dorcas... W 5612
      BLWt. 30593–160–55.
ALING. (See ALLEN.)
ALLCOX. (See ALCOCK.)
ALLEN, ALLIN, ALLING or ALLYN.
    Abel, Conn. & Cont., wid. Phebe (Conn. in 1818).............................. W 20595
    Abiel, Cont. (Conn.), wid. Lydia (N. Y. in 1818)............................... W 16807
    Abner, Conn. & Cont., wid. Lucy (Mass. in 1818).............................. W 20588
    Amasa, Conn. & N. Y. (N. Y. in 1818).. S 44547
    Amos, wid. Hannah... W 20582
    Amos, Conn. & Mass.. S 28619
    Asahel, wid. Eleanor... W 25346
      (Tolland Co. in 1832.)
    Asher, wid. Elizabeth.. W 9325
      (Ohio in 1818.)
    Azor, wid. Anna... W 20592
    Benjamin (N. Y. in 1818).. S 46171
    Cady, wid. Parthenia... W 16094
    Charles (Hartford Co. in 1832)... S 14916
    Cyrus, wid. Eleanor.. W 8094
    Daniel.. S 11956
    Daniel.. S 37656
    David... S 5241
    David, wid. Desire.. W 15533
    David... S 39930
    David, wid. Lydia... W 17212
    Diarea.. S 12917
    Ebenezer... S 11968
    Ebenezer... S 37662
    Ebenezer, wid. Huldah... W 8095
    Edward, wid. Abigail... W 20596
      BLWt. 682–100; BLWt. 87–60–55.
    Eleazer.. S 35171
    Elias, Conn. & Privateer.
      Wid. Amy.. R 99
    Eliphalet.. R 109
    Enos, wid. Mabel.. W 17207
      (New Haven Co. in 1832; wid. was 75 in 1840 in Wallingford.)
    Ezra, Conn. & Mass... W 27268
      Catharine Hunt, former wid. of.
    Gabriel, Conn. & Conn. Sea Service.. S 12915
      (New Haven Co, in 1832.)
    George, Conn. & Cont., wid. Sabra.. W 21606
      (Conn. in 1818.)
    Heman, Cont. (Conn.) & Green Mt. Boys... W 18285
      Abigail Wadham, former wid. of.
    Hezekiah.. S 23093
    Howard (N. Y. in 1818).. S 45204

4

ALLEN, ALLIN, ALLING or ALLYN—Continued.
Isaac, Cont. serv. Conn. res. & Agency.. S 37654
    (Conn. in 1818, as priv. Hazen's reg't. d Oct. 8, 1818.)
James.. R 12085
Jared, Conn. & R. I... S 11967
    (Windham Co. in 1832.)
Job, wid. Abigail.. W 17210
John, Conn. & Cont. wid. Electa... W 25347
    (Wid. was 79 in 1840, Plymouth.)
John, Conn. & Mass... S 17235
John. Conn. & N. Y... W 23429
    Persis Coolidge, former wid. of.
Jonathan... S 12910
Jonathan... S 32094
Jonathan, Conn. & Cont.. S 45203
Joseph.. S 11963
Joseph, wid. Lucy.. R 130
Lathrop, wid. Abigail.. W 17208
    (N. Y. in 1818 as Capt.)
Levi... S 11969
Luke.. S 16030
Luke.. S 18296
Othniel, wid. Phebe.. W 17202
    (Conn. in 1818.)
Parley, wid. Catherine.. W 17206
Phineas or Phinehas... S 45200
Phineas, Conn. & Mass.. S 45199
Reuben, wid. Rebecca... R 136
Reuben, Conn. & N. Y... R 137
Robert, BLWt. 29–200 Lieut. issued Aug. 3, 1796. No papers.
Samuel, wid. Susan... W 17201
    (N. Y. in 1818.)
Seth... S 11952
Sluman, wid. Hannah.. W 20576
    BLWt. 32226–160–55.
Stephen.. S 11964
Stephen.. S 12920
Stephen, Conn. & R. I... S 11965
Stephen, Cont. (Conn.)... S 37664
Timothy, Conn. & Cont... S 29580
    BLWt. 82–300.
Titus, wid. Abigail B.. W 25367
    BLWt. 19760–160–55.
William, wid. Rebecca... ----
William, wid. Rebecca... W 10353
    (Fairfield Co. in 1832; 75 in 1840, Westport.)
William Cornelius (N. Y. in 1818).. S 4519c
Wolcott.. S 18687
ALLIN, ALLING or ALLYN. (See ALLEN.)
ALTON, William, wid. Sarah.. W 17205
    (Wid. was 77 in 1840 in Thompson.)
ALVORD. (See ALFORD.)
AMADON. (See AMIDON.)
AMBLER, James, Cont., Conn. & N. Y... S 11977
Peter, Cont. service, Conn. res. & Agency, wid. Hannah.................................... W 25369
    (Hannah was 77 in 1840 at Danbury.)
Squire, Cont. service, Conn. res. & Agency, Jerusha Beers, former wid. of, BLWt. 194–60–55. W 205
    BLWt. 5373 & 12727 were issued June 27, 1791. Her former husband was Squire Ambler.
    Her later husband, Phineas Beers, was also pensioned, S 16635.
Stephen, Cont. (Conn.)... S. 37665
    (Conn. in 1818.)
AMEDON. (See AMIDON.)
AMES, Amos, Conn. & Cont., BLWt. 2396–100.. S 45505
Asa.. S 11973
Asahel.. S 45207
Daniel.. S 17237
    (New London Co. in 1832; 84 in 1840, Montville.)
David... S 11975
Elijah, wid. Cynthia, BLWt. 50810–160–55.. W 5615
Everit or Everitt.. S 37666
    (Conn. in 1818, as Everit.)
John, Navy (Conn.), wid. Sally or Sarah, BLWt. 28544–160–55........................... W 20601
Joseph, wid. Hannah, also EAMES.. W 17213
    (New London Co. in 1832; wid. 80 in 1840, Norwich.)
Nathaniel, BLWt. 5215–160–55.. S 11979
Samuel, wid. Axsa or Acksa.. W 25348
    (New Haven Co. in 1832.)
Zebulon (Vt. in 1818)... S 41413
See also EAMES and EMES.
AMIDON, AMADON or AMEDON.
Asenath, former wid. of Simon Skeels, Cont. (Conn.).. W 20605
Jacob, wid. Hannah.. W 23438
Jedediah or Jedidiah... S 14917
    (Windham Co. in 1832.)
Jonathan, wid. Keturah.. W 23441
    (Vt. in 1818, Amadon.)
Moses... S 11976

ANDERSON, Asa.. S 15732
   Daniel (Fairfield Co. in 1832).. S 14919
   James, wid. Abigail.. W 23451
     (Wid. was 81 in 1840 in Hartford.)
   James, Conn. & Cont.. S 37671
   John, wid. Linda.. W 20621
   Lemuel, wid. Rachel, BLWt. 14662–160–55................................... W 20615
   Robert (Middlesex Co. in 1832).. S 10325
   Samuel... R 200
   Thomas (Conn. in 1818).. S 37668
     BLWt. 28–200, Lieut., was issued Feb. 5, 1790. No papers.
   Thomas, Conn. & Vt., wid. Alice, BLWt. 12849–160–55..................... W 17216
   Timothy, Conn. & Privateer.. S 31522
     (Hartford Co. in 1832; 78 in 1840.)
ANDREAS, ANDRES, OR ANDRESS. (See ANDREWS.)
ANDREWS, ANDRES, ANDRESS, or ANDRUS or ANDRUSS.
   Abner Cont. (Conn.).. S 19899½
     (Middlesex Co. p. 648.)
   Amos (Conn. in 1818)... S 37679
   Andrew, wid. Mary... W 15538
   Benjamin... S 17239
   Benjamin... S 11988
   Clement, Conn. & Mass... S 44304
     (Ohio in 1818, as Andrus.)
   David... S 5244
   David... S 46495
   Ebenezer... R 221
   Eli... S 11989
   Elijah.. S 12935
   Elijah.. S 11983
   Elisha.. S 11985
   Elisha, wid. Anna, Cont. (Conn.), BLWt. 587–100........................... W 16172
   Ephraim, wid. Asenath R... W 1795
     (Tolland Co. in 1832.) BLWt. 26503–160–55.
   Ethan.. S 23515
   Giles... R 1493
   Hezekiah, wid. Rhoda.. W 17215
     (Wid. was 83 in 1840, Berlin.)
   James, wid. Lois... W 15542
   Jeremiah, wid. Cynthia, BLWt. 36630–160–55............................... W 25350
   John, wid. Sarah, BLWt. 16257–160–55..................................... W 5621
   John, Conn. & Cont.. S 11990
   John.. R 214
   John, Cont. (Conn.) & Mass.. S 38501
   John, Cont. (Conn.), wid. Lydia... W 23442
   Jonathan, Conn. & Cont., wid. Sopphia...................................... W 17214
     (Conn. in 1818; wid. was 76 in 1840 at Canton.)
   Joseph, Mercy... W 20612
   Josiah.. S 16032
   Josiah, Cont. (Conn.), BLWt. 86–100... S 37670
   Moses, Conn. & Mass... S 30247
   Nathan, Conn. & R. I.. S 19525
   Nathaniel, wid. Jerusha, BLWt. 19753–160–55.............................. W 4117
   Phinehas... S 12928
   Richard (N. Y. in 1832).. S 12931
   Richard, wid. Catharine (1818).. W 21616
     (Wid. was 87 in 1840, Simsbury.)
   Samuel, BLWt. 15424–160–55.. S 45218
   Samuel, wid. Mary Lee... W 25351
     Conn. & Privateer.
   Samuel, Conn. & N. Y.. S 11980
   Samuel, wid. Elizabeth... R 222
   Samuel J., Cont. (Conn.)... S 11982
   Theodore (Conn. in 1818).. S 37669
   Thomas... S 12933
   Thomas, Conn. & Cont... S 45219
   Thomas, Conn., Cont. & Privateer... S 5247
   Timothy, wid. Mary.. W 20620
     (N. Y. in 1818.)
   William.. S 11981
   William.. S 37678
   William, wid. Rosetta.. W 23450
   William, Conn. & Cont., BLWt. 19–200.
     Lieut. in Crane's reg't. Art. issued Aug. 12, 1789. No papers.
ANNABIL, Ebenezer, Conn. & Conn. Sea Service, wid. Ann.................... W 5629
ANNIS, Elizabeth, former wid. of Jason Harris................................ W 23443
ANSWERT, Appollos... S 32657
ANTHONY or ANTONY, Jack (colored), BLWt. 297–100.
   Samuel... S 14918
APLEY, Josiah (Litchfield Co. in 1832)... S 16607
APPELL, Peter, French Navy, Sea Service (Conn.), U. S. Revenue Service.... R 235
ARCHER, Amasa (Middlesex Co. in 1832)....................................... S 17242
   Crippen (Conn. in 1818) wid. Jemima.. W 21617
   Obadiah.. S 28623
ARES. (See AYRES.)
AREY. (See AVERY.)
ARMSBEY. (See ORMSBEE.)

ARMSTRONG, Daniel (Conn. in 1818)... S 37681
   Ebenezer, Conn. & Cont.. S 44298
   Jabez... R 250
   James, wid. Miriam, Conn. & Cont.. W 25360
     (Wid. was 84 in 1840, Washington.)
   James, Conn. & Cont., wid. Nabby... W 25372
     (Wid. was 75 in 1840, Franklin.)
   Jeremiah.. S 21610
ARNOLD, Fenner... S 5250
   Isaac (Tolland Co. in 1832; 76 in 1840, Mansfield)............................. S 31526
   Jabez, Conn., Cont. & Mass... S 14922
   John... S 19183
   Jonathan, wid. Polly, Conn. & N.Y... W 8102
     BLWt. 887–100. BLWt. 212–60–55.
   Jonathan, wid. Lucy, Cont.. W 17218
   Levi, former widow, Fanny Harris.. W 9050
     Conn. & Privateer, BLWt. 67536–160–55.
   Samuel B. P. (Middlesex Co., 1832).. S 31524
   Seth, Conn. & Privateer.. S 18690
   Timothy, Conn. & Mass., wid. Anna.. W 15549
ASHCRAFT, William, Conn. Cont. & Navy... S 37687
   (Conn. in 1818, as ASHCROFT; New London, 86 in 1840.)
ASHER, Gad (New Haven Co. in Conn. Men, p. 648).............................. S 17244
ASHLEY, Abner, Conn. & R.I.. S 18298
   Daniel, Conn. & R.I.. S 14928
     (Windham Co. in 1832; 82 in 1840, Hampton.)
   Joseph, Conn. & R.I.. S 14926
     (Conn. in 1818; Windham Co. in 1832; 84 in 1840, Hampton.)
   Samuel, wid. Lucy.. W 17219
ASK, Samuel... S 10327
ASPENWALL or ASPINWALL, Aaron (N.Y. in 1818)........................... S 44556
   Samuel, wid. Jane... W 20634
ATKINS, Chauncey or Chauncy.. S 10328
   David, Cont. (Conn.)... S 12013
   David, Cont. (Conn.)... S 45224
   Isaac.. S 22092
   Josiah.. 45223
   Josiah, former wid., Sarah Culver.. W 17673
   (See also ADKINS.)
ATTWATER or ATWATER.
   Holbrook, Cont. (Conn.), wid. Mehitable... W 16494
     (Conn. in 1818.)
   Ichabod, wid. Electa... W 699
     (80 in 1840, Norfolk.) BLWt. 26184–160–55.
   John, wid. Lucy... W 698
     BLWt. 26949–160–55.
   Jonathan.. R 298
   Russel or Russell... S 28238
   Stephen... S 12014
ATWELL, Oliver, Cont. (Conn.)... S 19526
   Samuel, wid. Betsey... W 1205
     BLWt. 19805–160–55.
   (Soldier in New London Co. in 1832; & 80 in 1840 in Montville.)
ATWOOD, Ebenezer, wid. Demarest... W 23469
     BLWt. 36626–160–55.
   Elijah.. S 39945
   Isaac, Conn. & Mass., wid. Elizabeth.. W 20636
   Jesse, Conn., Cont. & Mass., wid. Rachel.. W 17222
   John, wid. Candace... W 15718
   Jonathan.. S 15361
     (79 in 1840, Mansfield.)
   Philip, Conn. & Mass... S 18689
   Samuel, Conn., Mass., & Vt... S 14930
AUGER or AUGUR, Felix, wid. Esther... W 20610
   Justus, Conn. & Cont.. S 38507
AUGUSTINE, Joel, wid. Ann Taylor.. W 23166
   Also given GUSTENE.
AUSTIN or AUSTEN.
   Aaron (Conn. in 1818, as Capt.)... S 37692
   Amos.. S 22626
   Andrew D.. S 5257
   Apollos, wid. Sarah, BLWt. 56512–160–55... W 20644
   Benjamin, wid. Susannah... W 2514
   Catharine, former wid. of William Wooldridge or Woolbridge, BLWt. 80028–160–55.......... W 10359
     Conn. & War of 1812.
   Dan.. S 29594
   Ebenezer, wid. Amy... W 20642
     (N.Y. in 1818.)
   Edward, wid. Mary.. W 16171
     (N.Y. in 1818.)
   Elias.. S 12019
   Eliphalet, wid. Sibbell.. W 3918
   Eusebius, Cont. (Conn.).. S 45221
     (N.Y. in 1818.)
   Hannah, former wid. of Abel Tharp... W 20641
   James, wid. Hannah... W 20643
   James, Conn., N.Y., & R.I... S 19186

AUSTIN or AUSTEN—Continued.
Jedediah, Conn., N. Y., & R. I.. S 21616
    (78 in 1840, Stonington.)
John, wid. Esther... W 15674
    (Vt. in 1818.)
John, Conn., N. Y., & R. I... R 322
Nathan.. S 14932
Nathaniel... S 19902
Nathaniel, wid. Margaret... W 1695
Phineas... S 44557
Richard, former wid. Mary Phelps... W 17445
Samuel, Conn. & Cont.. S 2931
Seth, wid. Hannah... R 320
AVARY. (See AVERY.)
AVEREL, AVERELL, AVERIL or AVERILL.
Daniel (Conn. in 1818; New Haven Co. in 1832)... S 12027
Ebenezer, Conn. & Privateer.. S 28625
Jonathan, Conn., Navy & Privateer.. S 29333
Nathaniel... S 12938
William, wid. Abigail... W 20645
    Conn., Navy & Privateer.
See also AVERY.
AVERY, Abel, wid. Elizabeth... W 23476
    (79 in 1840, Cornwall.)
Abner.. S 12025
Abraham, Conn., Cont., Mass. & Privateer.. S 28626
Amos, wid. Betsey... R 12189
Amos, wid. Eunice... R 305
Amos, wid. Mary... W 25374
    He had a disability pension under act of 1816; and she lived in New London Co.
Amos, Conn. & Cont.. S 12023
    (Mass. in 1832.)
Benjamin (Conn. in 1818).
Caleb, wid. Mary.. S 44558
    (New London Co. in 1832.)   W 25363
Charles, wid. Mary.. W 23478
Christopher.. S 22627
Christopher, Conn. & Cont... S 49280
Constant, wid. Zipporah... W 1696
Daniel... S 19903
Daniel... S 44560
David.. S 12022
    (New London Co. in 1832; 75 in 1840, Lebanon.)
Denison, wid. Hannah.. W 23474
    (Tolland Co. in 1832 as Deneson.)
Ebenezer... S 19006
Ebenezer or Ebenzer, BLWt 782–160–55.. S 12021
Elihu, former wid. of Thankful Rogers.. W 15955
Elisha, wid. Sybil.. R 310
Ezekiel.. S 5261
George, Conn., Mass., & Vt., wid. Mary, BLWt. 26129–160–55........................... W 23477
Griswold... R 306
Jonathan, wid. Parmelia or Parmela... W 20646
    Conn. & Cont.
Jonathan, Conn., Navy & Privateer.. S 29333
    (Also given AVERILL.)
Joshua, wid. Rachel, BLWt. 11391–160–55; BLWt. 36616–160–55.......................... W 9335
    (Mass. in 1818, as AREY.)
Miles (Mass. in 1818, as Serj't.).. S 32666
Nathan... S 10331
Nathan, wid. Rebecca.. R 308
Nathan, Conn. & Cont., wid. Aliff.. W 17223
    (N. Y. in 1818 as AVARY.)
Nathaniel.. S 18693
Nathaniel, Conn. & Cont., wid. Amy, BLWt. 34521–160–55............................... W 700
Oliver (New London Co. in 1832; 83 in 1840, North Stonington)........................ S 16613
Park... S 19904
Peter.. S 12024
Roger (N. Y. in 1818)... S 44561
Rufus (New London Co. in 1832; 81 in 1840 in Groton).................................. S 12939
Samuel, wid. Lydia.. R 307
Simeon, BLWt. 1143–200.
Simeon, former wid. Sarah Bigelow.. W 23615
    Cont. (Conn.). BLWt. 5210–160–55.
Stephen.. S 12026
Stephen, Conn. & Cont., wid. Mary.. W 6890
    BLWt. 19764–160–55.
Thomas, Conn. & Cont.. S 5260
    BLWt. 313–200.
Uriah, Conn. & Navy... S 16612
AYER, AYERS or AYRES or ARES.
Ebenezer, Cont. (Conn.), wid. Achsa, BLWt. 26027–160–55............................... W 8589
John, former wid. of, Abigail Pelton, Rej. BL. This woman was pensioned as wid. of Joseph
    Pelton, Conn., W 26303, and that is why the BL was Rej.
John, wid. Martha, BLWt. 27614–160–55.. W 1357
Peter, wid. Temperance.. W 15872
William, Conn. & Cont... S 37685
    (Conn. in 1818 as ARES.)

8

NOTE.—The service for which a man was pensioned is not necessarily all of the service that he actually performed. Often, from old age, a man neglected to mention part of his service; and again he might be unable a.ter the lapse of years to prove it.

S means supervisor's file; W, widow's file; and R, rejected file. Often a man was pensioned and the widow's claim rejected for technical reasons—she may not have been married before 1794, or not have been a widow at the time of the passage of the act, etc. The case is marked by the last action, so that most of the cases marked R are really proven claims as far as the soldier is concerned.

BLWt. means bounty land warrant. Those issued before 1804 are marked first with the number of the warrant; then with the number of acres granted. Those issued later are marked first with the number of the warrant, second with the number of acres; third with 55, indicating that the act under which the warrant was issued was passed in 1855. This act allowed children as well as pensioners to obtain land.

ACKART, Solomon, 90 in 1840, Canton, Hartford Co., Conn.
    N. Y. not Conn. service, although pensioner lived in Conn. after the Revolution.
ALDRICK, Noah, Hartford Co. in 1832.
    This man served from Mass. and was pensioned in 1832, while a resident of Hartland, Vt., where he died. The mistake is found also in the Report of the Secretary of War in 1835.
ALEXANDER, Thomas, East Hartford, Conn., Conn. Men, p. 666.
    This man served in the Continental and Mass. service, but lived in Conn. after the Revolution.
ALLEN, Arnold, Hartford Co. in 1832; also 71 in East Windsor in 1840.
    This man served in Mass. not Conn. Line.
AMES, Smith, Hartford Co.
    No such name in files of Revolutionary pensioners. Probably served at a later date.
ANDREIS, Ephraim, Tolland Co. in 1832.
ANDREWS, Ephraim, Tolland Co. in 1832.
    Only one man pensioned of that name. He lived in Tolland Co. and spelled his name Andrus or Andrews.
ANGEVINE, Lewis (Conn. Men, p. 649.).
    No such name in files of Revolutionary pensioners. Probably served at a later date.
ARNOLD, Nathaniel, Windham Co., in 1832.
    R. I. not Conn. service.
ASHLEY, Elisha, Middlesex Co. in 1832.
    Only one pensioner of that name in the files. He lived in Vt. in 1832; service given as Green Mt. Boys and Vt.

B.

BABBET or BABBIT, or BABBETT.
    Edward.. S 31545
    (Conn. Men, pensioners 1832; also 77 in 1840.)
    Seth.. S 12956
    (Conn. Men, pensioners 1832, also 80 in 1840.)
BABCOCK, Amariah, wid. Sabra; Conn. & N. Y. BLWt. 3753–160–55............................ W 25198
    Beriah, Cont. (Conn.)... S 12034
    (Conn. Men, pensioners, 1818; pensioners, 1832.)
    Caleb, Conn. & R. I... S 23112
    Daniel.. S 12102
    Daniel, wid. Tryphena.. R 345
    Daniel, Conn. & R. I.. R 340
    Elisha, wid. Anna, BLWt. 26693–160–55.. W 681
    Ephraim.. S 37709
    (Conn. Men, pensioners, 1818.)
    George, wid. Content, Conn. & R. I., BLWt. 2350–160–55.................................. W 5210
    Horace, wid. Elcey.. W 23513
    Job, Conn. & Cont.. S 44576
    John, former wid. Lydia Barnard... W 25187
    John, former wid. Lydia Edgerton (Egerton)... W 17749
    Nathaniel... S 2367
    Oliver, former wid. Marcy Brown.. W 16865
    Conn. & Cont.
    Reuben.. S 28978
    or BADCOCK, Roger... S 12107
    Sherman, Conn., R. I., Vt.. S 17246
BACK, Elisha... S 44605
    (Conn. Men, pensioners, 1818.)
    Lyman, wid. Eunice.. W 23540
BACKUS, Abner, wid. Jemima, BLWt. 3794–160–55....................................... W 2049
    (Conn. Men, pensioners, 1818, 78 in 1840.)
    Elijah... S 38514
    (Conn. Men, pensioner in Vt. 1818.)
    Josiah... S 8058
    Ozias, wid. Elizabeth... W 17227
    (She was 74 in 1840, Conn. Men.)
    or BAKUS, Samuel... S 16036
    Stephen, Conn. & Privateer.. S 18704
BACON, Abner... S 37728
    (Conn. Men, pensioners, 1818. A BLWt. 2639–300 Capt. was issued Mch. 27, 1794, to Samuel Dorrance, assignee. No papers.)
    Ebenezer.. S 30849
    (Conn. Men, pensioners, 1818.)
    Ebenezer, 2nd., Conn. & Cont... S 44569
    (Conn. Men, pensioners, 1818.)
    Francis (Conn. Men, pensioners, 1832).. S 12981
    81 in 1840.
    Henry... S 29604
    BLWt. 2138–100; Conn. & R. I.
    (Conn. Men, pensioners, 1818.)

9

BACON, Jacob, Conn. & Privateer.. S 15306
  (Conn. Men, pensioners, 1832.)
 Joseph, wid. Betsey... R 355
 Joseph, Cont. (Conn.), wid. Eleanor... W 25190
 Josiah, Conn. & Mass.. S 17263
  (Conn. Men, pensioners, 1832.)
  (Conn. Men, 84 in 1840.)
 Nehemiah... S 45239
  (Conn. Men, pensioners, 1818.)
 William.. S 23525
 William, BLWt. 101-100.. S 37694
 William, Conn. & Cont... S 45566
BADCOCK, Amos... S 44577
 Jonathan.. S 12108
 Robert.. S 23105
BADGER, Benjamin, Conn. & Mass... S 12121
BADGER or BAGGER, John.. S 15301
 Jonathan.. S 22104
 Joseph, Conn. Cont. & Mass.. S 44336
BAGLEY, Barnard, BLWt. 73588-160-55... S 10341
 John, Conn. Cont., Mass., N. H.. S 12096
BAILEY, OR BAILY, or BALEY.
 Caleb, wid. Elizabeth.. BLWt. 77804-160-55
 Christopher... S 12098
  (Conn. Men, pensioners, 1818 & 1832.)
 David, wid. Eunice, BLWt. 71016-160-55.. W 18552
 Eliakim... S 17264
  (Conn. Men, pensioners, 1832.)
 Elijah.. S 44573
  (Conn. Men, pensioners, 1818.)
 Enoch... S 12072
BAILEY, Henry.. BLWt. 1594-100
 Hezekiah, Conn. Cont., wid. Adah, BLWt. 30596-160-55...................................... W 9340
  (Conn. Men, pensioners, 1818. Conn. Men, pensioners, 1832. Conn. Men, 85 in 1840.)
 Ichabod, wid. Patience.. W 20667
  (Conn. Men, pensioners, 1832.)
 Jacob, wid. Sarah... W 15875
 James, wid. Thedee or Theede... W 1799
  Conn. & Cont. BLWt. 3795-160-55.
  (Conn. Men, pensioners, 1832.)
 Jared, wid. Elizabeth, Conn. & R. I... W 4884
 Joshua.. S 10347
 Loudon, Conn. & Navy... S 37703
  (Conn. Men, pensioners, 1818.)
 Robert.. S 39953
  (Conn. Men, pensioners, 1818.)
 Timothy... S 44574
  (Conn. Men, pensioners, 1818.)
 William, former widow, Rachel Goodsell.. W 25640
  Conn. & Cont. (Conn. Men, pensioners, 1818.)
BAILEY. (See also BALEY.)

Note.—Silas Bailey of N. H. R. F. 390 had a wife (name not stated) who was the former wid. of Joseph Marks, who served in the Rev. from Conn. No papers in regard to his claim except what are in this envelope.

BAKER, Abel.. S 10338
 Alpheus... R-
 Andrew, former wid., Mary Walden... W 22524
 Asa... S 12127
 Asa, former wid., Zilla Pangburn.. W 21893
  Conn. & Cont.
 Daniel, wid. Jerusha.. W 3922
 Elijah, wid. Olive, Cont. (Conn.)... W 18569
  (Conn. Men, pensioners, 1818.)
 Enoch... S 17250
  (Conn. Men, pensioners, 1832.) (Conn. Men, 86 in 1840.)
 James... R 416
 Joshua.. S 12074
  (Conn. Men, pensioners, 1832.)
 Lovel, Conn. & Cont... S 37715
 Nathan.. S 12118
 Rebecca, former wid. of Marvin, Nathan... W 18558
 Robert, Cont. (Conn.), wid. Sarah... W 704
  BLWt. 255-60-55 & 286-60-55.
  (Conn. Men, pensioners, 1818.)
 Rufus, Conn. & Vt... S 16622
 Samuel, Conn., N. Y., & 1812.. S 9271
 Seth, Conn. & Conn. Sea Service... S 23106
 William... S 44323
  (Conn. Men, pensioners, 1818.)
BALCH, John, wid. Lucy... W 20685
  (Conn. Men, pensioners, 1818.)
 Joseph, Conn. & Cont. BLWt. 3641-160-55... S 12106
BALCOM (Balcam), Azariah.. S 16039
  (Conn. Men, pensioners, 1832.)
 Elias... S 44348
  (Conn. Men, pensioners, 1818.)
 Nathaniel... S 22108

BALDWIN, Aaron, Conn., Cont., & N. Y... S 12090
   Abel, wid. Molly.. W 20677
   Abiel (Abial), wid. Elizabeth.. W 8351
   Abner... S 12126
   Asa, Cont. & Conn. wid. Dolly... W 10372
     (Conn. Men, pensioners, 1832.) (Conn. Men, 84 in 1840.)
   Ashbel.. S 22629
   Asil (Azel)... S 19196
   Benjamin, wid. Lydia.. W 16498
   Brewen (Brewin).. S 12073
     (Incorrectly given Brewer. Conn. Men, pensioners, 1832.)
   Caleb, Conn. & Cont.. S 45517
     (Conn. Men, pensioners, 1818.)
   Daniel.. S 12036
     (Conn. Men, pensioners, 1832.)
   David, wid. Ruth.. W 23524
     (Conn. Men, pensioners, 1818; Conn. Men, soldier d 7-10-1819.)
   Desire, former wid. of Negus, John, who had Conn. & Conn. Sea service...................... W 17228
     Only one Desire wid., was in files. (Conn. Men, 83 in 1840.)
   Eleazer... S 2046
   Elijah, Conn. & Cont.. S 22103
     (Conn. Men, pensioners, 1818.)
   Elisha.. S 44306
     (Conn. Men, pensioners, 1818.)
   Elizabeth, former wid. of Gorham, Joseph................................... W 17247
     Cont. (Conn.)
   Henry, wid. Jane, Conn. & Cont... W 17240
     (Conn. Men, pensioners, 1818.) (She was 81 in 1840, Conn. Men.)
   Jabez, Conn. & Mass., wid. Hannah.. W 17261
   James, wid. Sarah.. W 12241
   James, Conn. & Cont., wid. Nabby... W 25203
   James, Cont. (Conn.)... S 12124
   Joel.. S 12067
   John.. R 447
   Jonathan, wid. Keziah.. W 25202
     (Conn. Men, pensioners, 1832.)
     (Conn. Men, she was 76 in 1840.)
   Jonathan, wid. Submit. BLWt. 26258-160-55............................... W 10402
   Joseph.. S 31530
     (Conn. Men, pensioners, 1832.)
   Joseph, wid. Rosanna... W 17256
   Josiah, former wid. Martha Hill... W 21326
   Nathan, Conn. Sea Service, wid. Avis..................................... W 25209
   Nathaniel... S 28982
   Peleg, wid. Anna or Anne... W 2050
   Philemon, Conn. & Cont.. S 18305
     (Conn. Men, pensioners, 1832.) (Conn. Men, pensioners, 1840.)
   Phineas, wid. Abigail.. W 17235
     (She was 77 in 1840.)
   Samuel.. S 10335
   Samuel.. S 12081
   Seth, Conn. & Vt... S 44307
   Stephen... S 23111
   Theophilus, Conn. & Mass.. S 37719
   Thomas... BLWt. 377-200
BALEY, John, Conn. & N. Y... R 454
   (See also BAILEY.)
   Stephen... R 392
BALL, Benjamin, Conn. & Cont.. S 12059
   Humphrey... S 39176
     (Conn. Men, pensioners, 1818.)
   John, BLWt. 143-200, Lieut., issued Feb. 4, 1797. No papers.
   Jonathan.. S 44320
     (Conn. Men, pensioners, 1818.)
   Wait.. R 460
BALLARD, Daniel, wid. Ruth. BLWt. 17702-160-55......................... W 474
   John, Conn. & Cont... S 44596
     (Conn. Men, pensioners, 1818.)
BALLOU, Jeremiah, Conn. & R. I... S 23102
     (Conn. Men, pensioners, 1832.)
BANCROFT, Oliver.. S 12980
BANISTER, George, Conn., Cont. & Penna............................... S 9095
BANKS, Benjamin.. S 12954
     (Conn. Men, pensioners, 1832.)
   Daniel.. S 9811
   Ebenezer... S 12038
     (Conn. Men, pensioners, 1832.)
BANKS or BANK.
   Elijah, wid. Mabel... W 20675
   Ezekiel O.. S 18303
     (Conn. Men, pensioners, 1832.)
   Gershom (Gershon) wid. Ruth... W 20669
     (Conn. Men, pensioners, 1832.) (Conn. Men, she was 86 in 1840.)
   Hyatt (Hyat)... S 12040
     (Conn. Men, pensioners, 1832.) (Conn. Men, 76 in 1840.)
   Jonathan, wid. Molly... R 476
   Joseph.. S 12973
   Joseph, wid. Esther.. W 20680

11

BANKS or BANK—Continued.
```
Moses O.............................................................................................. S 12035
    (Conn. Men, pensioners, 1832.)
Nathan, wid. Mabel. BLWt. 26131–160–55................................................ W 17236
Nehemiah............................................................................................ S 12974
    (Conn. Men, pensioners, 1832.)
Obadiah, Conn. & N. Y.......................................................................... S 12050
Obadiah............................................................................................... S 28272
Thomas............................................................................................... S 44602
    (Conn. Men, pensioners, 1818.)
BANNET (BENNET), Samuel.................................................................... S 15747
BARBER, Abraham, wid. Sarah................................................................ W 16832
    Conn. & Cont.
    (Conn. Men, pensioners, 1818.)
Amaziah, Conn. & Cont.......................................................................... S 44340
Bela, Conn. & Cont................................................................................ S 12071
    (Conn. Men, pensioners, 1832.)
Benjamin, wid. Sarah............................................................................. R 484
Daniel, Conn. & Cont............................................................................. S 8052
David, BLWt. 154–150 Ensign, issued Aug. 7, 1789, to James Noyes Barber, Adx. No papers.
Job..................................................................................................... S 15309
Job, Conn. & Cont................................................................................. S 12083
Joel, Conn. & Cont................................................................................ S 12099
Jonathan, wid. Abi................................................................................. W 17259
    (Conn. Men, she was 73 in 1840.)
Michael Conn. & Cont............................................................................ S 31531
    (Conn. Men, pensioners, 1832.)
Obadiah............................................................................................... S 15300
Rebecca, former wid. of Simons, Thomas.................................................. W 20679
Reuben................................................................................................ R 485
Reuben, Conn. & Cont. wid. Elizabeth...................................................... W 24624
    (Conn. Men, she was 86 in 1840.)
Reuben, Conn. & N. Y. wid. Hannah........................................................ W 10291
    BLWt. 11277–160–55.
Simeon................................................................................................ S 16037
    (Conn. Men, pensioners, 1832.)   (Conn. Men (Barbour), 87 in 1840.)
Stephen.............................................................................................. S 12030
BARCE, or BEARSE, or BASS, or BORCE, or BERCE.
Josiah, wid. Freelove............................................................................. R 489
BARDEN, Abraham................................................................................ R 1448
Ebenezer S........................................................................................... R 492
Samuel, Conn. & Cont. wid. Mary............................................................ W 16833
BARDSLEE (BEARDSLEE), Thaddeus........................................................ S 14952
BARDSLEY (BEARDSLEY), William, wid. Elizabeth...................................... W 23584
BARKER, Archelaus, Conn. & Conn. Sea Service, wid. Mary.......................... W 17225
    (Conn. Men, she was 78 in 1840.)
David, Conn. Privateer, Conn. Sea Service & Vt.......................................... S 6573
Ethan.................................................................................................. S 15308
    (Conn. Men, pensioners, 1832.)
Hananiah.............................................................................................. S 38519
James, wid. Lydia.................................................................................. W 21628
John, Cont. (Conn.) wid. Huldah............................................................. W 25215
    (Conn. Men, she was 80 in 1840.)
Jonathan.............................................................................................. S 28636
Joseph, wid. Susannah........................................................................... R 504
Oliver, wid. Ruth................................................................................... W 1698
    (Conn. Men, pensioners, 1818.)
Phineas, Conn. & Privateer..................................................................... R 501
Russell (Russel), wid. Elizabeth.............................................................. W 23528
Samuel................................................................................................ S 12977
Samuel................................................................................................ S 33990
    (Conn. Men, 1818.)
Samuel............................................................................... BLWt. 220–300
Timothy.............................................................................................. S 16615
William, wid. Phebe, BLWt. 9467–160–55................................................. W 24629
William, Conn. & Cont........................................................................... S 45223
    (Conn. Men, 1818.)
BARLOW, Aaron, wid. Rebecca................................................................ W 20665
David, wid. Lucy................................................................................... R 510
John, BLWt. 1416–100........................................................................... S 37732
    (Conn. Men, pensioners, 1818.)
Samuel, Conn. & Cont............................................................................ S 6585
Tempa, former wid. of Carter, Jonah, BLWt. 113033–160–55........................ W 10383
BARNABE, or BARNABEE, or BARNEBE or BARNEBEE.
Chandler, wid. Esther, Conn. & R. I.......................................................... W 20661
James, wid. Ann.................................................................................... W 20687
    (Conn. Men, pensioners, 1818.)
BARNARD, Cyprian, Conn., Cont., & Navy................................................ R 512
Dan..................................................................................................... S 23532
Grove, wid. Mary Ann............................................................................ W 17224
    (Conn. Men, pensioners, 1818.)
John, BLWt. 133–300, Capt., issued May 4, 1795.  No papers.
Lydia, former wid. of Babcock, John........................................................ W 25187
Moses, wid. Hannah............................................................................... W 16817
Moses, wid. Reliance.............................................................................. W 4634
Rufus, wid. Mary................................................................................... W 3644
Timothy, wid. Phebe, Conn. & Cont.......................................................... W 25214
William................................................................................................ S 12125
(See also BERNARD.)
```

BARNEBE or BARNEBEE. (See BARNABEE.)
BARNES or BARNS, Abel... S 44317
  Abel.. S 12055
  Abel.. R 514
  Ambrose.. S 44316
    (Conn. Men, pensioners, 1818.)
  Amos, Conn. & Cont.. S 44333
    (Conn. Men, pensioners, 1818.)
  Amos, wid. Elizabeth Cont. (Conn.).. W 17238
  Benjamin, former wid. of Abigail Clapp.. R 1957
  Daniel... S 12084
  Daniel, wid. Sarah.. R 527
  David.. S 12944
    (Conn. Men, pensioners, 1832.)
    (Conn. Men, 76 in 1840.)
  Elijah... S 12976
    (Conn. Men, 77 in 1840.)
  Eliphalet, Conn. & Cont... S 37695
    (Conn. Men, pensioners, 1818.)
  Enos, wid. Lucy, Cont. & Conn... W 20650
    (Conn. Men, pensioners, 1818.)
  Hartwell or Heartwell... S 44312
    (Conn. Men, pensioners, 1818.)
  Israel, wid. Susanna, Conn. & Cont.. W 25201
    (Conn. Men, pensioners, 1818, 1832, & 82 in 1840.)
  Ithiel, wid. Grissel.. W 23504
    (Conn. Men, pensioners, 1818.)
    BLWt. 5447, issued 1790.
  Jared, wid. Silence... W 25197
    (Conn. Men, pensioners, 1832.)
  Jared.. R 516
  Joel, wid. Dolly, BLWt. 3611-160-55... W 3497
  John... S 2047
  John, wid. Rachel... R 525
  John, Conn. & N. Y.. S 12105
  John, Conn. & N. Y.. S 23110
  John C., wid Abigail, Conn. & N. Y.. W 10385
  Jonah, wid. Abigail... W 20692
  Jonathan... S 44330
    (Conn. Men, pensioners, 1818.)
  Jonathan... S 44603
  Joshua... S 18302
    (Conn. Men, pensioners, 1832.)
  Josiah, wid. Olive, Conn. & Cont.. W 25213
    (Conn. Men, pensioners, 1818.)
  Moses.. S 2356
  Nathan... S 15307
    (Conn. Men, pensioners, 1832.)
  Nehemiah, Cont. (Conn.)... S 39965
    (Conn. Men, pensioners, 1818.)
  Orange, wid. Olive.. W 21647
    (Conn. Men, pensioners, 1818.)
  Reuben, Conn. & Cont.. S 12104
  Samuel... S 44318
    (Conn. Men, pensioners, 1832.)
  Simeon... S 37731
    (Conn. Men, pensioners, 1818.)
  Thomas, wid. Sibel, Cont. (Conn.)... W 4123
  Warner, wid. Elizabeth, Conn. & Cont. BLWt. 30611-160-55............................ W 25218
BARNET or BARNETT, Moses, Conn. & N. Y.. S 15303
  Nathan... R 536
BARNEY, Luther, wid. Ruth, Conn. & Privateer.. W 4124
  Samuel, wid. Sarah, Conn., Sea Service.. W 17233
BARNS. (See BARNES.)
BARNUM, Amos.. S 37707
    (Conn. Men, pensioners, 1818.)
  Daniel, wid. Hannah, BLWt. 3812-160-55.. W 1123
  Eli. BLWt. 144-200, Lieut., issued Oct. 12, 1789, to Eunice Barnum, Adx. No papers.
  Ezbon, Conn. & Cont... S 12979
    (Conn. Men, pensioners, 1832.)
  Jehiel... S 44334
    (Conn. Men, pensioners, 1818.)
  Josiah, wid. Abigail.. R 549
  Levi... R 552
  Noah, Cont. & Conn.. S 37722
    (Conn. Men, pensioners, 1818.)
  Samuel, Conn. & N. Y.. S 44335
  Seth, wid. Abigail.. W 21625
  Stephen, Conn. & Green Mt. Boys... S 39960
    (Conn. Men, pensioners, 1818.)
  Stephen.. S 4917
  Zenas.. BLWt. 1074-100
BAROTT. (See BARRETT.)
BARRET. (See BARRETT.)
BARRET, BARRETT, BARRIT, BARRITT, BAROTT.
  Bartholomew.. S 44579
  Benjamin, Conn. & Mass.. S 18697
  Hezekiah... S 10353
  Jacob.. S 6576

13

BARRET, BARRETT, BARRIT, BARRITT, BAROTT—Continued.

Jeremiah	S	37711
Jonathan	S	2049
Joseph, wid. Sally	W	21627
Oliver, Conn. & Mass	S	4920
Smith	S	29605
William	S	12048
(Conn. Men, pensioners, 1832.)		

BARROWS, Eleazer .... S 23101
Isaac .... S 17248
Isaac .... S 39162
Jacob, wid. Emela, BLWt. 32224–160–55 .... W 2515
(Conn. Men, pensioners, 1818.)
Lemuel, wid. Abigail, BLWt. 7445–160–55 .... W 5780
Thomas .... S 15297
BARRUS or BURRUS, Thomas, wid. Esther, BLWt. 57751–160–55 .... W 8402
(See also BURROUGHS.)
BARSTOW, Ebenezer .... S 15740
Job, Conn. & N. Y .... R 571
John .... S 12039
(Conn. Men, pensioners, 1832.)
Michael .... S 45519
(Conn. Men, pensioners, 1818.)
Samuel, wid. Lucinda, BLWt. 10241–160–55 .... W 25196
(Conn. Men, pensioners, 1832.)
(Conn. Men, 80 in 1840.)
BARTHOLOMEW, Charles, wid. Lenda or Belinda, BLWt. 1006–160–55 .... W 25195
Isaac, Cont. (Conn.) .... S 44590
(Conn. Men, pensioners, 1818.)
James, Cont. (Conn.) .... S 12943
(Conn. Men, pensioners, 1818.)
(Conn. Men, pensioners, 1832, & 80 in '40.)
Only James Bartholomew from any State.
Jonathan .... S 12068
(Conn. Men, pensioners, 1832.)
(Conn. Men, 85 in 1840.)
Joseph, wid. Lina, BLWt. 61241–160–55 .... W 9345
Moses .... S 15314
Luther, Cont. & Conn .... S 21625
Oliver, Conn. & Cont .... S 12086
Samuel, wid. Elizabeth .... W 20651
(Conn. Men, pensioners, 1818.)
William .... S 37717
(Conn. Men, pensioners, 1818.)
BARTISS, John .... R 575
BARTLET, BARTLETT, BARTLIT, BARTLITT.
Abraham .... S 28629
Christopher .... S 10340
Daniel C .... S 12077
Isaac (or W.), wid. Sybel, Cont. (Conn.), BLWt. 33570–160–55 .... W 517
Levi, Conn. & N. Y .... S 12082
Otis, Cont. (Conn.) .... S 10346
Samuel .... S 12982
(Samuel 2nd in 1832, Conn. Men.)
Samuel .... R 585
Stephen, Conn. & Cont .... S 44589
BARTMAN, Joseph, Conn. & Mass. & Sea Service & War against France & against Algiers & 1812 .... R 593
BARTON, Caleb, wid. Elizabeth, Conn. & Mass .... W 15565
Elkanah, Cont. & Conn .... S 37712
(Conn. Men, pensioners, 1818.)
Ruth, former widow of Josiah Conant .... W 17260
William, wid. Clarissa Cont. (Conn.), BLWt. 19779–160–55 .... W 10375
BARTOW, John, Cont. (Conn.) .... S 37718
(Conn. Men, pensioners, 1818.)
BARTRAM, Isaac, Cont. (Conn.) .... S 12110
(Conn. Men, pensioners, 1818.)
(Conn. Men, 88 in 1840, as Isaac H.)
James .... S 12066
(Conn. Men, pensioners, 1832.)
Job. Discharged. No papers.
Noah .... S 12043
BASCOM or WARD, Urial .... R 597
BASS, BARCE, BEARCE, BIERCE.
Joseph, Conn., Cont. & N. Y. Sea Service .... R 666
Josiah, wid. Freelove .... R 489
Samuel, Cont. (Conn. residence in 1802)—BLWt 87–100
(See also BEARS.)
BASSET or BASSETT, Abel .... S 45227
(Conn. Men, pensioners, 1818.)
Abraham, wid. Mary .... W 17253
(Conn. Men, pensioners, 1832.)
(Conn. Men, she was 81 in 1840.)
David, wid. Sarah .... W 17241
Edward, wid. Damaris, Conn. & Cont .... W 12234
Isaac .... S 12062
(Conn. Men, pensioners, 1832.)
James .... S 17259
(Conn. Men, pensioners, 1832.)
(Conn. Men, 83 in 1840.)

```
BASSET or BASSETT, Joshua, wid. Lydia, Conn. & Cont..........................  W 21634
    Nathan...................................................................................................  R 603
    Samuel..................................................................................................  S 15746
        (Conn. Men, pensioners, 1832.)
BATES, Benjamin, Conn. & Cont..........................................................  S 12148
    Eleazer..................................................................................................  S 23991
        (Conn. Men, pensioners, 1818.)
    Elias.....................................................................................................  S 12949
    Ezra......................................................................................................  S 12117
        (Conn. Men, pensioners, 1832.)
    Hinsdale...............................................................................................  S 16043
    John.....................................................................................................  S 40738
        (Conn. Men, pensioners, 1818.)
    Joseph, Cont. (Conn.)............................................................................  S 34642
    Phinehas, wid. Keziah...........................................................................  R 618
        BLWt. 84508-160-55.
    Samuel, former widow Deborah Wright..................................................  W 16798
        BLWt. 1534-100.
BATTERSON, BATTESON, Abijah.....................................................  S 12075
    George, wid. Mary, BLWt. 2356-160-55..................................................  W 17257
        (She was 77 in 1840, Conn. Men.)
    James, wid. Nancy.................................................................................  R 624
    John, wid. Sarah....................................................................................  W 17239
    Joseph, wid. Rebecca, BLWt. 1404-160-55..............................................  W 23536
        (Conn. Men, pensioners, 1818, Penna.)
    Stephen................................................................................................  S 40737
        (Conn. Men, pensioners, 1818.)
        (Conn. Men, 89 in 1840.)
    William.................................................................................................  R 625
BAXTER, Aaron...................................................................................  S 37714
        (Conn. Men, pensioners, 1818.)
    Benjamin, wid. Hannah..........................................................................  R 633
    Nathan.................................................................................................  S 6594
    Nathan.................................................................................................  R 637
    Simeon, Conn. & Mass...........................................................................  R 638
    William, wid. Deborah, Conn. & Vt........................................................  W 25207
BEACH or BEECH, Adna, wid. Sarah, BLWt. 16270-160-55...............  W 1212
    Asa.......................................................................................................  S 10362
    Asa, Cont. & Conn.................................................................................  S 35187
        (Conn. Men, pensioners, 1818, Ky.)
    Ashbel..................................................................................................  S 12173
    Daniel...................................................................................................  S 12178
    Daniel, wid. Comfort..............................................................................  W 17290
    Daniel or Dan, wid. Abigail.....................................................................  R 649
    David, wid. Elizabeth.............................................................................  R 650
    David, wid. Anna, Conn. & Cont.............................................................  W 15823
        BLWt. 146-200 Lieut. issued June 9, 1709, to Ezekiel Moore.  Assignee.  No papers.
    Edmund................................................................................................  S 10367
    Elihu, wid. Mary....................................................................................  W 4889
    Elnathan...............................................................................................  S 12162
    Ezekiel, wid. Azubah..............................................................................  W 4130
    Francis, Conn. & Mass. Sea service.........................................................  S 15323
        (Litchfield Co. 1832; 85 in 1840.)
    Israel....................................................................................................  S 12160
        (N. Y. in 1818.)
    Jabez, wid. Parthenia.............................................................................  W 17279
        (Fairfield Co. in 1832.)
    John.....................................................................................................  S 12138
    John, wid. Rhoda...................................................................................  W 23559
    John, Conn. & Green Mt. Boys................................................................  S 12200
    John H. wid. Phebe................................................................................  W 18575
        (Phebe was 82 in 1840.)
    Jonathan, wid. Martha, BLWt. 26392-160-55...........................................  W 5806
    Joseph, former wid. Hannah Harrison.....................................................  W 23187
    Julius....................................................................................................  S 12182
        (Litchfield Co. in 1832.)
        (75 in 1840.)
    Miles, wid. Sarah...................................................................................  R 653
    Nathaniel, Conn. & Cont., wid. Ruth......................................................  W 21655
        (1818 in N. Y.)
    Obiel or Obil.........................................................................................  S 4264
        (1818 in Ohio.)
    Reuben.................................................................................................  S 46366
    Robert, Conn. & Cont............................................................................  S 16046
    Roswell or Rosewill................................................................................  S 45315
        BLWT. 15412-160-55.
    Stephen, Conn. & Vt..............................................................................  S 28998
    Thaddeus, Navy (Conn.).........................................................................  S 37741
        or Mial Camp.
        (Marine, on frig. Alliance, Conn. Men, 1818.)
    Thomas, Conn. & Conn. Sea Service........................................................  S 14946
        (Hartford Co. 1832.)
BEADLE or BEDEL, Benjamin, wid. Rhoda..........................................  W 20705
BEAMAN, BEAMONT, BEAUMONT, BEEMAN, BEEMONT, BEMAN, BEMENT.
    Benjamin..............................................................................................  S 12179
        (New Haven Co. in 1832.)
    Caesar...................................................................................................  S 39190
        (Conn. Men, 1818.)
```

15

BEAMAN, BEAMONT, BEAUMONT, BEEMAN, BEEMONT, BEMAN, BEMENT—Continued.
Dan, wid. Lois... W 20703
Daniel, Conn., Mass., Green Mt. Boys, wid. Mary....................................... W 17295
  (Litchfield Co. 1832.)
Deodate, Cont. (Conn.)... S 12334
  (1818 in N. Y.)
  (1832 in New Haven Co.)
Friend.. S 12140
Isaac... S 6623
Isaiah, Cont. & Conn... S 9099
Lemuel... S 40741
Matthias, Conn. & N. Y.. S 37775
  (Conn. Men, 1818.)
Oliver, wid. Jane, BLWt. 2182–160–55... W 7361
  (1818 in N. Y.)
Samuel, Conn. & Cont.. S 37736
  (1818 in Ohio.)
Tracy, wid. Polly, BLWT. 26663–160–55... W 10404
  (1832 Litchfield Co.)
  (78 in 1840.)
Truman, Conn. & N. Y.. S 23121
William... S 32111
William, BLWt. 145–200, Lieut., issued Sept. 24, 1790, to Peleg Sanford, Assignee. No papers.
BEAN, Thomas, Conn. Sea Service & Mass.. S 21065
BEARCE. (See BASS.)
BEARD, Abijah, Conn. & Cont.. S 28640
Andrew, wid. Susan... W 17288
  (New Haven Co. 1832.)
David... S 12204
BEARDSEE or BEARDSLEE or BEARDSLEY or BEARDSLY, or BARDSLEE.
Aaron, wid. Sally... W 25237
  (Wid. was 73 in 1840.)
Abijah.. S 17278
Abijah, wid. Elizabeth or Betsey B.. W 8133
  BLWt. 5475–100 issued July 2, 1790. No papers.
  BLWt. 131–60–55.
Abijah (1750–1789), wid. Drusilla... W 17289
Benjamin, wid. Amelia.. W 24649
David, wid. Huldah.. W 25238
Elijah.. S 45265
Gershom, Conn. & Cont... S 44622
Ichabod.. S 12995
James, wid. Ruth, BLWt. 15180–160–55.. W 1364
  (Fairfield Co. in 1832.)
  (83 in 1840.)
John, wid. Margaret... W 17265
  (Fairfield Co. in 1832; wid was 78 in 1840.)
Joseph... S 14939
  (Fairfield Co. in 1832.)
Josiah.. S 16631
Moses, Conn. & Cont.. R 675
Robert Chauncey, wid. Huldah, BLWt. 26687–160–55................................... W 20710
Salmon Wheeler, wid. Abigail.. W 23585
BEARDSLEE, Silas, former wid. Catherine Whitaker...................................... W 3370
Thaddeus (also given BARDSLEE).. S 14952
Thomas, Conn. & Cont.. S 12142
  (85 in 1840.)
Whitmore, wid Dolly... W 24650
William, wid. Elizabeth... W 23584
  (Also BARDSLEE.)
  (See also BIRDSEYE and BIRDSLEY.)
BEARS or BEER or BEERS or BIERCE or BIERS, or BERIS.
Ann (see Samuel).. S 17267
Daniel.. S 12132
David... S 10365
David, wid. Molly, BLWt. 2055–160–55.. W 25212
Ezra.. S 12181
Fanton or Fenton, Conn. Line.. S 37750
Gershom.. S 18314
  (Fairfield Co. in 1832.)
Isaac... S 39182
Isaac... S 12198
Jabez.. S 12171
James.. S 12209
Jerusha, former wid. of Ambler, Squire, Cont. service, Conn. residence, BLWt. 194–160–55.... W 2056
Joel, Phebe Gardner or Gardiner, former wid., Conn. & Cont. service, BLWt. 3765–160–55..... W 19482
John, Conn. & Cont.. S 14949
  (Conn. Men, 1818, & 81 in 1840.)
  Only John Beers from any State.
Joseph... S 16632
  (Fairfield Co. 1832.)
Josiah, Conn. & Conn. Sea Service.. S 12197
Lewis, Conn. & Cont.. S 31547
BEARS, Matthew, wid. Phebe... W 8355
  BLWt. 26317–160–55.
  (Fairfield Co. in 1832.)
Nathan... S 12999
  (New Haven Co. in 1832.)
Nathan... S 15335
  (Fairfield Co. in 1832.)

BEARS, Nathan, wid. Mary Conn. & Cont... W 17269
    BLWt. 147-200 Lieut. issued Oct. 6, 1789. No papers.
    (Soldier was pensioner in 1818, and 87 in 1840.)
    Phineas (Litchfield Co, 1832).. S 16635
        Jerusha, wid. of the above received a pension as former wid. of Squire Ambler (Cont.).. W 2846
    Samuel, Conn. & Mass.. S 17267
        (Fairfield Co. in 1832.)
        Ann, wid. of the above, was pensioned as former wid of Thomas Phillips............... W 25233
    Silas... ·S 14935
        (Hartford Co. in 1832.)
    William... S 4265
    Zachariah or Zacheriah.. S 4946
BEAUMONT. (See BEAMAN.)
BECKLEY, Daniel... S 12199
    Richard Cont. Conn. residence in 1818.. S 39188
        (80 in 1840.)
    Solomon.. S 31583
    Zebedee, Conn. & Cont. wid. Elizabeth.. W 15579
        BLWt. 26807-160-55.
    (See also BUCKLEY.)
BECKWITH, Abner.. S 12158
    (New London Co. in 1832.)
    Amos Conn. & Cont. wid. Susanna.. W 17299
        (1818, Vt.)
    Jesse (New London Co. 1832)... S 16633
        (88 in 1840.)
    Job... S 12168
    John, Conn. & Cont.. S 28643
    Joseph.. S 9278
    Joseph, wid. Esther... W 17286
    Lemuel... S 12167
    Nathan, Cont. (Conn.).. S 39189
    Phineas.. S 40745
    Roswell, Conn. & Cont.. S 10358
    Samuel, Conn., Cont. & Sea Service, Polly Tinker, former wid of........................... W 25485
    Seth, wid. Esther... W 25234
    (New London Co. in 1832.)
    Silas, Conn. & N. Y... S 32115
    Thomas, Conn. & Conn. Sea Service.. S 12149
    Timothy, Conn. & Cont., wid. Lydia... W 25226
BEDEL. (See BEADLE.)
BEDEN or BEDON, William, Conn. & Cont... S 44620
BEDIENT, John, wid. Betsey... W 18576
    Mordecai or Mordica, wid. Polly... W 9354
        BLWt. 42882-160-55.
BEEBE, Amon, Conn. & Mass.. S 49302
    (1818, in N. Y.)
    Asa or Asahel, wid. Annabell Cont. (Conn.), BLWt. 1751-100............................... W 23576
    Daniel, wid. Jane... W 21656
    David... S 16045
    David... S 40746
    Hopson, Conn., Mass. & N. Y.. S 4262
    Joel.. S 40742
        BLWt. 5482-100, private issued Oct. 26, 1789. No papers
    Joseph.. S 12997
        (Fairfield Co. in 1832.)
    Lemuel... S 9097
    Paul, Conn. & Cont., wid Mary.. W 17274
    Peter, Cont. (Conn.) & Green Mt. Boys.. S 12157
    Reuben.•.. S 22638
    Richard, wid. Nancy, BLWt. 24608-160-55... W 2053
        (1818 in N. Y.)
    Richard Jeduthan, wid. Rachel, BLWt. 26330-160-55... W 5808
    Ruel.. S 12169
    William... R 705
    Zaccheus, Cont. (Conn.).. S 12196
BEEBEE, Comfort, wid. Lydia.. W 17268
    David, wid. Sarah... W 16838
    James, wid. Mehitabwl... W 10408
    Joseph.. S 17257
BEECHER or BUCHER, Jonathan.. S 36455
    Moses, Conn. & Privateer, wid. Dorcas.. R 707
    Nathan, Conn. & N. Y., wid. Lucy, BLWt. 6390-160-55.. W 20707
    Wheeler.. S 14943
    (Litchfield Co. in 1832.)
BEEMAN. (See BEAMAN.)
BEERS. (See BEARS.)
BELCHER, Elisha, Conn. & Cont., wid. Lydia.. W 9725
    Joseph, BLWt. 2113-100.
    Nathan, wid. Lucy.. W 17281
    (New London Co. in 1832; 82 in 1840.)
BELDEN, Azor, wid. Hannah, BLWt. 13737-160-55... W 8356
    Benjamin, wid, Sylvia... W 5819
    Bildad, Cont. (Conn.)... S 40744
        (Conn. Men, 1818.)
    Charles... S 10355
    David... R 714
    Ezekiel Porter, wid. Mary... W 17280
        (Ezekiel in 1818, prob.)

BELDEN, John (Hartford Co. in 1832).. S 12137
   Joshua... S 15326
   Leonard, wid. Anna... W 17275
   Othniel, Conn. & Cont., wid. Sarah... W 21660
   Richard, Conn. & Cont.. S 40740
     (78 in 1840.)
   Seth, Cont. (Conn.) wid. Christian.. W 17266
     (Is it Christiana, who was 85 in 1840?)
BELDING, Abraham, Conn. & Cont., wid. Mary... W 17285
   Othniel. (See BELDEN.)
   Simeon, BLWt. 142-200, Lieut. issued Sept. 1, 1789. No papers.
BELKNAP, Francis, Conn. & Vt.. S 31548
   Simeon, wid. Miriam or Miniam, BLWt. 4093-160-55...................................... R 717
     (See also BELNAP.)
BELL, Abraham or Abram... S 12195
   Andrew, Conn. & Cont.. S 12993
   Benjamin.. S 38538
   James (Conn. Men, 1818)... S 37735
   Jesse... S 22639
   Jonathan, wid. Agnes.. W 1362
     (Fairfield Co. 1832; 85 in 1840.)
   Oliver, Conn. & Vt.. S 23123
   Stephen... S 16636
     (Fairfield Co. in 1832.)
   Thaddeus.. S 17274
     (Fairfield Co. in 1832; 81 in 1840.)
BELLAMY, Asa.. S 42086
     (Ohio in 1818.)
   Justus.. S 17838
   Matthew... S 23117
BELLOWS, Isaac, wid. Mary, BLWt. 2354-160-55... W 18591
   Thomas, Conn., N. Y. & Vt., wid. Delia... W 17284
BELNAP, Jesse, Cont. (Conn.)... S 2068
BEMAN, BEMENT and BEMONT. (See BEAMAN.)
BENEDICT, Aaron (95 in 1840).. S 12133
   Abraham... S 10363
   Amos, Conn. & Mass., wid. Mary.. W 23568
   Darius (83 in 1840)... S 37744
   Ebenezer (Fairfield Co. in 1832).. S 12202
   Elisha, Conn. & N. Y.. S 12183
   Ezra.. S 12144
   Gamaliel (Fairfield Co. in 1832).. S 12983
   Isaac (Fairfield Co. in 1832)... S 17276
     (89 in 1840.)
   James (Fairfield Co. in 1832)... S 17273
   John, wid. Reunah... W 17287
   John, Conn. & Cont., wid. Chloe... W 23599
   Jonah, wid. Elizabeth... W 18587
   Jonathan, wid. Huldah, BLWt. 26709-160-55... W 23579
   Joshua.. S 23116
   Levi, wid. Elizabeth.. W 18589
     (N. Y. in 1818.)
   Nathaniel (Fairfield Co. in 1832)... S 17272
   Nimrod (Fairfield Co. in 1832).. S 15316
   Noah.. S 12987
   Noble... BLWt. 1256-300
   Samuel.. S 6625
   Thomas.. S 21064
   William, wid. Ruth.. W 18578
BENHAM, Ebenezer, wid. Elizabeth.. W 25230
     (Hartford Co. in 1832.)
   Elihu (New Haven Co. in 1832)... S 15748
   Isaac, Conn. & Cont... S 15320
   James... S 45247
   Jared, wid. Elizabeth... W 17267
   John, wid. Elizabeth.. W 16836
   Joseph (New Haven Co. in 1832).. S 17268
   Lemuel, wid. Margaret... W 21666
   Lyman, wid. Lois.. W 25325
     (Lois was 85 in 1840.)
   Samuel.. S 45269
   Silas... BLWt. 1295-200
   Thomas.. S 8068
BENJAMIN, Aaron, Conn. & U. S. A., wid. Dorothy.. W 25223
   BLWt. 149-200, Lieut., issued May 16, 1796. No papers. His pension was paid in D. C.
     and then transferred to Conn. (Fairfield).
     (Wid. was 72 in 1840.)
   Asa (of Preston, New London Co., 1832), wid. Mary, BLWt. 9489-160-55................... W 23586
   Asa (Fairfield Co., 1832)... S 12207
   Barzillai, Cont. (Conn.) & Mass, wid. Mary (Vt. in 1818).............................. W 17291
   James, former widow of Mary Crampton.. W 20935
   Jesse (N. Y. in 1818)... S 45275
   Phineas or Phinehas (N. Y. in 1818)... S 45259
   Samuel (Hartford Co. in 1832)... S 31546
     (83 in 1840.)
BENNET or BENNETT, Aaron... S 19206
   Aaron... R 748
   Ames or Amos, Conn. & Cont., wid. Wealthy... W 3377
   Benjamin.. S 12187
   Benjamin.. S 22645

BENNET or BENNETT, Benjamin, wid. Mercy... W 10405
Benjamin.. S 38529
    Betty Bennet, wid. of above soldier, was pensioned as the former wid. of Wolcott, Patchen
      or Patchin, W 25326.
   Caleb, wid. Freelove... W 18579
   Cromwell... R 751
   Daniel.. S 37734
   Daniel, Conn., Navy & R. I., wid. Delight... W 24653
   David... S 12201
   Ebenezer... S 23118
   Ebenezer... R 753
   Elias.. S 15319
   Elias, wid. Lydia... W 2908
   Elijah, Conn. & Cont., wid. Rebecca... W 20701
    (1818 in Vt.)
   Ezekiel, Cont. (Conn.)... S 45253
    (N. Y. in 1818.)
   Isaac (N. Y. in 1818)... S 45249
   Jabez, wid. Abigail... W 25328
   James, Conn. & N. Y., wid. Catharine.. W 16191
    BLWt. 150-200, Lieut., issued April 9, 1791. No papers.
    (N. Y. in 1818.)
   Jeremiah, Conn. & N. Y. wid. Lois.. W 23591
   Jesse, Conn. & N. Y... S 12184
   Jesse, wid. Temperance.. W 17263
    (Wid. was 95 in 1840.)
   John.. S 23119
   John, Conn. & R. I... S 23541
   John, Cont. (Conn.)... S 45252
   Joseph... S 37742
   Joseph, Conn., N. Y. & Vt... S 21639
   Josiah.. S 12136
    Spelled his name BENNIT.
    (Fairfield Co. in 1832.)
    (74 in 1840.)
   Joshua, wid. Esther... W 17298
    (Conn. Men, pensioner, 1818.)
    (Wid. was 79 in 1840.)
   Miles... S 12166
   Nathan... S 45258
   Oliver, wid. Catharine.. W 4886
   Rufus, wid. Martha.. W 3378
    (Penna. in 1818.)
   Samuel... S 10368
   Samuel... R 21769
   Samuel (also spelled BANNET).. S 15747
   Stephen.. S 37760
   Stephen, wid. Hannah.. W 25236
   Stephen, wid. Mary.. W 2906
   Thaddeus, wid. Martha... W 17278
   Thomas.. S 12143
   William.. S 23538
   William, wid. Elizabeth, BLWt. 26061-160-55...................................... W 25235
    (Elizabeth was 73 in 1840.)
   Wolcott, wid. Joanna.. W 17264
BENTLEY or BENTLY, Azel... S 29007
   Charles, Conn. & Cont., wid. Hannah.. W 14298
   Elisha, Conn., Mass. & R. I.. R 783
   George, wid. Lucy... W 17272
   John.. S 45262
BENTON, Adoniram, Conn. & Cont., wid. Betsey.................................. W 1360
    (New Hamp. in 1818.)
    BLWt. 19808-160-55.
   Chandler.. BLWt. 2430-100
   Elijah or Elisha, Conn. & Cont., wid. Sarah...................................... R 787
    He was living in 1818 in N. H. and was a Rev. pensioner. Signed his name Elijah. She
      called him Elisha; her claim was rejected.
   Jacob (Tolland Co. in 1832), wid. Sarah.. W 17276
    (80 in 1840.)
   Joel, Conn. & Vt., wid. Elizabeth... W 20711
   Jonathan.. S 29004
   Nathaniel W., wid. Susannah.. W 16186
    (N. Y in 1818.)
   Noah, wid. Phebe.. W 18574
    BLWt. 29037-160-55.
    (New Haven Co. in 1832.)
   Samuel, Conn. & Mass., wid. Mary.. W 5807
   Selah, BLWt. 137-300, Capt., issued Nov. 19, 1792. No papers.
   Zadock, wid. Lydia.. W 3926
   Zebulon, Conn. & Cont... S 34007
BERIS. (See BEARS.)
BERNARD, Phares, wid. Huldah... W 25229
BERRAY. (See BERRY.) (See also BARNARD.)
BERRY, Asahel, wid. Abigail... W 25225
   Barnabas.. S 12186
   Kellog (called Dr Kellog)... S 17279
    (Litchfield Co. in 1832; 77 in 1840.)
   Lemuel (Litchfield Co. in 1832)... S 10360
   Seth, wid. Anna, BLWt. 30610-160-55... W 24646

19

BETTS, Daniel (Fairfield Co. in 1832).. S 17275
    (84 in 1840.)
    David (Conn. Men, in 1818).. S 37737
    Hezekiah, wid. Grace.. W 29929
    Dau. Juliette obtained the pension.
    (He was pensioner in 1818.)
    (Fairfield Co. in 1832.)
    Isaiah... S 17277
    Isaiah, wid. Hannah.. W 23592
    Peter, wid. Bathsheba, BLWt. 26569-160-55.. W 25222
    Peter, wid. Phebe, Conn. & Cont... W 20700
    Reuben.. S 14947
    Silas... R 810
    Stephen, Conn. & Cont.. S 37749
    BLWt. 139-200 Capt. issued Mch. 18, 1789. No papers.
    (Conn. Men, 1818.)
    Uriah, wid. Lucy, BLWt. 27619-160-55.. W 476
    William Maltby, Cont. (Conn.)... R 811
BEVANS or BEVINS, Ebenezer, Conn. & Cont. Dis. No papers.
    Henry, Cont. & Conn... S 37754
    (Conn. Men, 1818.)
BEWEL, Matthew, wid. Mary (see also BUEL)... W 20810
BIBBENS or BIBBINS, Benjamin, Cont. (Conn.) & War of 1812, BLWt. 44801-160-55......... R 819
BICKNELL, Josiah.. S 37777
    (Conn. Men, 1818.)
BIDLACK, Benjamin, Cont. (Conn.) & N. J.. S 30991
    Philemon, Conn. & Penna., wid. Sarah, BLWt. 26086-160-55.............................. W 4895
BIDLOCK. (See BIDLACK.)
BIDWELL, Allen, Cont. (Conn.), wid. Anna... W 18600
    (New Hamp. in 1818.)
    Eleazer (88 in 1840)... S 14955
    Elisha.. S 12221
    John, Conn. & Cont., Sarah Potter, former wid. of..................................... W 16684
    Ozias (Conn. Men in 1818).. S 37766
    Phineas... S 12220
    Samuel, Cont. (Conn.) & Mass... R 826
    Thomas, Conn. & Cont., wid. Elizabeth... W 21672
    (Wid. was 83 in 1840.)
BIERCE. (See BASS and also BEARS.)
BIGELOW or BIGLOW, Eli, Cont. & Conn... S 37768
    Frederick... S 37767
    Joel, wid. Lucretia.. W 1535
    Josiah, wid. Lucy.. W 20716
    Sarah, former wid. of Avery. Simeon. Cont. (Conn.)................................... W 23615
    BLWt. 5210-160-55.
    Timothy... S 2074
BIGLOW. (See BIGELOW.)
BIGSBY. (See BIXBY.)
BILL, Abiel (New London Co. in 1832).. S 22648
    Azariah, Conn. & N. Y.. S 17283
    (New London Co. in 1832.)
    Benajah, Conn. & Privateer, wid. Content... W 1730
    (New London Co. in 1832.)
    Daniel (Hartford Co. in 1832).. S 15751
    Eleazer (New London Co. in 1832)... S 18316
    (81 in 1840.)
    Elijah, Conn., Cont. & Privateer... S 12218
BILL, Jonathan (N. Y. in 1818).. S 12222
    Jonathan, wid. Hannah.. R 834
    Joshua, Conn. & Privateer.. S 17282
    (New London Co. in 1832, 78 in 1840.)
    Phineas, wid. Mary... W 16844
    Roswell or Rozzell... S 37771
    (See also BILLS.)
BILLINGS, Benjamin, wid. Wealthy, BLWt. 541-160-55.................................... W 1702
    Elisha, wid. Lucretia.. W 17302
    (Wid. was 91 in 1840.)
    Ezekiel, Conn., Cont. & Navy, Privateer & R. I....................................... R 837
    James, Conn. & Cont.. S 45285
    (N. Y. in 1818.)
    John, Conn. & Cont., wid. Olive.. W 23601
    Joseph, Conn. & Cont... S 12210
    (Vt. in 1818.)
    Matthew, Conn. & Cont.. S 45282
    (N. Y. in 1818.)
    Stephen, BLWt. 135-300, Capt., issued Oct. 26, 1795, to Joseph Emerson, Assignee. No papers.
    Anna Dennis, former wid. of.. W 25523
BILLS, Sylvanus, wid. Lydia.. W 10414
    BLWt. 36611-160-55.
    (New Haven Co. in 1832, 74 in 1840.)
    (See also BILL.)
BINGHAM, Aaron (N. Y. in 1818).. S 45280
    Abel (Conn. Men, 1818).. S 37772
    Alvan, Conn. & N. H., wid. Elizabeth... W 5220
    Chester, Conn. & Mass... S 37765
    (Conn. Men, 1818.)
    Elias, Conn. & Cont... S 38543
    (Vt. in 1818.)
    Gurdon (Conn. Men. 1818).. S 37762

BINGHAM, Ithamar, wid. Hannah... W 17301
    Jeremiah... S 12211
    Johnson, wid. Anna, BLW. 26556-160-55.......................... W 18595
    Maltiah, wid. Marcy.. W 21667
      (Mercy was 97 in 1840.)
    Ozias.. S 22120
    Samuel... S 12230
    Silas, Conn. & Vt... S 2076
    Thomas.. S 38550
BINNS, Thomas, BLWt. 466-100.
BIRCH. (See BIRGE, BURCH, and BURGE.)
BIRCHARD, Daniel, wid. Anna, BLWt. 26920-160-55................... W 1379
    (Fairfield Co. in 1832; 80 in 1840.)
    Elias.. S 12216
    (See also BURCHARD.)
BIRDSEYE and BIRDSLEY, Ezra................................... S 14954
    (Fairfield Co. in 1832.)
    Thaddeus, wid. Helen, BLWt. 10242-160-55....................... W 25247
    (See also BEARDSLEY.)
BIRGE, David, Conn. & Cont. (Vt. in 1818)......................... S 38549
    Hosea, Cont. (Conn.) (N. Y. in 1818)............................. S 12224
    James (Litchfield Co. in 1832).................................... S 10364
    (82 in 1840.)
    John, wid. Lucy, BLWt. 26631-160-55............................. W 8362
    John, wid. Ruhama, BLWt. 9471-160-55........................... W 17309
    (See also BURGE.)
BISBY. (See BIXBY.)
BISHOP, Abraham, wid. Charity, BLWt. 26563-160-55................ W 5822
    Austin, wid. Annah.. W 17306
    (Hartford Co. in 1832.)
    David.. S 6652
    Hezekiah, wid. Polly, BLWt. 50857-160-55........................ W 2587
    Jacob (Fairfield Co. in 1832)..................................... S 17280
    (85 in 1840.)
    James.. S 16641
    James, wid. Elizabeth... W 25241
    (Wid. 71 in 1840.)
    Jared.. R 860
    Jared, Sarah Foot or Foote, former wid. of...................... W 17915
    Jesse, Conn. & Mass... S 41437
    (Vt. in 1818.)
    Joel, d. Oct. 23, 1843... R 862
    Joel, wid. Phebe... R 864
    John (N. Y. in 1818).. S 45281
    BLWt. 1667-100.
    John (New Haven Co. in 1832)..................................... S 12219
    John, wid. Sarah (pensioner, 1818)............................... W 17303
    Joseph, wid. Ruth BLWt, 10229-160-55............................ W 25245
    Josiah... S 29633
    Moses, wid. Jerusha... W 20714
    Nathaniel, BLWt. 231-200, Lieut. issued Dec. 31, 1795; also recorded as above under BLWt.
    269-2659. No papers.
    Newman (Mass. in 1818), BLWt. 24614-160-55.................... S 29634
    Richard, wid. Mercy, BLWt. 815-160-55........................... W 23613
    (N. Y. in 1818.)
    Seth (New London Co. in 1818).................................... S 12212
    (82 in 1840.)
    Simeon, Conn. & Cont... S 19910
    (Conn. Men, p. 648.)
    Stephen... S 37769
    Thalmeno, BLWt. 40-100.
    Thomas, d. 1801, wid. Amy.. W 17305
    Thomas F... S 14953
    (1818, & Hartford Co. in 1832; 76 in 1840.)
    Timothy... S 28646
BISSEL or BISSELL, Benjamin...................................... S 12214
    Benjamin.. S 37774
    Benjamin. wid. Elizabeth.. W 5825
    Calvin (Litchfield Co. in 1832)................................... S 14956
    Daniel, wid. Theoda... W 23604
    (N. Y. in 1818.)
    Daniel, Conn. & U. S. A. until 1821, wid. Deborah............... W 9735
    Eben Fitch.. S 18315
    (Eben F. in Conn. Men.)
    Elisha, wid. Rhoda.. W 17304
    Ezekiel (Litchfield Co. in 1832).................................. S 31553
    George.. S 12227
    George, wid. Lois.. R 871
    Jerijah (Hartford in 1832).. S 24064
    John, wid. Huldah... R 870
    Lemuel, wid. Sally, BLWt. 26639-160-55.......................... W 520
    (Hartford Co. in 1832.)
BISSELL, Leverett, Conn. & Cont., wid. Sarah, BLWt. 28540-160-55.... W 25248
    Noadiah... S 22647
    Ozias, Cont. & Conn... S 37764
    (Conn. Men, 1818.)
    Return (Litchfield Co. 1832)...................................... S 15257
    Thomas, wid. Eleanor, BLWt. 57522-160-55........................ W 12295
    (Hartford Co. in 1832; 82 in 1840.)

BIXBEE, BIXBEY, BIXBY and BISBY, and BIGSBY.
Aaron, wid. Mary.. R 877
   (Windham Co. in 1832; 79 in 1840.)
Benjamin, Conn. Cont. & Mass.. S 42618
   (In Ohio in 1818.)
Elias, wid. Grace.. W 20718
   (N. Y. in 1818.)
Jacob (New Hampshire in 1818).. S 49305
Joseph.. S 45284
Moses, wid. Mary or Molly.. W 25240
   (Windham Co. in 1832; wid. was 72 in 1840.)
Solomon, wid. Lucy, BLWt. 56972–160–55................................... W 23607
BLACK, Benjamin, wid. Patty.. W 24974
  also known as SIMMONS.
BLACKISTON OR BLACKSTONE, John... S 14963
  (New Haven Co. in 1832.)
BLACKLEACH, John... S 37786
  BLWt. 156–200 issued Nov. 19, 1792. No papers.
BLACKMAN, BLOCKMAN, BLAKEMAN, BLECKMAN, BLEEKMAN.
Chloe, former wid. of Hill, David.. R 15052
Dan (N. Y. in 1818).. S 45286
Daniel, wid. Mary.. W 16848
David, Conn. & Cont.. S 37791
Edward, wid. Hannah.. W 25249
Elijah, Cont. (Conn.).. S 42622
Elisha.. S 2084
Enoch, wid. Lydia.. W 2059
James, wid. Ann.. W 17312
   (Fairfield Co. in 1832.)
Jonathan (Mass. in 1818)... S 34038
Nehemiah, wid. Hannah was pensioned as former wid. of Terrill, Asahel, Conn. & N. Y.... W 17311
Phoebe, former wid. of Northrop, Joshua.................................. W 10419
Sampson (Conn. Men in 1818).. S 37787
Samuel, Conn. & Cont... S 37793
   (Conn. Men, 1818.)
Zachariah (N. Y. in 1818).. S 45295
Zachariah, Conn. & Cont., wid. Sarah..................................... W 20729
   (Wid. was 83 in 1840.)
BLACKMARR or BLACKMORE, John, Conn. & Navy. wid. Silence................. W 23637
BLACKSLE, BLACKSLEE, BLAKELEY, BLAKELY, BLAKESLEE, BLAKSLEY.
Abel, wid. Mary D., BLWt. 26691–160–55................................... W 8369
Ambrose... R 907
Caleb (Mass. in 1818).. S 34034
Eber, Conn. Sea Service.. S 23129
Enos (Conn. Men, p 649). Dis. No papers.
James... S 2085
Jared, wid. Rhoda.. W 20722
   (N. Y. in 1818.)
Jesse... S 37792
Moses, Conn. & Cont.. S 12232
Obed, Conn. Cont. & Mass... S 44629
Philip.. S 38610
Rebecca, former wid. of Hull, Henry...................................... W 3332
  BLWt. 2470–100.
Samuel.. S 45293
Samuel, Conn. & Vt... S 16052
   (Litchfield Co. in 1832.)
Zealous (Conn. Men, 1818).. S 37789
BLAKE, Christopher (N. H. in 1818.)...................................... S 45598
David... S 23128
Elijah (Litchfield Co. in 1832).. S 14964
Reuben, wid. Eunice, BLWt. 2184–160–55................................... W 25250
William, Sarah Miller, former wid. of................................... W 10502
BLAKEMAN, BLECKMAN and BLEEKMAN. (See BLACKMAN.)
BLAKSLEE, or BLAKESLEY. (See BLACKSLEE.)
BLANCHAR, Jedediah (see also BLANCHARD).................................. S 14961
BLANCHARD, Elias, Conn. & Cont... S 12247
   (Windham Co. in 1832.)
Jacob (Conn. Men, 1818).. S 37784
William, wid. Sarah.. W 17320
   (Conn. Men, p 649.)
   (See also BLANCHAR.)
BLANDIN, Jonathan, wid. Submit... W 1704
BLANDIN or BLANDEN, Samuel, Conn. & Mass................................. S 10339
BLATCHFORD, John C. (Va. in 1818).. S 37788
BLIN or BLINN, Justus (Conn. Men, 1818).................................. S 37790
Simeon, Conn. & N. Y... S 45292
William... S 41444
BLISH, Azuba, former wid. of Ransom, Joseph.............................. W 25255
  BLWt. 47614–160–55.
Ezra (Conn. Men, 1818.).. S 37785
   (72 in 1840.)
BLISS, Dan, wid. Eunice.. W 23626
   (New London Co. in 1832.)
David, wid. Jane... W 5829
Eli, Conn. & Cont.. S 34046
James, wid. Mehitable, BLWt. 814–160–55.................................. W 9728
John, Mary Freeman, former wid of.. R 3781
John, wid. Reliance.. W 18609

22

BLISS, Samuel.. S 18329
    Samuel, wid. Elizabeth... W 17314
        (Wid. was 75 in 1840.)
    William, Conn. & R. I... S 4953
BLODGET and BLODGETT, Artemas or Artomes.................................... S 45287
        (N. Y. in 1818.)
    Abisha, Conn. & U. S. A.. S 15752
    Benjamin.. S 16050
    Samuel, wid. Abigail... W 17316
        (Wid. was 87 in 1840.)
    Silas, Conn. & Mass.. S 44631
        (Lieut. in N. Y. in 1818.)
BLOGGETT. (See BLODGETT.)
BLOSS, Joseph... S 21071
    Zadok, Conn. & N. H.. R 960
BLOUNT or BLUNT, Asher... S 29016
    Elisha, wid. Sally.. W 16850
BLUSH, Joseph.. R 969
BOARDMAN or BORDMAN, Amos.. S 21077
    Elijah, wid. Mercy.. W 10433
    Elijah, wid. Nancy.. W 15754
    Elijah, Cont. (Conn.), wid. Mary Ann.. W 25262
    Jonas, wid. Elizabeth.. W 23549
    Jonathan (N. Y. in 1818).. S 46204
    Josiah, wid. Susannah.. W 16854
    Moses. Discharged. No papers.
    Samuel Allen, wid. Catherine... R 12576
    Seth (Conn. Men, 1818)... S 36419
    Timothy... S 22128
BOGUE or BOOGE, Jeffrey A., wid. Freedom.. W 18638
    (See also BOGE.)
BOLLES, BOLLS or BOWLES, James... S 36420
    Joseph, wid. Betsey.. W 17327
BOND, Jacob, Conn., N. J. & N. Y.. S 12273
BONFOY or BONFY, Benanuel, wid. Concurrence................................... W 17330
    (Pensioner in 1818; wid. 78 in 1840.)
    Henry, Conn. & Cont.. S 12266
        (N. Y. in 1818.)
BOOGE or BOUGE, Samuel Cook, wid. Tryphena.................................... R 1013
    (See also BOGUE.)
BOONE, Deidamia, former wid. of Davison, Ezra..................................... W 25260
BOOTH, David, wid. Betsey, BLWt. 26719-160-55.................................... W 1370
    Erastus (N. Y. in 1818)... S 44644
    Gideon, former wid. Hannah Lewis, BLWt. 5378-160-55........................ W 26206
    Isaac... S 14983
    Isaiah, Conn. & Cont. wid. Polly, BLWt. 8174-160-55........................... W 1809
    John, wid. Sarah... R 1022
        (New Haven Co. in 1832.)
    Lucretia, former wid. of Chapin, Frederick.. W 18626
    Nathaniel.. S 10381
    Ruth, former wid. of Jones, Isaac... W 20741
    Samuel.. S 12272
    Silas.. S 14969
    Thomas (Hartford Co. in 1832).. S 14970
    Walter, Conn. & Cont.. S 36422
        (Conn. Men, 1818.)
BORCE. (See BARCE.)
BORDEN, Benjamin, Conn. & R. I., wid. Sarah....................................... R 1028
    Joshua, wid. Betsey.. W 16855
BORRES or BURROUS, John Proctor, wid. Lydia................................... W 18636
    (In Conn. Men, Barres.)
BOSSET or BOSSETT, Isaac (Conn. Men, 1818)...................................... S 36426
    (Under name of BUSSETT; 82 in 1840.)
BOSTWICK, Amos, Cont. (Conn.).. S 45312
        (Ensign, N. Y. in 1818.)
    Andrew, Cont. (Conn.)... S 36915
        (Conn. Men. 1818.)
    David... S 36418
        BLWt. 2193-160-55.
    Doctor.. S 2384
    Ebenezer, BLWt. 32-100.. S 42090
        (Ohio in 1818.)
    Elisha, Conn. & Cont.. S 10376
        (Litchfield Co. in 1832.)
    Elizur or Eliezer... S 4269
    Jonathan... S 14978
        (Litchfield Co. in 1832.)
    Levi, wid. Anne or Anna.. W 21699
        (Wid. was 84 in 1840.)
    Medad, wid. Mary M., BLWt. 34591-160-55... R 1042
    Nathan.. S 40009
        (Ensign in 1818.)
    Oliver. Discharged. No papers.
    Reuben.. S 19551
BOSWORTH, Allen, wid. Sarah, BLWt. 50856-160-55.............................. R 1048
    Daniel, Conn. & Cont., wid. Rachel... W 447
    Jacob, BLWt. 1625-100... S
        (79 in 1840.)
    Nathaniel, Conn., Cont. & Vt.. S 38561

BOTSFORD or BOTCHFORD, Aaron, wid. Comfort.. W 23654
    Clement, wid. Mary... W 20742
      (Wid. was 82 in 1840.)
    Eli, wid. Polly... W 25264
    Samuel (New Haven Co. in 1832).. S 31560
    Simeon, wid. Esther.. R 1051
BOTTOM or BOTTUM, Abel.. S 45305
    Amaziah, wid. Wealthy.. W 17322
    Asahel or Asel (New London Co. 1832)... S 15341
    Darius (New Haven Co. in 1832)... S 14082
    Jabez L.. S 14068
    John, BLWt. 1396–100.. S 46459
BOUGE. (See BOOGE.)
BOUGHTON, BOUTON, BOWTON, Azor Cont. (Conn.), BLWt. 5537 issued in 1798......... S 45310
      (N. Y. in 1818.)
    David, wid. Dinah.. W 15755
      (In N. Y. in 1818.)
    Eleazer.. S 32130
    Joseph, wid. Zeruah.. W 21698
    Matthew, Conn., Cont. & N. Y.. S 10378
    Samuel, wid. Elizabeth, BLWt. 36512–160–55.. W 25271
      (Fairfield Co. in 1832.)
    Seth (86 in 1840).. S 12262
    William, wid. Sarah.. W 17324
      (Wid. was 88 in 1840.)
BOURN, Shubael.. S 22655
    (See also BOWEN.)
BOUTELL or BOUTTELL, James, wid. Chloe... W 20740
    Joseph, wid. Molly, BLWt. 36609–160–55.. W 893
      (New Hamp. in 1818.)
BOUTON. (See BOUGHTON.)
BOW, Edward, wid. Ruth... W 24776
    Samuel, wid. Mary... W 25269
BOWEN, Benjamin, Conn. & R. I.. S 15340
    Christopher, Cont. (Conn.), wid. Betsey, BLWt. 26803–160–55............................. W 1808
      (Mass. in 1818.)
    Eleazer (Windham Co. in 1832)... S 17290
      (86 in 1840.)
    John, wid. Catharine... W 20747
      (Wid. was 79 in 1840.)
    Shubael (also spelled BOURN).. S 22655
BOWER or BOWERS, Alpheus.. S 14977
      (Windham Co. in 1832; 85 in 1840.)
    Benajah or Banaiah... S 36424
    Ephraim (Conn. Men in 1818)... S 36423
    Joab, wid. Elizabeth, BLWt. 30–60–55.. W 8231
    John, wid. Sarah... R 1073
    Jonathan, wid. Rebecca, BLWt. 27666–160–55... W 25265
      (Conn. Men, p. 648; wid. was 82 in 1840.)
    Olive, former wid. of Kelly, John... W 393
    Zephaniah or Zepheniah (N. Y., 1818)... S 45306
BOYD, Joseph (N. Y. in 1818).. S 45299
BOYNTON, Bela (Tolland Co. in 1832).. S 18322
      (87 in 1840.)
    Eunice, former wid. of Rogers, Chester.. W 20744
BRACE, Charles, wid. Perses... R 1363
    David.. S 16658
    Elijah, wid. Catherine.. W 17339
    Jeffery, called also, Stiles, Jeff.. S 41461
    Joseph, wid. Lois, BLWt. 34525–160–55... W 25298
BRACKET, BRACKETT or BROCKETT, Benajah............................BLWt. 962–100
    Hezekiah, wid. Asenath, BLWt. 29–60–55... W 8167
    (See also BROCKETT.)
BRADFORD, Elisha, wid. Lucy... W 24676
      (N. Y. in 1818.)
    Hannah, former wid. of Lyon, Ephraim... W 17366
    Thomas, Conn. & Cont., wid. Philena... W 17351
      (She was 70 in 1840.)
BRADLEY, Aaron, Conn. & Cont.. S 17302
    Alexander, wid. Lydia.. W 17336
      (She was 87 in 1840.)
    Alling... S 36447
      (Conn. Men, 1818.)
    Aner, wid. Anna... W 17335
      (Conn. Men, p. 648.)
      (Wid. was 82 in 1840.)
    Ashbel, wid. Chloe, BLWt. 8172–160–55.. W 25225
    Daniel, Conn. & U. S. A. until 1802.. S 36442
      BLWt. 148–200, Lieut. issued Mch. 13, 1790. No papers.
    Daniel, BLWt. 2478–100... S 36443
    David.. S 34099
    Dimon, wid. Beulah.. W 14380
      (Mass. in 1818.)
    Elihu, wid. Sybel.. W 16864
    Elijah... S 15343
    Elijah, Conn. & Privateer, wid. Esther.. W 18664
    Elisha, Conn. & Vt... S 12310
    Elisha, wid. Ann ?... R 1129

BRADLEY, Gilead, Conn. & Cont... S 17293
    (New Haven Co. in 1832; 83 in 1840.)
    Joseph, Conn. & Vt... S 12347
    Lemuel... S 14990
    (New Haven Co. in 1832.)
    Moses.. S 23138
    Nathan... S 12301
    (Fairfield Co. in 1832.)
    Nathaniel.. R 1138
    Philip, Burr, wid. Ruth.. W 21702
    BLWt. 131–500, Lieut. Col., issued May 14, 1796. No papers.
    Reuben, Conn. & Mass... R 1139
    Stephen, wid. Mehitable... W 25301
    (New Haven Co. in 1832.)
    Sturgis.. R 1140
    Thadeus or Thaddeus, wid. Parnal, BLWt. 6394–160–55... W 5942
    Thomas.. R 1141
BRADSHAW, James.. S 29023
BRAINARD, BRAINERD, BRANARD or BRAYNARD.
    Amos, wid. Jerusha, BLWt. 27572–160–55.. W 5234
    Ansel, Conn. & War of 1812, wid. Mary.. W 8168
    BLWt. 83430–120–55; & BLWt. 70805–40–55.
    Bezaleel, wid. Lydia.. W 23671
    (Wid. was 82 in 1840.)
    Church, Conn. & N. H... S 29032
    Daniel... S 3099
    Elijah... S 10105
    Jabez.. S 4968
    Othniel (N. Y. in 1818)... S 44683
    Seba, wid. Anna... R 1146
    Simon (Middlesex Co. in 1832)... S 17296
    Stephen, wid. Rachel.. W 20794
    Timothy, wid. Sarah.. W 14392
BRAMAN or BRAYMAN, Daniel (Conn. Men, 1818)... S 46777
    Daniel (New London Co. in 1832).. S 12276
    James.. S 18746
    Sylvanus, Conn. & Mass... S 18743
BRAMBLE, Robert, wid. Hannah.. W 25297
    (New London Co. in 1832; 78 in 1840.   Only Robert Bramble in files from any State.)
BRANARD.   (See BRAINARD.)
BRANCH, Samuel, wid. Ruth, BLWt. 26155–160–55... W 2717
    Walter, Eunice Snow, former wid. of.. W 4076
    William, wid. Lucretia, BLWt. 73–60–55... W 1544
    (N. Y. in 1818.)
BRASHER, John, Conn. & N. Y... S 1605
BRATTLE, Dick, Conn. & Mass.. R 1167
BRAY, Sampson... S 28659
BRAYNARD.   (See BRAINARD.)
BREED, Jabez Sally Wheeler, former wid. of, BLWt. 1911–160–55.................................... W 19621
    Joseph, Conn., Navy & R. I., wid. Mercy.. W 2751
    Oliver... S 12298
    Stephen, wid. Esther.. W 16511
BREWER, Daniel, Conn. & Cont... S 36435
    (Conn. Men, 1818.)
    Daniel, wid. Molly.. W 25302
    Lois, former wid. of Ebenezer Drake.. W 20791
BREWSTER, Darius, Conn. Sea Service.. S 30900
    Elias (New London Co. in 1832).. S 15765
    Elisha, Cont. (Conn.), wid. Sarah H... W 14394
    (Conn. Men, 1818.   Mass.)
    Frederick... S 15346
    (New London Co. in 1832; 77 in 1840.)
    Hezekiah (Conn. Men, 1818).. S 36439
    Joseph, Conn., Cont., Mass. & R. I.. S 12286
    Justus, Conn. & Cont., wid. Joanna, BLWt. 7099–160–55... W 14354
    Morgan.. R 1189
    Nathaniel (see claim of Anna, wid. of Isaac Holmes).. W 7769
    Zadoc, Conn. Sea Service, wid. Lucy.. W 23685
BRIANT or BRYANT, Jacob, Conn. & Vt.. R
    (See also BRYANT.)
BRIDGEMAN, Gideon, Conn., Green Mt. Boys & N. H.. S 15002
BRIDGES, Samuel, wid. Content, BLWt. 31306–160–55.. W 10299
BRIGGS, Abial or Joseph, Conn. & R. I., wid. Jane... W 20764
    Ephraim, Cont. (Conn.), wid. Dilla.. R 1199
    Ephraom, Cont. (Conn.) & Vt., wid. Rhoda... W 23710
    Ezra (Conn. Men, 1818).. S 46788
    Isaac, wid. Lucy Ann.. W 23664
    (Conn. Men, 1818.)
    James (N. Y. in 1818)... S 44676
    John.. S 12331
    Joseph.   (See Abial.)
    Joshua, wid. Tryphena... W 20753
    (N. Y. in 1818.)
    Joshua, Conn. & N. Y.. R 1203
    Owen, Conn. & Mass., wid. Margery.. W 18644
    Polly, former wid. of Seth Holcomb.. R 1206
    Stephen, wid. Deborah... W 17337
    William.. S 12281
    Zephaniah (Fairfield Co. in 1832)... S 12336

BRIGHAM, Don C., wid. Polly... W 17350
   (Hartford Co. in 1832, as Dow C. 77 in 1840.)
  Elnathan (Tolland Co. in 1832)... S 14987
  Jonathan.. S 22665
  Mary, former wid. of Elisha Johnson.. W 17348
  Paul, wid. Lydia.. W 23695
BRIGHTMAN, Henry, wid. Mary... W 25293
   (wid. was 74 in 1840.)
BRINSMADE, Cyrus, wid. Sally, BLWt. 26611-160-55.............................. W 2559
   (Fairfield Co. in 1832.)
BRISCO OR BRISCOE, Nathaniel... S 12313
BRISTALL or BRISTOL, John... R 1217
BRISTER or BRISTEE, John, wid. Lilly, BLWt. 5461 issued 1790.................. W 20772
   (Candes Lilly was 83 in 1840.)
   (See also BRISTOR.)
BRISTOL, Austin.. R 1218
  Bezaleel, wid. Mary.. W 20781
  David (New Haven Co. in 1832).. S 17300
   (76 in 1840. Only David in files from any State.)
  Eli (also given BRISTOLL)... S 22664
  Gideon (New Haven Co. in 1832).. S 12323
   (Only Gideon Bristol in files from any State.)
  John. (See BRISTALL.)
  Jonathan (New Haven Co. in 1832)... S 12288
   (Only Jonathan from any State.)
  Nathaniel, Conn. & Cont.. S 12341
  Reuben, Conn. & Cont... S 12316
BRISTOR, Stephen.. S 36437
   (Given Brister in Conn. Men, 1818.)
   (See also BRISTEE or BRISTER.)
BROCK or BROCKE, John, wid. Hannah.. W 20767
   (Vt. in 1818.)
BROCKET, BROCKETT, BROCKIT, or BROCKITT.
  Enoch... S 12337
  Giles (New Haven Co. in 1832).. S 16661
   (79 in 1840. Only Giles Brockett from any State.)
  Hezekiah, wid. Asenath. (See BRACKETT.)
  Isaac (Conn. Men, 1818)... S 36441
  Joel, wid. Elizabeth... W 10452
   (New Haven Co. in 1832; 80 in 1840.)
   (See also BRACKETT.)
BROCKWAY, Asa (Litchfield Co. in 1832).. S 15350
  Benjamin (Conn. Men in 1818)... S 36428
  Ephraim... S 12278
  Gideon, wid. Tryphena.. W 20786
  John, wid. Irene, BLWt. 19716-160-55.. W 25280
   (New London Co. in 1832; 85 in 1840. Only John Brockway in files from any State.)
  Pardon, BLWt. 40907-160-55... W 12340
  Sarah, former wid. of Isaac Sill.. W 17358
  Semillus, Bridget Ely, former wid. of. This soldier was the first husband of Bridget Ely, and
   died in service. (See claim of Ely, Abner, Conn. W 21056.)
  Zebulon (New London Co. in 1832)... S 31565
BROGA, Andrew (Mass. in 1818).. S 34086
BROMLEY. (See BRUMBLEY.)
BRONSON, BROWNSON, or BRUNSON, Asa... S 36433
   (Conn. Men, 1818.)
  Asahel (80 in 1840).. S 12289
  Ashbel.. R 1359
  Elijah, wid. Delia or Deliverance.. W 17363
  Isaac.. S 40027
  Isaac, wid. Thankful.. W 10470
   (New Haven Co. in 1832; 78 in 1840.)
  Isaac, Cont. (Conn.), wid. Anne.. W 5932
   Soldier received no pension, but BLWt. 152-300 was issued to Isaac Brunson, Surg's.
   Mate, Col. Sheldon's reg't. of Cavalry, July 28, 1789, per Richard Smith, Assignee. No
   papers. Wid. was resident of N. Y. when she obtained her pension.
  Jabez, wid. Marilla.. W 25303
   (Tolland Co. in 1832; wid. was 71 in 1840.)
  Joel (Hartford Co. in 1832)... S 15006
  Joseph (N. Y. in 1818).. S 44685
  Joseph.. S 12295
  Levi... S 2100
  Luman (Vt. in 1818).. S 49297
  Michael, wid. Eunice... W 20773
  Pheneas or Phinehas.. S 32137
  Reuben, wid. Huldah.. W 25300
   (Litchfield Co. in 1832.)
  Samuel (Hartford Co. in 1832)... S 16055
  Selah, wid. Anna, BLWt. 61329-160-55... W 9367
   (New Haven Co. in 1832.)
   (Soldier was 77 in 1840.)
  Silas, wid. Sally... W 17365
  Titus, wid. Hannah... W 17356
   (Wid. was 85 in 1840.)
BROOKER, Isaac.. S 29655
  Samuel, wid. Polly, BLWt. 8151-160-55... W 5945
BROOKS, Ahira, BLWt. 26700-160-55.. S 29037
  Asa (N. Y. in 1818), wid. Betsey... W 16193
  Caleb E., wid. Jane E... R 1244
  David, wid. Jane... W 4148

BROOKS, Jabez-(Mass. in 1818), wid. Rhoda .... W 15601
James .... R 1249
James, Conn. & Cont., wid. Lydia .... W 3929
   (Washington's Guards, Conn. Men, p. 632. Soldier pensioned in 1818.)
John .... S 15003
John, BLWt. 26157-160-55 .... S 23557
Joseph B .... R 1254
Josiah (Hartford Co. in 1832), wid. Abigail .... W 20766
Lemuel, wid. Hannah .... R 1248
Reuben .... S 30294
Samuel, wid. Elizabeth .... R 1246
Samuel Lewis, Conn. & Cont .... S 44671
Silas (N. Y. in 1818) .... S 17861
Thomas, BLWt. 30-100; wid. Esther .... W 16871
Thomas, wid. Surviah or Zurviah .... W 23701
BROTHWELL or BROTHWILL, Benjamin (81 in 1840) .... S 14991
Joseph F (Litchfield Co. in 1832) .... S 15008
Thomas, wid. Nancy BLWt. 26802-160-55 (Fairfield Co. in 1832) .... W 5928
   (Soldier was 74 in 1840. Only Thomas Brothwell in files).
BROUGHTON, Ebenezer (Vt. in 1818), wid. Lois .... W 18650
John, wid. Hannah .... W 20769
Michael, wid. Sarah .... W 18666
BROWN or BROWNE, Aaron .... S 6733
Aaron .... S 36434
Amasa, wid. Mary .... R 1326
Amasa, Conn. & Cont., wid. Jerusha .... W 17344
   (Wid. was 76 in 1840).
Asher, wid. Mary .... W 25277
Austin (N. Y. in 1818), wid. Anne .... W 23697
Bridgham, wid. Mary .... W 17364
Charles .... S 18745
Charles .... R 1283
Charles F., Lucretia Hilliard, former wid. of .... R 1321
Christopher, Conn. & Privateer .... S 10411
Christopher, Cont. (Conn.), wid. Eunice, BLWt. 35844-160-55 .... W 12339
Cyrus, Conn. & N. Y .... S 6579
Daniel .... S 10408
Daniel, Conn. & Navy, wid. Lydia .... W 20787
Daniel, Conn. Sea Service .... R 1286
Daniel, Cont. (Conn.), wid. Anna
David .... S 22136
David .... S 28353
David, wid. Lydia .... W 10453
David .... Bl.Wt. 461-100
Ebenezer .... S 36446
Ebebezer .... S 44650
Ebenezer, wid. Abigail .... R 1270
Eleazer (Vt. in 1818) .... S 39231
Eli .... S 23548
Eli .... S 44659
Elias, Conn. & Cont. (N. Y. in 1818) .... S 12332
   (An Elias Brown was 81 in 1840; above was only Elias with Conn. service, but an Elias
   with R. I. service was pensioned from Conn.).
Elijah (N. Y. in 1818) .... S 44661
Elkanah .... S 44647
Ephraim .... R 1297
   (Is he the one who called himself a pensioner, and was 68 in 1840.)
Ezekiel, wid. Ruhannah .... W 16868
Ezra .... S 2391
Gershom, wid. Eunice, Conn. & Cont .... W 14389
Humphrey .... R 1302
Humphrey, wid. Olive, BLWt. 29010-160-55 .... W 18648
Ichabod .... S 28657
Isaac, Conn. & Cont., wid. Hannah .... W 17343
Isaac, Conn., N. Y. & R. I .... S 6745
Jabez, wid. Annis .... R 1278
Jacob (Vt. in 1818) .... S 39235
James, wid. Deborah .... W 21701
James, wid. Silence, BLWt. 347-100 .... W 3219
Jedediah, wid. Mary .... W 20763
Jedediah, Conn. & Cont .... S 36432
   (Pensioned in 1818 as Washington's Life Guards.)
Jepthah (New London Co. in 1832) .... S 12340
   (Given Jeptha, and 82 in 1840; only Jeptha or ah in files.)
Jeremiah, wid. Anna, BLWt. 6423-160-55 (Tolland Co. in 1832) .... W 25283
Jerusha H., daughter of Hayward, Samuel .... W 29934
John .... S 22660
John .... S 40749
John, born Aug., 1757, in Eng .... R 1314
John, wid Rebacca .... W 5871
John, wid. Elizabeth .... W 17357
John, Conn. & N. Y .... S 12339
John, Cont. (Conn.), wid. Phebe .... W 25284
Jonathan .... S 3058
Jonathan .... S 17294
Jonathan .... S 17295
Jonathan .... S 40751
Jonathan, wid. Esther, BLWt. 12826-160-55 .... W 5229
Josiah, Conn. & Cont .... S 45164
Jude (Vt. in 1818) .... S 40029

BROWN or BROWNE, Libbeus or Lebbeus, Cont. (Conn.).. S 36445
   (Conn. Men, 1818; 83 in 1840 as Lebius; only man of the name in the files.)
Marcy, former wid. of Oliver Babcock.. W 16865
Mary, former wid. of John Flint.. W 20785
Nathan.. S 23136
Nathan, wid. Philadelphia, BLWt. 36613-160-55... W 15603
Nathaniel, wid. Abigail... W 20757
Nathaniel, Conn. & Cont.. S 36427
Nathaniel..BLWt. 1772-100
   (Fairfield Co. in 1832.)
Nehemiah, Conn. & N. Y... S 17299
Obediah or Obadiah (N. Y. in 1818)... S 44649
Oliver (Ohio in 1818), Hannah Winslow, former wid. of, BLWt. 5446-160-55.................. W 1118
Peter, Mercy Gallup, former wid. of... W 25615
   Mercy's last husband, Nehemiah Gallup, was also a pensioner, Conn.................. S 13110
Reuben, wid. Matilda.. W 20775
Reuben, wid. Ruth, Cont. (Conn.).. W 17359
Robert, wid. Lorinda, BLWt. 9211-160-55.. W 1374
Robert, wid. Mary.. W 20771
Samuel.. S 10413
Samuel.. S 12283
Samuel.. S 44653
Samuel, wid. Anna.. W 16866
Samuel, Conn., Mass. & Vt.. S 8108
Solomon, wid. Betty.. W 5901
Stephen, wid. Lydia.. R 1323
Thaddeus.. S 44657
Thomas.. S 29022
Waldo, wid. Abigail.. W 25286
   (Windham Co. in 1832.)
William, Conn, & Cont., wid. Sarah.. W 10469
William.. S 10406
William, Conn. or Mass., wid. Miriam... R 1331
William, Cont. (Conn.), Elizabeth Tryon, former wid. of.. W 18164
Zebedee, Conn. & Cont., wid. Rosamund (1818 in R. I.).. W 23698
BROWNING, Daniel.. R 1354
BRUMBLEY, BRUMBLY, or BROMLEY, Alas, wid. Esther, BLWt. 34206-160-55............ W 9748
   (New London Co. in 1832; & 75 in 1840.)
William, Mary Hilliard, former wid. of... W 21324
BRUSH, Benjamin, wid. Semantha... W 10455
   (Fairfield Co. in 1832.)
Eli.. R 1375
John Cicero.. S 35789
Jonas, wid. Tamar... W 5924
BRYAN, Benajah, wid. Lucy.. W 17342
   (Litchfield Co. in 1832.)
Elijah, BLWt. 5519 issued Apr. 9, 1791; no papers to Elijah Bryon............................ S 17860
   (N. Y. in 1818.)
Jehiel, wid. Polly... W 10450
   (New Haven Co. in 1832.)
John.. S 12280
Oliver, wid. Esther... W 20762
   (New Haven Co. in 1832.)
BRYANT, Daniel D., wid. Bethiah... W 18652
Ebenezer (Hartford Co. in 1832)... S 17849
Fowler.. R 1335
Jacob. (See also BRIANT.)
Reuben (Conn. Men, 1818)... S 36444
   (Given as Briant, 77 in 1840.)
BRYDIA, David, Conn. & N. H... S 39234
BUBE. (See BEEBE.)
BUCHER. (See BEECHER.)
BUCK, Abner (N. Y. in 1818).. S 44694
Amasa.. S 17869
Asaph, wid. Phebe... W 2534
   BLWt. 26597-160-55.
Benton.. S 15330
Elijah, Conn. & Mass.. S 12387
George, wid. Agnes.. W 23737
Hepsibeth T., former wid. of John Swift, BLWt. 2505-100... W 8172
   Swift served from Conn., N. Y. & in 1812.
Joel.. S 44693
Jonathan... S 3108
Josiah.. R 1397
Thomas.. S 22666
Zebediah (Windham in 1832).. S 17316
BUCKINGHAM, Reuben.. S 44708
Stephen, wid. Polly, BLWt. 87018-160-55.. W 25306
Thomas.. R 1403
BUCKLAND, Alexander, Conn. & Mass., wid. Lois... R 1404
George (Hartford Co. in 1832).. S 23561
   (82 in 1840.)
Jonathan, wid. Laura, BLWt. 32240-160-55... W 25315
   (Hartford Co. in 1832; 76 in 1840.)
Joshua (Hartford Co. in 1832).. S 15332
BUCKLEY. (See BULKLEY.)
BUCKMAN, Stephen, wid. Abigail... W 17369
BUDD, Bristol, wid. Phebe, BLWt. 24772-160-55... W 25304
   Also known as Sampson, Bristol.

BUDLONG, Benjamin, Conn., N. Y. & R. I... S 15011
BUEL, BUELL or BEWEL, Asa, wid. Mercy.. W 21735
    (N. Y. in 1818.)
    Daniel... S 22149
    David.. S 12348
    David.. S 31584
    Deborah, former wid. of William Kircum or Kirkum, Conn. & Cont...................... W 20795
    Gideon (Vt. in 1818), wid. Lucy... W 2520
    Isaac, Cont. (Conn.)... S 10395
    (N. Y. in 1818.)
    James (Middlesex Co. in 1832)... S 17305
    Job, wid. Ruth... W 17375
    John... S 12363
    John H. BLWt. 136–300, Capt. issued Jan. 25, 1791. No papers.
    Joseph, wid. Lucy, Cont. (Conn.)... W 14408
    (Mass. in 1818.)
    Josiah.. S 44707
    Levi, Conn. & Vt.. S 18313
    Martin, wid. Sybil.. R 1413
    (He was pensioned from New Haven Co. in 1832. Her claim was rejected.)
    (Is he the one who is given in Conn. Men as Marlin, 81 in 1840?)
    Matthew. (See BEWEL.)
    Nathan.. S 23558
    Oliver, wid. Elizabeth... W 20801
    Orange.. R 1412
    Phebe, former wid. of Benjamin Thacher or Thatcher, BLWt. 26736–160–55............ W 2521
    Solomon... S 17318
    Solomon, wid. Sophia.. W 18670
    Timothy. (See also BEWEL).. S 15013
BUFFUM, Samuel, Conn. Sea Service & Mass. Sea Service.................................... S 12352
BUGBEE, BUGBEY or BUGBY, Amos, wid. Martha.. W 17388
    (She was 82 in 1840.)
    Benjamin (Conn. Men, 1818)... S 36461
    Benjamin (Vt. in 1818), wid. Mehitable.. W 23722
    Edward. BLWt. 312–200, Lieut. in Hazen's Reg't. issued Jan. 5, 1797 to Benjamin Dana,
    assignee. No papers.
    Elijah, wid. Sarah.. W 20802
    (Wid. was 88 in 1840.)
    James, wid. Thirza, BLWt. 28576–160–55... W 479
    (Conn. Men, 1818.)
    John, Conn. & Cont., wid. Hannah... W 17378
    (Wid. was 77 in 1840.)
    Pelatiah or Peletiah.. S 44698
    (Given as Patrick in Conn. Men.)
    Peter, wid. Isabel, BLWt. 7066–160–55.. W 21720
    Rufus... S 18751
BULKLEY, BULKLY, BUKELY, BUCKLEY, BULKELEY.
    Abraham or Abram, Conn. & Conn. Sea Service..................................... S 15331
    (Fairfield Co. in 1832.)
    Charles, Navy (Conn.)... S 12349
    (Lieut. Ship Alfred, pensioner, 1818, & New London Co. in 1832; & 87 in 1840.)
    Daniel, wid. Rhoda.. R 1407
    Edward, wid. Prudence... W 21727
    BLWt. 138–300, Capt. issued Apr. 22, 1796 to Prudence Bulkley, adx. No papers.
    Eleazer, Conn. & Conn. Sea Service.. S 18336
    (Fairfield Co. in 1832; 77 in 1840.)
    Francis, wid. Elizabeth, BLWt. 951–160–55.. W 1221
    Gershom, wid. Amelia.. W 17367
    (Wid. as Buckley, was 86 in 1840.)
    John, Conn. & Cont.. S 17314
    (1818, and 1832, New London Co.)
    Joseph.. S 23141
    Joseph, wid. Grizzel.. W 20799
    Nathan, wid. Jerusha, BLWt. 24773–160–55... W 25318
    (Fairfield Co. in 1832.)
    Seth, Mary Dayton, former wid. of... W 20956
    Solomon (Hartford Co. in 1832).. S 31583
    Turney, wid. Esther... W 17371
BULL, Aaron Cont. (Conn.) BLWt. 151–200, Lieut. in Sheldon's reg't, was issued June 25, 1789.
    No papers.
    Henry (pensioner, 1818; d Mch. 30, 1819)... S 36459
    Jeremiah, wid. Anne... W 17374
    John, wid. Martha... W 17377
    (Litchfield Co. in 1832.)
    (Wid. was 76 in 1840.)
    Reuben (Middlesex Co. in 1832)... S 17307
BUMFRIES, BUMPHRIES or BUMPHREY.
    Stephen, Conn. & N. Y. wid. Sarah, BLWt. 30623–160–55............................ W 8182
    (Mass. in 1818.)
BUMP, John, wid. Rebecca.. W 2590
    (Conn. Men in 1818.)
BUMPUS, Edward (Mass. in 1818)... S 34112
BURNAP or BUNAP, John, wid. Abigail.
BUNCE, Asa, wid. Sarah... W 24695
    Rory, wid. Elizabeth.. W 18673
    Timothy... R 1428
BUNDY, Joshua, wid. Elizabeth.. W 20817

BUNEL, BUNNEL, BUNNELL, Amos.. S 36460
  (Conn. Men, 1818.)
Daniel.. R 1432
Enos, wid. Naomi.. W 17385
  (New Haven Co. in 1832.)
Frederick (N. Y. in 1818).. S 44716
Jehiel, wid. Stetira.. R 1434
Joel (Hartford Co. in 1832)... S 15334
John... S 12382
John, wid. Pure.. W 20825
  (Pure was 85 in 1840.)
Joseph... S 10403
Joseph... S 36448
Patience, former wid. of Giles Andrews...................................... R 1493
William (New Haven Co. in 1832)... S 17317
  (See also BURNELL.)
BURBANK, Joel, wid. Eunice... W 21717
BURCH or BIRCH, Ebenezer, wid. Phebe................................... W 16204
BURCHARD, or BIRCHARD, Joseph... R 844
Sabra, former wid. of Hosea Gridley.. W 15992
  (See also BIRCHARD.)
BURDEN. (See BORDEN.)
Nathaniel, Conn. & Mass.. S 17313
BURDWIN, Samuel, wid. Lois... W 20814
BURGE, Lothrop.. S 12392
Lott, Conn. & Mass., wid. Hannah.. W 20804
  (See also BIRGE.)
BURGESS, Asa, Conn. & Cont., wid. Sarah................................ W 20798
  (Windham Co. in 1832.)
Ephraim... S 34114
BURKMAR, Nathan.. S 36947
BURLEY, Jacob (Conn. Men, 1818).. S 36451
BURNAM. (See BURNHAM.)
BURNAP, Jeriah, wid. Abigail; BLWt. 26311–160–55................... W 10472
  (Tolland Co. in 1832.)
John, wid. Abigail; BLWt. 24331–160–55..................................... W 25313
  (Windham Co. in 1832.)
Also given as BUNAP and BURNETT.
BURNELL, Samuel, wid. Sophia.. W 17390
  (See also BUNNELL.)
BURNET or BURNETT, James, wid. Phebe................................. W 25317
  (Windham Co. in 1832.)
John. (See BURNAP.)
BURNHAM or BURNAM, Abner... S 12390
Asa, Conn. & Cont.. S 12371
Asahel, BLWt. 447–100... S 44712
Eben or Ebenezer... S 15766
Gurdin, Conn., Cont. & Navy.. S 31585
Isaac (N. Y. in 1818).. S 42638
James, wid. Mehetabel... W 20823
  (Windham Co. in 1832; wid. was living in 1840.)
James, wid. Tamma.. W 17380
  (Wid. given BARNHAM, was 74 in 1840.)
James, Cont. (Conn.), wid. Eunice... W 14428
Jedediah... R 1479
John, wid. Bridget.. W 1548
John, Conn. & Cont.. S 18339
John, Cont. (Conn.)... S 46822
Joseph... S 12381
Joseph, Conn. & Cont.. S 17315
Joshua... R 1480
Josiah (Windham Co. in 1832).. S 12386
Nathan... S 36457
Nathan... S 36452
Oliver, Conn. & Cont.. S 15333
  (Conn. Men, p. 647.)
  (79 in 1840. Only Oliver Burnham in files from any State.)
Orrin.. S 28664
Roger (Hartford Co. in 1832; 79 in 1840).................................... S 23563
Stephen, Conn. & Cont... S 36450
  (Conn. Men, 1818.)
Sylvester, wid. Caroline... W 21728
  (New London Co. in 1832.)
William, wid. Marcy.. W 23742
  (N. Y. in 1818.)
Wolcott, wid. Sarah B., BLWt. 16259–160–55.............................. W 1220
BURNS, Daniel, wid. Martha... W 16519
William (Conn. Men, 1818)... S 36462
BURR, Asa, wid. Malinda.. W 16202
David, wid. Sarah Anna.. W 17373
  (Sarah A. was 78 in 1840.)
David, Jane Sherwood, former wid. of.. R 9502
Edmund, Conn. & Navy... S 37810
Hezekiah, wid. Mary... W 17382
  (Fairfield Co. in 1832.)
Jabez, wid. Mary.. R 1490
Joel.. S 12385
Nathaniel (Middlesex Co. in 1832).. S 16667
Roger, wid. Jane... W 20806

BURR, William, wid. Sarah, BLWt. 15421-160-55... W 25375
   (New Haven Co. in 1832.)
   (Wm. was 78 in 1840.)
   Zabina or Zebina (88 in 1840)... S 16064
BURRALL, or BURRILL, Ebenezer.. S 12395
   Jonathan.. S 29046
   (See also BURWELL.)
BURRETT or BURRITT, Andrew.. R 1496
   Anthony, wid. Abigail, BLWt. 34807-160-55.. W 2996
   (Surgeon, New Haven Co. in 1832.)
   Charles, wid. Hannah... W 23747
   (Lieut. in N. Y. in 1818.)
   Eben, wid. Sarah, BLWt. 82008-160-55.. W 17384
   (Litchfield Co. in 1832.)
   Elihu, wid. Elizabeth.. R 1497
   Israel, Conn. & Vt... S 19229
   Josiah, Mabel Curtis, former wid. of... W 25463
   Joseph, wid. Sally.. W 21627
   (Wid. was 79 in 1840.)
   (Also given as BARRETT.)
   Nathan (Fairfield Co. in 1832).. S 17306
   (77 in 1840.)
   Wakeman.. S 12942
   (Spelled BARRETT in Conn. Men.)
   Zalmon... S 16331
BURROUGHS, BURROWS, or BURRUS.
   Caleb, wid. Judith, BLWt. 11076-160-55... W 25311
   Elisha.. S 28406
   Hubbard, wid. Mary... W 25316
   Joseph, Conn. & Cont., wid Mary.. W 5237
   (N. Y. in 1818.)
   Josiah, wid. Sarah.. W 16518
   Nathan, former wid. of, Anna Cunningham... W 17674
   Paul, wid. Catharine... W 21724
   (New London Co. in 1832.)
   (Catharine was 82 in 1840.)
   Robert, BLWt. 26363-160-55.. S 28663
   Stephen... S 3110
   Stephen... R 1032
   Thomas, wid. Esther, BLWt. 57751-160-55... W 8402
   (Conn. Men, 1818.)
   (Also BARRUS.)
   William... S 19927
   William, Conn. & Navy, wid. Sarah.. R 1505
   William, Conn. & Vt... S 12396
   Zebulon, wid. Hannah... W 23751
   (See also BARRUS and BORRES.)
BURROUS. (See BORRES.)
BURT, John, wid. Eunice.. W 3653
BURTIS, Elizabeth, former wid. of Robert Eldredy...................................... W 1513
BURTON, Daniel, Conn. & Cont... S 12377
   Elijah, Conn., Cont., & Vt... S 18335
   Isaac, Conn. & N. Y., wid. Abigail, BLWt. 26393-160-55................................. W 2719
   James, wid. Naoma.. W 24682
   (Naomi was 92 in 1840.)
   Lewis (Fairfield Co. in 1832)... S 17310
   (78 in 1840.)
   Nathan (Litchfield Co. in 1832)... S 17311
   Seeley or Selah, or Othaniel Selah.. S 12394
BURWELL or BURWILL, Daniel, wid. Abigail... W 17386
   (Litchfield Co. in 1832.)
   Jere, wid. Lucy.. W 17381
   (Conn. Men, 1818.)
   (See also BURRALL and BURRELL.)
BURZETT, or BURZETTE, Charles, Cont. (Conn.)................................... S 44356
   (N. Y. in 1818.)
BUSH, George (Middlesex Co. in 1832; 83 in 1840)..................................... S 15768
   Rufus, Conn. & Cont... S 12374
   (Hartford Co. in 1832.)
   Samuel (Conn. Men, 1818).. S 36450
   Stephens, Conn. & Mass.. S 12357
BUSHNELL, Daniel (Middlesex Co. in 1832)... S 17319
   (Prob. also Conn. Men, p. 647.)
   David, BLWt. 141-300, Capt., issued Feb. 3, 1800. No papers.
   David, Conn. & Privateer... S 18752
   Elisha, wid. Lydia... W 17368
   (Middlesex Co. in 1832.)
   Ephraim.. S 12368
   Jason... S 2104
   Nathan, wid. Esther... W 17372
BUTLER, Benjamin, Conn. & Cont., wid. Lydia.. W 17376
   David... S 10397
   Eleazer... R 1543
   Ezekiel, wid. Lydia.. W 17392
   Ezra, wid. Mehitable.. W 17370
   George, Conn. & Mass... S 12375
   Isaac (Vt. in 1818)... S 39257
   Israel (N. Y. in 1818).. S 44329

31

BUTLER, Joel, Conn., Conn. Sea Service & Privateer... R 1546
    John.. S 44328
    John, wid. Patty.. W 20821
    Joseph (Vt. in 1818).. S 40775
    Josiah, wid. Hannah.. W 16517
    Matthew (New Haven Co. in 1832).. S 16673
    Peter.. S 37811
    Solomon.. S 21095
    Stephen.. S 12350
    Stephen.. S 37796
    Stephen, wid. Cata.. W 23724
    Stephen, Conn. & Cont., wid. Phebe.. W 4908
    Walter... W 16520
    William (Middlesex Co. in 1832).. S 12360
    Zebulon, wid. Phebe... W 5955
        BLWt. 132–500, Col., issued Sept. 15, 1791. No papers.
BUTTEN. (See BUTTON.)
BUTTOLPH, George or Georg... S 37809
    (Conn. Men, 1818.)
BUTTON or BUTTEN, Benjamin... S 44352
    Daniel, Conn. & R. I... R 1562
    Elijah... S 17312
    Isaiah, Conn. & R. I... S 21096
    Jonathan (Tolland Co. in 1832)... S 17870
    Mary, former wid. of Jonathan Hale.. W 17387
    Newbury... R 1563
    Samuel... S 38587
BUTTS, Esaias... S 37803
    (Is the one who is given as Isaac, 80 in 1840, the same as this?)
    John, former wid. of, Susanna Kirkland.. W 26724
    Josiah, wid. Eunice.. W 20800
    Josiah, wid. Lydia... W 14414
    Sherebiah.. S 29674
BUXTON, Peter, wid. Susanna... W 17383
BYINGTON, Ebenezer.. S 37814
    Isaac, wid. Elizabeth, BLWt. 6413–160–55.. W 1380
    (N. Y. in 1818.)
    John (Conn. Men, 1818.).. S 29051
    Justus, wid. Lucy.. W 23754
    Samuel, wid. Olive... W 15625
    Zuba or Zuby, former wid. of William Pratt... R 1570
BYRNE, Abigail, former wid. of Rogers, Stephen or Steven, BLWt. 2851–160–55........ W 25319

MEN WHO WERE PENSIONED FROM CONN. FOR THE MOST PART, AND ARE MENTIONED IN CONN. MEN AMONG
THE CONN. PENSIONERS, BUT ARE NOT SO CONSIDERED BY THE AUTHORITIES AT THE PENSION OFFICE IN
WASHINGTON; ALSO NAMES MISPRINTED IN CONN. MEN.

BABCOCK, Ichabod (R. I. in 1832), R. I. not Conn. service. (This man was living in Conn. in
    1840, and was 82 yrs. of age, his name being spelled BADCOCK.)
    Simon (82 in 1840), R. I. not Conn. Service.
    William, East Haddam, 54 in 1840. Not a Rev. pen.
BADLAM or BADLUM, Sylvanus (Conn. Men, 1818), Cont. and Mass. service, not Conn., widow
    Hannah, lived in Conn... W 25188
BAILEY, John, Jr. (C. Men, p. 649). No papers in files.
    Michael (Kent, 96 in 1840), as BARLEE in Pension Roll of 1835, but Mass. not Conn. service
    also Navy. (Conn. Men, 1818, as BARLEE.)
    William, Jr. (Conn. Men, p. 649). No papers on file.
BAKER, Windsor (Conn. Men, 1818), Mass. not Conn. Service.
BARBER, Timothy. Misprint in Conn. Men. This man was Timothy BARKER, and died
    before his pension was granted, and his wid., Irene, obtained the money due him to the date of
    his death.
BARDEEN, Aaron (Conn. Men, 1818), Mass. Service.
BARDWIN, Samuel. This is a misprint. It is either BURDWIN or BARDEN, both of whom
    were pensioners.
BARNES, Jonas. Misprint for Jonah.
BARRES, John Proctor (Conn. Men, 1818). Misprint for BORRES.
BARRETT, Wakeman, pensioned as BURRITT.
BARRON, Joseph (Conn. Men, 1818 in Vt.). He lived in Vt. in 1818, and N. Y. in 1820, where
    his wid. Magdaleine lived when she obtained her pension. But he only claimed Cont. and
    N. H. service, not Conn.
BATES, Asa (1832, pensioner), R. I. not Conn. service.
BASSETT, Howard or Hayward (Conn. Men, 1818), but he had Cont. (Mass.) not Conn. service. S 38521
BEDWELL, Eleazer, misprint for BIDWELL... S 14955
BEEBE, Alexander (N. Y. in 1818). His service was Cont., Mass. & Navy, not Conn.
    William C. (68 in 1840). Not in files, and probably not Revolutionary; too young.
BELLOWS, Elihu (Mass. in 1818). He is pensioned for Cont. (Mass.) service; had a wid. Sarah,
    who was also a pensioner. W 14296...BLWt. 488–100
BENJAMIN, Judah (N. Y. in 1818), Cont. (N. H. & N. Y.) not Conn. service................ S 39981
BENSON, Barak (Windham Co. in 1832), Cont. (Mass.), not Conn. service; had a wid. Sarah,
    also a pensioner who was 88 in 1840.. W 25329
BENTLEY, Ezekiel (New London Co. in 1832), R. I. not Conn. Service; had a wid. Anna, a
    pensioner, who was 83 in 1840... W 10407
BETTS, Aaron or Aron (Fairfield Co. in 1832), Mass. not Conn. service................... S 16634
BIGELOW, Abijah (Windham in 1832), Mass. not Conn. service, although he lived in Brooklyn
    after the Revolution.
BILL, Benjamin (Conn. Men, p. 649); no such name on files; is it Bell, Benjamin.......... S 38538
    Bozzell (Conn. Men, 1818); no such name on file, probably Rozzle or Roswell.......... S 37771
BILLINGS, John S.; he was pensioned from Conn. but his service was N. J. and Privateer; he was
    77 in 1840, and had a wid. Phebe, who got a Bounty Warrant, 30943.................. S 19909

BINGHAM, Ralph. No papers in files. (Conn. Men, p. 649.)
BIRDSEY, Ellen (79 in 1840). Probably Helen, wid. of Thaddeus BIRDSEYE (q. v.).
BITGOOD, John (Windham Co. in 1832), R. I. not Conn. service.
BLACKMAN or BLACKMAR, Jacob (Windham Co. in 1832), R. I. not Conn. service; had a wid. Zeruiah. (Jacob was 80 in 1840.)
BLISS, Isaac (Hartford Co. in 1832), Mass. not Conn. service (80 in 1840)......................... S 12246
    Moses (87 in 1840), Mass. not Conn. service.
BOUTON, Daniel (Conn. Men, p. 647). Not in files.
BOWERS, Michael (New Haven Co. in 1832), N. J. service not Conn. He did not move to Conn. until about 1790. Had a wid. Electa, also a pensioner, W 9360 and BLWt. 51880-160-55.
BOWMAN, Albert (Conn. Men, p. 649). No papers in files.
BRISTOL, Thomas (Conn. Men, p. 649). No papers in files.
BROWN, Ambrose (Conn. Men, 1818), Mass. not Conn. service; had a wid. Susannah, also a pensioner... W 25285
    BLWt. 13421-160-55. (He was 73 in 1840.)
    Edward (Conn. Men, p. 649); none from Conn. in files; one each from Mass., N. H., and Va. but none seem to have been residents of Conn.
    Joseph (Conn. Men, 1818), Mass. not Conn. service; had a wid. Sarah, also pensioned........ W 20777
    Othniel, Navy & R. I. not Conn. service; had a wid. Nancy, also pensioned.................. W 1135
    BLWt. 27620-160-55. (As Othaniel he was 81 in 1840.)
BRUSH, Gilbert (N. Y. in 1818). N. Y. not Conn. service.
BUCK, Aaron (Conn. Men, 1818). R. I. not Conn. service.
    (He was 86 in 1840.)
BUD, Solomon (Hartford Co. in 1832). In the printed report of 1835 the name appears BUEL, not BUD. That is a misprint in Conn. Men.
BUELL, Salmon (Conn. Men, p. 649). No papers on file.
BUGBEE, Patrick (N. Y. in 1818). Misprint in Conn. Men. Should be Peletiah, as given in U. S. Report.
BUKER, Windsor (82 in 1840). Mass. not Conn. service.
BUMFRIES, Edward (Mass. 1818). Misprint in Conn. Men, as shown by U. S. Report. Should be BUMPUS.
BURBECK, Henry (Conn. Men, 1818). Cont. & Mass. service not Conn.; had a wid. Lucy E., who also was pensioned W 10480, BLWt. 122-300, Capt. issued to him Dec. 3, 1789. No papers. He was 85 in 1840.
BURDICK, Walter (Conn. Men, p. 648). R. I. not Conn. service............................... S 19925
BURKMAR, Thomas (Maine, in 1818). Not Conn. service.
BURTCH, Billings (New London Co. in 1832), R. I. not Conn. service; had a wid. Jane, also pensioned.. W 20797

C.

CABLE, Abner (Conn. in 1818: Fairfield Co. in 1832)... S 10438
CADWELL, Aaron, wid. Mary.. W 17595
    John, Fabius, N. Y., 1832... S 12442
    John, Schaghticoke, N. Y., in 1818.. S 44365
    Phineas, Cont. (Conn.)... S 37822
    (N. Y. in 1818, as Corporal.)
    BLWt. 16127-160-55.
    Reuben, wid. Rebecca... W 18875
    Theodore, wid. Lucy, BLWt. 27637-160-55... W 22738
CADY, Abijah (Conn. 1818, d. May 16, 1819)... S 37818
    Abner, wid. Molly... W 17589
    (Tolland Co. 1832.)
    Elijah.. S 31591
    Elisha.. S 10433
    (Windham Co. 1832: 91 in 1840, Pomfret.)
    Elizabeth, former wid. of Obadiah Daley, Cont. (Conn.).. W 23757
    Ezra (Windham Co. 1832)... S 18434
    Jonathan, pensioned from R. I... S 17323
    Jonathan, Brooklyn, Conn. 1832... S 18344
    Luther, Conn. & N. Y.. S 28670
    Manasseh, Conn. & Navy, wid. Elizabeth.. W 20838
    Nedabiah, Conn. & Cont... S 12436
    Reuben (N. Y. in 1818).. S 44729
    Richard, wid. Alice... W 10571
    BLWt. 26991-160-55.
    (Soldier was in Windham Co. in 1832: and 78 in 1840, at Canterbury.)
CADY, Squire or Squier, wid Abiah.. W 1553
    BLWt. 26991-160-55.
    (Soldier was in Conn. 1818, as Serg't.; Windham Co. in 1832; 88 in 1840 at Plainfield.)
    William... S 39276
    Zadok, wid. Lucy... W 1714
CALDER, William, Conn. & Cont.. S 44725
CALKIN, CALKINS, CAULKINS, CAULKINGS.
    Daniel.. S 44374
    Darius (Penna. 1818), wid. Abigail.. W 6648
    Durkee.. S 22156
    Frederick, Navy (Conn.), wid. Annis.. W 5056
    James, wid. Esther.. W 23778
    Joel.. S 23567
    Moses, Conn. & N. Y... S 12426
    Nathaniel, wid. Lois.. W 16884
    Nathaniel Skiff, Conn. & Conn. Sea Service... S 15034
    Roswell, wid. Eunice... W 4915
    Solomon, Conn., N. H. & Vt... S 23568
CALL, John, d. Jan. 25, 1813; BLWt. 1727-100.
    or McCALL, John, wid. Loruhamah.. R 6599

CAMP, Abel, Conn. & Cont............ .... S 12435
    Chauncy... R 1613
    Elias (New Haven Co. in 1832).. S 17326
    Ephraim... S 12432
    Ezra (Litchfield Co. in 1832)... S 15033
    Israel... S 16689
    James, wid. Elizabeth.. R 1615
    John, Litchfield Co., Conn., in 1832... S 37819
    John.. R 1616
    John, New Milford, Conn., in 1832... W 23762
      Wid. Annis. BLWt. 31457–160–55.
    Manoah, wid. Clarissa.. W 1818
      (Middlesex Co. 1832; 79 in 1840 at Durham.)
    Mial. (See BEACH, Thaddeus.)
    Rejoice.. S 16066
      (Middlesex Co. 1832; 81 in 1840 at Durham.)
    Samuel, N. Y. in 1818, as Serg't... S 23148
    Samuel, Conn. in 1818 as private.. S 33590
    Sharp (Conn. 1919)... S 37821
CAMPBELL, Archibald, N. Y. in 1832.. S 12448
    (NOTE.—There was another pensioner by name of Archibald Campbell, who was born
    at Voluntown, Conn., May 11, 1873, and applied for pension in 1832 from Salisbury, Conn.
    He was living in Berkshire Co., Mass., in 1781 and enlisted in the N. Y. State Line. Both
    he and his wid. were pensioned. N. Y. Campbell, Archibald, wid. Eliza or Elizabeth,
    W 1138; BLWt. 13434–160–55.)
    Betsey or Betsy, former wid. of Seelye, John.. W 4419
    Isaac... S 12406
    John, Windham Co. in 1832.. S 17321
    Noble, wid. Janet.. W 16888
    Robert (N. Y. in 1818 as Serg't).. S 44373
CANADA, David (Conn. 1818), wid. Lucy, BLWt. 26313–160–55.................................. W 25388
CANDE or CANDEE, or CANDER, Job (New Haven Co. in 1832; 80 in 1840 in Oxford)...... S 13036
    Nehemiah.. R 1656
    Samuel (New Haven Co. in 1832; 87 in 1840 in Oxford).. S 17327
    Zacheus or Zaccheus.. S 29062
CANFIELD, Andrew, wid. Eunice... R 1658
    Daniel, Cont. (Conn.).. S 29696
    Elijah (Ohio in 1818).. S 2106
    Isaiah, Conn. & Service on Lake Champlain, wid. Anne.. W 16883
    Ithamar, wid. Betsey.. R 1657
    Oliver... S 23566
    Philo, wid. Mary P... R 1659
    Samuel, Conn. & Cont.. S 15772
CANNON, Mary, former wid. of John Heminger... W 23769
    BLWt. 67542–160–55.
CAPEN, Purchase, wid. Theodosia.. R 1670
    Timothy.. S 30313
CAPRON, Jeremiah, wid. Jerusha... R 1674
    BLWt. 2453–100.
    NOTE.—The soldier obtained a BLWt. It was the widow's claim that was rejected.
CARD, Elisha.. R 1676
CAREL, John (New London Co. in 1832; 79 in 1840 at New London)............................ S 12416
CAREY or CARY, Anson.. S 9148
    Hezekiah, Conn. & Cont... S 39279
      (Vt. in 1818. (BLWt. 33561–160–55.
    Jabez, wid. Mary, BLWt. 18952–160–55... W 25399
CAREY or CARY, John; BLWt. 578–100.
    Joseph, wid. Sarah... W 18865
    Levi, Conn. & Cont.. S 8157
    Oliver, Conn., Cont., & Mass... S 23149
CARLTON, Richard (Vt. in 1818 as Serg't.)... S 39280
CARMAN, John.. S 12409
CARPENTER, Allen (Vt. in 1818).. S 44367
    Comfort, Tolland Co. in 1832.. S 12422
    Comfort, Conn. in 1818... S 37823
    Daniel... S 42116
    David, Mass in 1832... S 29063
    David, New Haven Co. in 1832; wid. Azubah... W 16892
    Elias... S 21683
    Elijah, former wid. Sarah Sargeant... R 9204
    Eliphalet (Vt. in 1818).. S 23151
    Ephraim.. S 12670
    Esther, former wid. of Clement Stoddard, Conn. & War of 1812............................... R 10202
    Isaiah.. S 23672
    Israel... S 30315
    John.. S 15371
    Joseph... S 12411
    Joshua A., Cont. (Conn.)... S 45319
      (N. Y. in 1818.)
    Nathaniel, wid. Elfrida.. W 20839
    Phebe, former wid. of Solomon Eaton... W 8591
      BLWt. 30597–160–55.
    Simeon.. R 1718
    Timothy, BLWt. 26546–160–55.. S 12675
      (77 in 1840, at Ellington, Windham Co.)
    Uriah, wid. Elithal... W 25379
      (72 in 1840 at Ashford; is prob. this wid.)
    William, Cont. (Conn.)... S 37820
      (Conn. in 1818.)

CARR, Clement (Conn. 1818).. S 38597
   Ebenezer (N. Y. in 1818)... S 45318
   Robert.. S 44724
   William... S 39289
    NOTE.—Margaret Carr, wid. of above soldier, received pension as former wid. of William
    Brown, Cont. (Penna.), W 73.
   (See also KERR.)
CARRIER, David, wid. Rebecca... R 1727
   Hannah, former wid. of Guy Dodd... W 10573
   John.. S 12429
   (See also CURRIER.)
CARRINGTON, Jesse, former wid. Elizabeth Lewes or Lewis................................. W 20429
   Lemuel, former wid. Abigail Rice... W 17538
   Reverius, former wid. Loly Merrick.. W 9959
   BLWt. 17577–160–55.
CARTER, Aaron, wid. Rachel... W 22726
   Benjamin, wid. Phebe... W 1715
   Elihu, Cont. (Conn.)... S 12420
   (Hartford Co. in 1832.)
   Heman (N. Y. in 1818).. S 44358
   Ithiel, Conn. & Cont., wid. Lois.. W 17591
   (Conn. 1818, as Serg't.)
   Jirah.. S 23147
   John, Vt. in 1818, wid. Lucinda.. W 20840
   John, N. Y. in 1818 as Serg't., wid. Susanna.. W 10565
   Jonah, former wid. Tempa Barlow, BLWt. 113036–160–55................................... W 10383
   Ned or Chappel, Edward Carter, wid. Eunice (Conn. 1818, as Carter, Edward)........ W 20850
   Reuben, former wid. of Elizabeth Moss, BLWt. 571–100.
   Rufus... S 9208
   Samuel (Windham Co. in 1832).. S 10437
   Solomon.. S 18340
   Stephen (New Haven Co. in 1832).. S 12407
CARTRIGHT or CARTWRIGHT, Cyrus, wid. Mary.. W 6627
   (N. Y. in 1819.)
CARTY, or McCARTY, Clark, wid. Mabel.. W 20248
CARVER, Aldric, Cont. service, but Conn. Agency... S 38596
   Asa.. S 23150
   Joseph, wid. Tabitha... W 20829
   Nathaniel, wid. Lydia.. R 1763
CASE, Aaron, wid. Abigail.. R 1764
   Abel, Hartford Co. 1832.. S 12668
   Abel, Cont. (Conn.), N. Y. in 1818... S 44362
   Abner, wid. Hannah.. W 17588
   Asahel (Litchfield Co. in 1832).. S 16068
   Ashbel, wid. Azubah... R 1765
   Fithen, wid. Amarilla or Amrilles.. W 17586
   George.. S 3115
   Giles, wid. Dorcas.. W 17585
   Hosea, wid. Sarah.. W 17584
   (Hartford Co. in 1832.)
   Ichabod.. S 31602
   James, wid. Lydia.. R 1767
   John M., wid. Abigail... W 23770
   (Hartford Co. in 1832; BLWt. 26725–160–55; 77 in 1840 at Hartland.)
   Lemuel, wid. Mary, BLWt. 93530–160–55.. W 9766
   Micah, Conn. & Mass... S 17328
   (Hartford Co. in 1832.)
   Nathan, Conn. & Cont.. S 22159
   Oliver, wid. Amy.. W 17587
   (Hartford Co. in 1832.)
   Reuben... R 1769
   Richard, wid. Mary.. W 20833
   (Conn. in 1818.) BLWt. 264–100.
   Roswell (Conn. 1818).. S 38593
   Rufus, wid. Rachel, BLWt. 9062–160–55.. W 3655
   William, Conn. & Cont.. S 44361
CASEY, John, Conn., R. I. & Vt., BLWt. 85507–160–55... W 25378
CASH, Lois, former wid. of Zenas Goodrich... R 1780
CASHMAN. (See CUSHMAN.)
CASS, Moses, former wid. Abia Judd... W 20223
CASTLE, Joel.. S 8143
CASWELL, Ezra (Mass. in 1818)... S 34177
   Julius... R 1802
   Samuel... R 1803
CATLIN, Abel, Conn., Navy & Privateer.. S 3
   David (Litchfield Co. in 1832).. S 12430
   Eli, Conn. & Cont.. S 40812
   (Penna. in 1818 as Capt.)
   Elisha, wid. Roxanna.. R 1812
   Elizabeth, former wid. of Simeon Curtiss, BLWt. 14667–160–55.......................... W 10569
   Hezekiah, wid. Sarah.. W 18851
   Isaac (Litchfield Co. in 1832).. S 12433
   Lewis, Conn. & Cont.. S 17320
   Nathan, wid. Abigail... W 20827
   Phineas, Cont. (Conn.) wid. Sarah, BLWt. 545–100.. W 18872
   Putnam, wid. Mary or Polly.. R 1810
   Roswell (Vt. in 1818).. S 39278
   Simeon, Conn. & Cont.. S 10432
CAULKINGS or CAULKINS. (See CALKINS.)

CAVARLY, John, wid. Caroline.. W 17593
CAWDERY or CAWDRY. (See COWDERY.)
CHACE. (See CHASE.)
CHADWICK, James.. BLWt. 1458-100
    Nathan, Conn. & Vt.. S 16709
    Richard (New London Co. in 1832).. S 12690
CHAFE. (See CHAFFEE.)
CHAFF, CHAFEE, CHAFFE, or CHAFFEE.
    Abiel, wid. Hannah.. W 25401
      (Conn. in 1818; 79 in 1840 at Woodstock.)
    Calvin, wid. Ruth... W 16208
    Chester, wid. Caroline... W 17599
      (85 in 1840 at Thompson; Windham Co. in 1832.)
    Frederick (Hartford Co. in 1832).. S 17881
    Joel, wid. Eleanor, BLWt. 26046-160-55.. W 6909
      (Litchfield Co. in 1832; and 81 in 1840 at Sharon.)
    Jonathan, Conn. & Mass., wid. Olive.. W 2271
    Joseph.. R 1829
    Josiah, wid. Joanna, BLWt. 3531-160-55....................................... W 1887
    Serrill, Conn. & Mass.. S 18346
    Thomas (Conn. in 1818).. S 37833
    William, wid. Mary.. W 17619
      (Conn. in 1818.)
CHALKER, Jabez, wid. Hannah... W 20852
    (Middlesex Co. in 1832; and 83 in 1840 at Durham.)
    Jesse, wid. Elizabeth.. W 17596
    Moses (Middlesex Co. in 1832; 81 in 1840, at Saybrook)....................... S 31604
    Oliver (Middlesex Co. in 1832; 80 in 1840 at Saybrook)....................... S 17329
    Samuel, wid. Damaras... W 23802
CHAMBERLAIN, CHAMBERLIN or CHAMBERLINE.
    Aaron, wid. Wealthy... W 27394
    Ephraim, BLWt. 372-300, Captain, was issued Feb. 6, 1797. No papers.
    Isaac, Conn. & Cont... S 45836
    Jeremiah, wid. Sarah.. W 23790
      (Maine in 1818.) BLWt. 3516-160-55.
    Jireh... S 22170
    Joseph S.. S 37826
      (Conn. in 1818, where the name is incorrectly given as Joseph H.)
    Leander (Vt. in 1818) .... S 40826
    Nathaniel, wid. Rhoda... W 14474
    Pliney or Pliny, wid. Martha, BLWt. 17724-160-55............................. S 29708
    Samuel (Conn. in 1818).. S 37841
    Swift, wid. Mary, BLWt. 30694-160-55.. W 1555
    Theodore or Theodorus, wid. Fanny... W 1226
      (Conn. in 1818.) BLWt. 31893-160-55.
    William... S 44733
    Wyatt or Wayatt, wid. Dinah... W 17612
CHAMBERS, William (Ohio in 1818)... S 42644
CHAMPION, Elisha, wid. Phebe.. W 25406
    (Wid. was 75 in 1840 at Lyme.)
    Epaphroditus (Ass't. Deputy Commissary, Middlesex Co. in 1832).............. S 16711
    Ezra (Conn. in 1818) wid. Lucy.. W 6662
      BLWt. 110-60-55.
    Henry, Conn. & Cont.. S 12463
      (New London Co. in 1832.)
    Reuben, Lyme, 1818 & 1840.. S 38600
    Reuben, wid. Rhoda H... W 9783
      NOTE.—This pension was granted after both soldier and widow were dead, by special act
    of Congress to son, Reuben J., in Hillsdale, Mich. Soldier was son of Israel and grandson of
    Henry Champion, Commissary General.
    Salmon.. R 1839
    Samuel, Conn. & Cont... S 38604
CHAMPLIN, Caleb (New London Co. in 1832).................................... S 15043
    Charles (Windham Co. in 1832), wid. Mary................................... W 17614
    Silas, Conn. & Cont... S 18347
      (Conn. 1818; New London Co. in 1832; Lyme, in 1840.)
    Stephen... S 15040
      (New London Co. in 1832; 77 in 1840, at Lebanon.)
    William, Conn., Privateer & R. I... S 12473
CHANCE, Evans or Evens, Conn. & Vt... S 10441
CHANDLER, Daniel... S 13035
    Jacob, Conn. Sea service & Navy, wid. Anna.................................. W 14462
    Jonathan, Conn , Conn. Sea Service & Privateer.............................. R 21842
    Joseph (Ohio in 1818)... S 35206
    Josiah.. S 22167
    Robert (also given SHANDLER)... S 40399
    Simeon.. S 15774
CHAPEL, CHAPPEL, CHAPELL, CHAPPAL or CHAPPLE.
    Amaziah (N. Y. in 1818)... S 44749
    Curtis (N. Y. in 1818), wid. Sarah... W 17603
    Dan, wid. Experience.. W 20843
    Daniel, wid. Anna... W 17606
    Daniel, wid. Mary... W 2527
      BLWt. 6193-160-55.
    Edward Carter. (See CARTER, Ned.)
    Guy, wid. Delight... W 25407
      (New London Co. in 1832; and 81 in 1840 at Montville.)
    Hiram, Cont. (Conn.).. S 12474
    Jedediah, wid. Lucy, BLWt. 6287-160-55...................................... W 17597
    Noah (N. Y. in 1818).. S 40825

CHAPEL, CHAPPEL, CHAPELL, CHAPPAL or CHAPPLE—Continued.
Noah (N. Y. in 1818), wid. Lydia... W 16530
Samuel, wid. Abigail, BLWt. 26525–160–55... W 23385
Stephen, wid. Lucy, BLWt. 26012–160–55.. W 18880
Stephen, wid. Lydia.. W 16533
William... S 22677
William, wid. Lydia.. W 4154
CHAPIN, Asa (Tolland Co. in 1832)... S 15775
David (N. Y. in 1818), wid. Ruth, BLWt. 2490–160–55.................................... W 22768
Elias, wid. Dimmis, BLWt. 27621–160–55... W 2528
Frederick, former wid. of Lucretia Booth... W 18626
Ichabod... S 15372
John, Conn. & Mass., wid. Elizabeth, BLWt. 31438–160–55............................... W 10601
CHAPIN, Oliver wid. Elizabeth... W 25408
   (Tolland Co. in 1832; and 82 in 1840 at Somers.)
Phinehas, Conn., Cont. & N. H.. S 12701
Timothy, Cont. (Conn.), wid. Tacy.. W 18890
   (N. Y. in 1818.)
CHAPLIN, Ebenezer (Hartford Co. in 1832; and 90 in 1840 at Suffield)................... S 16075
CHAPMAN or CHOPMAN, Abner, Conn. & Cont... S 12461
   (Conn. in 1818, as Serg't. Middlesex Co. in 1832.)
Albert, Cont. service, N. Y. Agency, Conn. residence..................................... S 27612
Albert, BLWt. 367–400, Major, was issued June 6, 1797, to Nathaniel Satterlee, Assignee. No
   papers.
Asa, wid. Elizabeth.. W 17621
Ashbel, wid. Lydia.. W 25404
Caleb, Stephenson, N. Y. in 1832.. S 15309
   Conn. & Privateer.
Caleb, Steuben Co. N. Y. in 1832: wid. Lydia.. W 16209
Collins (Conn. in 1818), wid Mary.. W 17600
Comfort.. S 44377
Constant, wid. Jemima... W 6652
   (N. Y. in 1818.)
Dan, N. Y. in 1818.. S 23571
Daniel, New London Co. in 1832... S 12682
David.. S 22161
Ebenezer, wid. Mary... W 17618
   (Conn. in 1818.)
Edward, Conn. in 1818... S 38606
Edward, Conn. & N. Y. service; N. Y. in 1832, wid. Rebecca, BLWt. 30612–160–55.......... W 14466
Eliakim (Tolland Co. in 1832)... S 31603
Elijah (Conn. 1818, as Capt.)... S 37848
   BLWt. 375–300, Captain, was issued May 19, 1797, to Elijah Chapman. No papers.
Elijah (Cairo, N. Y. in 1818)... S 44739
   BLWt. 627–100.
Elijah, d. 1804; Conn. & Cont., wid. Esther.. W 17605
Elizabeth, former wid. of Joseph Smith... R 1865
Frederick or Frederik... S 24107
   (Hartford Co. in 1832; and 79 in 1840 at Windsor.)
Israel, Conn. & Navy.. R 1870
James, New London Co. in 1818.. S 37835
   (89 in 1840 in New London.)
James, Fairfield Co. in 1818.. S 37831
   Mrs. Ellen Turney, former wid. of James Chapman, was pensioned as former wid. of her
      first husband, Samuel Squires, Conn., W 22458.
Jason, wid. Mary.. R 1877
   (Soldier was pensioned and living in New London Co. in 1832, and 78 in 1840 at Waterford.)
Jedediah (Conn. 1818; Middlesex Co. in 1832; and 81 at Westbrook in 1840)............... S 12691
John... S 24108
Joseph, Preston, Conn. in 1832.. S 10445
Joseph, Conn. & Cont. Penna. in 1818, as Lieut.. S 40821
   BLWt. 377–200, Lieut. issued Sept. 24, 1790, to Peleg Sanford, assignee. No papers.
Joshua, wid. Lucy... R 1874
Lebbeus.. S 37842
   (Conn. 1818, as Libbeus, Lieut.)
Lydia, former wid. of William Cochran, BLWt. 27597–160–55.............................. W 23793
Michael.. S 42645
Nahum... S 44376
Oliver, wid. Eunice... R 1868
Richard.. S 22168
Robert, wid. Judith, BLWt. 27625–160–55.. W 24844
   (Litchfield Co. in 1832.)
Salathiel, wid. Amy, BLWt. 26440–160–55.. W 4920
   (Hartford Co. in 1832; and 80 in 1840, at Simsbury, as Salathel.)
Samuel... S 12472
Samuel... BLWt. 1954–100
Silas (Conn. in 1818)... S 37847
Simeon.. R 1879
Stephen.. BLWt. 186–100
Taylor... S 28675
Thomas, Conn. Cont. & Mass., wid. Phebe, BLWt. 1903–160–55............................. W 25405
Timothy, wid. Avis.. W 15881
Zachariah... S 28677
CHACE or CHASE, Isaac... S 37849
   (Conn. in 1818, and d. Oct. 20, 1818.)
Lot, wid. Rhoda... W 20846
   (Litchfield Co. in 1832.)
Mary, former wid. of Ziba Roberts.. W 22759
Samuel, BLWt. 103392–160–55.. S 19240

CHATFIELD, Dan... S 3783)
    (79 in Huntington, in 1840.)
  Isaac, Cont. (Conn.).. S 12475
    (Conn. in 1818.)
  John.. S 38605
CHATFIELD, Jonathan, wid. Dinah... R 1894
  Josiah (Conn. in 1818).. S 37837
  Levi (Conn. in 1818).. S 37843
CHATTERTON, Wait, Conn. & Privateer, wid. Melinda or Millinda, BLWt. 11096-160-55..... W 529
CHAUNCEY, Nathaniel W.. S 15044
  (Middlesex Co. in 1832.)
CHEADEL or CHEADLE, Elijah... S 11994
CHEESEBROUGH, CHESEBROUGH or CHESEBRO, or CHESEBRA.
  Asa.. R 1899
  Christopher.. R 1900
  Elijah, wid. Thankful, BLWt. 26591-160-55.. W 22748
  James... S 38607
  Lois, former wid. of Joseph Hilliard.. W 16901
  Nathaniel, Conn. & Cont.. S 37845
  Perez... S 15042
    (New London Co. in 1832; and 78 in 1840 at Bozrah.)
CHEEVER or CHEVER, Ebenezer, Conn. & Privateer................................ S 12452
CHENEY or CHENY, Elijah... S 37839
    (Conn. in 1818.)
  Joseph, Auburn, N. Y. in 1818... S 44754
  Joseph, d. 1790, wid. Rebecca.. W 20847
  Waldo, wid. Priscilla... W 20854
  William, wid. Sarah... R 1905
CHESEBRA, CHESEBRO, or CHESEBROUGH. (See CHEESEBROUGH.)
CHESTER, Christopher Conn. & Cont.. S 40043
    (R. I. in 1818.)
  Giles, Navy (Conn.), wid. Mary.. W 17611
    (Conn. in 1818, as Seaman on Brig *Calvert*.)
  John, Conn. & Navy... S 38603
CHEVER. (See CHEEVER.)
CHICHESTER, David, wid. Mary... W 17610
  Henry.. S 17330
    (Fairfield Co. in 1832; 77 in Norwalk in 1840.)
  Nathan, wid. Theodosia.. W 17607
    (Fairfield Co. in 1832.)
CHIDESTER, William, wid. Martha.. W 4918
CHIDSEY, Ephraim, wid. Hannah... W 17620
    (New London Co. in 1832.)
  Isaac, wid. Lydia... W 17601
CHILD or CHILDS, Cephas, Conn. & Cont.. S 12469
  Elias (Windham Co. in 1832)... S 31605
  Jesse... R 1919
  Lyman... S 21690
  Obadiah (Conn. 1818, as Ensign)... S 37832
  Penuel, Rutland Co. Vt. in 1832, wid. Sabra... W 716
  Penuel, d. 1813; wid. Sarah... W 20842
  Stephen, wid. Zilpha.. W 18886
    (Vt. in 1818.)
  Timothy, wid. Anna.. W 20859
  Willard.. S 10444
    (Windham Co. in 1832; and 82 in 1840 at Woodstock.)
CHIPMAN, John, Cont. (Conn.).. S 46351
    BLWt. 376-300, Capt. issued March 3, 1797, to Samuel Fitch, assignee. No papers.
  Nathaniel (Vt. in 1818 as Lieut.).. S 18780
  Thomas, Conn. & Cont... S 44741
    (N. Y. in 1818 as Serg't.)
  Timothy (Conn. in 1818).. S 37834
CHITTENDEN, CHITTENDON, CHITTINGTON, or CRITTENDEN.
  Abraham... S 16703
    (New Haven Co. in 1832; and 89 in 1840 at Guilford.)
  Asahel, former wid. of, Anna or Anne McFarland; BLWt. 28539-160-55.... W 25688
  Benjamin (Conn. 1818, as Ensign).. S 37836
  Calvin... S 17334
  Cornelius, BLWt. 11279-160-55... S 17880
    (Middlesex Co. in 1832; and 77 in 1840 at Westbrook.)
  Gideon... S 42660
  James (Vt. in 1818).. S 23570
  Jared or Jerard, Conn. & Cont... S 44742
  John, Conn. & Cont.. S 17332
    (Conn. in 1818; and Middlesex Co. in 1832; and 83 in 1840 at Westbrook.)
  Levi, wid. Hannah... W 17622
    (New Haven Co. in 1832.)
  Nathan (New Haven Co. in 1832; and 82 in 1840 at Guilford).................. S 17331
  Reuben.. S 44743
  Solomon, wid. Susanna.. R 1934
  William.. S 34197
CHOPMAN. (See CHAPMAN.)
CHURB, Joseph (N. Y. in 1818 as Serg't.)... S 44747
  William, Cont. service, but Conn. residence of daughter, who obtained BLWt. 917-100.
CHURBUCK, Ebenezer, wid. Lucina or Lusina... W 2919
CHURCH, Amasa, Conn. & Cont... S 12688
  Daniel... S 23155
  Ebenezer, wid. Eunice... W 3130
  Elihu (N. Y. in 1818)... S 44379
  Fairbanks, Conn. & Cont.. S 12470
  Gideon, wid. Abigail.. W 2755

CHURCH, James Cady... S 44380
   (Given James E. in N. Y. in 1818.)
  Joel W., Cont. (Conn.).. S 28674
  John Jonathan, John J., or Jonathan or Jonathan Ellis, wid. Abigail, BLWt. 39497–160–55... W 1143
  John, Conn., Green Mt. Boys & Mass.. S 15373
   (Litchfield Co. in 1832.)
  Joseph, Conn. & Cont., wid. Priscilla... W 23806
   (Conn. in 1818; and 80 in 1840 at Montville.)
  Nathaniel.. S 19933
  Parlly... R 1951
  Philemon (N. Y. in 1818)... S 42122
  Samuel, pensioned as Samuel 1st, at Dorset, Vt., in 1818.. S 40830
  Samuel, pensioned from Oneida Co., N. Y., in 1832; wid. Lydia................................... R 1950
  Samuel, Cont. (Conn.), pensioned as Samuel 2nd, Fletcher, Vt., 1818............................. S 39309
  Simeon, Conn., Mass. & N. H.. S 12471
  Uriah, Mass., 1818, as Serg't.. S 34185
  Uriah, Conn., in 1818 as Lieut... S 37844
  Willard (N. Y. in 1818).. S 44750
CHURCHILL, Jacob, wid. Lillis... W 14471
  John... R 1952
  Nathaniel, wid. Lydia.. W 22770
  Oliver, wid. Lydia, BLWt. 9433–160–55.. W 2560
  Samuel... R 1953
  Stephen, wid. Mary... W 1225
CLAP or CLAPP
  Abigail, former wid. of Benjamin Barnes or Barns... R 1957
  Oliver (Hartford Co. in 1832; 80 in 1840).. S 16718
  Samuel, Conn., Cont. & N. H.. S 39321
CLARK or CLARKE.
  Abel Farmington, Conn., in 1832; wid. Lois... W 1561
  Abel, d. 1788; former wid. Hannah Murray... W 21770
  Abel, wid. Sarah... R 13178
  Abraham or Abram (N. Y. in 1818)... S 44776
  Adna.. S 8209
  Amasa (Windham Co. in 1832; 76 in 1840 at Hampton)... S 17348
  Amos, Chatham, Conn., in 1832 as Sergeant and 83 in 1840....................................... S 23574
  Amos, Dryden, N. Y., in 1818, as 2nd... S 44774
  Amos, New Haven Co. as Amos, Jr.. S 37872
  Amos, Chaplin, Conn., in 1832; and 78 in 1840; wid. Hannah...................................... W 25419
   BLWt. 26492–160–55.
  Andrew, Middlebury, Conn., in 1832; wid. Anna.. W 17633
  Andrew, Norwich, Conn., in 1832; wid. Vashti, BLWt. 31890–160–55............................... W 480
  Andrew, Conn., N. Y. & Vt.; res. N. Y. in 1832... S 28687
  Asa, N. Y. in 1832.. S 12504
  Asa, Vt., in 1818... S 38611
  Augustus, wid. Anna... W 16211
   (N. Y. in 1818.)
  Barnabas.. BLWt. 1451–100
  Benjamin, Columbia Co., N. Y., in 1832... S 10455
  Benjamin, Tioga Co., N. Y., in 1832.. S 12502
  Benjamin, Conn. & Penna... S 41487
   Penna. in 1818.
  Benoni or Bennoni, Conn. & Mass.. S 12491
  Beriah.. S 34209
  Caesar, Negro... S 37871
  Champion.. S 16082
   (Litchfield Co. in 1832; and 79 in 1840 at Bethlehem.)
  Chipman... S 9181
  Comfort, wid. Esther.. R 1973
  Cyrenus (Conn. in 1818)... S 12695
  Daniel, Litchfield Co. in 1832... S 17341
  Daniel, New Haven Co. in 1832.. S 18354
  Daniel, Windsor Co., Vt., in 1832.. S 10457
  Daniel, Conn. & Cont., Windham Co., Conn., in 1832... S 23161
  Daniel, Cont. (Conn.), Bennington Co., Vt., in 1818.. S 17349
  David, Middlesex Co., Conn., in 1832... W 25424
  David, N. Y., in 1832; wid. Jane... R 2015
  David, wid. Sarah... S 15046
  Elias, Hartford Co., Conn., in 1832.. R 1970
  Elias, Conn. & N. Y... S 37867
  Elijah (Conn. in 1818).. S 44767
  Eliphalet, or Eliphlael, Berkshire Co., Mass., in 1832... S 12477
  Eliphalet, N. Y., in 1818... W 17630
  Elisha, Milford, Conn., in 1832; wid. Sraah.. W 718
  Elisha, Conn., in 1818; Cont. (Conn.); wid. Martha, BLWt. 8159–160–55.......................... S 18353
  Ezra, Conn., N. Y., R. I. & Vt.
   Vt. in 1832.
  Ezra, Cont. (Conn.), pensioned in 1818, as artificer, in Conn.; wid. Eunice.................... W 18911
  Flavel (Conn. in 1818).. S 12481
  Francis (Windham Co., Conn., 1832)... S 23165
  George, Conn. & Cont., Litchfield Co., Conn., in 1832.. S 12489
  George, Onondaga Co., N. Y., in 1832... S 28683
  George, Middletown, Conn., in 1818... S 37873
  Gershom, N. Y., in 1832.. S 23575
  Gershom, d. 1815; wid. Lavina.. W 20890
  Gideon, wid. Jemima... W 17627
   (Tolland Co. in 1832.)
  Giles, wid. Polly... W 2592
   (Conn. in 1818.)
  Hezekiah, wid. Lucy... W 6688
   (N. Y. in 1818, as Surgeon's mate.) 39

CLARK or CLARKE—Continued.
```
Ira (Conn., in 1818).................................................................. S  37854
Isaac, Milford, Conn., in 1832....................................................... S  16714
Israel, Conn. & Cont................................................................. S  42129
  (Ohio in 1818.)
Jabez (Windham Co., Conn., in 1832)................................................. S  12495
Jacob (New London Co. in 1832; 81 in 1840 at Lebanon)............................... S  10453
James.......................................................................... BLWt. 2045-200
James, Conn. & Cont., N. Y. City, 1832.............................................. S  12514
James, Conn. & Cont., in 1818....................................................... S  44768
James, d. 1816, Conn. & Cont.; wid. Jerusha......................................... W  20874
James W., wid. Betsey............................................................... W  20873
  (New Haven Co. in 1832.)
Jerome, Conn., Cont. & Privateer (N. Y. in 1818); wid. Nancy, BLWt. 14510-160-55..... W   4156
Jesse, wid. Olive................................................................... W  17632
Joel, wid. Susannah, BLWt. 1515-100................................................. W  22799
  (N. Y. 1818, Musician, as Clarke.)
John, Suffolk Co., N. Y., in 1832, BLWt. 32223-160-55............................... S  12500
John, b. 1754, res. Washington, Conn................................................ S  37857
John, enl. Windham, Conn., d. 1818; wid. Phebe...................................... W  17629
John, Conn. & Conn., Sea Service.................................................... R   1986
  b. 1746 in N. J.; claimed to have enlisted from New Haven, Conn.; res. N. Y.
John, Conn. & Cont., b. 1763, d. 1831; enl. from Lebanon, wid. Amy.................. W  14482
John, Conn. & Cont., b. 1752, d. 1841; enl. from Hampton & Mansfield; wid. Lucy..... W  25423
John, Cont. (Conn.), b. 1753, enlisted fr. Mansfield, res. Ashford, d. 1833......... S  44386
John, styled John Clarke, 2nd, of Middletown, N. H. Co., in 1818.................... S  37859
Jonas, Conn., Cont. & Mass., wid. Sarah............................................. R   2016
Jonathan............................................................................ R   1992
Jonathan............................................................................ R   1993
Jonathan, wid. Martha............................................................... R   2001
Jonathan, wid. Polly................................................................ W   9387
Joseph, Middlebury, Conn., in 1832.................................................. S  17347
Joseph, Windham Co. in 1818......................................................... S  37855
Joseph, Hartford Co. in 1818........................................................ S  37858
Joseph, former wid. Jemimah Spelman................................................. R   9969
Joseph, Middlesex Co., Conn., in 1832; wid. Sarah................................... W  20871
Joseph, d. 1814, Conn. & Mass., wid. Judith, res. Mass.............................. W  14479
Joseph, former wid. Rozina King..................................................... R  19377
Joseph, BLWt. 383-200 Lieut. issued Jan. 29, 1790, to Joseph Clarke.  No papers.
Joseph C., wid. Sally............................................................... R   2018
Lamberton or Lambert, wid. Martha................................................... W  18919
  (Vt. in 1818.)
Levi, Conn., 1818, as Corporal...................................................... S  37852
Levi, wid. Anna..................................................................... W   1146
Lydia, former wid. of Joseph Judson................................................. W  22782
Lyman (Conn. in 1818; and 89 in 1840 at Harwinton)................................. S  37851
Moses, Suffolk Co., N. Y., in 1832.................................................. S  10454
Moses, Musician, Niagara Co., N. Y., in 1832; wid. Patty............................ W   6684
Nathan, d. 1840, New London Co., wid. Miriam........................................ W  17635
Nathan, Mansfield, Conn., 1832, d. 1839; wid. Ruth.................................. W  25420
Nathaniel, wid. Sarah............................................................... W  20879
  (Conn. in 1818.)
Noah................................................................................ R   2008
Oliver, d. N. Y. 1825, wid. Betsey.................................................. W  23816
Oliver, Brookfield, Conn., 1832; wid. Huldah, BLWt. 33758-160-55.................... W    717
Phebe, former wid. of Samuel Husted................................................. W  16909
Reuben, New London Co. 1832......................................................... S  12506
Reuben, d. Conn. 1812; wid. Prudence, BLWt. 8171-160-55............................. W  10624
Reuben, d. Mass. 1813; wid. Zeruiah................................................. W  14483
Robert (Conn. in 1818).............................................................. S  37864
Roger (Conn. in 1818)............................................................... S  44773
Roswell, Hebron, Conn., 1832; wid. Dolly, BLWt. 8167-160-55........................ W   6686
Roswell, Vt. 1832; wid. Susannah, BLWt. 26590-160-55............................... W   6681
Rufus, wid. Lydia................................................................... W  10621
  (Middlesex Co. 1832; and 75 in 1840 at Saybrook.)
Samuel, Watertown, N. Y., in 1818................................................... S  44771
Samuel, Lewis Co., N. Y., in 1832................................................... S  12484
Samuel, Milford, Conn., in 1832..................................................... S  18350
Samuel, wid. Hannah................................................................. R   1976
Samuel, d. 1813; wid. Susannah...................................................... W  17626
Sarah, former wid. of Miles Dickson................................................. W  20881
Silvanus or Sylvanus................................................................ S  17342
  (New Haven Co. 1832 as Sylvanus.)
Smith, wid. Jane.................................................................... R   1981
Solomon, wid. Mahitable............................................................. W  16536
Stephen (Middlesex Co. in 1832; 83 in 1840 at Chatham)............................. S  17886
Thomas.............................................................................. S  19247
Waters or Watrous, Cont. (Conn.).................................................... S  38612
William, Columbia Co., N. Y., in 1818............................................... S  44758
William, Hampshire Co., Mass., in 1832..............................................    5009
William, Chaplin, Conn., in 1832.................................................... S  10458
William, Milford, Conn., in 1832.................................................... S  16713
William, Middletown, Conn., in 1818................................................. S  37863
William, Fabius, N. Y., in 1818..................................................... S  44760
William, Rensselaer Co., N. Y., in 1832; and d. in 1839; wid. Anner................ W  22791
William, Chenengo Co., N. Y., in 1832; and d. in 1840; wid. Eunice Ford, BLWt. 7082-160-55. W  18906
Zelotes............................................................................. S   3161
CLARY, Daniel (N. Y. in 1818)....................................................... S  23576
James, Conn., Cont. & N. Y.......................................................... S  44785
Samuel.............................................................................. S  44791
```

CLASON, Isaac. wid. Rachel, BLWt. 50859-160-55.. W 10619
CLEAVELAND, CLEAVLAND, CLEVELAND or CLEVLAND.
    Chester, wid. Elizabeth... W 20865
    Cyrus, wid. Mary.. W 20877
    Frederick, wid. Susannah.. W 20884
    Gardner, wid. Huldah, BLWt. 12715-160-55.. W 25425
    Isaac, wid. Mamre... W 22796
    Jacob (Windham Co., Conn., 1818).. S 37860
    John, Conn. & Mass., Whitehall, N. Y., in 1818... S 44780
    John, d. 1824, N. Y.; wid. Sarah, BLWt. 2334-160-55.. W 16535
    John, wid. Thankful.. W 20869
    Johnson (Conn. 1818).. S 37862
    Joseph, Conn. & Cont... S 10447
    Josiah, Conn. & Mass.; N. Y. 1818... S 44782
    Josiah, Conn. in 1818... S 37850
    Samuel, Windham Co. in 1818; wid. Lucy, BLWt. 6040-160-55.. W 720
    Samuel, Vt. in 1832... S 15378
    Silas, Conn. & Navy.. S 12486
        (Windham Co. in 1832; 84 in 1840 in Hampton.)
    Solomon, Vt. in 1818; wid. Martha... W 6699
    Solomon, d. 1823; wid. Hannah.. W 10617
    Squier, wid. Pamelia, Conn. & Cont... W 22798
        (Vt. in 1818.)
    Stephen, wid. Hannah... W 23815
    Timothy; BLWt. 442-200, Lieut. was issued Dec. 31, 1795; also recorded as BLWt. 2658. No
      papers.
    Tracy... S 2124
    William, N. Y. in 1818... S 12494
    William, d. 1799, former wid. Sarah Converse... W 23836
CLIFT, Lemuel; BLWt. 373-300, Capt. was issued Sept. 2, 1790. No papers.
    Wills, Conn. & Cont., wid. Mary.. W 22788
      BLWt. 368-400, Major, issued June 6, 1797, to Nathaniel Satterlee, Assignee. No papers.
CLINTON, Allen (Fairfield Co. in 1832), BLWt. 34501-160-55... S 12510
    Henry.. R 2052
    Isaac.. S 12498
    Joseph B., Conn. & Cont., former wid. Margaret More or Moore... W 6832
        (N. Y. in 1818.) BLWt. 1873-100 and BLWt. 313-60-55.
CLOCK, John, wid. Sarah... W 17623
        (Litchfield Co. in 1832.)
CLOSE, Abraham, wid. Mary... W 25414
        (Fairfield Co. in 1832.)
    Benjamin... S 27645
    Solomon (Fairfield Co. in 1832)... S 15377
CLOUD, DeForest or Forest, wid. Anna.. W 25415
CLOUGH or CLUFF.
    Isaac (Conn. in 1818).. S 37870
    Jonathan... R 2058
CLUXTON, Samuel (Conn. in 1818)... S 37866
COAN. (See CONE.)
COATES, COATS, or COTES.
    Amos. wid. Anna.. W 10643
        (Windham Co. in 1832.)
    Edward (New London Co. in 1832).. S 15780
    John... S 10474
    Robert, Conn. & Cont... S 12599
    Thomas, former wid. Lois Delano.. W 22925
COBANN. (See CORBIN.)
COBB, Benjamin, wid. Azubah... W 10661
    BLWt. 26248-160-55. (79 in 1840 at Chatham.)
    Henry S.. R 2073
    John, wid. Mary.. R 2076
    John, Conn. & Mass.; in 1818 he was living in Vt., pensioned as Corporal, in Conn. Line..... S 38618
    BLWt. 537-100.
    Simeon (Conn. in 1818)... S 38629
COBORN or COBURN.
    Daniel, Piermont, N. H., 1818.. S 34242
    Hezekiah... S 15054
    James, Ovid, N. Y., in 1818.. S 43401
    Lemuel, Vt. in 1818, d. 1839; wid. Sarah, who moved to Mass., BLWt. 34961-160-55.......... W 18946
        (See also COLBURN.)
COCHRAN, William, former wid. Lydia Chapman, BLWt. 27597-160-55.. W 23793
COE, Abner.. S 18364
    Asher, wid. Huldah... W 17639
    Ebenezer... S 2448
    Jedediah... S 21141
    John, wid. Lois.. W 23852
    Samuel (N. Y. in 1818)... S 43404
    Seth (Litchfield Co. in 1832).. S 18363
    Thomas... S 38630
    Timothy, wid. Abigail.. W 5250
        (Hartford Co. in 1832; and 79 in 1840 at Hartland.)
    Zachariah.. S 9195
COFFIN or COFFING, Isaac, former wid. Sarah Stiles... W 17876
COGER, Enoch, Cont. (Conn.), wid. Avis.. W 1654
    Joseph Cont. (Conn.)...BLWt. 1889-100
COGGESHALL, William, Conn. & Conn. Sea Service, wid. Eunice... W 17658
COGGSWELL or COGSWELL.
    Amos (Tolland Co. in 1832)... S 24127
    Benjamin, wid. Mercy... W 14523

COGGSWELL or COGSWELL—Continued.

Jesse.. S 12565
John... S 12613
William... S 17360
COHOON, John.. S 12705
COIT, Benjamin, Conn. & Conn. Sea Service, wid. Sarah, BLWt. 26047-160-55................. W 10639
   Farwell, wid. Anna.. W 17669
    (Conn. 1818, as Serg't.)
   Isaac, wid. Ruamy... W 14517
    (Mass. in 1818, as Serg't.)
   Richard (Litchfield Co. in 1832).. S 12521
COLBURN, Daniel, wid. Elizabeth.. W 17655
   Josiah.. S 10475
   (See also COBURN and CORBIN.)
COLE or COLL.
   Abner, Conn. & Cont.. S 38631
    BLWt. 382-150, Ensign, issued April 15, 1800. No papers.
    (Conn. in 1818, as Ensign.)
   Amos... S 12594
   Benjamin, wid. Jemima.. W 1236
    BLWt. 17701-160-55. (Vt. in 1818.)
   Benjamin, Cont. (Conn.), former wid. Rachel McMurphy.................................... R 6797
   Daniel, Conn. & Cont., wid. Edith.. W 22848
    (Conn. in 1818.)
   David.. S 38626
   Elisha, wid. Asenath, BLWt. 12578-160-55... W 18932
   Hendrick, wid. Phebe... W 17644
    (Middlesex Co. in 1832.)
   Jabez.. S 15053
   James.. S 23171
   John, wid. Mary, BLWt. 30595-160-55.. W 2068
   Jonathan, wid. Lois.. W 17643
   Levi... S 28694
   Nathaniel.. S 15048
   Samuel... S 23167
   Samuel, Cont. (Conn.).. S 10478
   Sands.. S 31619
   Solomon, wid. Lydia, BLWt. 26797-160-55.. W 1827
    (Conn. in 1818.)
   Thankful, former wid. of William Fancher.. W 22811
   Thomas, wid. Mary.. W 17637
COLEMAN or COLMAN, John (Tolland Co. in 1832) (87 in 1840 at Bolton).................... S 17350
   Nathan, wid. Deborah... W 17652
    (Conn. in 1818.)
   Noah, BLWt. 369-400, Surgeon, issued March 1, 1797. No papers.
COLES. (See COWLES.)
COLFAX, Jonathan, wid. Elizabeth... W 262
   Robert... S 34219
   William, Conn. & Cont., wid. Esther.. R 2174
    BLWt. 378-300, Capt., issued Dec. 9, 1796. No papers.
COLL. (See COLE.)
COLLAR or COLLER.
   John, Cont. service, Conn. res. in 1818.. S 38623
   Norris or Narris, Conn. & Cont... S 12576
COLLARD or COLLERD, Thomas T... R 13363
COLLENS. (See COLLINS.)
COLLEY, George (New Haven Co. in 1832)... S 18361
COLLIER, Joseph (N. Y. in 1818)... S 43399
   Oliver... S 12555
COLLINS, COLLINGS, or COLLENS.
   Ambrose (Litchfield Co. in 1832)... S 17892
   Daniel, Conn. & Cont., wid. Anna... W 20899
   Daniel, wid. Eunice, BLWt. 16104-160-55.. W 17648
   Elisha, Conn. & Mass., wid. Roxa, BLWt. 96060-160-55..................................... W 10305
   Jabez.. S 16088
   Jonathan... S 23577
   Lois, former wid. of Nathaniel Wood, Conn., Green Mt. Boys & Vt.......................... W 16925
   Nathaniel, Cont. (Conn.)... S 12585
    (Hartford Co. in 1832.)
   Samuel, wid. Betsey.. W 17645
    (N. Y. in 1818.) BLWt. 41-100 and BLWt. 17622-160-55.
   Sarah, former wid. of Thomas H. Hooker... W 24442
   Stephen or Stephens.. S 10484
   William, Ill. in 1832.. S 32184
   William, N. Y. in 1818... S 43350
   William Lock... S 36472
COLMAN. (See COLEMAN.)
COLENEY or COLONY, Isaac, BLWt. 26464-160-55... S 12564
COLT, Jabez or Jabish.. S 9321
    (N. Y. in 1818 as Jabez.)
   John, Conn. & Conn. Sea service.. S 18769
   Peter, wid. Sarah.. W 5880
COLTON, Mehitable D., former wid. of Pownal Deming, BLWt. 8463-160-55...................... W 20894
   Samuel, Conn. & Cont., wid. Lois... W 17663
COLVER. (See CULVER.)
COMBS, John, Conn. & Cont.. R 2185
COMES, Ebenezer.. R 2188
COMINS, COMMINGS or COMMINS. (See CUMMINGS.)
COMSTOCK, Aaron, wid. Ann.. W 17647
    (Fairfield Co. in 1832.)
   Abner.. S 12575

```
COMSTOCK, Achilles, wid. Sarah..................................................................... W 20900
    Ansel, wid. Betsey............................................................................... W 18950
        BLWt. 32222-160-55.
    Anson.............................................................................................. S  1253
    Caleb, wid. Lucy.................................................................................. W 67252
    David............................................................................................... S 12589
    Elisha.............................................................................................. S 12570
    James, wid. Amy.................................................................................. W 17651
        (New London Co. in 1832; and 90 in 1840 at Montville.)
    Jason, wid. Sarah................................................................................ W 17646
        (New London Co. in 1832.)
    John, wid. Charlotte.............................................................................. W 25434
        (New London Co. in 1832.)
    Martin L........................................................................................... S 19260
    Nathan.............................................................................................. R  2194
    Oliver, wid. Amy, Conn., Cont. & Navy (Conn. in 1818)......................................... W 17660
    Samuel, N. H. in 1832............................................................................. S 22693
    Samuel, Wilton, Conn. in 1818.................................................................. S 36471
        BLWt. 374-300, Capt., issued Jan. 16, 1797.  No papers.
        (Conn. in 1818, as Brevet Major.)
    Samuel, Saybrook, Conn. in 1818................................................................ S 36475
    Samuel, former wid. Else Scofield.............................................................. W 22163
        BLWt. 10029-160-55.
        (Soldier was from Fairfield Co. Conn., but d. in 1788 and never received a pension.)
    Serajah or Sarajah, former wid. Clemina Austin............................................... W 16170
        (Pensioned in 1818 in N. Y. as Saragah.)
    Simeon (Conn. in 1818 as Corporal; 86 in 1840 at Groton)..................................... S 36463
    Stephen............................................................................................ S 12573
    Theophilus......................................................................................... S 43379
        (N. Y. in 1818 as Serg't.)
CONANT, Ebenezer..................................................................................... S 29095
    Josiah, former wid. of, Ruth Barton............................................................ W 17260
    Silvanus or Sylvanus, Conn. & Cont............................................................. S 16737
CONE or COAN, Beriah................................................................................. S  9237
    Daniel (Mass. in 1818)........................................................................... S 17352
    Daniel, H. (Conn. in 1818; 87 in 1840 at Winchester).......................................... S 36473
    Henry, wid. Waitstill............................................................................ W 25432
        (Wid was 79 in 1840 at Lyme.)
    Israel (Conn. in 1818, as Serg't................................................................ S 36477
    Jesse (Conn. in 1818 as Corporal)............................................................... S 36478
    John (New Haven Co. in 1832 as Coan; 77 in 1840 at Guilford)................................. S 31628
    Joseph, Conn. & Cont............................................................................. S 12569
        (N. Y. in 1818.)
    Joshua, East Haddam in 1832, wid. Sarah, BLWt. 81566-160-55............................... W 25428
    Joshua, Conn. & Cont. d. 1807, wid. Mehitable................................................. W 18933
    Nathaniel, Cont. (Conn.)......................................................................... S 36476
        (Conn. in 1818.)
    Noadiah, wid. Polly.............................................................................. W  1030
        BLWt. 30696-160-55.  (Middlesex Co. 1832; 80 in 1840, Haddam.)
    Oliver.............................................................................................. S 12525
    Ozias (N. Y. in 1818), BLWt. 1317-100.......................................................... S  4334
    Reuben, Cont. (Conn.), former wid. of, Esther Edwards........................................ R  3256
    Robert, wid. Sarah............................................................................... W 18961
        (Mass. in 1818.)
    Samuel, Maine in 1818............................................................................ S 36988
    Samuel, Conn. & Cont., wid. Betsey............................................................. W 16538
        (N. Y. in 1818.)
    Timothy............................................................................................ S  9197
    William, Conn. & Cont............................................................................ S 38635
CONGAR or CONGER.
    Elijah (Fairfield Co. in 1832)................................................................... S 12544
    Joseph.............................................................................................. S  9223
CONGDON, John (N. Y. in 1818)........................................................................ S 43388
CONNELL, Benoni, Conn & Cont., wid. Sarah........................................................ W 20914
    (See also CORNWELL.)
CONNELY, CONNOLY, or CONNOLLY, James............................................................ S 34229
CONVERS or CONVERSE.
    Benjamin (Windham Co. in 1832)................................................................. S 12549
    Demon Read........................................................................................ R  2241
    Dyer (Conn. in 1818, and d, Sept. 11, 1818).................................................... S 36479
    Elisha, Conn. & Cont............................................................................. S 12517
    Jeremiah, Conn. & Mass........................................................................... R  2242
    Jonathan, wid. Zurnah or Zuruah................................................................ W   722
        (Windham Co. in 1832; and 80 in 1840 at Thompson.)
    Nathaniel, wid. Abigail.......................................................................... R  2240
    Sarah, former wid. of William Cleaveland..................................................... W 23836
    Solvin, wid. Sarah............................................................................... W 25436
    Stephen, Conn. & Mass., wid. Sarah............................................................. W 22847
    Thomas, BLWt. 371-300, Capt., issued Feb. 14, 1791.  No papers.
CONWAY, Elizabeth, former wid. of Stephen Hill, Cont. service, Conn. res. & Agency......... W 18885
COOK or COOKE, Abial or Abiel, Conn. & N. Y., wid. Julia Anna, BLWt. 24761-160-55...... W  6704
    Abraham. wid. Elizabeth......................................................................... W  3224
    Archibald (Vt. in 1818)........................................................................... S 15781
    Atwater, wid. Mary............................................................................... W 16914
    Ebenezer or Ebenezer H., wid. Jemima, BLWt. 24330-160-55................................ W  6929
    Elisha, wid. Lois................................................................................ W  2066
    Elijah.............................................................................................. S 29085
    Ezekiel............................................................................................ S 12526
    George ............................................................................................ R  2254
```

43

COOK or COOKE, George... BLWt. 665-100
   Gideon, wid. Huldah... W 20924
   Jesse, BLWt. 385-300, Capt. issued April 23, 1798, to Jesse Cook. No papers.
   Joel, Penna. 1818 and 1832... S 3182
   Joel, Ohio in 1818.. S 43392
   Johnson, Serg't. Ohio 1818... S 10461
   Johnson, Fairfield Co., Ohio.. S 42141
   Johnson, Serg't. BLWt. 5572 issued in 1791.
   Jonah.. S 19948
   Joseph, wid. Mercy... R 2269
   Lemuel (N. Y. in 1818)... S 23173
   Lucy, former wid. of John Priest... W 16539
      BLWt. 2227-100.
   Merriman or Marimon, BLWt. 26126-160-55..................................... S 2453
   Miles (N. Y. in 1818).. S 43366
   Moses, Windsor, Conn., in 1832... S 15056
   Moses.. R 2270
   Nathan (Conn. in 1818)... S 36482
   Nathaniel, wid. Anise.. W 17642
   Oliver, wid. Submit.. W 16929
   Richard, Utica, N. Y., in 1832... S 12545
   Richard, Oneida Co., N. Y., in 1818.. S 43368
   Samuel, Vt. in 1832.. S 22187
   Samuel, Conn. & Cont., wid. Mary.. W 15829
      N. Y in 1818.
   Serad.. S 12533
   Shubael, wid. Sarah.. R 2274
   Trueworthy... S 43395
   Urijah... R 2279
   Warren, Conn. & Cont., wid. Lois, BLWt. 49466-160-55.......................... W 18926
   William, Middletown, Conn., 1818... S 36467
   William, Vt. in 1818... S 38641
   William, Green Co., N. Y., in 1818, BLWt. 1415-100............................. S 43381
   William, Pompey, N. Y., in 1818, wid. Asenath, BLWt. 11421-160-55............. W 1723
   William, Mexico, N. Y., in 1818, wid. Keziah.................................. W 23871
COOLEY, or COOLY, Reuben (Conn. in 1818).. S 36469
   Thomas, wid. Elizabeth... R 2282
COOLIDGE, Persis, former wid. of John Allen, Conn. & N. Y....................... W 23429
COON, Daniel... S 12568
   James, Cont. (Warren's reg't.), BLWt. 381-200 Lieut., issued March 18, 1790, to Deborah
      Beach (late Coon), Adx. Also recorded BLWt. 2548. No papers.
   Joseph, Conn. & R. I... S 12583
      (New London Co. in 1832.)
COOPER, Abner.. S 22178
   Abraham (Conn. in 1818).. S 36468
   Isaac, wid. Lydia.. W 3946
   Price.. S 43349
COPELAND, COPELIN or COPLAND.
   Amasa, Conn. & Cont.. S 36464
      (Conn. in 1818 & 82 in 1840 at Pomfret.)
   Asa, wid. Abilene.. W 2594
   Jonathan (Windham Co. in 1832)... S 31616
COPLEY, Daniel, Conn. & Cont... S 12518
      (Litchfield Co. in 1832 & Milford in 1840.)
   Samuel... S 18362
COPP, Ebenezer, wid. Deborah... W 20911
      (Conn. in 1818.)
   Joseph (N. Y. in 1818, as Drum Major).. S 43398
      BLWt. 569-100.
CORBIN or COBANN, Clement, wid. Sabra.. W 3661
      (N. H. in 1818.) BLWt. 9418-160-55.
   Joseph... S 34601
   Joseph, Conn. & Mass... S 9323
   Peter, wid. Villette, BLWt. 13412-160-55....................................... W 24836
   (See also COBORN and COBURN.)
CORBITT, Joseph, wid. Hannah... W 17661
COREY or CORY, Benedick, Conn. & R. I.. R 2317
   Jerusha, former wid. of Eliphaz Parrish.. W 1563
CORLISS, Bliss, wid. Phebe... W 17650
CORNELIUS, John, Conn. res. in 1821.. R 2324
CORNING or CORNNING.
   Allen (Conn. in 1818).. S 36480
   Bliss.. S 22684
   Uriah, Conn. & Navy.. S 15262
      (New London Co. in 1832; Preston, 1840.)
CORNISH, George (Hartford Co. in 1832; 79 in 1840 at Simsbury).................. S 15058
   Joel... S 12561
CORNWALL or CORNWELL.
   Amos... R 2334
   Ashbel, Conn. & Privateer, wid. Roxana, BLWt. 15192-160-55.................... W 27665
   Benjamin (N. Y. in 1818)... S 43393
   Daniel, wid. Rachel, BLWt. 7061-160-55... W 25427
   Isaac.. S 23584
   John (Middlesex Co. in 1832; 80 in Middletown in 1840)......................... S 10485
   Nathaniel, wid. Anna... W 17653
   Richard.. BLWt. 1586-100
   Samuel, wid. Sarah... W 23844
      (See also CONNELL.)

CORTIS or CORTTIS. (See CURTIS.)
CORWIN, Amaziah... S 12582
    Selah, wid. Joanna.. W 22805
    (N. Y. in 1818.)
CORY. (See COREY.)
COSSIT, Timothy.. S 23170
COTES. (See COATES.)
COTTEN or COTTON.
    Bibye, L... S 12571
    George, BLWt. 380–150, Ensign, was issued Feb. 15, 1799. No papers.
    Rowland, Conn., Cont. & War of 1812... S 11170
    Samuel, Conn. & Navy... R 2356
    Ward, wid. Nabby.. W 22826
    William (Vt. in 1818)... S 34244
COUCH, Abraham... S 36481
    (Conn. in 1818 and 73 in 1840 at Reading.)
    Amos, wid. Phebe (Conn. in 1818)... W 20901
    Daniel.. S 29086
    Ebenezer (Conn. in 1818).. S 36483
    Ebenezer, wid. Asenath, BLWt. 27599–160–55... W 23839
    John, wid. Lois... W 17640
    John, wid. Prudence... R 2360
    Joshua, wid. Patty, Conn. & Conn. Sea Service.. W 17656
    Samuel, Conn., Cont. & Mass.. S 29717
    Stephen, Poliphena.. W 14508
    Thomas, wid. Sarah... W 20906
    William, or FREEMAN, William, colored.. R 2358
CONNEY, Michael, Cont. (Conn.), wid. Mehitable.. W 16919
COVEL, or COVELL or COVIL or COVILL.
    Abraham, wid. Mehitable.. R 2378
    David, wid. Sarah (N. Y. in 1818)... W 18952
    Ebenezer (N. Y. in 1818)... S 31625
    Ebenezer, Conn. & Cont.. S 15261
    (Windham Co. in 1832 as Covel; 81 in 1840 as Covill.)
    Eliphalet, Conn., Mass. & Privateer... S 10477
    Ephraim... S 12597
    Henry Conn. & Mass... S 30954
    James, wid. Lucy.. R 2377
    James, Cont. (Conn.), wid. Margaret, BLWt. 6256–160–55... W 5251
COVERT, Jeremiah... S 10466
COWDERY, COWDRY CAWDERY or CAWDRY.
    Ambrose (Hartford Co. in 1832).. S 15050
    Asa (Hartford Co. in 1832; and 82 at Hartland in 1840)... S 10479
    Edward, wid. Submit.. W 23863
    (Vt. in 1818.)
    Samuel, Cont. (Conn.)... BLWt. 132–100
    William... R 2392
COWEL or COWELL, Samuel... S 10476
COWLES, COWLS or COLES.
    Asa (Conn. in 1818)... S 36466
    Cynthia, former wid. of Ezekiel N. Root... W 4927
    Ezekiel (Hartford Co. in 1832)... S 12614
    Isaac (Hartford Co. in 1832).. S 16089
    Jabez (84 in 1840, Hartford Co.)... S 15057
    Noah.. R 2394
    Phineas... S 23197
    Samuel.. R 2395
    Solomon, Conn., Cont. & N. Y... S 15049
    (Hartford Co. in 1832.)
    Thomas, wid. Tamer, BLWt. 9202–160–55... W 23851
COX, Robert, Vermont in 1818... S 43400
COY or COYE.
    David (N. Y. in 1818)... S 43364
    David... R 2413
    Edee, Cont. (Conn.).. S 43376
    (Mass. in 1818 as Corporal.)
    Ephraim, wid. Rebekah... W 17638
    (Windham Co. in 1832.)
    Joseph, Conn. & Cont.. S 43371
    (N. Y. in 1818 as Serg't.)
    Nehemiah, wid. Anne.. W 20909
    (N. Y. in 1818.)
    Vine... S 19262
CRAFT or CRAFTS.
    Benjamin, wid. Jane, BLWt. 202–60–55... W 5258
    (N. Y. in 1818.)
    Joseph, Cont. (Conn.), BLWt. 51–100.. S 46352
    Samuel, wid. Lucy.. BLWt. 56948–160–55
CRAIN. (See CRANE.)
CRAMER, CRAMMER or CREAMER.
    Henry, Conn. & Cont., wid. Jemima.. R 2436
CRAMPTON or CRAMTON.
    Elon (Litchfield Co. in 1832).. S 10502
    Jonathan, wid. Elizabeth, BLWt. 8453–160–55.. W 1725
    (New Haven Co. in 1832.)
    Mary, former wid. of James Benjamin.. W 20935

CRANDAL, CRANDALL, CRANDEL, CRANDELL, CRANDOL or CRANDOLL.
Amariah or Ammariah, BLWt. 26081–160–55. .... S 16090
Azel.. S 12633
Christopher, Conn. & R. I .... S 15269
Edward, Conn. & Cont .... S 43410
    (N. Y. in 1818.)
Ezra.. S 12618
Gideon, Conn. & R. I .... S 15272
Isaiah, Conn. & R. I .... S 12636
Jeremiah, Conn., N. Y. & R. I .... S 10506
John.. R 2438
Richmond, Conn. & Conn. Sea Service.. W 20930
    Wid. Lucretia. BLWt. 34962–160–55.
CRANE or CRAIN, Amariah, wid. Tryphena... W 17688
    (N. Y. in 1818 as fifer.)
Curtis, wid. Elizabeth... W 16547
Daniel, Conn. & Cont .... S 12713
    (Tolland Co. in 1832 as Crain.)
Ebenezer, Conn. & Mass. .... R–
Elihu... S 21134
Elijah, wid. Susannah.. W 16223
Elisha.. S 15236
Elizabeth, former wid. of Ozias Hanford... W 25449
Enos, former wid. of Sophia Williams, BLWt. 101838–160–55.............................. W 11832
    (N. Y. in 1818.)
James... S 23588
John, N. Y. in 1818.. S 43415
John, Cortland Co., N. Y., in 1832, wid. Phillis, BLWt. 26324–160–55 .... W 8192
Jonathan, wid. Sybil... W 23882
Nathaniel (Conn. in 1818 as Serg't.).. S 36484
Roger, Conn. & Mass., wid. Sarah.. W 18981
Rufus, wid. Rachel... W 23877
Silas, wid. Clarissa, BLWt. 85080–160–55.. R 13483
Simeon, Conn. & Mass., wid. Anne.. W 18977
    (New London Co. in 1832.)
CRARY, Joseph, Conn., Privateer & R. I., wid. Lucy...................................... W 23867
Nathan, Conn. & Vt., wid. Lydia.. R 2456
CRAW. (See CROW.)
CRAWFORD, James, wid. Hannah... W 17685
Jason, former wid. of, Bethsheba Strobridge or Strowbridge............................. W 19110
    (N. Y. in 1818.)
    NOTE.—Bethsheba's other husband, George Strobridge or Strowbridge, was also a Revo-
lutionary soldier.
CREAMER. (See CRAMER.)
CRESEY, CRESSEY or CRISSEY.
Gould, wid. Eunice... R 2483
John.. S 12965
Jonathan, Cont. (Conn.).. S 34262
    (Mass. in 1818.)
CRIPPEN, Silas, Conn. & N. Y., wid. Elizabeth.. W 20929
CRITTENDEN, Gideon (also given CHITTENDEN)... S 42660
CROCKER, David, Conn. & Navy... S 42146
Dyer.. S 22710
James, wid. Mary... R 24921
John (Conn. in 1818)... S 36485
Peter... R 2493
Zebulon, wid. Sarah.. W 25453
    BLWt. 26682–160–55.
CROFOOT or CROFUT.
Elizabeth, former wid. of Lewis Hunt.. W 17686
Ephraim, Cont. (Conn.), wid. Lois... W 20927
    (Conn. in 1818.)
John.. R 2497
Seth, wid. Sarah... W 22859
    BLWt. 26319–160–55.
CROOK, Joseph... S 15271
CROSBY, David (Ohio in 1818 as Corporal)... S 43413
Ebenezer.. BLWt. 7759–400
Obed, wid. Jerusha.. W 25446
Sawney, or YORK, Sawney... S 36862
Simon (N. Y. in 1818)... S 43420
Thomas, Conn. & N. Y., wid. Diantha.. W 3516
CROSLEY, Prince, wid. Caroline... W 24833
CROSMAN. (See CROSSMAN.)
CROSS, Eunice, former wid. of Isaac Tubbs.. W 16937
Joseph, Vt. residence... S 39385
Joseph, N. Y. in 1818, wid. Serviah.. W 16940
Nero (Vt. in 1818.) .... S 39370
Solomon... S 21148
Stephen, wid. Sarah... W 23892
Uriah, Conn., Cont. & Green Mt. Boys.. S 10499
CROSSMAN, Trobridge, wid. Phebe.. W 25448
CROSWELL, John.. S 22703
CROUCH, Christopher (Tolland Co. in 1832)... S 17904
David, former wid. of, Eleanor Wiley.. W 18354
    Conn. & N. Y. BLWt. 33553–160–55.

CROW or CRAW, David, N. Y. in 1832.. S 12622
    Elias.. R 2458
    Jacob... S 12631
    Reuben, Conn. & Cont.. S 38643
        (Vt. in 1818 as Craw.)
    Shubael, Cont. (Conn.), wid. Huldah.. W 25447
        (Wid. was 74 in 1840 at New Hartford.)
CROWELL, Edward, wid. Rachel.. W 17684
        (Middlesex Co. in 1832.)
    Samuel, d. 1811, Bedford Co., Penna., wid. Jerusha... W 4931
    Samuel, Middletown, Conn., in 1832, wid. Sarah. BLWt. 27631-160-55....................................... W 25451
    Solomon... S 23587
CRUMB, Joseph, former wid. of, Oliviet Tuthill. BLWt. 99761-160-55 .... W 11675
CRUMBIE, Aaron or Aron, Conn. & Mass.. S 34716
        (Vt. in 1818 as Corporal.)
CUFF, Cato (Conn. in 1818; 83 in 1840 in Stonington)... S 36487
    Samson or Sampson... S 34616
CULVER or COLVER.
    Aaron, wid. Phebe... R 2569
    Abel.. BLWt. 2128-100
    Christopher... S 12660
        (New London Co. in 1832; 87 in 1840 in New London.)
    David, Conn. & Cont., wid. Mary, BLWt. 14514-160-55.. W 4933
    Eliakim... S 23184
    Enoch, wid. Lucy.. W 25464
    James, wid. Hannah.. W 23900
    John.. S 45713
    Nathaniel, wid. Catharine, BLWt. 92083-160-55... W 10697
        (Also given, COLVER, Nathan.)
    Reuben.. R 2572
    Sarah, former wid. of Josiah Atkins.. W 17673
    Thomas.. S 23185
    Timothy, Conn. & Cont... S 40871
        (Penna. in 1818 as Serg't.)
CUMMINGS, CUMMINS, COMINS or COMMINGS.
    Asa, wid. Cathelina... W 18992
        (N. Y. in 1818.) BLWt.. 31442-160-55
    John.. S 23582
    Simeon, former wid. of, Naomi Lilly... W 26217
    Stephen (N. Y. in 1818)... S 43342
    William, Vt. in 1818.. S 39389
    William, Mansfield, Conn., in 1832, wid. Rhoda.. W 17671
    William... BLWt. 13-100
CUNE, or McEWEN, John.. S 11056
CUNNINGHAM, Anna, former wid. of Nathan Burrows.. W 17674
    John.. S 18367
    Peter, Conn. & Mass. sea service, wid. Elizabeth.. W 17672
    Robert, wid. Hannah... R 2584
CURRIER, Joseph... S 43426
    (See also CARRIER.)
CURTICE, CURTIS, CURTISS, CORTIS, or CORTISS.
    Agur, 1760-1844, wid. Huldah, BLWt. 26316-160-55... W 25456
    Agur, 1755-1838, wid. Mercy... W 25465
        NOTE.—Both of the above soldiers lived in Fairfield Co., Conn.
    Amos.. S - 36488
    Andrew, Conn. & N. Y., wid. Eunice.. R 2597
    Benjamin, wid. Amelia, BLWt. 9206-160-55.. W 6900
    Caleb, wid. Catharine... W 17682
    Chauncey or Chauncy, Conn. & Cont... W 6746
        Wid. Mary Ann. BLWt. 1986-100.
    Daniel, Conn. & Cont., wid. Mary.. R 2605
    Davis, wid. Lois.. R 2603
    Ebenezer.. S 18789
    Eli (Conn. 1818 as Ensign).. S 37001
    Elijah.. S 12641
    Everard... S 17368
    Felix (N. Y. in 1818)... S 43429
    Frederick, wid. Persis.. W 17676
        (N. Y. in 1818.)
    Gideon, wid. Hannah... W 9400
        (Vt. in 1818.) BLWt. 5440-160-55.
    Giles, wid. Hannah, BLWt. 26794-160-55.. W 22874
    Giles, wid. Lucy.. W 637
        BLWt. 379-200, Lieut. was issued Nov. 10, 1789. No papers.
    Hull, Conn. & Cont.. S 18787
    Isaac (Ohio in 1832).. S 16094
        NOTE.—The Isaac Curtis who lived in Conn. after the Revolution served from R. I.
    Jacob... S 12657
    James, Conn. & Mass. Sea service.. S 12659
    James, d, 1811, wid. Sarah.. W 17679
    Japheth, wid, Mary.. W 17649
    Joel, Ohio in 1818, wid. Sally, BLWt. 26318-160-55... W 25460
    Joel, N. Y. in 1818... S 43428½
    Joseph, wid, Lydia.. W 25457
    Jotham, wid. Elizabeth, BLWt. 33760-160-55.. W 6745
    Lysander.. S 17367
    Mabel, former wid. of Josiah Burrit... W 25463

47

CURTICE, CURTIS, CURTISS, CORTIS, or CORTISS—Continued.
Martin... S 22711
Philip... S 12658
Robert, wid. Clara, BLWt. 40943–160–55...................................... W 25466
Robert W... S 28698
Samuel, Conn. Sea service & Navy, wid. Zipporah........................... W 3956
Samuel.. R 2608
Sarah, former wid. of Robert Lewis... W 20939
Silas, Cont. (Conn.) & War of 1812.. S 43436
Simeon, former wid. of, Elizabeth Catlin, BLWt. 14667–160–55......... W 10569
Solomon, Conn. & Mass., wid. Hannah... W 23895
Thomas, Conn. or Mass., wid. Eunice.. R 2598
Timothy, wid. Rebecca... W 20943
William, Conn., Cont., N. H. & Vt., wid. Charry............................. W 23902
Zadock, wid. Rosy... W 17681
Zerah or Zarah, wid. Abigail.. W 282
(Ohio in 1818.) BLWt. 205–60–55.
This woman's claim for BL on acc't. of her former husband (Elias Edward or Edwards, War 1812) was rejected. See papers in this file.
CUSHMAN, CUSHMON or CASHMAN.
Benjamin, Conn. & Cont., wid. Elizabeth....................................... W 22883
Charles, former wid. of, Desire Gates.. W 17003
Daniel, Cont. (Conn.)... S 23183
Eliphalet (N. Y. in 1818)... S 44389
Frederick, Conn. & Vt... S 10512
Joab, wid. Hannah... W 17683
Jonah, wid. Rachel.. W 14557
Joseph, wid. Tabitha, BLWt. 14501–160–55................................... W 20938
Joshua.. S 43437
Nathaniel, Vt. in 1818... S 38648
Nathaniel, wid. Hannah... W 25459
CUTLER, Jonathan.. S 15794
Joseph.. S 43432
Joseph, Conn. & R. I... S 12643
Seth... S 28700
CUTTING, Bille, BLWt. 26077–160–55... S 16355
Zebedee... S 12645
CYRUS, Exeter (Conn. in 1818)... S 36491

D.

DABALL or DABOLL, Benjamin, wid. Prudence............................... W 6991
NOTE.—This woman was also pensioned on account of the service of her former husband, Joseph Moxley, Conn., who received a pension for disability and died Nov. 10, 1815. No papers in his claim. See her papers within.
John, act of 1816, Conn. Agency... S 19950
John, Groten, Conn., 1818, d. 1830, N. Y. from which State wid. Anstiss (or Austiss) was pensioned, Conn. & Cont. service.. W 24033
DAGGETT, Henry, wid. Anna.. W 17709
BLWt. 539–200, Lieut. was issued Aug. 21, 1789. No papers.
John, Conn. & Vt... S 23595
Nathan, Conn. Sea service & Mass. Sea service............................. R 21987
Silas, Conn. Sea service & Mass. & Mass. Sea service; wid. Deborah.. W 22899
DAILEY or DAILY or DALEY.
David.. S 43445
Giles... S 36500
James.. S 43465
Johnson or William Johnson, wid. Lydia, W 1393, and BLWt. 7212–160–55.
Obadiah, Cont. (Conn.) former wid. Elizabeth Cady....................... W 23757
Samuel.. S 44128
DAINS, Asa, Conn. & Privateer, wid. Jane..................................... W 6960
Ephraim Cont. (Conn.), wid. Irene, BLWt. 15128–160–55................. W 4937
Jesse, wid. Chloe... R 2624
DALIBA, DALLABY or DALLIBA, George, Conn. & Cont., BLWt. 943–100... S 43461
DAMAN. (See DEMING.)
DAN or DANN, Squire, wid. Rhoda, BLWt. 50901–160–55.................. W 2439
DANA, David.. S 22194
Joseph.. S 28705
DANIELS, Daniel.. S 43471
David, wid. Lucina... W 3959
Ezekiel, Conn. 1818... S 36498
Ezekiel, N. Y. in 1818... S 43454
Job, wid. Jane... W 4662
John... S 38653
Jonathan... R 2652
Nathan.. S 12730
Nehemiah, wid. Elizabeth.. W 2074
Peletiah, wid. Huldah.. W 25513
Reuben... S 36499
Samuel, New Haven Co., Conn., in 1832.. S 16753
Samuel, N. Y. in 1832; wid. Lydia, BLWt. 11179–160–55................. W 25510
DANN. (See DAN.)
DARBE, or DARBEE or DARBY.
Asa.. S 15396
Jedediah, Conn. & Cont... S 43455
Moses, wid. Dorothy... W 3339
(See also DERBY.)
DARLING, Benjamin, Jaffrey, N. H., 1818, then N. Y. & Vt............. S 43452
Benjamin, d. 1820, Conn., wid. Mary.. W 17705

DARRANCE. (See DORRANCE.)
DARRIN, Daniel, Conn. & N. Y., wid. Martha, BLWt. 26924–60–55................................ W 19141
DARROW, Benjamin, Tenn. 1828, BLWt. 1945–100.. S 46229
   Benjamin, Conn. Sea service & Navy, Conn. 1818; d. 1827; wid. Grace...................... W 24850
   Christopher, Conn. & Cont., wid. Bridget.. W 16554
   Daniel... S 36492
   Ebenezer, Waterford, Conn., 1832... S 18369
   Ebenezer, Cont. (Conn.), Litchfield, Conn., in 1818, as Corporal......................... S 15072
   James, wid. Sarah.. W 1394
   Nathan... S 15075
   Samuel... S 23186
   William, wid. Sally.. R 2670
DART or DEART, Caleb, wid. Margaret.. W 16943
   David.. S 18368
   Dolphin.. S 36496
   Ebenezer, Cont. (Conn.), wid. Hannah, BLWt. 10305–160–55................................ W 1243
   Elias, wid. Ruth... R 2673
   Jonathan... S 17922
   Levi, wld. Elizabeth... W 24046
   Thomas, Conn. & N. H... R 2674
DASKAM, John.. S 43453
   William.. S 36495
DAUD. (See DOWD.)
DAVENPORT, or DEAVENPORT, or DEVENPORT, Benjamin, former wid. of, Elizabeth
   Judson... W 7948
   Charles, wid. Mabel.. W 17706
   David, wid. Patience... R 2682
   Eliphalet, wid. Elizabeth.. W 16233
   Hezekiah... BLWt. 2329–200
   Humphrev, Conn. & Cont., wid. Jerusha.. W 20952
   John, d. 1830, not pensioned; wid. Mary S., from Fairfield.............................. W 17711
   John, N. Y. 1818; d. 1830, wid. Polly, from Wayne Co., N. Y............................. W 24031
   Noah, wid. Lydia... W 22911
   Phebe, former wid. of Yale Todd, Cont. (Conn.), q. v.
   Squire... S 44148
DAVIDSON, DAVISON or DAVISSON.
   Benjamin, Conn. & Cont. (Mass.), wid. Roxy... W 16946
   Douglas or Douglass, wid. Asenath, BLWt. 31287–160–55.................................. W 19145
   Ezra, former wid. of, Deidamia Boone... W 25260
   Hezekiah... R 2689
   John, N. Y. in 1832... S 32209
   John, Conn. & N. Y. serv... BL Rej.
   Joseph, wid. Lydia... W 25517
   Paul, wid. Sally... W 20962
   Peter.. S 15063
   Thomas... S 15066
   Zachariah, wid. Hannah... W 17712
DAVIS, Abel, Conn., Green Mt. Boys & Vt.. S 12902
   Cornelius, wid. Ruth, BLWt. 31897–160–55... S 10716
   Daniel, Fairfield Co., Conn., 1851, aged 87.. S 17915
   Daniel, Groton, Conn., 1818, wid. Deborah.. W 20947
   David.. S 23592
   Ebenezer... S 34292
   Elijah... S 10548
   Elisha, wid. Flizabeth, BLWt. 29736–160–55... W 1730
   George, Northumberland Co., Penna., 1832... S 22193
   George, never pensioned; wid. Deborah, Fulton Co., N. Y................................. R 2712
   Hannah, former wid. of Stephen Palmer, q. v.
   Jacob, wid. Catherine, BLWt. 2–60–55... W 19136
   James, Harwinton, Conn., 1832.. S 17378
   James, New Haven Co., Conn., 1832; d. 1852; son of James, also Rev. sol., wid. Ruth, BLWt.
     10239–160–55... W 10706
   Jesse, former wid. of, Mary Ginnings... R 3971
   John, N. Y. in 1832.. S 12720
   John, Fairfield Co., Conn., 1832; d. 1840; wid. Eunice................................. W 17699
   John, Cont. & Conn., Vt. in 1818... S 39402
   John, Conn. & Cont., Warner, N. H., in 1818, BLWt. 765–100............................. S 45716
   Jonathan... S 36494
   Joseph, Conn. & Cont., Conn. in 1832... S 17373
   Joseph, Conn., Mass. & Vt., Franklin Co., Mass., 1832, & died Dec., 1832; wid. Azubah...... W 14581
   Josiah, wid. Annis F., BLWt. 26658–160–55.. W 20961
   Kitteridge, Conn. & Mass... S 10537
   Lathrop, wid. Mary... W 20958
   Lois, former wid. of Elihu Judd, q. v.
   Micajah, wid. Betsey... R 2703
   Nancy, former wid. of Abner Lee, q. v.
   Nathan, Cont. (Conn.), wid. Betsa.. W 19142
   Nathaniel.. R 2751
   Samuel, Ohio in 1832... S 9380
   Samuel, not pensioned; wid. lived Mich... R 2752
   Samuel, Conn. & R. I., d. 1826; wid. Lucy, New London Co., Conn., 1838, BLWt. 30700–160–55. W 17701
   Silas, Conn. & Cont., wid. Matilda... W 10709
   Solomon, wid. Mary... R 2765
   Stephen B.. S 36497
   Thomas... R 2769
   Thomas, d. Fairfield Co., Conn., 1827; wid. Abigail, applied from N. Y.................. W 19152
   Thomas, Windham Co., Conn., 1832, & died there Nov., 1832; wid. Rebecca................ W 17703
   Willard.. BLWt. 67513–160–55
   William.. S 42668

DAVISON or DAVISSON. (See DAVIDSON.)
DAWSON, Titus.. S 15070
DAY, Comfort, wid. Esther... W 16232
    Isaac, Cont. (Conn.), wid. Sarah, BLWt. 11–60–55................................. W 6954
    John, wid. Annis.. W 17694
    Noah... S 23591
    Russell, wid. Anna... R 2780
    Samuel.. S 10530
    Solomon... S 22725
    Thomas, wid. Susannah.. S 17695
    Westbrook.. S 39405
DAYTON, Andrew, wid. Jerusha... W 17708
    Benjamin.. S 17369
    David, wid. Elizabeth.. R 2793
    Ephraim, wid. Mary, BLWt. 91508–160–55.. W 10707
    Jonah.. S 13691
    Mary, former wid. of Seth Bulkley, q. v..
    Nathaniel... S 10527
    Samuel, wid. Naomi.. W 20955
DEAN, DEANE or DEANS, or DEIANS, or DEEN.
    Aaron, BLWt. 28523–160–55.. S 9384
    Benjamin. NOTE.—BLWt. 1988–100 was given his daughter, who resided in Conn., for Cont.
      service of her father.
    David, Vt. in 1818.. S 39424
    David, Tolland Co. Conn. in 1832; wid. Mary, BLWt. 26489–160–55............. W 1246
    Ebenezer.. S 31647
    Elijah, wid. Anna, BLWt. 3766–160–55... W 19162
    Enos, Conn. & Vt... S 15400
    Hopestill or Hoptill, former wid. of Ephraim Johnson, q. v.
    James L., BLWt. 56505–160–55... S 22200
    Joel, Conn. & Mass.. S 15083
    John, wid. Martha.. W 17714
    Phineas or Phinehas, Conn. & Cont., wid. Ruth, BLWt. 17576–160–55......... W 25527
    Reuben, Litchfield Co., Conn., in 1818; died in 1821; wid. Lucretia............ W 25524
    Reuben, Norfolk, Conn. in 1832; died in 1836; wid. Roxalana.................... W 17713
    Samuel, Conn. & N. Y., wid. Hannah, BLWt. 71027–160–55...................... W 25520
    William, Cont. services but Conn. res. after Rev.; N. Y. when pensioned; wid. Anna........ W 20977
DE ANGELIS, Paschal Charles Joseph, Conn., Conn. Sea Service & Privateer; wid. Elizabeth.. W 17715
DEAR, Jonathan... S 34740
DEART. (See DART.)
DEAVENPORT. (See DAVENPORT.)
DEEN. (See DEAN.)
DE FOREST, Abel... S 15086
    Ebenezer.. S 31643
    Gideon, N. Y. in 1832; wid. Hannah... R 2842
    Mary, former wid. of Thomas U. Ruland, q. v.
    Mills... S 13046
    Reuben, Conn. & N. Y. (also given DEFREES).................................... S 17380
    Samuel, BLWt. 538–200, Lieut. was issued June 3, 1789. No papers.
    Samuel, wid. Mary... W 16559
DE FREES, Reuben. (See DE FOREST.)
DEIANS. (See DEAN.)
DELANO, Aaron, Conn., Cont. & Mass., wid. Anna .... W 19171
    Jonathan.. S 39429
    Lois, former wid. of Thomas Coats, q. v.
    Thomas.. S 23194
DELANOY, Ellen, former wid. of Abraham Resseguie, Conn. W 24054; also former wid. of Richard
    Hill, Mass.. R 2853
DELLEBER. (See DILLEBER.)
DEMING or DEMMING or DENING, or DAMAN.
    David, wid. Ann, BLWt. 14961–160–55... W 2599
    Davis, wid. Elizabeth Ann.. W 17716
    Edmund or Edmond, wid. Bethiah... W 10313
      Given also DAMAN.
    Elijah, wid. Lucy... W 17717
    Gideon, Conn. & Mass... S 10552
    James.. R 2866
    John, b. 1749, wid. Elizabeth... W 14606
    Jonathan, BLWt. 745–100.. S 17381
    Julius.. S 39428
    Pownal, Conn. & Cont., former wid. of Mehitable D. Colton..................... W 20894
      BLWt. 8463–160–55 and BLWt. 537–200, Lieut. was issued Apr. 22, 1796 to Mehitable
      Deming, Adx., marked "Entered Feb. 22, 1816." No papers.
    Stephen... S 37883
    Theron.. S 31648
    Wait, former wid. of, Ruth Morey... W 17135
DEMMON, Thomas.. R 2880
    Also given DENNISON.
DENING. (See DEMING.)
DENISON or DENNISON, Abigail, former wid. of Asa Gillet, q. v.
    Amos... S 39438
    Avery, wid. Prudence.. W 20984
    Bebee or Bebee... S 9328
    Chauncy, wid. Sarah... W 24055
    Daniel, wid. Lucy.. W 17718
    David, Conn. & Vt.. S 5335
    George, Madison Co., N. Y., in 1832... S 10551
    George, Conn. in 1832.. S 12768
    Gilbert.. S 15805
    Henry, Conn., Cont. & Navy, wid. Mary.. W 15890

50

DENISON or DENNISON, James	S	37881
James P	S	15079
Jedediah	S	15084
Joseph, Cont. (Conn.)	S	10564
Nathan	S	22203
Samuel	R	2878
Thomas	R	2880
Also given DEMMON.		
DENMARK, Burnardus or Barnardus	S	43482
DENNIS or DENNISS.		
Anna, former wid. of Stephen Billings, q. v.		
Russell	S	15804
Samuel, Navy service, Conn. res	S	37884
DENNY, Absalom, wid. Bethia	W	20969
DENSLOW, Benjamin	S	27671
Eli, wid. Polly, BLWt. 104-60-55	W	25528
Elijah	S	15087
Martin, former wid. of, Roxarene Wright	W	6593
BLWt. 3191-160-55 and BLWt. 540-200, Lieut. issued (no month) 26, 1790. No papers.		
DENSMORE, Thomas, wid. Hannah	W	2601
DENTON, Daniel, BLWt. 1747-100	S	43486
DERBY, Benjamin, d 1830, never pensioned; wid. Constant, Albany, N. Y., 1838	W	20979
Benjamin, fifer, never pensioned; died 1829; wid. Esther, pensioned from Vt	W	26207
(See also DARBE.)		
DEVENPORT. (See DAVENPORT.)		
DE WITT, Garret or Garrit, wid. Elizabeth	W	25522
Jacob, wid. Martha	W	20970
DE WOLF, DE WOLFE, DEWOOLF or D'WOLF.		
Benjamin, Conn. & Navy	S	43490
Daniel, Michigan in 1832	S	29117
Daniel, Conn. in 1832, died 1834; wid. Hannah, BLWt. 14507-160-55	W	1245
Edward, Conn. & Privateer	S	15089
Elisha, Cont. (Conn.)	S	29756
Joseph	S	3280
Levi or Levy, wid. Huldah, BLWt. 3519-160-55	W	25521
Peter	S	18377
Samuel, wid. Susannah	W	20978
Seth, wid. Hannah, BLWt. 26504-160-55	S	2562
Stephen, wid. Abigail	W	2600
DEXTER, Abigail, former wid. of Aaron French, q. v.		
John	S	23192
Nathan	S	37889
Warham	R	
DIBBLE, DIBLE or DIBOL.		
Abraham	R	2928
Benjamin	S	15098
Daniel, wid. Susannah	W	17723
Israel	S	20337
John, Darian, Conn., in 1832	S	15097
John, N. Y. in 1818	S	39445
Moses, wid. Elizabeth	W	27931
DICKENSON or DICKERSON. (See DICKINSON.)		
DICKEY, Peter	S	23600
DICKINSON, DICKENSON or DICKERSON.		
Asahel, wid. Lucy	W	19179
Benjamin	S	27691
David, wid. Sybil	W	17725
Friend	S	44147
Ichabod, Conn. & N. Y	S	17385
Jesse	S	42157
Josiah, wid. Lucy	W	24062
Levi, Conn. & Privateer, wid. Bethiah	W	14619
Nathaniel, wid. Lucy	W	25540
Oliver, wid. Anna	W	17726
Ozias, wid. Mary W	W	17721
Samuel, wid. Hannah	W	16955
Silvanus, Cont. (Conn.), wid. Mary	W	17724
Simeon, Conn. & Privateer	S	17386
Solomon, wid. Elizabeth	W	1736
Waitstill, Conn. & Cont	S	17928
DICKS, David	S	43500
(See also DIX.)		
DICKSON or DIXON, or DIXSON.		
Amos	S	23602
BLWt. 26588-160-55.		
David	S	43499
Jared	S	39441
John, Cont. & Conn., Dutchess Co., N. Y., in 1821 as Drummer, BLWt. 1021-100.		
John, Monroe Co., N. Y., in 1832, as private; wid. Jane	W	25544
Joseph, wid. Mercy	W	22939
Miles, former wid. of, Sarah Clark	W	20881
Robert	S	10571
Thomas, wid. Lydia	W	1397
DIGGINS, Martin, wid. Lydia P., BLWt. 9187-160-55	W	540
DIKE, William	S	10572
DIKEMAN, Daniel	S	15408
Eliphalet, wid. Huldah, BLWt. 7056-160-55	W	25542
Frederick or Frederic	S	39447
Hezekiah, wid. Esther	W	25545
Levi, wid. Rebecca	W	24857

51

DILLEBER or DELLEBER, John... S 12747
DILLINGHAM, Benjamin, Conn. residence in 1819... R-
DIMICK, DIMMICK, or DIMOCK.
  Amasa, wid. Matilda... W 3396
  Benjamin, N. Y. in 1818.. S 43501
    BLWt. 541-200, Lieut. was issued Sept. 11, 1789. No papers.
  Benjamin, former wid. of, Miriam Raymond, soldier d. 1797, Vt., BLWt. 27575-160-55...... W 18787
  David, Conn., Cont. & Vt.. S 5347
  Edward, wid. Esther... W 4427
  Elias... S 21737
  Jeduthan.. S 37890
  John.. S 12775
  Joseph, Vt. in 1818... S 39448
  Joseph, N. Y. in 1832, died in 1845; wid. Fanny.. W 22942
  Peter... S 23197
  Shubael, Conn. & Mass... R 2962
  Simeon, wid. Priscilla.. W 4942
DINER, James.. S 37891
DISBRO, DISBROW, or DESBRO, Asa... S 9385
  Henry, wid. Hannah, BLWt. 11260-160-55.. W 9408
  Joshua.. S 37882
  Justus.. S 37885
  Simon, wid. Philama, BLWt. 821-160-55... W 17722
DIX, Benjamin... S 39446
  Samuel, former wid. of, Sarah Willson... W 18414
  (See also DICKS.)
DOAN or DOANE or DONE.
  Joel, wid. Jemima; BLWt. 6108-160-55.. W 3525
  Josiah, wid. Lois. .... W 16239
  Oliver, Conn. Sea service & Mass.. S 20339
  Richard... S 43510
DODD, Bishop.. S 37894
  Guy, former wid. of, Hannah Currier... W 10573
  John, wid. Anna, Conn. residence in 1843.. R 2989
  John, former wid. of, Hannah Mansfield.. W 17092
  Timothy, wid. Susannah.. W 20991
DODGE, Benjamin, wid. Tabitha.. W 16956
  Daniel, former wid. of, Irena Hubbs... W 8963
  Elihu, wid. Lucretia.. W 17730
  Ira... S 8335
  Joel.. S 15099
  Reuben, wid. Dolly or Dorothy... W 20994
  William... S 43512
DOLE, James, Conn., Cont. & N. Y... S 43518
  BLWt. 542-200, Lieut. was issued Dec. 1, 1789. No papers.
DOLPH, Stephen.. S 35897
DOND. (See DOWD.)
DONE. (See DOANE.)
DONNELLY, Robert.. R 3008
DOOLITTLE, Benjamin, wid. Sarah.. R 3015
  Charles... S 12796
  David, Conn. & N. Y., wid. Ann Elizabeth; BLWt. 35832-160-55................................... W 25537
  Eber, former wid. of, Mary Doolittle; BLWt. 26686-160-55...................................... W 26974
  Mary's second husband was also pensioned. (See Doolittle, Obed, S 16766.)
  Ezra, wid. Sarah.. R 3016
  George, wid. Grace.. R 3014
  John, wid. Hannah... W 19194
  Joseph.. S 37893
  Obed.. S 16766
  Thomas.. R 3017
  Uri... S 10577
DORCHESTER or DORCKESTER.
  Alexander, Cont. (Conn.), wid. Anna... W 19190
  Reuben.. S 10576
  Stephen, wid. Abigail... W 19192
DORMAN, David, wid. Mabel... R 3021
DORR, Elisha.. R 3023
  Samuel, Cont. (Conn.), wid. Abigail... W 14632
DORRANCE, David, Conn. & Cont.. S 45331
  BLWt. 535-300, Captain was issued March 5, 1793, to Samuel Dorrance, Assignee. This war-
  rant was issued under DARRANCE.
DOTA, John, Conn. & N. Y.. S 12791
DOTEY or DOTY, Benjamin... S 45327
  Danforth, wid. Sarah.. W 19193
  Daniel, wid. Talitha or Talatha... W 22952
  John.. S 12781
  Joseph, wid. Mary... R 3034
  Samuel.. S 45326
  William... S 10584
DOUBLEDAY, Ammi, N. Y. in 1832; wid. Lois.. S 3037
  Asahel.. S 18803
  Jacob... R 3036
  Joseph, Sharon, Vt., in 1818.. S 39453
  Joseph, Mass. in 1818 & 1832; wid. Lucy... W 14625
  Seth.. S 10580
DOUD. (See DOWD.)
DOUGAL or DUGAL, Thomas, former wid. of, Ann Page or Paige....................................... W 17417
DOUGLAS or DOUGLASS, David.. S 10579
  James, Rockland, N. Y., in 1832... S 46033
  James, d. 1817, not pensioned; wid. Elizabeth... R 3045

DOUGLAS or DOUGLASS, Joseph, wid. Hannah .... R 3046
  Nathaniel .... S 45333
  Richard, wid. Lucy .... W 730
    BLWt. 536-300, Capt., was issued Jan. 25, 1790. No papers. Sarah, former wid. of Lebbeus Harris, q. v.
  Skeen or Sacket, Skene Douglas, wid. Lorrilla .... W 4619
    BLWt. 18019-160-55.
DOW, Nathan .... S 23202
DOWD, or DAUD, or DOND, or DOUD.
  Benjamin .... S 21739
  Daniel, Conn. & R. I .... S 12789
  Moses, former wid. of, Abigail Smith. See papers in claim of Elijah Smith, R 9676, Navy (Mass.) and Sea Service.
  Richard, Cont. (Conn.), former wid. of, Rebecca Wilcox .... W 22641
  Samuel .... R 3038
  Solomon, BLWt. 419-100 .... S 38663
  William, wid. Hannah .... W 19183
DOWER. (See DOWNER.)
DOWN or DOWNS, David .... S 17392
  Elijah, wid. Ruth .... W 10755
  Jabez .... S 45643
  James .... S 38664
  Joseph .... S 12785
  Nathaniel .... S 15813
DOWNER, Avery, Conn. residence .... R 3063
  Elisha, Conn. & Cont .... S 12786
  James (also given DOWER) .... S 21741
  Jason, Conn. & Vt .... S 16769
  Zaccheus or Zacheus, Conn. & Vt .... S 12782
DOWNING, Daniel .... S 15414
  John .... S 39451
  Jonathan, Conn. & Cont., wid. Huldah .... W 24868
  Phineas .... S 31651
  Stephen .... S 29122
DOWSETT, Amos, wid. Mary .... W 17728
  (See also DUSETT.)
DRAKE, Abial, wid. Anna, applied from N. Y .... R 3071
  Abiel, Conn. 1818 .... S 38674
  Ebenezer, former wid. of, Lois Brewer .... W 20791
  Elihu .... S 38673
  Gideon, wid. Annah .... W 14643
  Lemuel .... S 31655
  Lory or Lowry, not pensioned; wid. Sarah applied from Penna., BLWt. 43879-160-55 ...... R 3078
  Moses, wid. Abigail .... W 17731
  Noah .... S 12802
  Phinehas .... S 31657
DREW, Samuel, Conn., Green Mt. Boys, Mass., N. H. & N. Y .... S 45238
DUCIT. (See DUSETT.)
DUDLEY or DUDLY, Benajah .... S 12824
  Eber or Ebor, wid. Hannah .... W 21016
  Harman .... S 27737
  Isaac, wid. Anne .... R 3101
  Jared, wid. Anna .... W 17737
  Medad .... R 3104
  Roswell .... S 10592
  Samuel, Conn. & Privateer .... S 6806
  Thomas .... S 22222
DUGAL. (See DOUGAL.)
DUGLASS. (See DOUGLASS.)
DUMMER, Stephen .... R 3116
DUNBAR, Joel .... S 43525
  Miles, wid. Tryphosa .... W 16962
  Robert .... S 39463
  Thomas, Conn. Sea Service & R. I., wid. Eunice, BLWt. 29039-160-55 .... W 24081
DUNCAN, Jared, pensioned for disability in 1810; wid. Dolly R .... R 3122
DUNCOMB or DUNCOMBE, Edward, wid. Anna .... W 25553
DUNHAM, Cornelius .... S 12828
  Daniel, BLWt. 10235-160-55 .... S 43523
  Elisha, wid. Mehitable .... W 25546
  Gershom, wid. Mary .... W 21013
  Gideon, wid. Anna .... W 16565
  Hannah, former wid. of John Lawrence .... W 26662
  James .... S 31658
  Salathiel, wid. Lucy .... W 19202
  Samuel, Ontario Co., N. Y., 1832; former wid. of, Asenath Turner, BLWt. 114388-160-55 .... W 27795
  Samuel, Cont. (Conn.), Stillwater, N. Y., 1818 .... S 45346
  Stephen .... S 12804
DUNING. (See DUNNING.)
DUNMORE, Jane, former wid. of James Merrill, q. v.
DUNN, Samuel, Conn. & N. J., wid. Barbara, BLWt. 26927-160-55 .... W 7048
  Timothy, wid. Mehitable, BLWt. 11176-160-55 .... W 1249
DUNNING or DUNING, David .... S 15103
  Edmund .... S 15819
  James, Conn., Cont., & N. Y .... S 12830
  Josiah, Conn., N. Y., & Vt .... S 23207
  Luther .... R 3151
DUNWELL, Stephen .... S 2188
  William .... S 34772
DUNWORTH, George, wid. Abigail W., BLWt. 26314-160-55 .... W 9416
DUPLEX, Prince, wid. Lement .... W 16963

53

DURAND, Alexander, wid. Elizabeth.. W 21014
    Andrew.. S 2528
    Ebenezer, wid. Polly, BLWt. 13202–160–55... W 25547
    Eleazer... S 45354
    Fisk or Fish.. S 12807
    Isaac.. S 19961
    John, Derby, Conn., in 1818.. S 37898
    John, Service in Navy; Conn. residence; Milford, Conn., in 1818................. S 37900
    Joseph, Conn. & N. Y.. S 12829
    Lemuel, wid. Catharine.. W 1248
    Samuel, wid. Susanna.. W 17734
    William, Conn. & Sea Service, wid. Mary.. W 25552
DURFEE, DURFEY, or DURPHEY.
    Ebenezer, wid. Abigail, BLWt· 13187–160–55.. W 2080
    Elijah, wid. Elizabeth, applied from Knox Co., Ohio.................................... R 3156
    John, Conn. & Privateer, wid. Mary.. W 21011
    Joseph, wid. Experience, BLWt. 6415–160–55... W 1839
DURHAM, Simeon... S 10595
DURKEE, Asahel or Asel, wid. Sarah, BLWt. 9453–160–55............................... W 19201
    Benjamin, Conn. & Cont., BLWt. 420–300.. S 39473
    Daniel.. S 22742
    Ebe.. S 2524
    John, wid. Jemina; BLWt. 100834–160–55, soldier, a private, died in 1838.
    John, Conn. & Cont.; BLWt. 580–500, Colonel; Soldier died May 30, 1782.
    John, Conn. & Cont.; BLWt. 533–300, Captain, was issued July 7, 1791, to John Durkee,
        Captain, and son of Col. John Durkee.
    Nathaniel, wid. Melinda, BLWt. 19729–160–55... W 25548
    Phineas... BLWt. 606–100
    Robert... BLWt. 432–300
    Sally (Sarah), former wid. of Walter Tiffany, q. v.
    Solomon, Cont. (Conn.)... S 42682
    William.. S 18385
DURPHY. (See DURFEE.)
DUSETT or DUCIT, John... S 45351
    (See also DOWSETT.)
DUTTON, Amasa, wid Elizabeth.. W 1399
    Asa... S 39464
    Joseph, wid. Mary.. W 25551
    Oliver, Serg't, Bristol, Conn., 1818, & died 1826 in N. Y., from which State wid. Ruth was
        pensioned.. W 24861
    Oliver, Conn., Cont. & Mass., Hampden, Mass., in 1832, wid. Phebe, BLWt. 9437–160–55.... S 18383
        This woman's former husband was also pensioned for service in the Revolution. See
        Mass. Powers, Stephen, W 25550.
    Thomas.. R 3170
    Titus, Conn. & Cont.. S 45344
DWIGHT, Alpheus, wid. Fanny, BLWt. 29738–160–55....................................... W 25554
    Timothy, Cont. (Conn.), wid. Mary... W 21025
D'WOLF. (See DE WOLF.)
DYAR or DYER, Benjamin, former wid. of, Ann Mills....................................... W 18520
    Ebenezer.. R 3177
    Joseph, wid. Charlotte, BLWt. 9203–160–55.. W 25555
DYGART, Orpha, former wid. of Solomon Welch, q. v.
ESTABROOK. (See ESTABROOK.)
EASTEN. (See EASTON.)
EASTMAN, Asahel, wid. Mary... W 19210
    Clark, wid. Betsey, BLWt. 36638–160–55.. W 9421
    Deliverance.. S 8389
    Eli, Conn. & Vt.. S 18810
    Joseph, wid. Elizabeth, BLWt. 26434–160–55... W 7101
    Nathaniel, Conn. & N. H., wid. Ruth.. W 22992
EASTON, Giles, Cont. (Conn.), wid. Anna... W 22997
    Julian, BLWt. 1209–100.. S 37902
    Obadiah.. S 21171
EATON, Abigail, former wid. of Ashbel Merrell, q. v.
    Benjamin, Conn., Cont., & N. J., also War of 1812...................................... S 45359
    Cyril or Cyrel... S 32227
    Daniel, wid. Mary... W 19211
    Ebenezer, Conn., Mass., & R. I.; in 1832 was in Chenango Co., N. Y.; wid. Polly Ann....... W 7067
    Ebenezer, never pensioned; wid. Lois, Windham Co., Conn......................... W 21038
    Eunice, former wid. of Joseph Walker, q. v.
    James, d. 1814; wid. Anna, from Conn... W 25556
    James, d. 1807, Mass., wid. Eleanor... W 21037
    Josiah, Conn. & Cont.. S 12839
    Luther, wid. Sally.. W 21034
    Maverick.. S 18809
    Nathan.. S 15821
    Samuel... S 12837
    Solomon, former wid. of, Phebe Carpenter... W 8591
        BLWt. 30597–160–55.
    Stephen... S 23209
ECCLESTON or ECCLESTONE, David, wid. Catharine...................................... W 19217
    (See also EGGLESTON.)
EDDY, Asa, wid. Rebecca... W 25561
    BLWt. 26789–160–55.
    Gilbert, Conn. & Privateer, wid. Prudence; also in War of 1812................... W 25560
        BLWt. 15046–160–55 for service of above soldier as Brig. General N. Y. Militia from Sept. 1
        to Sept. 19, 1814.
    Levi, wid. Rhoda.. W 21046
    Sarah, former wid. of Samuel Waterous, q. v.
    Seth... S 39483

EDER, Anthony, or NEEDAR, Toney, Conn. & Cont., wid. Phillis, BLWt. 19813–160–55..... W 7073
EDGAR, Thomas, Navy (Conn.).. S 37905
EDGECOMB or EDGECOMBE.
  Jabez.. S 37906
  Roger, Conn., Cont. & Navy... S 10615
  Samuel, Conn. & Privateer.. S 20743
EDGERTON or EGERTON.
  Abel, Conn. & Cont.. S 10613
  Ariel, Conn., Cont. & Privateer... S 18816
  David, Conn., Conn. Sea service & Privateer... S 15110
  Ebenezer, pensioned as Jr. in Conn. in 1818, and transferred to Mass.................... S 34793
  Ebenezer, pensioned as Senr.—Granby, Conn. in 1818.................................... S 37904
  James, Conn. & Privateer.. S 18391
  Jediah, Richford, N. Y., in 1832 as Serg't., wid. Sarah.................................... R 3235
  Jedediah, Vt. in 1832.. S 21743
  Lydia, former wid. of John Babcock, q. v.
  Roger, Cont. (Conn.), wid. Betsey.. W 19219
EDMOND, EDMONDS, EDMUND or EDMUNDS.
  Andrew, Capt. & Lieut. Train Band, wid. Esther.. R 3247
  Andrew, wid. Elizabeth.. R 3248
    Pension applications of both soldier and widow were rejected.
  Esther, former wid. of Peter Rose, q. v.
  George, Cont. (Conn.), wid. Abigail.. W 17744
  William.. S 20472
EDSON, Benjamin, wid. Anne, BLWt. 39494–160–55....................................... W 19220
  Eliab... S 15419
  Josiah.. S 39486
  Lydia, former wid. of Timothy Harrington, q. v.
  Nathan... S 39482
  Seth, Conn. & Cont... S 10614
EDWARDS, ABEL, wid. Sarah... W 17745
  Clark, Conn. & R. I., wid. Catharine... W 14671
  Daniel, Conn. & Privateer; Tomkins, N. Y., in 1832...................................... S 8395
  Daniel, Delaware Co., N. Y., in 1832, & died in 1836; wid. Hannah...................... W 17743
  Esther, former wid. of Reuben Cone, q. v.
  Hezekiah... S 16780
  Isaac, wid. Mary, BLWt. 26586–160–55.. W 25558
  Jabez... S 10607
  Jonathan... S 42696
  Mercy or Marcy, former wid. of Joel Judd, q. v.
  Nathaniel.. S 44797
    BLWt. 659–200, Lieut. was issued Dec. 14, 1792, to Nathaniel Edwards. No papers.
  Samuel... S 12855
EELS, ELLES or ELLS.
  Daniel.. R 3267
  Edward, wid. Abigail.. BLWt. 102–300
  Jeremiah... S 44798
  John... S 29132
  John... R 3268
  Samuel, Conn. & Cont.. S 37912
EGERTON. (See EDGERTON.)
EGGELSTON, EGGLESTON or EGLESTON.
  Benedict, BLWt. 6381–160–55... S 38694
  Gershom or Garshom, wid. Avis.. W 1739
  James, Conn. & Cont., wid. Jemima.. W 17747
  Joseph, Conn. & R. I., wid. Elizabeth.. W 17748
  Samuel... R 3270
  Timothy, Conn. & Cont.. S 42698
ELDERKIN, Elisha, Conn. & Conn. Sea service, wid. Mary................................. W 17758
ELDRED or ELDRID, John, Conn. & Cont... S 42705
  Judah.. S 6817
ELDREDG, ELDREDGE, ELDRIDG, ELDRIDGE or ELDRIGE.
  Elisha, wid. Cynthia... W 23007
  Henry, Conn. & R. I., wid. Elizabeth... W 23004
  James.. S 22231
  John... S 37911
  Jonathan... S 39487
  Joseph, Cortland, N. Y., in 1832.. S 23213
  Joseph, not pensioned, d. 1830, Hartford, Conn., wid. Rhoda............................. W 17756
  Robert, former wid. of, Flizabeth Burtis.. R 1513
  Zoeth, wid. Bethiah.. R 3280
ELEY. (See ELY.)
ELITHORP, ELLITHORP, ELITHROP or ELLITHROP.
  Azariah.. S 10618
  Samuel, Conn. & Cont. wid. Amy.. W 21064
ELLES. (See EELS.)
EILLIOT or ELLIOTT.
  George, wid. Percy... W 25612
  Henry.. R 3296
  Richard, Cont. (Conn.)... S 12864
  Thomas... S 31664
ELLIS, Asa... S 29138
  Nathan, wid. Phebe.. W 17752
  Phenix Carpenter, Conn. & Cont.. S 17941
  Stephen, wid. Rebekah... W 6716
  William, Conn. & Conn. Sea service... S 28720
ELLITHORP or ELLITHROP. (See ELITHORP.)

55

ELLSWORTH or ELSWORTH.

Benjamin.. S 37910
Eliphalet, Cont. (Conn.), wid. Jemima... R 3332
   Also War of 1812.
Job, wid. Huldah, BLWt. 9078-160-55... W 7103
John, liv. Farmington, Conn. in 1832, & moved to Pittsburgh, Ohio............................. S 2196
John, Conn., N. H. & R. I. serv., liv. Montgomery Co., N. Y., in 1832........................... S 9854
   Mary, former wid. of William Gillespie, q. v.
Moses... S 37909
ELLWOOD. (See ELWOOD.)
ELMER, Elijah.. R 3328
Joel, wid. Zillah.. W 24112
Joseph, wid. Ruth... W 19224
Samuel.. S 31665
Stephen... S 23617
ELMORE, Daniel, wid. Elizabeth.. W 21060
Joel... S 30399
ELSWORTH. (See ELLSWORTH.)
ELTON, Bradley, wid. Grace... W 17751
ELWELL. Ebenezer.. S 43527
ELWOOD or ELLWOOD.
Abijah.. W 25562
Abram... S 44803
Isaac.. S 44804
Joseph, wid. Naomi... W 21058
Nathan, wid. Abigail... W 15765
Stephen, wid. Betty.. W 17757
Thomas, Navy serv. Conn. res.. S 37907
ELY or ELEY, Abner, Conn. & Conn. Sea service, wid. Bridget...................................... W 21056
   Bridget's first husband, Semilius Brockway, died in service.
Andrew, Cont. (Conn.)... S 44801
Daniel.. S 31663
Gabriel, wid. Eunice... W 2775
Gurdon.. S 17404
Jabez... S 44802
Jacob... S 15111
John.. S 3329
Wells... S 44800
William... S 42706
EMERSON or EMMERSON.
Catharine, former wid. of John Skinner, q. v.
Joseph.. R 3343
Nathaniel, wid. Mary... W 21068
Stephen... S 22754
EMES, Joseph, wid. Hannah; also given AMES.
EMMONS or EMONS, Arthur.. S 29140
Daniel Spencer, wid. Luna.. W 17760
Jonathan.. S 22755
Phineas or Phinehas, Conn. & N. Y., wid. Keziah.. W 21071
Samuel, wid. Sarah, BLWt. 26995-160-55... W 7106

Solomon... S 22753
ENO, Isaac, Conn. & Vt... R 3356
Levi.. S 31667
Reuben, wid. Lois.. W 25564
ENOS, Alexander.. S 15113
David, Hartford Co. in 1818... S 37914
David, N. Y. in 1818, moved to Vt... S 39497
Elisha, wid. Sarah... W 16252
Erasmus, not pensioned: wid. Anna... R 3358
Matthias or Mathias, Conn. Sea service & R. I., wid. Anna... W 16251
   Olive, former wid. of Joseph Holcomb, q. v.
Roger, wid. Jerusha.. W 24127
ENSIGN, Daniel, wid. Elizabeth... W 10957
Eliphalet... S 12874
James... S 37913
Otis, wid. Hannah, BLWt. 6421-160-55... W 9428
ENSWORTH, Jesse.. S 15114
John, wid. Mary.. W 17761
ESTABROOK, ESTBROOK or EASTABROOK, Nehemiah.. S 44809
ETTICK, George J., Conn. & N. Y.. S 10635
EVANS or EVENS, or EVINS.
Abiathar or Abiather, wid. Mary... W 21080
Allen... S 37916
Benjamin Stacy, wid. Sybil, BLWt. 6268-160-55.. S 22759
Benoni.. S 43535
Cotton Daniel.. S 23623
Daniel, wid. Sarah... W 17766
David... S 12887
Isaac... S 44813
Josiah.. S 43533
Moses, wid. Thirza... W 7121
Randall or Randol, Conn. & N. H... S 12879
William, Conn. & N. Y.. S 12880
EVARTS or EVERTS.
Daniel, Conn. & N. Y... S 10637
Eber, Conn., Cont. & Green Mt. Boys... S 12881
Ezra, wid. Lorrain... W 21078
Nathaniel, wid. Mary... W 21077
Reuben.. S 23624

EVARTS or EVERTS, Solomon .... S 12888
   Stephen, Bergen, N. Y., in 1818. .... S 44811
   Stephen, Cont. (Conn.). .... S 21768
      Conn. in 1816, N. Y. in 1827.
EVENS. (See EVANS.) :
EVEREST, Daniel, wid. Eunice .... W 21082
   Elisha .... S 43534
EVERETT, EVERIT, EVERITT or EVRIT.
   Abner .... S 15827
   Andrew .... S 12884
   Daniel .... S 22758
   Ebe .... S 15417
   Eliphalet, wid. Rhoda .... W 19234
   Jeremiah, Navy (Conn.), wid. Maria, BLWt. 26585-160-55. .... W 21081
   Oliver, wid. Mary, BLWt. 265-60-55. .... W 1583
EVENS. (See EVANS.)
EVERTS. (See EVARTS.)
EVRIT. (See EVERETT.)

F.

FAIRBANKS, Samuel .... S 16788
FAIRCHILD, Abel .... S 12892
   Clement, wid. Jerusha .... W 1741
   Ephraim, wid. Mary .... W 2929
   Gilbert .... S 15116
   James, wid. Mary .... W 21093
   John, Conn. & N. Y. .... S 10641
   Joseph .... S 43542
   Nathan, wid. Sarah .... W 25568
   Peter, Newtown, Conn., 1818 .... S 38688
      Also given FAIRFIELD.
   Peter, Fairfield, Conn., as Corporal in 1818; wid. Rachel .... W 7248
FAIRFIELD. (See FAIRCHILD.)
FARMAN, Daniel .... S 12894
   Roswell or Roswill, wid. Anna, BLWt. 26372-160-55. .... W 645
FAIRWEATHER or FAYERWEATHER, Samuel .... S 37917
FANCHER, Rufus .... S 43540
   William, former wid. of, Thankful Cole .... W 22811
FANNING, Asa, wid, Jerusha, BLWt. 34996-160-55. .... W 19247
   Charles .... S 13001
      BLWt. 723-200, Lieut.; was issued Dec. 24, 1799, to William Wells, Assignee. No papers.
   John, wid. Abigail .... W 1585
   Jonathan, Conn. Sea Service & Navy .... S 23214
   Thomas, wid. Susannah .... W 17891
FARGO or FERGO, Ezekiel .... S 10650
   Samuel, wid. Hannah .... W 24178
   Thomas .... S 29152
   Timothy, wid. Betsey .... W 25569
   William, wid. Polly .... W 19240
FARLOW, Hulaah, former wid. of Joseph Moger, q. v. .... S 43546
FARMER, Thomas .... S 43546
      BLWt. 722-200, Lieut., was issued Oct. 7, 1789. No papers.
FARNAM or FARNAN or FARNHAM or FARNUM.
   Abial, wid. Chloe .... W 21089
   Benjamin, Conn. & Cont., former wid. of, Ann Griffin .... R 4305
   Bezaleel or Barzaleel .... S 40058
   Elijah .... S 10643
   Eliphalet, wid. Hannah .... W 24175
   John, wid. Mary .... W 5273
   Joseph .... S 13003
   Levi, former wid. of, Dorcas Taylor .... W 16752
      Dorcas' second husband, Ebenezer Perry, Conn. or Mass., also served in the Revolu-
      tion. Her third and last husband, Taylor, Thomas, S 46202, was a Rev. pensioner....
   Peter, Newtown, Conn. in 1832 .... S 17405
   Peter, d. 1817, Hebron, Conn., wid. Sylvia .... W 25571
   Rufus, Conn. & Navy, wid. Priscilla, BLWt. 26181-160-55. .... W 10073
   Thomas, Conn. & Cont. .... S 17408
   Zedediah .... S 38689
FARRAND, Joseph, Conn. & Vt. .... S 18396
FARWELL, Isaac .... S 12893
   Thomas .... S 34831
FASSET or FASSETT, Adonijah .... R 3459
FAULKNER or FAULKNOR.
   Caleb, wid. Martha .... W 19239
   Thomas .... R 3467
FAY, John .... S 43543
   Moses, Conn. & Cont., wid. Mary .... W 21086
   Nathan, Conn. & Vt., wid. Mary .... R 3471
   Sherebiah, Conn. & Mass .... S 10647
   Timothy, Conn., Cont. & Mass., former wid. of Sarah How .... W 13469
   William .... S 43538
FAYERWEATHER. (See FAIRWEATHER.)
FEERO, Peter .... S 16792
FELLOWS, Abial, Conn. & N. Y., wid. Dorcas, BLWt. 92023-160-55 .... W 25576
   Isaac, Conn. & Cont .... S 13006
   Rosel, wid. Molly .... W 17899
   Samuel .... S 34840
   Sarah, former wid. of Benjamin Fenn .... q. v.
   Varney, wid. Anna .... W 23027

```
FENN, Benjamin, Middlebury, Conn., in 1832.................................................... S 13011
       Benjamin, Lieut. not pensioned; former wid. of, Sarah Fellows............................. W 17898
       Daniel....................................................................................... S 37918
       David........................................................................................ R 3490
       Edward, Conn. & Cont....................................................................... S 13012
       John......................................................................................... S 2545
       Thomas...................................................................................... S 13010
       Titus........................................................................................ R 3491
FENTON, Adonijah..................................................................................... S 23217
       Asa.......................................................................................... S 31674
       Elijah....................................................................................... S 10662
       Gamaliel, wid. Elizabeth, BLWt. 26989-160-55............................................... W 4951
       John, former wid. of, Lucy Scott........................................................... W 26957
       Jonathan, Conn. Sea service, wid. Rosalinda................................................ R 3496
            Both soldier and widow were rejected.
       Jotham....................................................................................... S 37919
       Nathaniel, Chataqua Co., N. Y., in 1832.................................................... S 13014
       Nathaniel, Mass., in 1832.................................................................. S 18398
       Solomon, Willington, Conn., in 1818........................................................ S 13007
       Solomon, Conn. & Cont., Unadilla, N. Y., in 1818, d. 1831, & arrears of pension were given
            his children—Polly McFarland, Solomon & Washington Fenton, & Fanny Johnson—in 1832 W 17120
FERGO. (See FARGO.)
FERGUSON, FORGASON, or FURGESON.
       Daniel....................................................................................... R 3500
       Samuel....................................................................................... S 29151
FERIN or FERRIN, Zebulon............................................................................. S 21752
FERRE. (See FERRY.)
FERRIS, Gould....................................................................................... S 28726
       Jeremiah, wid. Nancy........................................................................ W 17897
       Jonah, wid. Anne............................................................................ W 25572
       Oliver, Conn. & Conn. Sea service, wid. Abigail............................................ W 16254
FERRIS, Rainford A., or Ramford A................................................................... S 20751
       (See also FORRIS.)
FERRY or FERRE, Eliphalet, wid. Mercy............................................................... W 21104
       Moses, Conn. & Cont., wid. Jerusha......................................................... W 19255
FIDDIS, Hugh E., Conn. Sea service & Navy, BLWt. 75105-160-55........................................ R 3525
FIELD or FIELDS.
       David........................................................................................ R 3526
       Edmond...................................................................................... S 37920
       George....................................................................................... S 43556
       Ichabod...................................................................................... S 16800
       James, wid. Anna or Anna Hurd.............................................................. W 25582
       Joarab....................................................................................... R 3528
       John......................................................................................... S 13018
       Pardon....................................................................................... S 43555
       Samuel, wid. Huldah......................................................................... W 17907
FILER, Orris........................................................................................ S 23632
       (See also FISLER and FYLER.)
FILLEY, FILLY, & PHILLEY.
       Mark, wid. Elinor........................................................................... W 17901
       Moses........................................................................................ S 13016
       Remembrance, Conn. & Cont., wid. Hannah.................................................... W 17903
            BLWt. 193-60-55 & BLWt. 5817-100, issued April 21, 1791. No papers.
       Sylvanus, wid. Jemima....................................................................... W 17906
FILIMORE or FILMORE.
       Cyrus, Conn. & N. Y., wid. Jemima.......................................................... R 3539
       Henry........................................................................................ S 28538
FILLOW, Adams. (See PHILO.)
       Isaac........................................................................................ S 17416
FILLY. (See FILLEY.)
FILMORE. (See FILLMORE.)
FINCH or FINCHE.
       Abraham or Abram............................................................................ S 28727
       Ezra......................................................................................... R 3541
       Jeremiah, Serg't., Fairfield Co. Conn. 1818................................................ S 37923
       Jeremiah, N. Y., in 1818, as private....................................................... S 43560
       Jonathan, Conn. & N. Y. service............................................................ S 37924
       Samuel, pensioned as priv., Corp. & Serg't., N. Y., in 1832; wid. Polly.................... R 3543
       Stephen, wid. Mindwell...................................................................... W 24187
       Timithy...................................................................................... R 3544
       William, Ohio, in 1832, as priv............................................................ S 3359
       William, Conn. & N. Y., pensioned in Penna., in 1832 as priv. & Serg't..................... S 22768
FINCHLEY, George, wid. Sarah............................................... S 43557 & W 19261
FINNEY, FINNY, or PHINNEY.
       Eleazer...................................................................................... S 17415
       Jonathan, Conn., Cont. & Mass., wid. Sarah, BLWt. 34594-160-55............................. W 19262
       Joseph, wid. Mary........................................................................... W 16688
       Josiah....................................................................................... S 15280
       Sylvester, Conn. & N. Y..................................................................... S 16114
FISH, Aaron, Conn. & Navy........................................................................... S 10673
       Aurelia. (See FISK.)
       David........................................................................................ S 13019
       Esther, former wid. of John Ladd........................................................... q. v.
       John, wid. Eunice; also given FISK.
       Moses........................................................................................ S 13029
FISHER, Asahel, wid. Anna........................................................................... W 19236
       Jeremiah, wid. Sabra, BLWt. 11424-160-55................................................... W 7270
       John......................................................................................... S 13020
       Timothy...................................................................................... S 38695
```

FISK or FISKE.
Abijah, Conn., Conn. Sea service & Mass.. S 5394
Aurelia, former wid. of Nathaniel Stowell... q. v.
James, Conn. & Mass.. S 21199
John, wid. Eunice... W 17900
Jonathan, pensioned in Otsego Co. N. Y., in 1818; wid. Mehitable...................... R 3578
Samuel.. B 3580
FISLER, Jacob... S 2551
  (See also FILER and FYLER.)
FITCH, Andrew, wid. Abigail... W 2116
  BLWt. 721-300, Capt. was issued August 7, 1789. No papers.
Cordilla, former wid. of, Joanna Walker, BLWt. 31740-160-55............................ W 18263
Daniel, BLWt. 38-60-55... S 37922
Darius, wid. Lydia, BLWt. 17587-160-55.. W 1162
Elnathan.. S 45134
Giles... S 13408
Hannah, former wid. of Robert Williams... q. v.
James, wid. Esther.. W 17905
James, Conn. & Vt... R 3582
Jesse... S 10668
John, N. Y., in 1832 as Serg't... S 13028
John, Vt., in 1832 as priv... S 13030
John, Chittenden Co., Vt., in 1832, as priv. of Dragoons & infantry..................... S 10664
Luther, Conn. & Privateer.. S 16794
Nathaniel, N. Y., in 1832, d. 1837; wid. Caty.. W 23035
Nathaniel, Serg't, Artificers, d. 1814; "Cont. service but Conn. residence," wid. Abigail..... W 21122
Prentice.. S 44818
Rufus, Conn. & Cont... S 44817
William, N. Y., in 1832 as priv., wid. Mary.. W 19265
William, Surgeon, Conn. & Conn. Sea service, not pensioned; wid. Elizabeth.............. W 16990
FLAGG, Abijah, wid. Thankful... W 17909
Jonathan, wid. Christiana... W 14726
FLEMING or FLEMMING, Benoni, wid. Louisa... W 19288
FLETCHER, Jonathan... S 22771
FLING, Abel, wid. Susanna.. W 24214
Lemuel, pensioned in N. H. as Ensign, moved to N. Y., wid. Sarah........................ R 3611
FLINT, Aaron... S 15124
Asel or Asael, Conn. & Conn., Sea service, wid. Sally, BLWt. 3823-160-55................ W 25597
Daniel.. S 38703
Davis, wid. Lucy.. W 16991
Jabez... S 10681
James... R 3613
James or James L., wid. Jerusha.. W 17911
John, Conn. & Cont., former wid. of, Mary Brown.. W 20785
Jonathan.. S 15834
Joshua, Cont. (Conn.), wid. Sarah.. W 17910
Luke.. S 42195
Nathaniel... S 38702
Zacheus, wid. Sarah... W 16260
FLOWER, Abdiel... S 46361
Zephon, Conn. & Cont., BLWt. 3-60-55... S 6856
FLYNN, Michael, wid. Fanny... W 24212
FOARD. (See FORD.)
FOBES, Nathaniel... S 2218
Simon, Cont. & Mass... S 161/9
FOLKER, Chloe, former wid. of William Russell, q. v.
Ebenezer.. S 37938
FOLLET, Robert... S 8509
FOORD. (See FORD.)
FOOT or FOOTE.
Abraham, wid. Abby.. R 14246
Ambrose... S 13059
Amos.. S 13069
Beeri... S 13074
Bronson, wid. Thankful.. W 21144
Darius, Conn. & N. Y.. S 17957
Ebenezer or Ebenezer E., N. Y. in 1818, as priv.. S 44841
Ebenezer, Serg't, Capt. & Inspector of Cattle; d. N. Y. in 1829; wid. Matilda, BLWt. 34276-160-55... W 25583
Elihu, Conn. & Sea service.. S 15838
Ezra, former wid. of, Mercy Parson or Parsons.. W 19962
Hannah, former wid. of Robert Kimberley, q. v.
Heli, Conn. & Conn. Sea service, wid. Ruth... W 21142
Isaac, Cont. (Conn.).. S 44839
Jacob, wid. Lucy.. R 3641
Jesse, Cont. (Conn.).. S 29157
John.. R 3640
Prudence, former wid. of James Knowles, q. v.
Sarah, former wid. of Jared Bishop, q. v.
Stephen, wid. Hannah.. W 17912
Susannah, former wid. of Benjamin Johnson, q. v.
Timothy... S 17958
FORBES or FORBS.
Eli... S 15837
Elisha.. S 27801
James... S 37928
John, Vt. in 1832... S 15427
John, Conn. & Cont., d. 1786; daughter, Mary Blinn, got BLWt. 1298-100. Wid. was Mary Adams.
Levi, wid. Sarah.. W 21133

FORCE, Ebenezer... S 34873
FORD, or FOARD or FOORD.
   Amos, Windham Co., Conn., in 1832 as Jr... S 15428
   Amos, Hampton, Conn., in 1818.. S 37936
   Amos, Milford, Conn., in 1832, d. in 1835; wid. Eunice, BLWt. 26167-160-55............. W 25585
   Benjamin.. S 44842
   Hezekiah.. S 45538
   John, wid. Anna... W 14743
   John Morrison, Privateer (Conn.)... R 3656
   Jonathan, Genesee Co., N. Y., in 1832... S 23222
   Jonathan, Rensselaer Co., N. Y., in 1818.. S 44844
   Jonathan, d. 1829; son Eliakim got BLWt. 1498-100.
   Martin.. S 37932
   Nathan.. S 2557
   Nathaniel... S 13049
   Phinehas.. S 37929
   Stephen... S 16807
FORDHAM, Nathan, Conn., Sea service & N. Y... S 6848
FORGASON. (See FERGUSON.)
FORRIS, Peter, wid. Mary or Mony, BLWt. 1331-100 & 53-60-55................................. W 19281
FORSTER. (See FOSTER.)
FORSYTH, Latham, wid. Abigail, BLWt. 26049-160-55... W 2442
   William, wid. Prudence.. W 11007
FORTUNE, Richard... S 37933
FOSDICK, James... S 38707
   Thomas U., Cont. (Conn.) BLWt. 1239-150.
   William... R 3678
FOSTER or FORSTER.
   Alpheus, wid. Esther.. W 21129
   Asa, wid. Sarah... W 5277
   Benjamin.. S 37931
   Chauncey, wid. Charlotte.. W 17917
   David... S 44835
   Edward.. S 37935
   Faith, former wid. of John O. Waterman, q. v.
   Giles... S 13051
   Isaac, wid. Esther.. R 3683
   Jacob, wid. Susanna... W 24219
   Jesse... S 37934
   John, b. Mass., enl. from Conn. & liv. Conn. 1832... S 13047
   John, Conn. & N. Y. serv., Lieut. liv. N. Y. in 1832.. S 17962
   John, Fairfield Co., Conn., in 1818; wid. Pruella... R 3692
   Jonathan.. S 22247
   Joseph, Conn. & Mass. service, liv. Conn. in 1832, pensioned as priv. & fifer.............. S 16802
   Joseph, Conn. & Vt. service, liv. Vt. in 1832; wid. Dolly, BLWt. 9043-160-55............... W 736
   Peter, d. 1805, Mass., wid. Tammy... W 14745
   Peter, Conn. & Conn., Sea service... R 3691
   Samuel, Catskill, N. Y., in 1832.. S 13043
   Samuel, S., Conn., Sea service & Privateer.. S 13071
   Saul.. S 16808
   Timothy, wid. Desire.. W 16577
   Wareham, Conn. & Cont., wid. Lucretia... R 3688
FOWLER, Abiathar, wid. Asenath... W 14746
   Amos, Warren, Conn., in 1832 as Serg't.. S 15839
   Amos, priv., Corp. & serg't under Capt. Cook in Lebanon, Conn., in 1832; d. 1837; wid. Rebecca. W 17914
   Caleb, former wid. of, Olive Pratt.. W 4057
   Daniel.. S 10685
   Ebenezer.. S 10689
   Eli... R 3702
   Elisha A., Serg't in Bethel, Vt., in 1818; wid. Mary.. R 3710
   John, wid. Anna... W 17919
   Jonathan, Conn. & Cont.. S 41542
   Nathaniel, wid. Ruth.. R 3713
   Reuben.. S 44851
   Samuel, Conn. Sea service... R 3715
   Silas... S 13072
   Theophilus, wid. Sarah.. W 17916
FOX, Aaron, wid. Lydia... W 4437
   Allen, wid. Chloe, BLWt. 1315-100... W 19275
   Amon.. R 3722
   Amos, d. 1794, wid. Jemima or Jamima.. W 11009
   Amos, Conn. in 1818; wid. Mary.. W 25590
   Appleton.. R 3723
   David, Ohio in 1832... S 2217
   David, N. Y. in 1832 as drummer... S 23223
   Ebenezer, Washington, Vt., in 1832, as priv. & teamster, moved to N. Y.................... S 13066
   Ebenezer, Milton, Vt., in 1818.. S 39539
   Elijah, Cont. (Conn.)... S 22774
   Elisha, Penna, in 1832 as priv.. S 22777
   Elisha, Conn. & Cont., N. H. in 1832.. S 10093
   Eunice, former wid. of Marshall Palmer, q. v.
   Ezekiel, wid. Susan... W 25592
   Isaac... S 37937
   Israel.. S 4288
   Jabez... S 13053
   Jacob, Conn, in 1832 as priv.. S 17956
   Jacob, N. Y. in 1818 as Lieut... S 44829
     BLWt. 725-200, Lieut. was issued April 5, 1793, to Reuben Murray, Assignee. No papers.
   Jedediah.. S 44830
   Jesse, New London Co., Conn., in 1832; wid. Ruth.. R 3732

```
FOX, Joel, wid. Mercy................................................................................. W 4673
    John, N. Y. in 1818 as priv., wid. Louisa, BLWt. 7203–160–55........................ W 2091
    John, Conn. in 1832 as priv. & Serg't. Conn. & Cont. service....................... S 15426
    Lemuel, wid. Prudence.............................................................. W 11018
    Peter.............................................................................. S 22245
    Reuben............................................................................. S 32225
    Robert....................................................................... BLWt. 2177–100
    Roswell, former wid. of, Martha Hall............................................... W 17051
    Samuel, Dryden, N. Y., as Corp. in 1818............................................ S 44832
    Samuel, Sherburne, N. Y., in 1818, as priv. "Samuel 2nd".........................  S 44834
    Simeon............................................................................. S 44831
    Stephen, wid. Mary................................................................. W 10031
        Soldier also in Harmar's Indian War, 1790.
    Thomas, b. Glastonbury, Conn., son of David & Sarah, Hartford Co., Conn., in 1846... S 13048
    Thomas, Penna. in 1832 as priv., d. 1834; wid. Cloe................................ W 3673
    Vaniah or Vernia, Conn. & Cont..................................................... S 9335
    William, Conn. & Cont.............................................................. S 9334
FRANCES or FRANCIS.
    David, wid. Anna................................................................... W 21148
    Elijah, wid. Jane................................................................. W 25610
    James, wid. Mary.................................................................. R 3743
    James, wid. Sarah................................................................ R 3747
    James, Killingworth, Conn., in 1832............................................... S 15841
    James, Cont. (Conn.) Litchfield Co., Conn., in 1818 as Corp....................... S 37942
FRANCES, FRANCIS or FRANSSESS.
    Job, BLWt. 26395–160–55........................................................... S 13084
    Justus, former wid. of, Abi North................................................ W 10822
    Robert, wid. Lydia Deming......................................................... W 25606
        BLWt. 2496–160–55.
    Titus............................................................................. S 16813
    William........................................................................... S 37944
FRANCOIS, Anthony.  (See O'CAIN, Anthony Francis.)
FRANK, Joshua........................................................................ S 37945
FRANKLIN, Abel....................................................................... S 37948
    Ezra.............................................................................. S 16812
    Jehiel or Jeile................................................................... S 44863
    Samuel............................................................................ S 37940
FRANKS, John, Conn. & Mass........................................................... S 34884
FRANSEWAY.  (See O'CAIN, Anthony F.)
FRANSSES.  (See FRANCIS.)∗
FRANSWOI.  (See O'CAIN, Anthony F.)
FRARY or FRERY, Seth................................................................. S 29517
FREEDOM, Cato........................................................................ S 44849
    Dick......................................................................... BLWt. 590–100
    Ned............................................................................... S 37946
FREEMAN, Andrew, wid. Elizabeth...................................................... W 21149
    Call.............................................................................. S 36513
    Caser or Caesar................................................................... S 43567
    Chatham........................................................................... S 36524
    Cuff, Conn. in 1818............................................................... S 36522
    Cuff, d. 1800, Litchfield, Conn.; not pensioned, wid. Amelia...................... W 19298
    Daniel............................................................................ S 45543
    David............................................................................. S 36511
    Devonshire........................................................................ S 36519
    Enoch, wid. Sarah................................................................. W 21157
    Jack.  (See ROWLAND, Jack.)
    James, New London Co. in 1818, as priv............................................ S 36518
    James, Washington Co., R. I., in 1818, as priv................................... S 38708
    Jethro............................................................................ S 36520
    John.............................................................................. S 36517
    Joseph, Conn. & Cont., BLWt. 1540–100............................................. S 39548
    Mary, former wid. of John Bliss, q. v.
    Peleg, Conn. & Privateer.......................................................... R 3782
    Peter, Hartford Co. in 1818....................................................... S 36516
    Peter, New London Co. in 1818, as priv............................................ S 36521
    Philemon.......................................................................... S 36523
    Phoebe, former wid. of London Wallace or Wallis, q. v.
    Plymouth or Plymmouth............................................................. S 44852
    Prince............................................................................ S 39549
    Providence, wid. Azuba, BLWt. 31307–160–55........................................ W 739
    Roger............................................................................. S 43574
    Samuel, wid. Jemima, BLWt. 1413–100............................................... W 17926
    William........................................................................... S 13085
    William.  (See COUCH, William (colored).)
FRENCH, Aaron, former wid. of, Abigail Dexter........................................ W 22037
    Abel, Cont. (Conn.)............................................................... S 13087
    Comewell or Cromwell, wid. Elizabeth.............................................. R 3790
    Ebenezer, Conn., Mass. & N. Y..................................................... S 13090
    Francis, wid. Sylvia.............................................................. W 17928
    James............................................................................. S 1200
    James R........................................................................... S 15844
    Jonathan, Conn. Sea service....................................................... S 28737
    Levi, Cont. (Conn.), BLWt. 5826, issued 1792.
    Nathaniel H....................................................................... S 18827
    Samuel, Trumbull, Conn., in 1832 as Serg't........................................ S 16814
    Samuel, priv. in Fairfield Co. in 1818............................................ S 36515
    Truman............................................................................ S 36512
    William, former wid. of, Lucy Smith............................................... W 3609
        BLWt. 1200–100.
```

FRERY. (See FRARY.)
FRINK, Isaac .... S 10705
    Jabish or Jabesh or Jabez.. S 28736
    Nathan, wid. Clarissa .... W 24251
    Nathaniel Lothrop, former wid. of, Rebecca Gilbert................................. W 25623
    Thomas.. BLWt. 506-100
FRISBE, FRISBEE or FRISBIE.
    Abraham, wid. Olive.. W 3341
    Asahel.. S 10708
    David.. R 3807
FRISBE, FRISBEE or FRISBIE, or FRISBY.
    Ichabod C... S 15842
    Israel, wid. Esther... R 3808
      Heirs allowed claim by special act.
    John, wid. Rachel... W 17921
    Josiah, Conn. & Conn. Sea service... S 17425
    Joseph, wid. Diantha... R 3806
      His commission as Serg't. is on file in the Dep't. He never applied for a pension. The
      wid. was rejected.
    Luther, Cont. (Conn.).. S 4273
      Sally Frisby, wid. of above soldier, was pensioned on account of service of her first hus-
      band, Elizur or Eleazer Talcott, Conn. W 27522.
    Noah.. S 23227
    Philemon, wid. Rhoda... R 3809
    Reuben.. S 36514
FRISSELL or FRIZZLE, John, wid. Martha.. W 19293
    BLWt. 11268-160-55.
FROST, Amos, BLWt. 5790 issued 1796.
    Joseph... S 29164
    Solomon... R 3816
FROTHINGHAM, Ebenezer, Cont. service, but Conn. residence of heirs in 1827 when they ob-
    tained BLWt. 1229-200.
    Samuel.. S 46253
FRY, Peleg, Conn. & R. I., wid. Barbara... W 17924
FULLER, Abijah, Conn. & Cont., wid. Abigail... W 17928
    Abraham.. R 14329
    Asa, wid. Abigail... W 24258
    Benajah, wid Catharine.. W 4675
    Benjamin, Hampton, Conn., in 1832, brother of John, who d. in 1807; soldier d. in 1840; wid.
      Clarissa, BLWt. 26625-160-55.. W 1746
    Benjamin, Rome, N. Y., in 1832; wid. Polly.. W 21163
    Daniel, wid. Sarah... W 19302
    Darius.. S 22782
    David, wid. Eunice... W 17931
    Dayton.. S 29136
    Ebenezer, wid. Juan Fernandis.. W 21162
    Edward.. S 36528
    Eleazer, Litchfield Co., Conn., in 1818, moved to Mass................................ S 32707
    Eleazer, Conn. & Mass. service; d. 1819, Hampden, Mass., was priv. & corp., wid. Rachel... W 14762
    Eli... S 36527
    Ezra... S 36526
    Isaac, wid. Elizabeth, BLWt. 24155-160-55.. W 11029
    James... S 36525
    John, Litchfield Co. in 1832 as serg't... S 13115
    John, Tolland Co. in 1832 as priv... S 31684
    John... R 3834
    John, d. 1813, New London Co., wid. Wealthy... W 17929
    John, Conn. & Cont., N. Y. in 1818... S 43580
    Joseph.. S 17428
    Joshua.. S 43579
    Josiah... S 16815
    Lemuel, wid. Polly, BLWt. 26490-160-55.. W 648
    Luther, Conn. & Mass.. R 3837
    Nathan, Windham Co., Conn., in 1832.. S 17427
    Nathan, N. Y. in 1832, d. 1840; wid. Hannah... W 19301
    Noah, wid. Lucy.. W 23073
    Samuel, d. 1821, priv. under Capt. Millard, Otsego Co., N. Y., in 1820; wid. Lydia........... W 17932
    Samuel, d. 1826, Herkimer Co., N. Y.; priv. under Capt. Holmes; wid. Mary............... W 25603
    Samuel, Cont. (Conn.) & N. H., pensioned in 1818, as res. of Burlington,Vt., moved later to
      N. Y. State.. S 44869
    Shubael... R 3841
    Timothy, former wid. of, Hannah Hayes or Hays...................................... W 17974
      This woman's second husband, Benjamin Hays, also served in the Revolution.
FURBECK, John, Cont. (Conn.)... S 13108
FURGESON. (See FERGUSON.)
FYLER, John, Colebrook, Conn. in 1832; wid. Asenath; BLWt. 26014-160-55............. W 2379
    John, d. 1810, Guilford, Conn., wid. Ruth (given also as TYLER)....................... W 17936
    (See also FILER and FISLER.)

G.

GAGE, Moses.. R 3861
    Thaddeus, Livingston Co., N. Y., 1832; wid. Judith................................... R 3860
GAGER, Samuel R., wid. Lucretia, BLWt. 26045-160-55................................. W 7495
GAINS, Jude, wid. Anner.. W 17004
GALLOP, John... S 10721
GALLUP, Amos... S 13116
    Andrew... S 17430
    Benadam, wid. Mary, BLWt. 24441-160-55.
    Ezra... S 29168
    George, former wid., Freelove Kinne... W 21532

GALLUP, Isaac, Conn. & Cont., former wid., Anna Williams. .... W 26032
 Joseph. .... S 15137
 Levi. .... S 8544
 Nehemiah. .... S 13110
  Mercy, wid. of above soldier, was pensioned as former wid. of Peter Brown (q.v.).
 Robert, BLWt. 28531-160-55. .... S 23651
 William. .... S 15581
GALPIN, Amos, Conn. & Cont. .... S 13129
 Daniel, Cont. (Conn.), BLWt. 253-100. .... S 13113
 Jehiel, former wid., Lucy Morgan. .... W 17161
 Samuel. .... S 15132
GALUSHA, Abiram. .... S 43583
 Jacob, wid. Dinah. .... W 24270
 Thomas. .... S 23648
GANSEY, Seth, BLWt. 897-100. .... S 39565
 (See also GARNSEY and GUERNSEY.)
GANTT, Erasmus. .... S 10727
GARDENER, GARDINER, GARDINIER or GARDNER.
 Abijah. .... S 44154
 David, New London Co., Conn., in 1818. .... S 36532
 David, New Haven Co., Conn., in 1818; wid. Fanny, BLWt. 31909-160-55. .... W 1850
  Elizabeth. former wid. of Ezekiel Tinker (q. v.).
 Isaac, wid. Esther. .... W 7499
  BLWt. 26788-160-55.
 John, Conn. & N. Y. .... R 3903
 Jonathan. .... S 17429
  Phebe, former wid. of Joel Beers (q. v.).
 Sherman. .... S 5176
 Thomas, wid. Esther. .... W 16020
 William, Conn. 1818, d. 1826, N. Y. Co., N. Y.; wid. Hannah. .... W 25618
 William, Elmira. N. Y., in 1818; d. 1823; wid. Margaret. BLWt. 8387-160-55. .... W 1750
GAREY or GEAREY or GARY.
 Eneas. .... S 13128
 Gilbert. wid. Nancy or Anna. .... R 3961
 Josiah. Cont. (Conn.). .... S 37003
GARNSEY, Chauncey. .... S 13120
 David. .... S 22785
 Joel. .... S 15136
 Samuel. .... S 13111
 (See also GANSEY and GUERNSEY.)
GARRET, GARRETT, GARRIT.
 Abigail, former wid. of Gideon Scofield (q. v.).
 Francis. .... S 16124
 John, Oneida Co., N. Y., 1832. .... S 43581
 John. Litchfield Co., Conn., in 1818. .... S 44159
GATES, Asa, Conn. & R. I. .... S 21214
 Cyrus, Conn. & R. I. .... S 22262
 Daniel. .... R 3871
  Desire, former wid. of Charles Cushman (q. v.).
 Ezra, Conn. & N. Y. .... S 10726
 Freeman. .... S 42735
 James, wid. Polly. .... W 23083
 Jehiel. .... S 44875
 Joseph, wid. Mary. .... W 4203
 Luther, wid. Ann. .... W 21168
 Marvin. .... S 15138
 Nathan. .... S 21764
 Nathaniel, Navy (Conn.). .... S 41562
 Nehemiah, wid. Ruth. .... W 25614
 Oliver, Conn. & Sea Service, Bradford, Penna., 1832; wid. Jemima. .... R 3941
 Samuel. .... S 18833
 Thomas, wid. Rachel. .... W 11040
 William. .... S 43584
 Zebulon Waterman, wid. Alice. .... R 3939
GAY, Asahel, wid. Temperance. .... W 17940
 Edward. .... S 13172
 Jason. .... S 44871
 Richard. .... S 16817
GAYLARD or GAYLORD.
 Ambrose, wid. Eleanor, BLWt. 290-100. .... W 4677
 Chauncy. .... S 13112
 Deodate. .... S 17433
 Eleazer, wid. Sylvia. .... W 17941
 Elijah, BLWt. 9465-160-55. .... S 15139
 Jedediah or Jedidiah. .... S 22784
 Joel, Conn. & Mass., BLWt. 374-100. .... S 46357
 John, wid. Charlotte. .... W 17005
 Jonathan. .... S 44876
 Jonathan, Conn. & Navy. .... S 42736
 Joseph. .... S 15848
 Josiah, wid. Mary Ann. .... W 19483
 Justus, wid. Lucretia. .... W 3342
 Lemuel. .... R 3958
 Levi, Conn. & Cont. .... S 4293
GEAR, George. .... S 36534
GEAREY. (See GAREY.)
GEDDINS, John, wid. Achsah. .... W 25624
 (Also given GIDDINGS.)

63

GEER or GEERE.
Allyn, Conn. & Mass... S 17972
Amos... S 23230
Asa.. S 41571
Benajah.. S 43588
David.. R 3965
Ebenezer Steel, wid. Catherine, BLWt. 31910-160-55................................ W 1265
Elihu, wid. Eleanor.. W 21180
George... S 17434
Gurdon, Cont. (Conn.)... S 42738
Jedediah... S 42741
John, wid. Onnah... W 14782
Nathan... S 16126
Nathaniel.. S 15849
Richard.. S 13132
Robert... S 13131
Roger.. S 8552
GENNINGS, Mary, former wid. of Jesse Davis (q. v.).
GEORGE, Amos... S 43593
Prince... S 43594
GEORGIA, Simon.. BLWt. 1289-100
GERALD, GERALDS, GERRALD or JERALDS, Thomas, Cont. (Conn.)..... BLWt. 1034-100
GERMAN or JARMAN, Charles, wid. Betsey.. W 20169
GHADEN or GLADING, Joseph.. S 36548
GIBBS, David... S 13141
Eldad.. S 29176
Gershom, Conn. & Cont... S 15144
Ithamar.. S 44161
Moore, Conn. & Cont., wid. Patience... W 25628
    (Consolidated with S 36546.)
Philo, wid. Lois, BLWt. 19524-160-55.. W 7518
Samuel, private, Berkshire Co., Mass., in 1818; wid. Caty, BLWt. 29731-160-55...... W 689
Samuel, Capt. Conn. in 1818; wid. Julia F... W 7519
    BLWt. 822-200, Lieut. was issued July 27, 1789. No papers.
Simeon, wid. Esther.. W 17008
Solomon.. S 17439
Spencer.. S 36542
Stephen, Hartford Co., in 1818; wid. Ruth... R 3989
Sylvanus, wid. Betsey.. W 24276
William.. S 13145
GIBSON, Roger.. S 29827
GIDDINGS, Benjamin, wid. Apphiah... W 17946
John, wid. Achsah. (Given also GEDDINS (q. v.).)
Joseph, Norwich, Conn., in 1818, d. 1832; wid. Mary............................... W 25625
Joseph, Conn., Cont. & N. Y. service; Litchfield Co., Conn., in 1832, living in 1836........... S 10736
Joshua... S 3396
Niles.. S 10738
Thomas, wid. Anna, BLWt. 29021-160-55... W 1410
GIFFEN, Ezra, Conn. & N.J... S 16136
    (Also given GRIFFIN.)
GIFFIN, Simon, Cont. & Conn.. S 36543
GIFFORD, Absalom... S 13134
Jeremiah, wid. Sally... W 1411
William, Conn. & R. I... S 2236
GILBERT, or GILBUT.
Allen.. S 44162
Asa, Conn. & Cont., wid. Mary... W 17944
Asahel, Cont. (Conn.)... S 32268
Benjamin, Conn. & Cont.. S 13139
Burr, former wid., Clarissa Turney.. W 18165
Butler... S 43607
David, wid. Molly.. W 25621
Ebenezer, Brooklyn, Conn., 1818... S 36539
Ebenezer, d. 1798, wid. in Fairfield Co., wid. Ruth............................... W 17945
Ebenezer, Navy (Conn.) service; surgeon, Revenue Cutter; son Joseph M............ S 27
Gardner, Conn. & Cont., wid. Mary, BLWt. 91126-160-55............................. W 13265
Gershom.. S 10743
Hooker... W 4966
Heber, wid. Lucina.. S 13136
Isaac.. S 13137
Jesse.. S 36544
John, Grafton Co., N. H., in 1832... S 15585
John, d. 1816, Westchester Co. N. Y.; wid. Elizabeth.............................. W 16268
Joseph, Bloomfield, N. Y. in 1818... S 43605
Joseph, Corp. & Serg't. Conn. & Cont. service; d. 1812, Livingston Co., N. Y.; wid. Miriam.... W 23112
Lemuel, wid. Amorillis... W 21185
Lewis.. S 22265
Moses.. S 15145
Nathan... S 17440
Obadiah.. S 39579
Rebecca, former wid. of Nathaniel Lothrop Frink (q. v.).
Samuel... S 16127
Solomon, wid. Thankful.. W 17009
Thaddeus... S 43596
Theodore, Conn. & Mass. service; Madison Co., N. Y., in 1818...................... S 10739
Theodore, Volney, N. Y., in 1818.. S 43601
Thomas... S 31689
Truman... S 18417
William, wid. Hope.. W 24275

64

GILES, Thomas.. S 15141
GILL, John... S 39576
  Samuel.. R 4025
GILLBERT. (See GILBERT.)
GILLESPIE, William, Cont. (Conn.); former wid., Mary Ellsworth................. W 16249
GILLET, GILLETT, GILLETTE or GILLIT.
  Adna... R 4033
  Alpheus or Alphius, Cont. (Conn.)..................................... S 41577
  Asa, former wid., Abigail Denison..................................... R 4032
  Asa, Cont. (Conn.), Mich. res. & Agency............................... S 34898
  Benjamin, Conn. & Privateer... S 15143
  Benjamin, Cont. service, Conn. res. & Agency; ch. David W., Polly Gillett, & Sally Derrick
    (Mrs. John) obtained.. BLWt. 437-100
  Benoni, 62 yrs. New Haven, Conn., in 1819, d. June, 1844, wid. Phebe...... W 25630
  Benoni, Granby, Conn. in 1832, d. April, 1844; wid. Polly, BLWt. 29022-160-55........... W 2607
  Elijah.. S 17436
  Ephraim... S 36538
  Isaac... S 17978
  Jabez, Conn. & N. Y., wid. Hannah..................................... W 19501
  Jeremiah, Burlington, Conn. in 1818................................... S 36535
  Jeremiah, N. H. in 1818... S 45554
  Joel.. S 36540
  John, wid. Mary... S 36537
  John, d. 1810, Cortland, N. Y.; former wid., Mercy Hoar............... W 18035
  Jonathan, Mus. & Corp. 1832... S 15851
  Joseph, Lyme, Conn. in 1832... S 15850
  Joseph, Del. Co. Ohio in 1832; wid. Parcey, BLWt. 9546-160-55......... W 7524
  Luther.. S 6890
  Nathan or Nathaniel... S 42744
  Othniel... S 36536
  Reuben.. S 21228
  Reuben, Conn. & Cont.. R 20374
  Rufus, wid. Ellen... W 17948
  Samuel.. S 22789
  Stephen, Conn. & Cont... S 13143
  William, Conn. & Mass. service, wid. Abigail.......................... W 2930
GILMAN, Calvin, wid. Hannah... W 19506
GILSON, Eleazer... S 17973
  Jacob... S 39584
GLADDEN, Azariah, Conn. & Navy service.. S 29828
GLADDING, Jedediah, wid. Elizabeth.. W 25634
GLADING, Joseph. (See GHADEN.)
GLASS, Alexander, wid. Jemima... W 15770
GLAZIER, Eliphalet, wid. Rachel... R 4060
  John, wid. Hannah... W 4208
GLEASON or GLESON, Benjamin, Conn. & Cont. service, BLWt. 642-100............... S 39589
  James, wid. Lovina.. W 24280
  John.. S 31694
  Joseph, Conn. & N. Y., wid. Elizabeth................................. W 17949
GLENNEY, GLENNY or GLINNEY.
  Isaac, Cont. (Conn.) & Mass., wid. Sarah.............................. W 17015
  William, wid. Polly or Mary... W 17950
    BLWt. 815-200, Lieut. was issued Aug. 5, 1789. No papers.
GLESEN. (See GLEASON.)
GLINNEY. (See GLENNEY.)
GODARD or GODDARD.
  Ebenezer, priv. & Serg't. Hartford, Conn., in 1832................... S 15153
  Ebenezer, Conn. & Navy service; Hartford, Conn., Serg't. Marines, in 1832................. S 15857
  Edward.. S 44166
  Isaac, Granby, Conn. in 1832; wid. Rosanna............................ R 4079
  John.. S 15148
  Levi, wid. Mary... W 19521
  Rufus, wid. Mindwell.. W 17958
    (Given also as GOSSARD.)
  Tilley.. R 4080
GODFREY, Isaac.. S 17444
  Jonathan.. S 16834
  Reuben, Conn. Sea service & Navy...................................... S 15152
  Stephen... S 13071
GOFF, Charles, Conn. & Cont... S 13178
  Comfort... S 28744
  David, wid. Elizabeth... W 690
  Ezekiel, Conn. & Cont... S 15149
  Gideon.. S 36558
  Hezekiah, Conn., Conn. Sea service, Mass. & 1812; Vt. in 1818; wid. Rebecca............... R 4087
  James, wid. Mary.. W 7539
  Richard, Conn., Navy & Privateer; wid. Polly.......................... W 24287
  Samuel.. S 36551
  Samuel D.. S 39598
  Solomon... S 42749
GOLD. (See GOULD.)
GOLDSMITH, James... S 22794
GOODALE, Chester, wid. Asenath.. W 19522
    BLWt. 26983-160-55.
  Ebenezer, wid. Jerusha.. W 4967
    (Also given GOODALL.)

GOODALL, GOODELL or GOODDELL.
Alvan or Alvin, Conn. & Cont., former wid. Alice Potter........................ W 18769
Asa... S 15865
Ezra.. S 43608
Jabez, wid. Peninah... W 14800
Jacob... S 45562
Silas, Conn. & Cont... S 36559
   BLWt. 813–200, Lieut.
   (See also GOODALE.)
GOODFAITH, David.. S 36553
GOODHARD, David... R 4106
   (Also given GOODFAITH.)
GOODMAN, Moses, Cont. (Conn.)... S 36550
Richard... S 13165
GOODRICH, Abel.. S 13181
Abner, Conn. & Cont... S 42754
Allen... S 18418
Bethuel.. S 38740
   BLWt. 5833–100 was issued April 19, 1790. No papers.
Crafts.. R 4115
David, former wid. Penelope Hillyer... R 5026
   NOTE.—Widow's second husband, Elijah Hubbard, and her third husband, James Hillyer,
   also served in the Revolutionary War. David died in service at Fort Lee, N. J., in
   1776, and her pension was rejected because she was unable to prove that he had served
   six months before he was killed.
David, Conn. & Cont... S 10760
Elisha.. S 43612
George.. S 32755
Gideon.. S 10753
Ichabod... S 36556
Isaac, d. 1847, not pensioned; wid. Electa; BLWt. 21835–160–55..................... R 4116
Isaac, d. Del. Co., N. Y., in 1834; wid. Sarah.................................... W 17016
James, Conn., Conn. Sea service & Privateer....................................... S 15864
Jared, Conn., & Cont., wid. Deborah... W 17954
John, Conn. & Cont.. BLWt. 1607–100
   (Also given GOODRICK.)
John, Conn. & Cont., wid. Mabel.. W 24292
John H., wid. Mary... W 4682
Levi, Conn. & Cont., wid. Julia Ann... R 4118
Micah... S 15858
Michael.. S 43628
Nathan... S 32276
   (Given also GUTRICH.)
Ozias, BLWt. as Ensign, 821–150.
   (Given also GOODRIDGE.)
Roswel or Roswell, Glastonbury, Conn., 1832, as musician.......................... S 31696
Roswell, Conn. & Cont., N. Y. in 1818, as artificer............................... S 13182
Simeon, Vt. 1832, Serg't. Artificers.. S 21772
Simeon.. R 4119
Solomon P., wid. Anna.. W 2095
Stephen, Conn. & Cont... S 38735
William, wid. Phebe.. W 17019
Zenas, former wid. Lois Cash.. R 1780
GOODRICK. (See GOODRICH.)
GOODRIDGE. (See GOODRICH.)
GOODSEL, Ephraim, Conn. & Navy.. S 29182
Isaac, former wid. Elizabeth Webster BLWt. 40502–160–55.
John, wid. Abigail... W 17952
Rachel, former wid. of William Bailey (q. v.).
Samuel, wid. Abigail.. W 21192
Thomas... S 10756
GOODSPEED, Nathaniel, Conn., Mass. & N. H., wid. Abigail........................... W 23117
GOODWIN, Hezekiah, wid. Polly... W 27873
Joseph... S 29180
Levi... S 17442
Moses.. S 13157
Nathaniel.. R 4130
Seth, wid. Mahitable, BLWt. 28557–160–55.. W 1412
Solomon, wid. Anna.. W 24283
Zebedee, Cont. (Conn.), wid. Caroline... W 21198
GOODYEAR, Edward.. S 43623
Stephen.. S 16832
GOOKINS, Samuel, wid. Polly... W 10064
GOOLD. (See GOULD.)
GORDON, Alexander, Conn. & Privateer.. R 4137
George, Conn. & Cont.. S 39599
Samuel... S 43614
GORE, Obadiah.. S 39601
   BLWt. 817–200, Lieut. was issued Feb. 22, 1791. No papers.
GORHAM, Daniel, Conn. & Cont.. S 13159
George, Cont. (Conn.)... S 13161
Joseph, Cont. (Conn.), wid. Elizabeth Baldwin..................................... W 15150
Nathan, Conn. & Conn. Sea service... S 15150
Nehemiah... S 36552
   BLWt. 814–200, Lieut., issued Feb. 25, 1800 to Jones Stansbury, Assignee. No papers.
Seth, Castleton, Vt. in 1832; private under Capt. Hubbell, Col. Silliman........... S 15587
Seth, Rutland, Vt. in 1832; private under Capt. Godding, Col. Beardsley; wid. Lovisa, BLWt.
   26199–160–55... W 9467
GORTON, Benjamin, Cont. (Conn.)... S 13154
Joseph... S 31698

GOSLEE, or GOSLEY, Solomon .... S 31697
  Consolidated with S 36554.
GOSS, Andrew .... S 32747
GOSSARD, Rufus. (See GOSARD.)
GOUGE, Phebe, former wid. of Eli Smith (q. v.).
GOULD, GOLD and GOOLD.
  James, wid. Mary .... W 17022
  John, Conn, & R. I .... S 16128
  John, Windsor Co. Vt. in 1818; private Capt. Durkee .... S 39605
  Nathan, Conn. & Navy, wid. Patience .... W 17957
  Noah M .... S 37013
  Samuel, wid. Sarah .... W 21201
  Silas .... S 37023
  Thomas, Cont. (Conn.) .... S 22271
  Willard, Conn., Cont. & Mass .... S 13180
  William, Conn., Cont. & Mass .... S 42752
GOWDY, Alexander .... S 10750
  Hill, wid. Roxana .... W 17951
  John .... S 31066
  Samuel .... S 15151
GRAHAM, Jesse, wid. Elizabeth .... W 25663
  John .... S 42755
  Oliver .... S 22797
  William .... S 13222
GRANGER, Bildad .... S 36561
  Ebenezer, wid. Patience .... W 1169
  Ithamar, wid. Jemima .... W 14812
  Jacob, Cont. (Conn.), wid Esther .... R 4189
    Soldier was a pensioner in Galen, N. Y., in 1818.
  Moses, wid. Lucy .... W 15907
  Moses, Conn. & Vt .... R 4190
GRANNES or GRANNIS or GRANNISS.
  David, wid. Clarissa .... W 24302
  Elle .... S 17449
  Enos, Conn. & Cont .... S 39613
    BLWt. 818-200, Lieut. of Art. Artificers was issued Mar. 10, 1796, under name of Eneas
    Grannis, and also recorded as above BLWt. 2663. No papers.
  Jared, Conn. & Privateer .... S 31704
  Robert .... R 4192
  Samuel, Cont. service, former wid. Charity Irion or Trion or Tryon, res. Conn ...... W 26154
GRANT, Aaron, wid. Lucy .... W 17967
  Andrew .... S 18847
  Azariah .... S 38775,
  David .... S 15870
  Elihu .... R 4194
  Elnathan .... S 13193
  Gideon .... S 36565
  Gustavus, wid. Phebe, BLWt. 9204-160-55 .... W 2101
  Hamilton, wid. Lucy, BLWt. 2521-160-55 .... W 1417
  Hezekiah .... S 30446
  Isaac .... R 4195
  James .... S 38759
  Jehu .... R 4197
  Jesse, BLWt. 823-300, Capt. was issued Feb. 18, 1793. No papers.
  Oliver, wid. Hannah .... W 25126
  Reuben, wid. Anna .... W 21228
  Roswell, b. Aug. 18, 1762, priv .... S 15161
  Roswell, b. Mch. 20, 1746, Capt. & Paymaster .... S 31710
  Thomas .... S 8605
  William, Conn. & Mass. Sea service, wid. Polly .... W 19531
GRAVE or GRAVES.
  Amos, Conn. & Mass., wid. Hannah .... W 7579
  Asahel .... R 4205
  Bela .... S 9344
  Benjamin, Conn. & Cont., wid. Sarah, BLWt. 157-60-55 .... W 4972
  Elijah, Herkimer Co., N. Y., in 1832 as Serg't .... S 8596
  Elijah, N. Y. in 1818, as private .... S 44173
  Gilbert, wid. Elizabeth .... W 25649
  Hobart .... S 28746
  John, wid. Hannah .... W 25661
  Josiah .... S 29842
  Peter .... S 43640
  Seth, wid. Elizabeth .... W 21222
  Simeon .... S 43641
  Thaddeus, Conn. & Mass .... S 16134
  Timothy, private, Madison, Conn. in 1832 .... S 31705
  Timothy, priv. & Serg't, Hoosick, N. Y., in 1832 .... S 15162
  Whitney .... S 15159
GRAW. (See GROW.)
GRAY, Daniel .... R 4219
  Ebenezer, BLWt. 812-450 Lt. Col. No papers. No date of issue.
  Eliphalet, wid. Lydia .... R 4223
  Jabesh .... S 43643
  James, Conn., Cont. & N. Y .... S 2245
  Joseph, Weston, Conn., priv. Militia, d. 1840, Fairfield Co., wid. Eunice .... W 21226
  Joseph, Conn. & Mass. service; priv. & Corp., d. 1833, Ridgefield, Conn., wid. Lydia ...... W 21225
  Samuel, former wid. Abigail Hadley (soldier never pensioned) .... R 4415
    Abigail Hadley's second husband, Joseph Hadley, also served in the Revolution, and
    Abigail was pensioned for his service, so was rejected for her first husband's service.
  Samuel, Conn., Cont. & N. Y. private, 1818 .... S 43638
  Samuel, Cont. (Conn.), Deputy Commissary General .... S 13188

67

GREEN or GREENE.

Abel	S	43642
Abner	S	17448
Amasa, Cont. (Conn.), wid. Lurena	W	4684
Amos, wid. Lavina	W	25646
Asahel, wid. Grace	W	17962
Benjamin, Conn. & R. I.	S	21783
Caleb, wid. Rebecca	W	21206
Dorastus	S	36564
Ebenezer	S	13217
Eleazer or Elezer	S	44885
Ezra, wid. Amy	W	17965
Gideon	R	4255
Henry, Conn. & Cont	S	13187
Jabez, Conn. & R. I.	S	13189
Jack	S	43631
Jacob	S	44176
James, Conn., in 1832	S	10770
James, Orange Co., N. Y., in 1832; wid. Sarah, BLWt. 36502-160-55	W	25644
Joel	R	4257
John, N. Y., in 1832, as private	S	23659
John, wid. Esther	R	4251
(Soldier not pensioned.)		
Joseph, Conn., Cont. & Mass. & Vt., former wid. Jerusha Morey	W	17148
Josiah, former wid. Susanna Holbrook	W	21395
Noah	S	29840
Obadiah	S	18422
Roswell, BLWt. 9403-160-55	S	28749
Samuel, Madison Co., N. Y., in 1832; priv	S	13196
Samuel, Milford, Conn., d. 1843, wid. Polly, BLWt. 8179-160-55	W	25662
Samuel, Elmira, N. Y., in 1818, private, Col. Chandler, wid. Tamazen	W	21223
Sebra, former wid. of Stephen Harrington (q. v.).		
Timothy, wid. Jane	W	21207
Willard	S	13198
Zachariah, Conn. & Cont., BLWt. 13732-160-55	S	28747
GREENFIELD, Enos	S	44177
James	S	13192
William, Conn., Cont. & Green Mt. Boys (soldier not pensioner), wid. Prudence	R	4283
GREENOLD. (See GRINNELL.)		
GREENSLET or GREENSLIT.		
Benjamin, wid. Martha	W	25659
Joel, Conn. & Cont	S	10765
John, Cont. service, Conn. residence in 1820	S	36563
John, private under Durkee; Washington, Vt., in 1832; wid. Saloma, BLWt. 34327-160-55	W	9465
GREGG, David, Conn. & Mass. & N. H	S	15590
GREGGS or GRIGGS, Ephraim, wid. Hannah	W	16024
GREGORY, Daniel	S	17453
Elias, wid. Elizabeth	W	17960
Elnathan	S	29841
Ezra, wid. Huldah, BLWt. 15197-160-55	W	4971
Jabez, wid. Mercy	W	21213
James	S	17445
John, wid. Jerusha	W	1419
Joseph, wid. Deborah	W	1596
Josiah, wid. Ellen	W	24308
Matthew	S	46360
BLWT. 819-200, Lieut, was issued Dec. 5, 1799. No papers.		
Moses, wid. Abigail	W	25655
Nathan	S	13214
Nathaniel	R	4296
Nehemiah	S	22803
Samuel, wid. Charity	W	17970
Silas, wid. Sarah	W	25653
Stephen, Bradford Co., Penna., in 1832, private	S	22274
Stephen, Conn. & Cont., N. Y. in 1832	S	13191
Uriah, Conn. & N. Y	S	15157
William	S	29191
GRENELL or GRENNELL. (See GRINNELL.)		
GRIDLEY, Asahel, wid. Chloe	W	15771
Ashbel, wid. Jemima	W	17961
Elijah, wid. Abigail Eliza	W	4968
BLWt. 29725-160-55.		
Elisha, wid. Lois	W	19545
Hosea, former wid. Sabra Burchard	W	15992
Obediah, wid. Elizabeth	W	16274
Seth	S	15588
Silas	S	4304
Theodore, wid. Amy	W	5287
BLWt. 11281-160-55.		
Thomas	S	29186
GRIFFEN, GRIFFIN or GRIFFING.		
Ann, former wid. of Benjamin Farnam (q. v.).		
Ezra, Conn. & N. J	S	16136
Joel	R	4319
John	S	37037
Joseph, Conn. & Cont	S	8615
Martin, wid. Anna	W	21210
Samuel	S	23666
Stephen, Conn. & N. Y., wid. Elizabeth	W	19549
Thomas, wid. Polly, BLWt. 26598-160-55	W	19537

GRIFFETH or GRIFFITH.
Eli, Conn. & N. Y. .... R 4324
George .... S 43648
Jeremiah, Conn. & N. Y., wid. Mary .... W 19532
Lucy, former wid. of Ebenezer Hitchcock (q. v.).
GRIGG, Henry, wid. Elizabeth .... W 11087
(See also GREGG.)
GRIGGS, Joseph .... S 30445
(See also GREGGS.)
GRIMES, Abraham, Conn. & Mass .... S 13200
Joseph, wid. Jemima .... W 21234
GRINNEL, GRINNELL, GRINNIEL, GRENELL or GRENNELL.
Amasa .... S 43650
Michael, BLWt. 26451–160–55 .... S 2251
William .... S 29843
(Also given GREENOLD.)
William B., wid. Sarah .... W 17968
Wise .... S 45573
GRISWOLD, Aaron, wid. Polly .... W 747
Abel .... S 17447
Alexander .... R 4342
Andrew, Conn. in 1818, d. 1825; wid. Anna, BLWt. 1068–200 .... W 17963
Andrew, d. New London Co., Conn., never pensioned, 1813, wid. Eunice .... W 21205
Asa .... S 37028
Constant .... S 16133
Daniel, Conn. & Mass., wid. Nancy, BLWt. 40938–160–55 .... W 11086
Edmund, wid. Jane, BLWt. 508–160–55 .... W 7608
Edward, wid. Asenath .... W 19553
Elihu, Conn. & Sea Service .... R 1204
Elijah, Windsor, Conn., in 1818 .... S 37032
Elijah, Hartford Co., Conn., in 1832, d. 1846; Ensign, wid. Lydia .... W 25650
Francis .... S 23245
George, priv .... S 17456
George, Serg't. Conn. Line, 1818 .... S 31703
Janna, wid. Lucy .... W 21220
Joel .... S 31708
John .... R 4345
John, Rome, N. Y. in 1818; wid. Vashta, BLWt. 2346–160–55 .... W 9466
John, Fairfield, N. Y. in 1818; wid. Lydia, BLWt. 10237–160–55 .... W 25654
Joseph, Ontario Co., N. Y., in 1818 .... S 43652
Joseph, d. 1829, Hampden Co., Mass.; wid. Mehitable .... W 14811
Midian, Cont. (Conn.), wid. Annis .... R 4343
Nathaniel .... S 31706
Samuel .... R 4348
Samuel, wid Hannah .... W 21230
BLWt. 336–100 and BLWt. 235–60–55.
Selah, Conn. & Cont .... S 17454
Simeon, Conn. & Cont .... S 13092
Sylvanus, wid. Mary Maria .... W 25648
Zenas .... S 15158
GROSE. (See GROSS.)
GROSS, John, wid. Susannah .... W 21212
Josiah .... S 32774
Samuel .... S 49283
Thomas .... R 4356
GROSVENOR, Asa .... S 10762
Joshua .... S 15156
Lemuel .... S 15154
Polly, former wid. of Elihu Mather (q. v.).
Thomas .... R 4361
Thomas, Conn. & Cont .... S 37033
BLWt. 811–500, Lieut. Col. Commandant was issued Jan. 28, 1790. No papers.
GROVENOR. (See GROSVENOR.)
GROVER, Amasa .... S 38751
Amaziah, Conn. & N. H., wid. Joanna, BLWt. 9520–160–55 .... W 746
Daniel .... R 4369
Ebenezer, Conn. & N. Y., wid. Mary .... W 17964
Jabez, wid. Jerusha, BLWt. 27644–160–55 .... W 7604
Jacob, BLWt. 748–100.
Joseph, Conn. & Cont .... S 39631
Luther .... S 21777
Peter, resided in Conn. in 1789; wid. Diadama .... R 14578
Phineas, BLWt. 816–200, Lieut. was issued April 18, 1796 to Thomas Lloyd, assignee to Jabin
Strong & Ruth Strong, Administrators. No papers.
Stephen, wid. Mary .... W 268
GROW, Ambrose, Conn. & Vt., wid. Amy, BLWt. 26560–160–55 .... W 1416
David, wid. Martha, BLWt. 6285–160–55 .... W 2609
Ebenezer, BLWt. 1426–100 .... S 36560
John .... S 13211
GRUMON, Moses .... R 4373
GRUNDEY or GRUNDY, Edmund .... S 38772
GUERNSEY, Southmayd .... R 3921
(See also GANSEY and GARNSEY.)
GUILD, Richard, wid. Eleanor Rice, BLWt. 15444–160–55 .... W 1420
GUILE or GUYLE, Abraham, wid. Deborah .... W 1421
GUNN, Abel .... S 44887
GURNEY, Asa, wid. Sarah, BLWt. 9416–160–55 .... W 7616
Bazaliel .... S 44993

69

GUSTENE, GUSTINE or AUGUSTINE.
Edward... S 13234
Joel. (See AUGUSTINE.)
GUTHRIE, James, wid. Mehitable.. S 20777
Consolidated with... W 25667
GUTRICH. (See GOODRICH.)
GUYANT, Luke, Conn. & Cont... S 17990
GUYLE. (See GUILE.)

H.

HADLOCK, Samuel, Conn., Cont. & Navy, wid. Sarah, BLWt. 860–100.................... W 25757
Thomas, wid. Lovina, BLWt. 28589–160–55... W 487
HADSALL or HADSELL, Elijah, wid. Anna, BLWt. 5070–160–55............................. W 1859
HAIL. (See HALE.)
HAINES. (See HAYNES.)
HAIT. (See HOYT.)
HAKES, Caleb, Conn. & R. I.. S 23247
George, Conn., Cont. & R. I.. S 44911
Jonathan, Conn. & R. I... S 23255
HAIL or HALE, Aaron, Conn., Cont. & N. Y., wid. Hannah, BLWt. 1203–200............... W 17041
Ebenezer, wid. Theda.. W 17896
Gershom... S 22283
(Also given Garshom HAIL.)
Jonathan.. S 21257
Jonathan, former wid. Mary Button... W 17387
Matthew, wid. Ruth... W 25749
Reuben.. S 44898
Thomas.. S 44899
HALL, Aaron, priv. Capt. Hall; in 1818 & 1832 Wallingford, Conn...................... S 13330
Aaron, priv. Capt. Leavenworth; in 1832, in N. Y., wid. Em............................ W 16286
Abner.. S 13273
Alpheus, wid. Marcy.. W 19717
Amos, Serg't. Col. Swift; Vt. in 1832... S 18015
Amos, d. 1827; Serg't. Capt. Hall; wid. Phebe... W 16289
Anan, wid. Comfort... W 21250
Andrew, priv. Conn. State troops; Norwich, Conn., in 1832............................. S 13258
Andrew, priv. Militia; New Haven, Conn., in 1832.. S 13335
Asa, wid. Elizabeth... R 4460
(Soldier never pensioned; wid. applied from Ohio.)
Asa, Cont. (Conn.), N. Y., in 1818.. S 44892
Asahel... R 4455
Benajah, wid. Ruth... W 17980
Caleb.. S 13292
Christopher, Conn. & N. Y... W 27521
Former wid. Sarah Benedict. BLWt. 8155–160–55.
Sarah's other husband, James Benedict, was a Rev. pensioner from Mass. but her applica-
tion was refused. (See BENEDICT, James, Mass., R 742.)
Clarissa, former wid. of Solomon PINTO.
Daniel, priv. Mass., in 1832.. S 30472
Daniel, Conn. & Cont., Serg't., N. Y., in 1832... S 10789
David, priv. Capt. Leavenworth; Conn. in 1818, wid...................................... S 37084
David, d. 1824, Sapper & priv., wid. Ann, was pensioned in 1840 & moved to N. Y...... W 17053
Ebenezer.. S 31721
Elihu or Ellehu.. S 29210
Elisha.. S 13249
Enoch, wid. Esther... W 25762
Enos... S 10806
Ephraim, Conn. & Mass.. S 13238
Gad.. S 23679
Hezekiah, Cont. (Conn.)... S 16138
Hiland, Conn. & Cont... W 23371
Former wid. Hannah Hulbard or Hulburd.
Hiram.. BLWt. 2352–100
James... S 10784
Jesse, Conn. & Mass.. S 5432
John, priv. Litchfield, Conn., in 1832; wid. Damaris...................................... W 24400
John, priv. Col. Burrill, Rome, N. Y., in 1818, d. 1832; wid. Sarah..................... W 16282
John, Conn. & R. I. service; priv. & serg't. Ohio in 1832................................ S 2588
John B.. S 10814
Jonathan.. S 29866
Joshua, wid. Rhoda.. W 17050
Jotham.. S 44964
Levi, Middletown, Conn., in 1832... S 10818
Levi, Conn., Cont. & Mass. & R. I. service; N. H. in 1832................................ S 16850
Lyman or Lymon, wid. Charity... W 17983
Martha, former wid. of Roswell FOX.
Martha, former wid. of Gamaliel PARKER.
Moses, never pensioned, d. 1827, priv. Col. Meigs; wid. Lucy, in N. Y. in 1838....... W 23193
Moses, priv. Col. Baldwin; Meriden, Conn., in 1832; wid. Rebecca...................... R 4484
Moses, R.. R 4480
Nathaniel, Lieut. Capt. Brewster; N. Y. in 1818... S 44891
Nathaniel, pensioned as Nathaniel, Jr., drummer, Capt. Eldridge; wid. Elizabeth; BLWt.
28606–160–55.. W 7637
Peter, Conn., Cont. & Vt.. S 13268
Richard... S 45580
Robert... S 37079
Samuel, N. Y. in 1832; d. 1836, Wayne Co., N. Y., wid. Esther......................... W 21260
Samuel, priv. Capt. Burwell; Vt. in 1832; d. 1849; wid. Lucy........................... W 19673
Seth.. S 10812

HALL, Stephen, Serg't. Conn. in 1818.. S 37058
   Stephen, Capt. 7th reg't., dau. Rachel obtained BLWt. 1193–300.
   Talmage.. BLWt. 1232–300
   Titus, Conn. & Cont., wid. Olive... W 21283
   Wildman.. S 13344
HALLADY or HALLIDAY.
   Eli.. S 2605
   Roger... S 31723
   (See also HOLLADAY.)
HALLAM, John... S 13283
   Robert, wid. Lydia.. W 19731
HALLET, Thomas, Conn. & Cont.. S 37064
HALLOCK, William, wid. Ruth.. W 25754
HALLOW, Richard. (See PENHALLOW.)
HALLSTED, HALSTEAD, HALSTED or HOLSTED.
   John.. S 44908
   Joseph.. S 10811
   Richard, BLWt. 205–100... S 44909
   Timothy.. S 2625
HALSEY, Philip, Conn. & N. Y.. S 16845
   Stephen, Conn. & N. Y., wid. Hamutal.. W 24413
HAMBLIN. (See HAMLIN.)
HAMES, Samuel, wid. Jemina.. W 24411
   (Also given HAWES.)
HAMILTON, David, Conn. & Cont.. S 23678
   James, wid. Jemina... W 2111
   BLWt. 28597–160–55.
   Joshua, wid. Mary.. W 21263
   Samuel, wid. Wealthy.. W 2794
HAMLEN. (See HAMLIN.)
HAMLIN, HAMLEN or HAMBLIN.
   Benjamin... S 10815
   Cornelius... S 37050
   Elisha.. S 10816
   James... S 29196
   John, Cont. (Conn.), priv. Rutland Co., Vt., in 1832...................................... S 18428
   John, Conn. & Privateer; Middletown, Conn., in 1832; d. 1834; wid. Caroline............. W 17985
   John, Cont. (Conn.), priv. pensioned in 1818, d. 1825; wid. Lucy in Ill. in 1839......... W 23219
   Joseph, wid. Rhoda, BLWt. 26684–160–55... W 9057
   Levi, priv. Col. Wyllys; Ohio in 1818.. S 41617
   Levi, Cont. (Conn.), priv. & corp., wid. Mary; BLWt. 13440–160–55....................... W 23168
   Mark.. S 23680
   William... S 37068
HAMMOND, David, wid. Phebe, BLWt. 67686–160–55.. W 11243
   Isaac, Conn. & Cont., Seneca, N. Y., in 1818; wid. Dorcas................................. R 4532
   Jason, wid. Mary... W 16287
   Robert, priv. Col. Starr, Essex Co., N. Y., in 1832; wid. Ruanah.......................... R 4539
   Thomas... S 18865
   Titus, wid. Charity, BLWt. 26058–160–55... W 7653
HANCHET, HANCHETT or HANCKETT.
   Ezra.. S 13291
   Jonah... S 9568
HANCOCK or HANCOX.
   Edward... S 16843
   Elihu... BLWt. 1760–100
   Nathan, wid. Phebe... W 19706
HAND, Edmund, wid. Huldah... W 27775
   Ichabod.. S 31722
HANDFORD. (See HANFORD.)
HANDY. Nathaniel, wid. Martha... R 4560
   William, Cont. (Conn.), wid. Martha... W 23241
HANFORD or HANDFORD.
   Ebenezer... S 31720
   Levi.. S 23676
   Matthew, wid. Elizabeth... W 21288
   Ozias, former wid. Elizabeth Crane... W 25449
HANKS, Elijah, wid. Mary.. W 4688
HANNAH, James, Conn. & Cont.. S 43653
HANSON or HENSON, Christopher.. S 37059
   William, BLWt. 1446–100.. S 43669
HARDIN or HARDING.
   Ephraim, wid. Susan.. W 17054
   George, wid. Martha.. R 4602
   Israel, wid. Lydia... W 2791
   James... S 44194
   Jeremiah.. S 13286
HARDY or HARDEY, Nathaniel.. S 41598
HARDYEAR or HARGER, Elijah.. R 4605
HARMAN or HARMON, Jacques or Jaques. BLWt. 969 for 150 acres issued for Ensign, May 26,
   1790. No papers.
   Jehiel, wid. Betsey E.. W 25759
   BLWt. 26615–160–55.
   Joseph.. R 4622
HARPER, Godfrey.. S 29202
HARRINGTON, HERINGTON, HERINTON, HERRINGTON.
   Anna, former wid. of Elijah PORTER.
   Andrew... S 37051
   Benjamin... S 32813
   Benjamin... R 4638

HARRINGTON, HERINGTON, HERINTON, HERRINGTON—Continued.
Eber, Conn. & R. I., wid. Susannah.. W 23229
John, Oxford, N. Y., in 1832.. S 28759
Parley.. S 44183
Samuel, BLWt. 953-100.. S 44195
Stephen, Sebra Green, former wid. of, BLWt. 128-60-55.. W 19541
Timothy, Lydia Edson, former wid. of.. W 17742
William, wid. Elizabeth, BLWt. 33741-160-55... W 19726
HARRIS, Andrew, wid. Elizabeth... W 27423
Asa, Conn., Navy & N. H., wid. Rachel.. W 19667
Daniel.. S 10797
David... S 37062
Ebenezer.. R 4651
Fanny P., former wid. of Levi ARNOLD, BLWt. 67536-160-55................................... W 9050
Jason, Elizabeth Annis, former wid. of... W 23443
Jedediah or Jedidiah.. S 16844
John, b. Preston, Conn., 1766, son of Job & brother of Joshua; priv. & cook, Capt. Latham;
     Vermont in 1832... S 10787
John, priv. Capt. Warner: Conn. in 1818... S 37049
John, Conn. & Cont., BLWt. 1608-200. Served under Lieut. Col. Webb & killed 1777 in N.
     J., wid. Irene, of New London Co.; granson Zebulon Lee obtained BLWt. in 1830.
Joseph, wid. Anna... R 4647
Lebbeus, Sarah Douglass, former wid. of.. R 3049
Paul.. S 31719
Pearly, wid. Aby.. W 21287
Philip, Conn. & Cont., wid. Anna, BLWt. 26553-160-55.. W 25755
Robert, wid. Lucretia.. W 10076
Thomas, Conn. & Cont., wid. Elizabeth.. W 21270
Water, Cont. (Conn.), wid. Jane A., BLWt. 30787-160-55.. W 2106
William... S 38811
HARRISON, Daniel.. S 15165
Hannah, former wid. of Joseph BEACH.
Jairus.. S 37081
Justus, Conn. & Conn. Sea Service, wid. Sarah.. W 19742
Lemuel, BLWt. 31644-160-55... R 4680
Nathan.. S 13343
Silas, Conn. & Cont... S 13281
Solomon... S 16137
Stephen, Conn., Mass., N. H. & Vt.. S 18433
Theodore, Conn. & Cont.. S 13251
HART, HARTT, HEART or HEARTT.
Aaron, wid. Sarah... W 19707
Ard, wid. Lucy... W 8894
     BLWt. 949-160-55.
Benjamin.. S 37080
Bliss, wid. Silva or Sylvia... W 7630
Elias, Conn. & Cont... S 17462
Elisha.. S 44408
Frederick A., wid. Sally; BLWt. 1912-100... W 1603
     (Also given John HART.)
Gilbert, Conn. & N. H.. S 13304
Hezekiah.. S 15167
Hosea... R 4696
Ithurel... S 15872
James... S 10793
Job... S 44196
John, Fairfield, Maine, in 1818... S 36011
John, Cont. (Conn.), Saybrook, Conn., in 1818... S 37054
John. (See Frederick A.)
Jonathan, BLWt. 955 for 300 acres, Capt. was issued Sept. 7, 1790. No papers.
Lent.. S 13257
Lewis, Cont. service, Conn. residence in 1810; BLWt. 497-100.
Martin.. S 5438
Munson.. S 13252
Peleg, wid. Hannah... W 17990
Pharaoh or Pharo or Pharoh.. S 34392
Reuben.. S 41633
Reuben, wid. Ruth.. W 1972
Samuel, wid. Patience, BLWt. 9472-160-55... W 1176
Selah, Canaan, Conn. in 1832... S 17471
Selah, wid. Ruth... W 21286
Stephen, BLWt. 2373-100.
Thomas, Chenango Co., N. Y., in 1832... S 13325
Thomas, d. 1829; wid. Mary, Guilford, Conn., in 1838... W 17982
Titus... S 13282
HARTSHORN or HARTSON.
Hezekiah, wid. Mary.. W 19733
Joshua, wid. Huldah.. W 21279
Oliver, wid. Hannah.. W 21256
HARTWELL, Oliver.. S 44187
Samuel.. R 4705
HARVEY, Anna, former wid. of Joseph STEWART.
Jonathan.. S 13270
Nathan.. S 13272
Robert, wid. Asenath... R 4706
     (Soldier was pensioned from Litchfield, Conn., in 1832 as private.)
Thomas.. S 13288
William, Conn. & Conn. Sea Service, wid. Jane.. W 4225
HARVY, George, Conn., Mass. & R. I., wid. Philena... W 1037

HASKEL or HASKELL.
David, Conn., Mass. & N. H., wid. Mary, BLWt. 16110–160–55........................ W 7650
Jacob, wid. Diantha... W 21298
John... S 21809
Stephen, Conn. & Mass... S 29859
HASKIN or HASKINS.
Abraham... S 44923
Benjamin, Conn. & Mass., wid. Mary, BLWt. 31697–160–55..................... R 21635
(Did not serve long enough for a pension.)
HATCH, Asa, Conn. & N. H., wid. Ruhamah, BLWt. 26958–160–55............. W 752
Dan, Lucy Northrup, former wid. of.. W 19922
Ede.. S 44918
Gilbert, wid. Martha, BLWt. 9521–160–55.. W 225
Heman.. S 34393
Ichabod.. S 38813
Isaac, wid. Polly, BLWt. 26194–160–55.. W 17993
John... S 13250
Joseph.. S 37057
Josiah... S 5437
Moses, Conn. & Cont., wid. Abigail.. W 25745
Oliver, Conn., Cont. & N. Y., wid. Phebe... W 21137
Timothy, Hartford, Conn., in 1818; wid. Lucinda................................... W 2109
Timothy, Chenango Co., N. Y., in 1832.. S 13296
William, Conn. & Mass... S 13237
HATHAWAY, HATHEWAY or HATHWAY.
Ebenezer... S 23675
Guilford.. S 13287
John, Conn., Cont., Mass. & N. Y.. S 13271
Zenas or Zenus... S 44905
HAUGHTON. (See HORTON.)
HAULEY. (See HAWLEY.)
HAVEN or HAVENS.
Cornelius... S 37093
John, wid. Mary, BLWt. 11258–160–55... W 25760
Peleg, Conn. & R. I... S 9349
HAWES or HAWS, Benjamin, Conn. & Mass., wid. Sarah....................... W 24410
Samuel, wid. Jemima. (Also given HAMES.)
Zenas... S 37053
(Also given HOWES.)
HAWKINS, Amaziah.. S 23254
David, Conn., Conn. Sea service & R. I., wid. Sarah.............................. W 21264
Ebenezer... S 29208
Isaac, wid. Anna... W 17987
James, wid. Nancy.. W 19746
Job, wid. Hannah.. W 19714
Joseph.. S 23689
Moses... S 23683
Rodolphus, wid. Tryphena.. W 11230
Samuel, wid. Hannah... W 13387
William, Conn. & N. Y.. S 44900
HAWKS, William.. R 4769
HAWLEY, Abel, N. Y. in 1832.. S 9346
Abel, wid. Sarah... W 11245
Conn. in 1832; BLWt. 26992–160–55.
Abraham... S 28753
Daniel, Cont. (Conn.).. S 6970
Ebenezer, wid. Lucy, BLWt. 26511–160–55.. W 1760
Ebenezer Rice, Conn. & Cont.. S 9572
Elijah... S 16847
Elisha, wid. Charity, BLWt. 26508–160–55... W 11251
Gad.. S 10805
Hezekiah, wid. Anne.. W 17989
Israel.. S 17470
James, wid. Martha.. W 19705
Joseph, wid. Phebe.. W 19686
Joseph C.. S 44906
Liverius, wid. Anne.. W 19715
Nathan, priv. & corp.; wounded, 1777; invalid pension, 1790................... S 20779
Nathan, Del. Co., N. Y., in 1832, d. 1835; wid. Ruamy........................... W 7656
Nero... S 20784
Ozias, wid. Sarah.. W 4484
Robert, wid. Mary Elizabeth.. W 17984
Salmon. (See Solomon.)
Samuel, Conn. sea service & Mass. sea service; wid. Lucy...................... W 21295
Seth.. S 23277
Solomon or Salmon.. R 4471
Thomas, Ridgefield, Conn., in 1832; d. in 1840; wid. Keziah................... W 25761
Thomas, Trumbull, Conn., in 1832; died in 1850, wid. Mary; BLWt. 26652–160–55.......... W 7657
Zadock or Zadok... S 44907
HAWS. (See HAWES.)
HAYDEN, HEYDON or HEYDEN.
Allen or Allyn.. S 29220
Charles, Conn. & Cont., wid. Molly.. W 23243
(Given also HEATON.)
Daniel, wid. Zerviah.. W 21262
David.. S 43668
Ezra, wid. Olive.. R 4781
Jacob.. S 43654
Samuel.. S 16144

HAYES or HAYS.

Aaron.. S 9345
Amos.. S 10810
Asa.. S 37060
Benajah, Conn. & Cont... S 9565
Benjamin, wid. Alathea... W 21285
Benjamin, wid. Hannah.
    Asa.. S 3706
Benajah, Conn. & Cont... S 95650
Benjamin, wid. Alathea... W 21285
Benjamin, wid. Hannah.
    Is found in case of Fuller, Timothy, widow's former husband.
Dudley, wid. Beda, BLWt. 3815–160–55.. W 17975
Elijah.. S 13280
Enoch, wid. Louisa, BLWt. 28577–160–55... W 11252
Ezekiel.. S 31724
Hezekiah.. S 37055
Jesse, Conn. & N. Y.. S 15168
Joseph, Conn., Cont. & Privateer.. S 13327
Levi.. S 4328
Obadiah, wid. Ahinoana or Ahinoam.. W 17973
Oliver.. S 2262
Samuel, wid. Eunice.. R 4784
Seth, Conn., Cont. & Mass., wid. Mehetable.. W 23207
Zenas, wid. Sarah, BLWt. 71154–160–55.. W 25752
HAYFORD, Ira, wid. Sarah, BLWt. 31569–160–55.. W 660
HAYNES or HAINES, John.. S 13240
Margere, former wid. of Lovell or Lovewell HURD.
HAYS. (See HAYES.)
HAYT. (See HOYT.)
HAYWARD, Ebenezer.. S 13248
Samuel, wid. Sarah, BLWt. 29061–160–55.. W 29934
    Samuel's daughter, Jerusha H. Brown, was pensioned for her father's services under
    Special Act of Congress. Later she was dropped from the rolls and pensioned by Special
    Act, as the wid. of Lt. Col. Edward M. Brown, 8th Vt. Vol. Inf. (See Civil War, Wid.
    Cert. 608657.) She had not been reported as dead Sept. 30, 1910.
Simeon, wid. Hannah.. W 14882
    (Also given as HOWARD.)
HAZARD or HAZZARD, Stewart, Conn. & N. Y.. S 13262
HAZEN, Andrew, wid. Polly.. W 23170
Jacob, Conn. & Cont... S 17459
HEADY, Daniel, wid. Mary.. W 25764
HEALY, George, wid. Bethia.. W 17065
John.. S 23691
HEARD. (See HURD.)
HEARICK. (See HERRICK.)
HEART or HEARTT. (See HART.)
HEATH, Aaron, Conn. & Mass., wid. Rhoda.. W 13440
John, Conn. & Cont.. S 23693
    Peleg, BLWt. 957 for 200 acres, Lieut. was issued Feb. 5, 1790. No papers.
Samuel C., wid. Leah.. W 21311
Thomas, priv. Col. Welles, Copiah Co., Miss., in 1832................................... S 46041
Thomas, Sharon, Conn., in 1832; priv. Col. Allen; wid. Polly........................... W 24423
William, priv. Col. Sage; Berkshire Co., Mass., in 1832................................. S 29219
William, d. 1794, wid. Mary, lived Groton, Conn., in 1833.............................. W 17997
HEATON, Charles. (See HAYDEN.)
HEBARD. (See HIBBARD.)
HECOCK and HECOX. (See HICKOX.)
HEDGES, Henry... R 4839
HELMAGE, John... S 43667
HEMINGER, John, Mary Cannon, former wid. of, BLWt. 67542–160–55............... W 23769
HEMINGWAY, Enos... S 10827
Jacob... S 10677
HEMPSTEAD or HEMSTEAD.
Nathaniel, wid. Elizabeth.. W 14902
Stephen... S 24612
HENDEE, Caleb, Conn. & Cont... S 13349
HENDER or HENDOR, Thomas, wid. Sally.. W 17994
HENDERSON, David.. S 43658
Joseph... S 43661
HENDRAKE, HENDRICK or HENDRIX.
Andrew.. S 39667
Coe... S 18441
David.. S 37098
Nathaniel.. S 38015
HENMAN or HENMON. (See HINMAN.)
HENRY, John, priv. Capt. Dunlap, Hamilton, N. Y., in 1832; wid. Esther.............. R 4890
John, priv. Capt. Hotchkiss, Wallingford, Conn., in 1832; wid. Fanny................. W 19763
HENSEY, Andrew, wid. Sarah.. W 8922
HENSHAW, Benjamin, wid. Elsa or Sarah.. W 21307
William, BLWt. 962–200.
HENSON. (See HANSON.)
HERICK. (See HERRICK.)
HERINGTON, HERINTON. (See HARRINGTON.)
HERRICK or HEARICK or HERICK.
Abel... R 4919
Daniel, wid. Olive.. W 25765
Ephraim, Conn. & Navy.. S 13346
Hezekiah, Conn. & Mass... S 10828
Israel, wid. Ruth... W 17061

HERRICK or HEARICK or HERICK—Continued.
John, Avis Howe, former wid. of.. W 21387
Joseph.. S 13368
Lemuel, wid. Lucy.. W 19756
Libeus... S 41634
Robert, wid. Alice, BLWt. 835–100.. W 11287
Simeon... S 13375
Stephen, Conn. & Cont., wid. Rebecca... W 27784
HERRINGTON or HERRINTON. (See HARRINGTON.)
HERRON, John... S 37099
HEWES. George R. T., Mass. & Privateer (Conn. & R. I.).. S 13367
   (See also HUGHES.)
HEWET, HEWETT, HEWIT or HEWITT.
   Alice Rogers, former wid. of Josiah Rodgers or Rogers.
Andrew, wid. Julia... W 27860
Daniel, Serg't under Capt. Buck, pensioned from Conn. & transferred to N. Y. in 1823; wid.
   Sarah... R 4930
Edmund or Edward, Conn. & N. Y., wid. Hannah.. W 15774
Elisha Cont. (Conn.).. S 16151
Elkanah, wid. Desire.. W 1280
   BLWt. 26930–160–55.
Gershom... S 31735
Henry... S 29218
Israel, wid. Sally.. W 2796
John.. S 43660
Joseph.. S 43659
Lewis, Conn. & Conn. Sea service, wid. Charlotte.. W 17066
Randal.. S 43664
Richard, BLWt. 26032–160–55.. S 23258
Richard, wid. Experience... W 16599
Robert, wid. Abigail, BLWt. 5251–160–55.. W 3683
Simeon, wid. Mehala... W 25766
Sterry, Conn. & Cont.. S 13354
Thomas, Conn. & Conn. Sea service.. R 4939
HEWLET or HEWLETT. (See HULETT.)
HEYDON. (See HAYDEN.)
HIBBARD, HIBBERD, HEBARD, HEBBARD or HEBBERD.
Aaron, wid. Sarah... W 16602
Andrew, in Col. Meigs' reg't., father of Gen. Daniel F. Hibbard, who in 1829 obtained BLWt.
   1488–100.
Andrew, Serg't. under Col. Durkee; in 1790 was in Hampton, Conn.; wid. Ruth was in Vt.
   in 1838.. W 19774
Asa... S 32824
Bushnell, wid. Rebecca or Rebekah.. W 21190
David, Conn. & Cont... S 10835
Diah, wid. Zerviah or Zeviah.. W 21306
Ebenezer.. S 15170
Ebenezer.. S 13412
Jabez... S 18442
Jedediah.. S 43666
Joseph, wid. Lydia, BLWt. 26703–160–55... W 23260
Ozias, wid. Mary, BLWt. 26783–160–55... W 7722
Rufus... S 10840
Timothy, under Col. Bradley, Bath, N. H., in 1818.. S 44422
Timothy, d. 1804, Rutland, Vt., under Col. Swift; Abigail Noble, former wid. of............. W 19931
Uriah... S 43686
Vine Timothy, wid. Dorcas, BLWt. 24755–160–55.. W 662
William... S 13400
   Arminda Hebard or Hibbard, wid. of above soldier, was pensioned as former wid. of
    Obadiah Phelps, Cont., W 4985.
HICKCOX. (See HICHOX.)
HICKMAN, Michael.. R 20514
KICKOX, HICOCK, HICOK, HECOCX, HECOX, HICKCOX or HICKOK.
Aaron... S 16867
Amos.. R 4957
Asa, wid. Esther.. W 2798
Asher... S 46384
Daniel.. S 13402
Darius, Lucinda Miles, former wid. of.. W 18521
David... S 41637
Ebenezer, under Capt. Brown, Col. Waterbury, Amherst Co., Va., in 1832....................... S 5541
Ebenezer, under Capt. Dayton, Col. Baldwin; Ravenna, Ohio, 1832.............................. S 2617
James, wid. Hannah.. W 18011
Nathaniel... S 2316
Samuel.. S 43673
Samuel, Cont. (Conn.), wid. Lucena, BLWt. 51754–160–55....................................... W 1036
Truman.. S 2304
HICKS, John... S 13406
Samuel, Conn. & Cont.. S 18446
HIDE. (See HYDE.)
HIGBY, Nathaniel, wid. Nancy.. R 4972
   Both soldier and wid. were rejected.
   (Also given HIGLEY.)
Samuel, wid. Hannah... W 11301
HIGGINS, Benjamin, wid. Jane.. W 16600
Cornelius, Conn. & Cont., wid. Esther.. W 21325
Ebenezer, wid. Mary... W 21320
Hawes... S 16873
Isaac, Conn. & N. Y., wid. Hannah.. W 19773
   BLWt. 35839–160–55.

HIGGINS, Joseph, BLWt. 971-300, Surgeon's Mate, was issued Dec. 13, 1796. No papers.
Timothy.. S 37109
William, BLWt. 963-200, Lieut., was issued May 17, 1796, to Wm. Higgins. No papers.
HIGLEY, Brewster, Conn. & Vt., wid. Naomi.. W 7742
Nathaniel, wid. Nancy. (See HIGBY.)
Obed, Conn. & Cont... S 17481
Roswell, Conn. & N. Y... S 13411
HILL or HILLS, Abner.. S 37100
Asahel, Cont. (Conn.).. S 38829
Abram, wid. Lydia... W 25770
BLWt. 9429-160-55.
Benajah.. S 23699
Daniel, Conn. & Cont... S 10838
David, Chloe Blackman or Blackmore, former wid. of.. R 15052
Soldier never pensioned; wid. rejected.
Ebenezer, priv. Capt. Belcher; Conn. in 1818; BLWt. 1691-100................................. S 43691
Ebenezer, BLWt. 974-300, Captain was issued June 14, 1790. No papers.
Ebenezer, Jr., Conn. & N. Y. service; also in 1786; Albany, N. Y., in 1832; wid. Mary....... W 7735
Ebenezer or Primus... S 43677
Elijah, wid. Esther.. W 13457
Erastus.. S 43675
George, Elizabeth Conway, former wid. of, Cont. service but Conn. res. and Agency........... W 18885
Grey... S 13405
Henry.. S 15455
Ichabod, Cont. (Conn.), wid. Anna, BLWt. 2353-160-55.. W 2549
Isaac.. S 31747
Jacob.. S 18447
Jedediah, wid. Abigail, BLWt. 26491-160-55.. W 23274
John, wid. Rhoda... W 11302
Joseph, under Capt. Wells; East Hartford, Conn., in 1832...................................... S 17477
Joseph, Conn. Line: Farmington, Conn., in 1818... S 37107
Josiah, Conn. & R. I., wid. Ellen... W 13456
Nathan... R 5018
Peleg, wid. Mary.. W 23281
Philemon, BLWt. 961-200, Lieut. was issued July 14, 1789, to himself. Warrant, via G. L.
Office returned to ditto June 23, 1827. No papers.
Primus, or Ebenezer, Colored, under Col. Hewett; Augusta, N. Y., in 1818.
Reuben... R 5007
Samuel... S 13407
Seth, wid. Karine... W 19779
Thomas... S 43678
Uri, Conn. & Mass... S 19331
Zimri... S 27996
Zimry, wid. Mille... W 3992
HILLARD. (See HILLIARD.)
HILLER, Timothy. Conn. & Mass... S 10833
HILLIARD, HILYARD, or HILLARD.
Azariah.. S 13386
Barnabas, wid. Martha, BLWt. 27669-160-55.. W 7749
Daniel, Conn., Con. Sea service & Mass., wid. Rebecca, BLWt. 10230-160-55.................... W 23294
John... S 37102
Joseph, Lois Cheesbrough, former wid. of... W 16901
Joshua, wid. Elizabeth, BLWt. 31273-160-55.. W 549
Lucretia, former wid. of Charles F. BROWN.
Mary, former wid. of William BRUMBLEY or BRUMLEY.
Minor.. S 22302
Sarah, former wid. of John STEELE.
William, Cont. (Conn.), wid. Hannah... W 18010
HILLYER or HILLER.
Andrew, wid. Lucy.. W 8933
BLWt. 17720-160-55.
(Also served in the British Army.)
Asa.. S 37105
James, wid. Penelope.
(See case of widow's former husband, Conn., GOODRICH, David, R 5026.)
Pliny, wid. Jane.. R 5025
Soldier never applied; widow R.
Seth, wid. Sibil.. W 4696
Theodore... S 37104
Timothy, Conn. & Mass... S 10833
HILYARD. (See HILLIARD.)
HINCHER. Isaac, wid. Marcy or Mary.. W 19780
HINCKLEY or HINKLEY.
Benjamin, wid. Puanna... W 18000
David.. S 13388
Ebenezer... S 13397
Gershom, Conn. & N. Y., wid. Prudence... W 25771
Gillet, wid. Tryphena or Typhena, BLWt. 14669-160-55.. W 5297
Ichabod, BLWt. 951-300, Capt. was issued Oct. 16, 1789 to Theodosius Fowler, Assignee. No
papers.
Jared.. S 19338
John, wid. Rachel, BLWt. 17895-160-55... W 691
Wiat or Wiatt... S 13360
HINE, Benjamin... S 28744
Hezekiah, Cont. (Conn.)... S 37106
Hollingsworth... S 31741
Newton, wid. Mary... R 5031
Samuel... S 16874
Titus (also given HINES).. S 37103

HINKLEY. (See HINCKLEY.)
HINMAN, HENMAN or HENMON.
    Benjamin, Conn. & Cont., wid. Anna, BLWt. 21602–160–55........................... W 23364
    Enoch.. S 30486
    Ephraim, wid. Sylvania... W 17999
    Husted, wid. Mercy.. W 17998
    Isaac, wid. Martha, BLWt. 5452–160–55....................................... W 4986
    Joel, wid. Sarah, BLWt. 30771–160–55... W 21332
    Jonas, wid. Caty.. R 5035
        Soldier was pensioned from N. Y. in 1832.
    Lewis, Conn. & N. Y., wid. Lucy.. W 18001
    Samuel, wid. Elizabeth... W 21334
    Timothy, wid. Phebe, BLWt. 14765–160–55................................... W 1607
    Wait or Weight, wid. Eunice.. BLWt. 52615–160–55
HINSDALE, Abel.. S 13363
    Elias.. R 5037
    Elisha... S 41640
    Jacob, Litchfield Co., Conn., in 1832; wid. Sarah............................... R 5038
HITCHCOCK, HITCHCOK or HITCHOCK.
    Abel, wid. Mary... W 21327
    Ashbel.. S 13398
    Daniel, wid. Lydia, BLWt. 15422–160–55...................................... W 1180
    Ebenezer, Lucy Griffith, former wid. of....................................... W 7588
    Ichabod, wid. Lucy, BLWt. 95681–160–55..................................... W 11293
        Widow was also allowed pension as wid. of Charles TUTTLE, her former husband, who
        died in service in War of 1812.
    Ira, Cont. (Conn.), wid. Hannah... W 23276
    Jared, wid. Irene.. W 16601
    John, Lucy Manley, former wid. of.. W 9929
    John L., wid. Eunice.. R 5053
        (Soldier never applied.)
    Jonathan.. S 7009
    Lemuel... S 43679
    Levi, priv. Capt. Leavenworth; Oneida Co., N. Y., in 1832...................... S 10837
    Levi, priv. Col. Chandler; Colebrook, Conn., in 1818; wid. Mary................. W 8936
    Samuel, under Capt. Stanley; Hartford Co., Conn., in 1832...................... S 13404
    Samuel, Cont. (Conn.), BLWt. 1185–100 was issued in 1826 for soldier's service in Sheldon's
        Dragoons, to brother Ambrose et al.
HIXON, Sarah, former wid. of Joseph WOLCOTT or WOLCUTT; she was wid. of Elkanah
    HIXON, Mass... S 39614
HOADLEY or HOADLY.
    Culpeper, BLWt. 11397–160–55.. S 17492
    Ebenezer... S 37122
    Philo... S 2624
    Silas, Conn. & Privateer... S 13355
HOBART, John, BLWt. 966 for 200 acres, Lieut. was issued July 6, 1795 to Eneas Munson Jr. No
    papers.
    Mason.. S 17487
HOBBY, Hezekiah... S 17488
    Thomas.. BLWt. 1543–450
HOCKHISS. (See HOTCHKISS.)
HODGE, Asahel, Saratoga Co., N. Y., in 1818................................... S 43702
    BLWt. 954 for 300 acres, Captain was issued May 8, 1792 to Amos Muzzy, Assignee. No
    papers.
    Asahel, wid. Martha, BLWt. 43876–160–55.................................... R 5080
        Soldier was b. 1766, and son of Capt. Asahel H., under whom he enlisted; pensioned in 1832
        from Portage Co., Ohio, wid. R.
    Benjamin, Conn. & Privateer... R 5081
    Benjamin, Conn. & R. I.. S 39720
    David, Conn. & Cont... S 44201
    Levi.. S 33320
    Philo, Conn. & Cont., wid. Lucy.. W 24447
        (Also given HODG.)
    Thomas, Cont. (Conn.).. S 44426
HODGES, Job... S 37123
    Leonard, wid. Sarah, BLWt. 11092–160–55.................................... W 19815
HODGKIN, Ambrose... S 17493
HODGKINS, Nathaniel.. S 23261
    Thomas, Conn. & Cont., wid. Tryphena....................................... W 23352
HOGAN, Benoni, Cont. (Conn.), wid. Anna...................................... W 19802
HOIT. (See HOYT.)
HOLBROOK, Abel, wid. Hannah, BLWt. 31274–160–55......................... W 11343
    Calvin.. S 10873
    Ebenezer... S 21820
    Nathaniel, wid. Allice... W 18061
    Susannah, former wid. of Josiah Green.
HOLBURTON or HULBERTON, William, wid. Eunice............................. W 21346
HOLCOMB or HOLCOMBE.
    Abel, wid. Elizabeth... W 18034
    Abner.. S 13433
    Abram.. S 17489
    Asahel, priv., Capt. Hoagland; Hartford, Conn., in 1818........................ S 37112
    Asahel, priv. Capt. Phelps; Granby, Conn., in 1832; Hannah Holcomb, former wid. of....... W 7795
        Hannah was allowed Bounty land for the services of her third husband, Jacob Holcomb
        (BLWt. 47422–160–55).
    Dose... S 29910
    Ebenezer, wid. Chloe.. W 25794
    Elijah, priv. Capt. Phelps; Hampden Co., Mass., in 1830; Cont. (Conn.)......... S 32853
    Elijah, priv. in Sheldon's Dragoons; d. 1815; wid. Mary....................... W 21353

HOLBCOMB or HOLBCOMBE, Ezekiel, wid. Susannah.. W 21358
    Increase, wid. Mary.. W 18017
    Jacob, wid. Hannah.. BLWt. 47422–160–55
      (See HOLCOMB, Asahel, wid. Hannah.)
    Joel, wid. Sarah... W 3685
    John... S 31751
    John G.. S 37116
    Joseph, Berkshire Co., Mass., in 1832.. S 30489
    Joseph, Cont. (Conn.), d. 1797; Corp. in Sheldon's Dragoons; Olive Enos, former wid. of..... W 17762
    Levi.. S 21818
    Luther, wid. Sally.. R 5134
      (Applications of both soldier & wid. R.)
    Nahum.. S 16879
    Noah... R 5131
    Obed, Conn. & Indian Wars of 1783 & 1784; priv. Capt. Case; Essex Co., N. Y., in 1832; Elizabeth Worden or Wordin, former wid. of.. R 11866
    Peter.. S 15175
    Phinehas.. S 10862
    Roger, Conn. & Mass... R 5133
    Seth, Polly Briggs, former wid. of... R 1206
      (Soldier never applied for pension.)
    Timothy... S 15892
HOLDEN or HOLDIN, Amos.. S 32851
HOLDRIDGE, Hezekiah, BLWt. 947 for 450 acres, Lieut. Col. was issued Mch. 28, 1797. No papers.
    Robert, BLWt. 12720–160–55... S 37124
    Rufus, wid. Hannah.. W 18053
HOLISTER. (See HOLLISTER.)
HOLLADAY or HOLLIDAY, Amos... S 10858
    (See also HALLADAY.)
HOLLAND, Joseph, priv. Col. Ledyard; Dutchess Co., N. Y., in 1832........................... S 5567
    Joseph, priv. Col. Burrall; Macomb Co., Mich., in 1832.................................... S 29240
HOLLENBACK, HOLLENBEAK, HOLLENBECK or HOLOMBACH, John, wid. Esther. W 23353
HOLLEY or HOLLY, Abraham, priv. Capt. Hoyt, Stamford, Conn., in 1818.................. S 37110
    Abraham, priv. Col. Chandler, Fairfield Co., Conn., in 1818............................... S 37114
    Elijah, Conn., Mass. & R. I... S 32857
    John, priv. Capt. Watson, Fairfield Co., Conn., in 1818................................... S 37111
    John, d. 1824, Fairfield Co., Conn., wid. Tammy.. W 21396
    Joseph, under Capt. Holley, Cortland Co., N. Y., in 1829................................ S 45386
    Joseph, under Capt. Spicer, d. 1813, Columbia Co., N. Y., wid. Dorothy.............. W 18037
    Robert, wid. Hannah... W 21391
    Stephen, under Col. Burrall; Addison Co., Vt., in 1832.................................. S 21819
    Stephen, under Capt. Hughes; d. 1833, Fairfield Co., Conn., wid. Deborah.......... W 21354
HOLLIDAY. (See HOLLADAY.)
HOLLISTER or HOLISTER, Asahel, wid. Elizabeth... W 7803
    Ashbel, Conn. & Cont.. S 15461
    David, Tioga Co., N. Y., in 1832; d. 1836; wid. Hope, BLWt. 26704–160–55........... W 21409
    David, under Capt. Hubbard, Delaware Co., N. Y., in 1832, d. 1843; wid. Sarah....... W 21347
    Elijah.. S 22315
    Innett, Conn. & Mass... S 10846
    Joseph, Conn. & Navy... S 16880
    Josiah, Conn. & Cont.. S 31748
    Josiah, Conn. & N. Y.. R 5158
    Lucy, former wid. of Gideon NOBLE.
    Nathan, Conn. & Cont... S 4406
HOLLOW, Richard P. (See PENHALLOW, Richard.)
HOLMAN, Thomas, Conn. & Mass., wid. Mary, BLWt. 2695–160–55.......................... W 7787
HOLMES or HOLMS, David.. S 33309
    Ebenezer, wid. Abigail.. W 18058
    Edward, Conn. & Mass... S 13423
    Eliphalet... S 10859
    Elisha.. S 15178
    Ezra, Conn., Cont. & Mass... S 13421
    James, wid. Rhoda J., BLWt. 13886–160–55... W 25780
    John, Conn. & Cont., wid. Rachel... W 21386
    Joshua, wid. Lucretia... R 5176
      (Soldier did not apply.)
    Lemuel.. S 13459
    Levi.. S 37117
    Nathaniel, Cont. (Conn.)... S 45380
    Samuel... S 45389
    Seth, wid. Rhoda, BLWt. 61310–160–55.. W 7770
    Silas, Cont. & Conn., Louisa Palmer, former wid. of...................................... W 8282
    Simeon... S 31754
    Thomas, Conn. & Cont... S 13466
    Titus... S 18880
HOLOMBACH. (See HOLLENBACK.)
HOLSTED. (See HALLSTED.)
HOLT, Ebenezer, wid. Elizabeth... W 25790
    George... S 10875
    Jesse... S 37121
    Jonathan, wid. Anna.. W 21360
    Samuel, Conn. & Navy, wid. Margaret... W 3141
    Silas.. BLWt. 177–200
HOLTON, Elisha, wid. Lydia.. W 7801
HOMISTON. (See HUMISTON.)
HOOKER, Brainard, wid. Molly... W 16297
    Daniel.. S 31360
    Gilbert, Conn., Mass. & N.Y... S 9353
    Ira, Cont. (Conn.)... S 15180

HOOKER, James, Corp. Col. Chandler; Poultney, Vt., in 1818... S 39735
James, Military Store-keeper, together with Horace Hooker in 1778-9; wid. Mary............. W 25800
Martin.. S 9919
Roger.. S 37120
Thomas, wid. Mary, BLWt. 8169-160-55.. W 19804
Thomas H., Sarah Collins, former wid. of... W 2442
William, Cont. (Conn.), wid. Hannah.. W 21349
William, Conn & Vt... R 5199
HOPKINS, Charles.. S 37119
Consider... S 13443
Elisha, BLWt. 956 for 300 acres, Capt. was issued August 9, 1798. No papers.
Frederick, wid. Susan, BLWt 45961-160-55... R 5215
Soldier was pensioned by Special Act of Congress in 1847 for two years   He was living
then in Chenango Co., N. Y.   This pension was not allowed his widow, but Bounty
land was granted in 1855.
George, Cont. (Conn.), wid. Rachel W.. W 18068
John, Conn. & Mass.. S 13447
Rhoderick, Cont. (Conn.).. S 44929
Robert, Conn. & Penna., wid. Elizabeth... W 8946
Timothy, wid. Phebe.. W 4238
HOPSON, Rew., wid. Sarah.. R 5224
(Soldier never applied.)
HORSAM or HORSOM, Ebenezer, BLWt. 886-100.. S 22314
HORSKINS. (See HOSKINS.)
HORTON, HOSTON, or HAUGHTON.
Henry.. S 41652
James, Cont. (Conn.).. S 44930
Lebbeus.. S 37094
(Spelled also HAUGHTON.)
Samuel, Conn. & Cont., wid. Adah, BLWt. 26931-160-55... W 4700
HOSKINS or HORSKINS.
Asa, Hitty Adams, former wid. of... W 25366
Ashbel, wid. Rachel... W 5302
David... S 23708
Elijah... S 5568
John... S 21298
Timothy, wid. Rhoda.. W 21344
Zebulon, wid. Kezia.. W 18026
HOSMER, Ashbel, wid. Polly... R 5248
(Ashbel was an Invalid Pensioner; and as such recorded on the rolls of Conn.)
David, wid. Sarah, BLWt. 30784-160-55.. W 668
Graves, Conn & Navy... S 44938
John... S 45390
Prentice, BLWt. 959 for 200 acres, Lieut., was issued Dec. 12, 1789, to Theodosius Fowler,
Assignee of Elizabeth Hosmer, Adx . No papers .
Prosper, wid. Catharine... W 23339
Timothy, BLWt. 970 ⌐ or 400 acres, Surgeon, was issued Feb. 15, 1799, to Timothy Hosmer.
No papers.
HOSTON. (See HORTON.)
HOTCHKISS, HOCHKISS or HOTCHKIS.
Abraham, wid. Rosetta... W 18057
Ambrose, wid. Lucretia.. W 23321
Asahel, wid. Ruhamah, BLWt. 30770-160-55... W 25787
Eben... S 36582
Eldad, Conn. & Privateer.. S 13432
Elihu, wid. Sally.. W 21397
Elijah... S 10864
Ezekiel, Cont. (Conn.).. S 36585
Harris, Conn. & Navy.. S 2632
Ira.. S 36581
Isaac, priv. Col Swift; New Haven Co., Conn., in 1818; wid. Ann....................................... W 18021
Isaac, Serg't. of Artillery; Conn. & Cont.; N. Y. in 1818; wid. Olive................................. W 18032
Jared, wid. Betsey.. W 368
Jeremish, wid. Mabel.. W 24450
Rej. BLWt.
(This woman was also pensioned as former wid. of Nathaniel TYLER, Conn. & Cont.
W. 24450.)
Joseph, wid. Temperance... W 18051
Josiah, wid. Asenath, BLWt. 30768-160-55... W 18030
Levi, wid. Susannah... W 18054
Lodowick or Lodwick... S 36583
Medad, Cont. (Conn.).. S 36586
Rueben, wid. Thankful... W 18062
Roswell.. S 13453
Samuel, priv. Capt. Hooker, Col. Wolcott; Burlington, Conn., in 1832.................................. S 10877
Samuel, priv. Capt. Watson, Col. Burrall; Steuben Co., N. Y., in 1832; wid. Chloe, BLWt.
8154-160-55... W 7811
Samuel, priv. Capt. Hand, Col. Walcott; Guilford, Conn., in 1832; d. 1835 in New Haven,
Conn., wid. Chloe... W 18047
Simeon... S 10868
Stephen, wid. Tamar... W 18040
Thebus (also given HOTCHKIS).. R 5249
Titus, Conn. & Navy, wid. Rachel... W 18049
Trueman, wid. Ruth.. W 18064
(Also given as Truman HOCHKISS.)
HOUGH, Azel... R 5253
Bede, former wid. of Baldwin WOODRUFF.
David, Conn. & N. Y., wid. Abigail... R 5252
(Soldier never pensioned.)

79

HOUGH, Erastus.. S 13456
    Jabez, wid. Eunice.. W 21357
    Joel... S 17495
    John, wid. Susannah.. W 15685
    Samuel, Cont. (Conn.).. S 36580
    Walter, wid. Martha.. W 3687
HOUGHTON, Ephraim, wid. Mary, BLWt. 26829–160–55................................ W 2550
HOUSE, Abner.. R 5259
    Benjamin.. S 18032
    Eleazer.. R 5262
    Eleazer, Conn. & Cont.. S 10847
    George, Cont. (Conn.), wid. Mary.. W 23317
    Joel, Conn. & Cont., wid. Lois, BLWt. 2482–100.. W 18023
    John, Cont. (Conn.), wid. Esther... W 18041
HOVEY, Azel, wid. Lucy, BLWt. 39223–160–55... W 1770
    Dudley.. S 18451
    Ivory, Conn. & Mass.. S 32842
    Jacob.. S 45394
    Nathaniel, Betsey Mason, former wid. of... W 21778
    Roger, wid. Martha... R 5270
        (Soldier was pensioned from Orange Co., Vt., in 1832; wid. R.)
    Samuel.. S 46641
    William, wid. Lucinda.. W 4995
    Zaccheus... S 18882
HOW. (See HOWE.)
HOWARD, Benjamin, wid. Freelove.. W 18055
    Darius, Conn. & N. H., wid. Susan, BLWt. 26030–160–55.............................. W 27713
    James, wid. Sarah... W 18094
    Jeremiah, wid. Sally.. W 18043
    John... S 41658
    Simeon, wid. Hannah.
        (Also given HAYWARD.)
    Solomon, Conn., Cont. & Vt., wid. Anna.. W 7789
    William, priv. Windsor Co., Vt., in 1832.. S 15463
    William, Capt.; never pensioned; wid. Lucy, BLWt. 2027–160–55.................... W 4699
HOWD, Benjamin... S 20798
    Daniel, wid. Johannah.. W 11329
HOWE or HOW, Asa, wid. Priscilla, BLWt. 9526–160–55................................. W 2552
    Avis, former wid. of John HERRICK.
    David, wid. Phebe... R 5290
        (Soldier never pensioned.)
    Israel, wid. Hannah... W 25795
    Jazamiah, wid. Mary.. W 21381
    Joseph.. S 45373
    Nathan.. S 15466
    Sarah, former wid. of Timothy FAY.
    Zadock or Zadok, Conn. & Cont... S 32866
HOWEL or HOWELL, Nicholas, BLWt.. 1517–100
    William, Conn. Sea service, Mass., Mass. Sea Service & Privateer.................. S 18039
HOWES or HOWS, Benjamin... S 30499
    John, wid. Lucy... R 5293
        (Soldier never pensioned.)
    Zenas.
        (Also given HAWES.)
HOWLAND, Joseph... S 39734
HOWS. (See HOWES.)
HOYT, HAIT, HAYT or HOIT.
    Daniel, priv., corp., fifer & serg't. Fairfield Co., Conn., in 1832.................... S 16881
    Daniel, Serg't., d. 1777; former wid. Sarah Treadwell................................. W 18155
        Sarah was also pensioned as wid. of Daniel TREADWELL.
    David, Conn. & Vt., wid. Sarah... W 23301
    Ebenezer, Darien, Conn., in 1832... S 16882
    Ebenezer, Norwich, Conn., in 1818... S 36588
    Eleazer, Conn. & Cont., wid. Clarissa, BLWt. 24993–160–55.......................... W 4990
    Ezekiel... S 13448
    James, wid. Sally, BLWt. 51755–160–55.. W 11342
    Jared, Cont. (Conn.), wid. Mary, BLWt. 5991–100, issued 1789..................... R 5311
        (Soldier never pensioned.)
    Jesse, wid. Lydia.. W 21370
    Joel, Cont. (Conn.), wid. Abigail... W 21378
    John, wid. Ruth... W 25786
    Jonathan, Artillery, Capt. Jackson; Sullivan Co., N. Y., in 1832.................... S 10869
    Jonathan, under Capt. Benedict; New Haven, Conn., in 1832......................... S 13428
    Joseph.. S 36587
        BLWt. 946 for 450 acres, Lieut. Col., was issued Dec. 14, 1789. No papers.
        (Name recorded as HAIT.)
    Joseph, Hannah Weed, former wid. of... R 11273
        (Soldier not pensioned.)
    Mary, former wid. of
    Moses... S 10860
    Nathan.. R 5312
    Nathan.. S 13426
    Nathaniel.. S 31750
    Samuel, fifer under Capts. Scofield & Lockwood; b. 1762, Stamford, Conn........ S 17491
    Samuel, Conn. & Cont., wid., Hannah.. W 11328
        BLWt. 953 for 300 acres, Capt., was issued June 27, 1789. No papers.
    Samuel.. S 46004
        BLWt. 967 for 200 acres, Lieut., was issued June 27, 1789. No papers.
        (Also given HAIT.)

HOYT, HAIT, HAYT, or HOIT—Continued.
Stephen, wid. Hannah.. W 16290
Walter, wid. Grace.. W 18052
Warren. wid. Mary. BLWt. 10238-160-55... W 25782
    (Also given HOIT.)
William, priv. Artillery. Capt. Bean, d. 1828; wid. Anna............................... W 11338
William, priv. Col. Mead; Greene Co., N. Y., in 1832; wid. Anna..................... R 5309
William. Artificer, Col. Baldwin, Cont. (Conn.), Fairfield Co., 1832................... S 15177
HUBBARD or HUBBART, Abijah, Cont. (Conn.).. S 44962
    BLWt. 5986-100, private, was issued Dec. 14, 1792. No papers.
Abner, wid. Esther... W 19846
Asa.. S 2333
Bathsheba, former wid. of Zebulon MYGATT.
David.. S 17504
Elihu, wid. Martha.. W 16610
Elijah, Penelope Hillyer. former wid. of.
    (See case of her former husband, David GOODRICH.)
Elijah, State Commissary, d. 1808, Middlesex Co., Conn., wid. Abigail................ W 21425
Elisha, Conn. & Cont.. S 18457
George, Corp. under Capt. Hinckley; New Hamp. in 1818................................ S 44451
George. priv. & serg't. under Col. Meigs; Granville, Mass., in 1832; wid. Emily; BLWt.
    26536-160-55.. W 7828
Hezekiah, BLWt. 964-200, Lieut., was issued Nov. 19, 1789. No papers.
Jedediah.. S 10897
Joel. Conn.. Cont. & Privateer.. S 10886
John, fifer, Capt. Abbott; Otsego Co., N. Y., in 1832................................... S 5593
John. priv. under Capt. Church; Otsego Co., N. Y., in 1832............................ S 23715
Jonas... S 38858
Josiah, wid. Mary.. W 19847
Lucretia, former wid. of John R. WATROUS.
Nehemiah, Conn. & Cont.. S 10882
Philip, wid. Ambrillis.. W 19843
Robert, Poebe Skeel, former wid. of... R 9629
    (Soldier not pensioned.)
Thomas, wid. Silence... W 15916
Titus, Cont. (Conn.)... S 5572
HUBBEL or HUBBELL, Aaron, wid. Sarah.. W 11360
Abijah... S 10890
Amos, wid. Lucy... W 18073
David. wid. Abiah... W 18075
    (Soldier died 1820, Fairfield Co., Conn.)
David, wid. Elizabeth... W 19849
    (Soldier pensioned in 1818 from Litchfield Co., Conn.; d. 1836.)
Ezbon.. S 44943
Gershom, wid. Sarah.. R 5316½
    (Neither soldier nor wid. applied for pension, but daughter Priscilla.)
Gideon... S 31763
Isaac, Conn. & N. Y... S 36601
Salmon.. S 36604
    BLWt. 960 for 200 acres, Lieut., was issued June 16, 1789. No papers.
Samuel, wid. Mary.. W 18076
Seth, wid. Salome... W 2115
    BLWt. 1500-100 and BLWt. 67677-160-55.
Silliman, wid. Polly, BLWt. 26869-160-55... W 1774
Thaddeus.. S 13482
William, Conn. & Cont., wid. Margaret... W 8952
HUBBS, Irena, former wid. of Daniel DODGE.
HUDSON, Joshua, wid. Celia... R 5326
    (Soldier was pensioned from Cuyahoga Co., Ohio, in 1832, as priv. in State troops.)
Obadiah, Conn. & N. Y.. R 5337
HUGG, Isaac... S 13492
HUGHES, William, Conn. & Cont.. S 36599
    (See also HEWES.)
HULBARD or HULBURD, Hannah, former wid. of Hiland HALL.
HULBERT. (See HURLBERT.)
HULBERTON. (See HOLBURTON.)
HULBURT and HULBUT. (See HURLBERT.)
HULET, HULETT, HEWLET or HEWLETT.
Aaron, wid. Cynthia, BLWt. 18365-160-55.. W 19831
Daniel, Conn. & Vt.. S 18864
Phinehas.. S 34932
Seth.. S 29249
HULL, Abner... S 2535
Asahel... S 16159
Benjamin.. S 13510
Chester, Cont. (Conn.).. S 44965
David, priv.; called David 2d when pensioned in Otsego Co., N. Y., in 1832............ S 22843
David, First Lieut., Mass., in 1818.. S 32871
David, priv. Conn. Line, Otsego Co., N. Y., in 1818; d. there 1842; wid. Abigail...... W 19795
Eli.. S 18041
    Priv. Col. Meigs; Monroe Co., N. Y., in 1832; applied, but pension not paid until 1850,
    when it was made payable to David Hull, his only surviving child.
Eli, priv. Col. Swift; N. Y. in 1818, d. 1828; wid. Sally, BLWt. 6114-160-55.......... W 26663
Eliakim, wid. Rachel.. W 19840
Ezra, wid. Mary... W 8959
George... S 44967
Henry, Rebecca Blakeslee, former wid. of, BLWt. 2470-100............................. W 3332
Jehiel, wid. Rachel, BLWt. 18022-160-55.. W 25813
Jeremiah, wid. Phebe.. W 19718
Joseph, priv. Lampeter, N. H., in 1818... S 23272

81

HUEL, Joseph, Conn. & Cont., wid. Freelove .... W 7815
  BLWt. 980 for 200 acres, Lieut., was issued Feb. 24, 1791. No papers.
Josia or Josiah, wid. Mehitable .... W 16608
Prince .... S 36596
Samuel, priv. Capt. Morgan; Candor, N. Y., in 1832 .... S 13496
Samuel, priv. Col. Webb; N. Y. in 1818 .... S 44966
Samuel, priv. Col. Webb; Conn. in 1818, d. 1835; wid. Mabel .... W 21284
Wakeman, wid. Esther .... W 7816
Zalmon .... S 15472
Zephaniah, Cont. (Conn.), wid. Rachel, BLWt. 521–100 .... W 25801
HULTS, Stephen, Conn. & N. Y .... S 10880
HUMASON, HUMASTON, HUMASTUN, HUMISTON, HUMMISTON or HOMASON.
Abraham .... R 5369
Daniel, Cont. (Conn.) .... BLWt. 305–100
David .... S 17725
Jesse, wid. Abi .... W 25809
Joel, wid. Ann .... W 4244
HUMPHREY, HUMPHREYS, HUMPHRIES or HUMPHRY.
Abraham .... S 23273
Asahel, Cont. (Conn.), wid. Prudence .... W 21424
David, BLWt. 948 for 450 acres, Lieut. Col., was issued Feb. 28, 1795. No papers.
Elijah, Conn. & Cont., wid. Anna .... W 18092
  BLWt. 952 for 300 acres, Capt., was issued Feb. 5, 1800, to Anna Humphreys and John
  Humphreys, Adx., in trust for the heirs and legal representatives of Elijah Humphreys.
  No papers.
Israel .... BLWt. 1600–100
James, wid. Abiah .... W 19829
Joel, wid. Amelia, BLWt. 13413–160–55 .... W 4245
Levi, wid. Polly .... W 2619
Lot .... S 31762
Nathaniel, Conn. & Cont .... S 36594
Noah, wid. Hannah Cyrene .... W 18099
Roswell, wid. Elizabeth .... W 4998
Samuel .... S 28771
Solomon .... S 17498
Timothy, Cont. (Conn.), wid. Rhoda .... W 18070
HUNGERFORD, Elijah .... S 13494
Green .... S 46048
James, priv. Capt. Fenn; Chanango Co., N. Y., in 1832 .... S 15182
James, priv. Col. A. Ward; Jefferson Co., N. Y., in 1818 .... S 44946
Jehiel .... S 13489
Joseph .... S 13285
Lemuel .... S 16160
Mary, former wid. of Ashbel UPSON.
Robert or Robart, wid. Olive .... W 19793
Uriel, wid. Hannah .... W 18090
HUNN, Samuel .... S 13508
HUNT, Catharine, former wid. of Ezra ALLEN.
Charles, Conn. & Conn. Sea service, BLWt. 6379–160–55 .... S 9920
Daniel, Cont. (Conn.) .... S 39749
Israel .... S 17499
Joel .... S 36605
Lewis, Elizabeth Crofut, former wid. of .... W 17686
Russell, priv. Capt. Burrall; Litchfield Co., Conn., in 1832 .... S 13474
Russell, Serg't., Litchfield Co., Conn., in 1818, d. 1831; wid. Hester .... W 25810
Sampson R .... S 37125
Walter .... S 44853
HUNTER, Daniel .... R 5400
Elizabeth, former wid. of Seth JACKSON.
Joseph .... S 32873
Nathaniel, Conn. & N. Y., wid. Sarah, BLWt. 26031–160–55 .... W 19835
HUNTINGDON or HUNTINGTON.
Andrew, priv. Capt. Baldwin, Col. Sheldon; Monroe Co., N. Y., in 1832 .... S 23716
Andrew, Asst. Commissary of Purchases; d. 1824, New London, Conn.; wid. Hannah A ..... W 21429
Azariah .... S 10888
Christopher, wid. Eunice .... W 7853
  BLWt. 57526–160–55.
Ebenezer, Conn. & Cont .... S 36595
  BLWt. 949 for 450 acres, Lieut. Col., was issued Oct. 13, 1789. No papers.
Hezekiah or Hesekiah, Conn. & Cont .... S 15475
Hiram .... S 23722
Jedediah, BLWt. 945 for 850 acres, Brigadier General, was issued Oct. 26, 1791. No papers.
John, wid. Rebecca .... W 18081
John S., wid. Keturah .... W 19844
Joseph, wid. Susannah .... W 19839
Roger, priv. infantry; Windham, Conn., in 1832 .... S 10901
Roger, priv. Col. Durkee; Vt. in 1818, then moved to N. H .... S 44449
Samuel .... S 23274
Theophilus .... S 44960
Thomas .... S 44961
Wightman .... S 5411
William .... S 13490
HUNTLEY or HUNTLY, Abner, Conn. & Cont .... S 13480
Adriel, Lucy Stedman, former wid. of .... R 10092
  (Soldier never pensioned.)
Andrew, wid. Zelinda .... R 5413
  BLWt. 85067–160–55.
  (Soldier's application rejected as he did not serve six months.)
Dan .... R 5414

HUNTLEY or HUNTLY, Elihu, wid. Naomi .... W 19791
 Ezekiel .... S 13511
 Hoel .... S 18043
 Jabez .... S 36600
 Jehiel, Conn. & N. Y .... S 10894
 Jonathan .... S 18893
 Martin .... R 5415
 Moses .... S 21308
 Reuben, Cont. (Conn.) .... S 13501
 Reynold .... R 5416
 Rufus .... S 45404
 Solomon, wid. Abigail A., BLWt. 7438–160–55 .... W 27854
 Zadock .... S 23270
HURD or HEARD, Abijah .... S 44947
 Adam, Conn. & Vt .... S 18463
 Benjamin .... S 10885
 Cooley, wid. Sarah, BLWt. 26432–160–55 .... W 431
 Crippen or Crippin, wid. Elizabeth .... W 24458
 David .... S 20804
 Elijah, wid. Polly .... W 1773
 Elnathan, Conn. & Cont .... S 13505
 Graham, wid. Love .... W 23242
 Isaac, wid. Mary .... W 1184
  (Also given as HEARD.)
 Jacob, BLWt. 13021–160–55 .... S 17505
 Lewis .... S 18886
 Lovell or Lovewell, Margere Haynes, former wid. of .... W 25763
 Mead or Mede .... S 29250
 Philo .... S 36597
 Robert, Conn. & Cont., wid. Olive .... W 18095
 Roswell .... R 5431
 Wilson .... S 17506
HURLBERT, HURLBURT, HURLBUT, HURLBUTT, HULBERT, HULBUT.
 Abiram, Conn. & Cont .... S 10887
 Alfred, wid. Lydia .... W 25804
 Amos .... S 15896
 Bartholomew .... R 5424
 Daniel .... S 44454
 Daniel, wid. Esther .... W 18077
 David .... S 45401
 Elijah, wid. Ruth .... W 19845
 Eliphalet, wid. Mehitabel .... W 18093
 George, BLWt. 978– for 300 acres, Capt., was issued March 3, 1797, to Ann Welsh, Devisee;
  also recorded as above under BLWt. 2680. No papers. (Given also HURLBRETT.)
 Gideon .... S 36598
 Gideon, wid. Sarah .... W 18087
 John, priv. Col. Wyllys; Onondaga Co., N. Y., in 1818; wid. Judith .... W 16612
 John, wid. Sarah .... R 5426
  (Neither soldier nor wid. applied, but son Stephen, whose application was R.)
 Jubilee A., Cont. (Conn.), wid. Polly or Molly .... W 21423
 Matthias, wid. Clemence .... W 21426
 Seymour .... S 13500
 Shadrack, Conn. & Cont .... S 29915
 Silas, wid. Sarah .... W 18074
 Stephen .... R 5427
 Stephen, d. 1807; wid. Abigail .... W 25812
 Thomas, wid. Eunice .... W 21422
 Timothy, wid. Olive, BLWt. 2028–160–55 .... W 25807
 Wait .... S 39757
HURLEHOY or HURLEROY, or HURLEROI, John .... BLWt. 270–100
HUSTED, Nathaniel, wid. Ruth .... W 18089
 Samuel, Phebe Clark, former wid. of .... W 16909
 Thaddeus, Conn. & N. Y .... S 16158
HUSTON, William, wid. Elizabeth .... W 7847
HUTCHINS, Amasa, wid. Hannah .... W 19790
 John Church, wid. Irene .... R 5448
  (Soldier not pensioned.)
 Nathan, Conn. & Vt., wid. Lois, BLWt. 10236–160–55 .... W 1614
 Shubael, wid. Avis .... W 21428
 Zadoc .... S 13478
HUTCHINSON or HUTCHISON, Abijah, Conn. & Cont .... S 13491
 Amos, wid. Lucy .... W 18088
 Eleazer, wid. Huldah .... W 18079
 Job .... S 13493
 John, priv. Col. Durkee; d. 1804; Mary Adams, former wid. of .... W 20571
 John, wid. Tryphena .... R 5455
  (Soldier not pensioned.)
 John, priv. Col. Wyllys; Windsor Co., Vt., in 1818 and 1832 .... S 22321
 Jonathan .... S 17503
  (Also given as HUTCHISON.)
 Samuel .... R 5453
HUTINACK, Francis .... S 13488
HUXFORD, John .... S 13504
HYATT, Abraham, Conn., N. Y. & Privateer, wid. Anna .... W 16613
 Alvan .... S 18049
 Hezekiah .... R 5461
 Isaac, wid. Esther .... W 18098
 Samuel, Conn. & Cont., wid. Judy or Judia .... W 15776
 Stephen, wid. Eunice .... W 25818

HYDE or HIDE, Agur.. S 36610
    Alexander... S 36609
    Andrew.. S 15477
    Azel, Corp. Col. Reed.. S 46464
    Azel, priv. Col. Wells; Lebanon, Conn., in 1832; wid. Arethusa....................... W 25817
    Benjamin... S 13515
    Clark... S 45407
    Ebenezer... S 13516
    Elihu, wid. Hannah.. W 25814
    Elijah, Conn. & Cont... S 5597
    Elisha, wid. Abigail.. W 25815
    Ichabod... S 15476
    James, BLWt. 958-200, Lieut., was issued Oct. 22, 1789, to Theodosius Fowler, Assignee. No
        papers.
    James, priv. Col. Webb; Vt. in 1818; Conn. & Cont.; wid. Eunice......................... W 5000
        BLWt. 258-60-55.
    Jedediah, Capt. under Col. Durkee; Grand Isle, Vt., in 1818............................. S 39759
    Jedediah, Qr. Mr. Serg't under Col. Parsons; d. 1824, Chittenden, Vt.; wid. Elizabeth...... W 25816
    Joel.. S 13514
    John.. S 10902
    Jonathan.. S 23723
    Joseph... R 5463
    Joseph, Conn. Sea Service, wid. Betsey.. W 1186
    Moses, wid. Sarah.. R 5465
        (Soldier never pensioned.)
    Oliver.. S 45406
    Phineas, Navy (Conn.)... S 32

I.

IAMS, John Frederick, wid. Mary.. W 434
INGALLS, Luther, BLWt. 26079-160-55... S 44972
INGERSOLL, Briggs, wid. Abigail.. W 1188
    BLWt. 9438-160-55.
    John.. S 10904
    Rosannah, former wid. of Abraham PARKER.
INGHAM, Daniel.. S 29255
    David.. S 35458
    Holladay.. S 45409
        (Also given INGRAHAM.)
    Isaac, wid. Lucy... W 16305
    Samuel, wid. Zillah, BLWt. 34285-160-55... W 297
    Solomon, wid. Molly.. W 13527
INGRAHAM, Amos... S 44971
    Hezekiah, wid. Mary, BLWt. 6266-160-55... W 26152
    Holladay. (See INGHAM.)
    James.. S 17509
    Jonathan.. S 30505
    Samuel... S 22325
    Simeon... S 21835
IRION, Charity, former wid. of Samuel GRANNIS.
ISAACS, Isaac, Chloe Wilcox, former wid. of.. W 6541
ISBEL or ISBELL, Garner, wid. Mary... W 20160
    Joel, wid. Mary.. R 5500
        Soldier pensioned as priv. in 1818, Wayne Co., Ohio, later Michigan.
ISHAM, Daniel.. S 15592
    George I, or J... S 41682
    Isaac, wid. Faith.. R 5491
        Soldier never applied for pension.
    Jehiel or Jehial... S 39766
    Jirah... S 18466
    John, wid. Lois.. W 16304
    Joshua, wid. Martha.. W 26791
    William.. S 39765
IVES, Amos... S 15186
    Charles.. S 13319
    Ichabod... S 18050
    John, Conn. & Cont.. S 44974
    Lent, priv. Col. Matthew Meade; N. Y. in 1822... S 28048
    Lent, Conn. & Vt., priv. Capt. Kimball, Col. Chandler, Vt. 1818; d. 1838; wid. Mary......... W 26812
    Levi.. S 15187
    Phineas, wid. Martha... W 20161

J.

JACK, John, wid. Hannah... W 20167
JACKLIN, Ebenezer... S 32891
JACKSON, Archibald, Conn., Cont. & R. I.. S 13521
    Benjamin, Cont. (Conn.), wid. Sabrina... W 26157
    Daniel, priv. under Col. Webb; Stratford, Conn., in 1818.................................... S 36615
    Daniel, Conn. & Conn. Sea Service, Lieut. under Col. St. John; Fairfield, Conn., in 1832...... S 17512
    David, priv. under Capt. Betts; N. Y. in 1818... S 45412
    David, priv. under Capt. Hawley; d. 1814, Sullivan Co., N. Y., in 1814; wid. Olive.......... W 20170
    Elias, Conn. & R. I., wid. Agnes (or Nancy).. W 4002
    John, priv. N. Y. in 1832.. S 22851
        (Claim suspended.)
    John, priv. Capt. Davis, Col. Burrall; d. 1820, Litchfield, Conn.; wid. Delight, pensioned in
        1836.. W 21445
    Joseph... S 10907
    Matthew, Conn. & Mass., wid. Jane... W 10142

84

JACKSON, Michael, wid. Deborah .... W 16033
    Robert, Conn. & R. I. .... S 9994
    Samuel BLWt. 1167-100
    Seth, former wid. Elizabeth Hunter, BLWt. 5447-160-55. .... W 10131
JACKWAY. (See JAKAY.)
JACKWAYS. (See JAKWAYS and also JAQUES.)
JACOBS, Asa, Conn. & R. I., wid. Phebe, BLWt. 21819-160-55. .... W 9070
    Asahel or Ashael. .... S 15478
    Enoch wid. Lois. .... R 5532
    (Soldier never applied for pension.)
    Ezekiel. .... S 10908
    Gershom, wid. Mary. .... W 16309
    (Also given as JACOCKS.)
    Nathaniel, Conn. & R. I. .... S 13520
    William. .... S 23278
JACOCKS. (See JACOBS and JACOX.)
JACOX, JAYCOX or JACOCKS, Joshua. .... S 45432
JACQUES or JACKWAYS, William, wid. Ann. .... W 2118
JAKWAY, JACKWAY or JAKWAYS, Daniel, wid. Olive. .... W 20166
    William. .... S 5612
JAMES, Amos, Conn., Mass. & R. I., wid. Phebe. .... W 1615
    Jeffery. .... S 36616
    Paul. .... S 44983
    Rhoda, former wid. of Billy TROWBRIDGE.
    William, wid. Lovisa. .... W 20168
JAMESON, JAMESSON or JAMISON, Samuel, Cont. (Conn.), wid. Rosana. .... W 16032
JANES, Seth. .... S 28772
JAQUA, Gamaliel, wid. Eleanor, BLWt. 26826-160-55. .... W 7888
JAQUES. (See JACQUES.)
JARMAN or GERMAN, Charles, Conn. & Cont., wid. Betsey. .... W 20169
JARRARD, Benjamin. .... R 5556
JARVIS, Henry. .... R 5559
JAYCOX. (See JACOX.)
JEFFERS, George, wid. Martha. .... R 5562
JEFFERY, Charles. .... S 13539
JELLIFF, James. .... S 17514
JENCKS. (See JENKS.)
JENINGS. (See JENNINGS.)
JENKINS or JINKINS, Calvin. .... S 36624
    John, wid. Bethiah, BLWt. 448-200. .... W 7895
    Samuel, BLWt. 2203-100. .... S 44461
JENKS or JENCKS, John or John S., BLWt. 1821-100. .... S 39775
JENNINGS, Aaron. .... S 13535
    Abijah, wid. Eleanor. .... W 26669
    Abraham, wid. Charity. .... W 21455
    Burritt, Navy (Conn.). .... S 36625
    Daniel. .... S 36628
    Eliphalet. .... S 18468
    Esbon, BLWt. 2208-100. .... S 41695
    Jonathan, priv. under Capt. Benton; Dyberry, Pa., in 1818. .... S 39778
    Jonathan, Cont. (Conn.), in Sheldon's Dragoons six yrs., Addison Co., Vt. in 1818. .... S 38871
    Joshua, wid. Sarah. .... W 20181
    Justus. .... S 44987
    Nathan. .... S 31775
    Nathan B., wid. Ann or Nancy. .... R 5577
    (Soldier was pensioned in Phila. in 1818, for service as Serg't. under Col. Meigs.)
    Noah. .... S 23727
    Peter, wid. Sarah. .... W 24746
        BLWt. 30766-160-55.
    William, private under Capt. Lacy; born 1765; Fairfield Co., Conn., 1835. .... S 13537
    William, priv. under Col. Webb; 62 in 1820, Fairfield Co., Conn. .... S 36622
JERALDS. (See GERALD.)
JEROME, David. .... S 36627
    Thomas. .... S 17513
JESSUP or JESUP, Ebenezer, wid. Rebecca. .... R 5582
    (Soldier was pensioned in Greenwich, Conn., in 1832 as priv. under Capt. Lockwood.)
    Jonathan, Continental service, resided in N. Y. in 1818, and Conn. in 1820. .... S 36626
    Joseph, wid. Eunice. .... W 16310
JEWETT or JEWITT, Alpheus, Conn. & N. Y., wid. Abigail. .... W 24734
    Joseph, wid. Rachael. .... W 21454
    Joseph M. .... S 4438
    Nathan H. .... S 13541
    Zebulon, Conn., N. Y. & Vt. .... S 18900
JINKINS. (See JENKINS.)
JOHNSON, Abner, wid. Anna. .... W 21481
    Abraham. .... S 36650
    Amos, priv. Col. Canfield, d. 1828, Cayuga Co., N. Y., wid. Lucene or Luceny. .... W 21473
    Amos, priv. Capt. Berry, Col. Enos; Oswego Co., N. Y., in 1832, BLWt. 26779-160-55. ... S 13575
    Benjamin, former wid. Susannah Foot. .... W 7299
    Benoni. .... S 13578
    Bristol or Briston, wid. Vira, BLWt. 1592-160-55. .... W 20207
    Caleb, wid. Naomi. .... W 26802
    Calvin, wid. Sally, BLWt. 31283-160-55. .... W 20205
    Constant, wid. Thankful. .... R 5668
    (Soldier did not apply.)
    Daniel, priv. under Col. Wyllys; Lewis Co., N. Y., in 1818. .... S 45423
    Daniel, priv. Capt. Meigs, Col. Hooker; Chenango Co., N. Y., in 1832. .... S 46051
    Daniel, Cont. (Conn), priv. under Capt. Barton, Col. Flowers; Hartford, Conn., in 1828. ... S 36644
    David, priv. under Col. Webb; d. 1827; Vt. in 1818; wid. Eunice. .... W 15779

JOHNSON, David, d. Tolland, Conn., in 1806; wid. Mary... W 21463
  David, Conn. & Cont., priv. under Capt. Hubbard, Col. Huntington; Lexington Heights,
    N. Y., in 1832.. S 13547
  Ebenezer, teamster, Hartford, Conn., in 1837... S 13570
  Ebenezer, priv. Col. Whiting; Monroe, Conn., in 1832.. S 17519
  Ebenezer, priv. under Capt. Collins; Greene Co., N. Y., in 1832; wid. Elizabeth, BLWt. 30765–
    160–55... W 1294
  Edward... R 5609
  Edward... S 13572
  Elias... S 29263
  Elijah.. S 44463
  Eliphalet... R 5611
  Elisha, Northampton, Mass., in 1818, as priv. under Col. Wyllys............................. S 29933
  Elisha, priv. Col. Sage, died in 1813 at Tolland, Conn., former wid. Mary Brigham.......... W 17438
  Elisha, Conn. & Cont., priv. under Col. Lamb, enlisted from Litchfield, Conn., Tioga Co.,
    N. Y., in 1818.. S 45425
  Ephraim, former wid. Hopstill Dean.. W 16237
  Fenn, wid. Rebecca... W 20212
  Gideon... S 17515
  Henry, wid. Holdah... R 5619
    (Soldier was pensioned from N. Y. in 1818 as priv. under Col. Meigs.)
  Hezekiah, Conn. & War of 1812.. S 19353
  Ichabod.. S 10928
  Isaac, priv. Col. Mead; Cayuga Co., N. Y., in 1832.. S 10920
  Isaac, priv. Capt. Bull, Col. Meigs; Huron Co., Ohio, in 1829; wid. Lucy...................... W 20209
  Isaac, priv. under Capt. Blackman, Col. Enoch; wid. Rebekah, Middlesex Co., Conn., in 1832. W 20211
  Isaiah.. S 13581
  Israel, priv. under Col. Wyllys; N. Y., in 1818.. S 43726
  Israel, priv. under Capt. Hall, Col. Swift; d. 1820; wid. Huldah.............................. W 26681
  Jacob, Cont. (Conn.) & Mass. Sea service... R 5623
    (Also given as JONSON.)
  James, priv. Capt. Dana, Col. Ward; Albany Co., N. Y., in 1832.............................. S 43720
  James, priv. under Col. Wyllys; Bath, N. Y., in 1818.. S 45417
  James, priv. under Col. Webb; Norwich, Vt., in 1818; wid. Phebe, BLWt. 39212–160–55.... W 26163
    (Also given as JONSON.)
  James, Cont. (Conn.), Middletown, Conn., in 1832, as priv. under Capt. Sumner.............. S 13557
  Jedediah, wid. Lucy, BLWt. 27671–160–55.. W 7943
  John, priv. under Col. Wyllys; Greenup Co., Ky., in 1818.................................... S 36027
  John, priv. under Col. Swift; Highgate, Vt., in 1818.. S 38877
  John, ensign; d. 1832, Middlesex Co., Conn., wid. Abigail.................................... W 20198
  John (1745–1834), priv. Serg't., Ensign, Lieut. & Capt. Broome Co., N. Y., in 1832; wid. Clarissa,
    BLWt. 7439–160–55.. W 27621
  John, priv. Col. Talcott; Middlesex Co., Conn. 1832; wid. Mary.............................. W 7933
  Jonathan, BLWt. 1136–450, Lieut. Col., was issued Nov. 19, 1789. No papers.
  Joseph... R 5637
  Joseph, Conn. & Cont. priv. under Col. Wyllys; Oswego Co., N. Y., in 1832.................. S 13550
  Joseph, Conn. & Cont.; priv. under Col. Webb; BLWt. 1277–100 granted in 1829 to daughter
    of deceased soldier, Elizabeth Fitch.
  Josiah, priv. under Col. Talcott; Middletown, Conn., in 1832................................ S 16893
  Josiah, Conn. & N. Y... R 5641
  Justus... S 13566
  Lawrence, wid. Grace... W 20202
  Levi, wid. Ruth, BLWt. 9231–160–55.. W 1777
  Miles.. S 22855
  Nathaniel, priv. under Col. Webb; Cazenovia, N. Y., in 1818................................ S 45418
  Nathaniel, priv. under Col. Penn; Derby, Conn., in 1832; wid. Rebekah...................... W 1979
  Nathaniel, wid. Sarah.. R 5662
    (Soldier never applied.)
  Phinehas... S 36639
  Reuben... S 16167
  Reynolds, BLWt. 26472–160–55.. S 13544
  Rufus, priv. under Col. Durkee; Canterbury, Conn., in 1832.................................. S 13576
  Rufus, Conn. & Mass., wid. Mary... R 5647
    (Soldier did not apply.)
  Samuel, BLWt. 1141–400, Major, was issued July 23, 1789 to Samuel Johnson. No papers.
  Samuel, priv. under Capt. Belcher; Tioga Co., N. Y., in 1832................................ S 13569
  Samuel, priv. under Capt. Heath; Tolland Co., in 1832...................................... S 15481
  Samuel, priv. under Col. Huntington; Batavia, N. Y., in 1818............................... S 43710
  Samuel... R 5659
  Samuel, ensign under Col. Burrall; Delaware Co., N. Y., in 1818; wid. Rebecca.............. R 5655
  Samuel, Cont. (Conn.), priv. in Hazen's reg't.; Batavia, N. Y., in 1818..................... S 45420
  Seth, wid. Abigail... W 1295
    Abigail was also pensioned on account of the services of her former husband, Edmund
    CARLETON, Mass.
    (Seth, b. 1748, Middletown, Conn.; served under Capt. Hubbard, and died 1833 in N. H.)
  Shadrach, wid. Hannah... W 20201
  Silas... S 5636
  Solomon, BLWt. 430–100.
  Stephen, priv. Capt. Chapman, N. Y., in 1832.. S 10919
  Stephen, Conn. & Cont., Sheldon's Cavalry; d. 1831, Windha Co., Conn.; wid. Persis....... W 21487
  Stephen W., Conn., Conn. Sea service & Navy.. S 28776
  Theodata, wid. Ruth... W 26672
  Timothy, priv. Col. Durkee; Wayne Co., N. Y., in 1832...................................... S 22853
  Timothy, priv. Col. Webb; New Haven Co., in 1818.. S 36645
  Turner... S 43724
  Uzal, Conn. & R. I., wid. Mehetable.. W 26161
  William, priv. Capt. Meigs, Col. Spencer; Warren Co., Ohio, in 1832......................... S 8762
  William, priv. under Capt. Brown; Stamford, Conn., in 1818................................ S 36635
  William, priv. Capt. Wolcott; Windham Co., Conn., in 1818................................. S 36651
  William, priv. Capt. Mills, Col. Webb; Cayuga Co., N. Y., in 1832; former wid. Anna White,
    BLWt. 102200–160–55... W 27500

JOHNSON, William, priv. under Col. Bradley; died in 1838; Harpersfield, N. Y., in 1818; wid.
Hadassah, BLWt. 30762-160-55.. W 5305
William, Navy (Conn.)... S 36634
JOHNSTON, Benjamin, Cont. (Conn.), wid Clarissa; BLWt. 25781-160-55........................ W 1435
John, Navy (Conn.), wid. Ruth... W 26673
JOINER, Hepsibah, former wid. of James SUTLIEF.
JOLIFF, Eunice, former wid. of John LOCKWOOD.
JOLLY, William, wid. Desire.. W 20196
JONES, Amos, wid. Lydia.. W 20183
Asa, Serg't under Col. Durkee; in 1818 in Ohio; in 1832 in Tolland Co., Conn.................. S 13558
Asa, Conn. & N. Y., priv. & Serg't under Col. Waterbury; Greene Co., N. Y., in 1832....... S 13568
Asaph, wid. Hannah, BLWt. 17704-160-55.. W 1293
Augustus... S 18059
Benjamin, priv. under Capt. Edwards, Col. Waterbury; Preble, N. Y., in 1832................. S 13565
Benjamin, priv. Capt. Brigham; Chenango Co., N. Y., in 1831... S 45428
Crocker or Croker... S 41702
Daniel, Serg't under Col. Huntingdon; Morris Co., N. J., in 1832... S 2297
Daniel, priv. Col. Huntingdon; Rensselaer Co., N. Y., in 1818... S 45429
David.. S 28777
Deodate Pratt.. S 36649
Eaton, Cont. (Conn.), wid. Mary.. W 20187
Elkanah... S 16170
Epaphras.. S 16889
Ephraim, wid. Anna.. W 2620
Ethel... S 22854
Ezekiel... S 28778
Ezra... R 15464
George, wid. Lucretia.. W 21484
Harris... S 36655
Isaac, priv. under Col. Wells; Hebron, Conn., in 1832... S 18058
Isaac, died 1793 in Fairfield, Conn.; priv. under Col. Whiting; Ruth Booth, former wid. of.. W 20741
Issacher, wid. Eleanor.. W 21472
James, BLWt. 1141-100.
Joel, Conn. & Mass... S 43730
John, priv. under Capt. Sherwood, Col. Lewis; Delaware Co., N. Y., in 1832.................. S 13573
John, priv. under Capt. Kirtland, Col. Ledyard; Saybrook, Conn., in 1832..................... S 31871
Joseph.. S 45845
Moris or Morris, Conn. & Cont... S 13571
Oliver, wid. Hannah.. W 20185
Philip.. R 5734
Phineas or Phinehas... S 43707
Reuben, priv. under Col. Swift; Plymouth, Penna., in 1832.. S 2292
Reuben.. R 5737
Richard L., wid. Elizabeth, BLWt. 5439-160-55... W 765
Samuel, priv. in Col. Sheldon's Cavalry; Genesee Co., N. Y., in 1818; and Linklaen, N. Y.,
in 1832.. S 28775
Samuel, priv. under Col. Ely; died in 1827 in Saybrook, Conn.; wid. Mercy was living in
Ulster Co., N. Y., in 1838.. W 21485
Samuel, priv. under Capt. Hutchinson, Col. Hofford; Pompey, N. Y., in 1832; wid. Tabitha.. W 26685
BLWt. 6396-160-55.
Samuel, Conn. & Cont., priv. under Capt. Smith, Col. Parsons; Rensselaer Co., N. Y., in 1832. S 13559
Samuel L., wid. Elizabeth... R 5700
(Soldier never applied.)
Simeon.. S 16894
Solomon... S 32903
Squire, Cont. (Conn.) & N. Y., wid. Polly... W 21471
Stephen.. S 43728
Thomas, Conn. & Cont... S 43716
Timothy, wid. Lydia... W 20186
William, b. Jan. 18, 1764; priv. under Capt. Lathan; Madison Co., N. Y., in 1832........... S 13577
William, Serg't under Col. Durkee; New Haven Co., Conn., in 1818.................................... S 36640
William, priv. under Col. Bradley; Middlebury, Vt., in 1818... S 38875
William, priv. under Capt. Chamberlin; Whitehall, N. Y., in 1818; pensioned as William 1st. S 39784
William, priv. under Col. Webb; pensioned as William 2d in 1818.. S 43715
William C... S 18473
JONSON. (See JOHNSON.)
JORDAN, John; also given KENEA, John Jordan.
Stephen, wid. Mary... W 20220
JOSLEN, JOSLIN or JOSLYN, David.. S 13543
Joseph, Conn. & R. I.. S 17518
Reuben, wid. Mary... W 20219
JOSTIN. (See JUSTIN.)
JOY, Anna, former wid. of Clement MINOR.
Benjamin.. S 40888
Ebenezer.. S 22337
JOYCE, David, Conn. & N. Y.. S 13548
Abia, former wid. of Moses CASS.
Anthony... S 23282
Calvin, wid. Mary.. W 26801
Dan.. S 13590
Demas... S 10932
Eben W., wid. Lydia... W 26706
Elias, Conn. & Cont.. S 17520
Elihu, Lois Davis, former wid. of... R 2743
(Soldier never applied.)
Freeman, Conn. & Cont., wid. Deborah.. W 21500
Isaac.. R 5781
James, wid. Esther... W 20222
Jehiel... S 20816
John, wid. Mary, BLWt. 26116-160-55... W 10160

JOYCE, Joel, Marcy or Mercy Edwards, former wid. of.. W 17746
    John, Cont. (Conn.), wid. Hannah.. W 26707
    Levi.. S 18067
    Nathan... S 44467
    Reuben.. R 5782
    Samuel, Phebe Waters, former wid. of.. R 11184
      (Soldier never applied.)
      It is alleged that Phebe's other husband, Oliver WATERS, also served in the Rev. War.
      See papers in this case.
    Solomon.. S 23736
    Stephen, wid. Sarah... W 21499
    Thomas.. S 31785
    Walter, wid., Margaret.. W 20221
    William, priv. under Capt. Edwards; Jefferson Co., N. Y., in 1832.................................... S 19724
    William, BLWt. 1137-300, Capt., was issued July 1, 1790. No papers.
JUDSON, Aaron.. S 17522
    Agur... S 15594
    David, wid. Elizabeth.. W 21504
      BLWt. 1138-300, Capt., was injured October 7, 1789. No papers.
    Elizabeth, former wid. of Benjamin DAVENPORT.
    John B., wid. Hepsy... R 5784
      (Soldier never applied.)
    Joseph, Lydia Clark, former wid. of.. W 22782
    Lemuel.. S 17521
    Nathaniel... S 13592
    Nehemiah, Conn. & Cont... S 16899
    Phineas, Conn. & Cont.. S 13591
    Solomon.. S 29266
    Stiles, wid. Naomi... W 21498
JUNE, Israel.. S 36670
    Joel.. R 5787
    Reuben, wid. Mary.. W 2555
    Seth, wid. Hannah.. W 20224
JUSTIN or JOSTIN, Charles, BLWt. 1172-100.. S 36669
    George, wid. Lucy... W 20226
    Gershom, Conn. & Navy, wid. Susannah.. R 5791
      (Soldier was pensioned as Mariner in Vt. in 1832.)
    Walcut or Walcot.. S 45433

K.

KALLAN, Luther, Conn. & R. I.. S 13594
KANNEDY. (See KENNEDY.)
KAPLE, John... S 13593
KAULL, John, Cont. (Conn.).. R 5800
KEARN. (See KERN.)
KEATOR, Eunice, former wid. of Josiah PATCHEN or PATCHIN.
KEELER, Aaron, wid. Chloe.. R 5806
      (Soldier never applied.)
    Aaron, Cloriana Olmstead or Ollmstead, former wid. of... W 21867
      BLWt. 1191-150, Ensign Wm. Fisher; August 17, 1775. No papers.
    David, priv. under Col. Canfield; Brooklyn, Conn., in 1832... S 16904
    David, priv. under Col. Chandler; Onondaga Co., N. Y., in 1818.. S 45442
    Ebenezer, wid. Lucy.. W 3261
    Henry, Conn. & R. I., Martha K. Miller, former wid. of... W 7452
      BLWt. 355-60-55.
    Hezekiah, wid., Mercy.. W 12005
    Isaac... S 45440
      BLWt. 1188-200, Lieut., was issued May 9, 1789. No papers.
    Isaac, matross, died 1814; wid. Deborah.. W 20314
    Isaac, Conn. & Cont., priv. & Corp. under Capt. Hoyt, Col. Webb; New Canaan, Conn., in
      1832; wid. Catherine.. W 26178
    Jeremiah.. S 45441
      BLWt. 6052-100, private, was issued January 16, 1797. No papers.
    Levi, wid. Dorcas.. W 20294
    Lewis.. S 4471
    Mathew, wid. Ruth.. R 5809
      (Priv. under Col. Enos; Fairfield Co., Conn., in 1832; wid. only was rejected.)
    Nathan, wid. Huldah... W 20302
    Nehemiah... S 15494
    Philip.. S 15493
    Samuel, BLWt. 201-300.
    Thaddeus, BLWt. 1187-200, Lieut., was issued January 16, 1797. No papers.
    Thomas, BLWt. 639-100.
    Uriah, wid. Lydia... R 5810
      (Soldier was pensioned in Onondaga Co., N. Y., in 1818 as a priv. under Col. Chandler.)
KEENEY or KENEY, Ashbel, wid. Sarah.. W 20300
    Ethel.. R 5813
    James, wid. Anne.. W 20326
      (Also given as KINEY & KINNEY.)
    Richard.. S 13620
    Thomas, Conn. & Penna.. S 9366
    William.. S 18072
KEITH, Barak.. S 13613
    John, Conn. & Mass... S 44479
    Peter... S 45447
KELLEE, KELLEY or KELLY.
    Charles.. S 45445
    Craig, wid. Sibbel... W 20304
    Jeremiah M.. S 15911
    John, Olive Bowers, former wid. of.. W 393

KELLOGG, Daniel.. S 10944
   Eldad, Conn. & Mass., wid. Elizabeth.. W 7977
      BLWt. 523-160-55.
   Elijah, priv. under Capt. Mead, Col. Waterbury; Carlisle, N. Y., in 1832.............. S 23738
   Elijah, Conn. & Mass., priv. under Capt. Swift, Col. Butler; Essex Co., N. Y., in 1832....... S 13599
   Enoch.. S 45439
   Helmont... S 21847
   Horace or Horrace... S 45437
   Josiah... S 41722
   Martin.. S 10940
   Medad, Conn. & Mass.. S 15492
   Noah.. S 45436
   Phineas... S 42774
   Samuel.. S 39806
   Solomon... S 40896
   Stephen, wid. Lydia... W 21506
KELSEY or KELSY, Benjamin... S 36676
   Ezra.. S 15491
   Heth or Heath... S 13611
   Joel.. S 16432
      BLWt. 26777-160-55.
   John, wid. Lucy... W 20301
   Merry Seymour, Conn. or R. I., wid. Sarah.. R 5852
   Noah, wid. Margaret.. R 5851
      (Soldier never applied.)
   Reuben.. S 10937
   Samuel.. S 13622
   Seymour. (See Merry Seymour.)
   Stephen, wid. Lois.. W 26168
KENDAL, KENDALL, KINDAL or KINDALL.
   Ebenezer, wid. Elizabeth.. R 5930
      (Neither soldier nor wid. applied.)
   Isaac, wid. Rachel.. W 12007
   John, Conn. & Cont.. S 39812
   Joshua.. S 13615
KENEA, John Jordan, Conn. & Cont., wid. Obedience...................................... W 26177
KENEDY. (See KENNEDY.)
KENEY. (See KEENEY.)
KENNEDY, KANEDY or KENEDY.)
   Hugh, Conn. & R. I.. S 42777
   Joseph, wid. Agnes.. W 13600
   Robert, Conn. & N. Y., wid. Eunice... R 5868
      (Soldier never applied.)
   Seth, Conn., Cont., Mass. & Navy... S 31789
   William, wid. Mary... W 15783
KENT, Bela, Cont. (Conn.), wid. Lucretia... W 7962
   Cato, wid. Beulah... W 26169
      (See also NEGRO.)
   Charles... S 13618
   Darius.. S 31791
   Elihu, wid. Elizabeth... W 26172
   Jacob... R 20388
   John, wid. Mary... W 3559
      BLWt. 8384-160-55.
   Jonathan K.. S 31792
   Joseph.. S 42764
   Samuel, wid. Mary... W 5306
   Titus (colored), BLWt. 1665-100.
KENTNER, John P... R 5876
KENYON, Payne... S 42767
   Zephrah, former wid. of William PRENTICE.
KERN or KEARN, Michael, Conn. & N. Y., wid. Mary..................................... W 7964
KERR, Robert.. S 31793
KETCHAM, Ezra... S 42768
KEYES or KEYS, Daniel, wid. Abigail.. W 20309
   David... S 13623
   Ebenezer.. R 5897
   Elias, Conn. & N. H... S 15912
   John, Conn. & Cont.. S 42766
   Marshal or Marshall... S 42771
   Sampson, Conn. & Mass.. S 13606
KIBBE, KIBBEE, KIBBEY, & KIBBY.
   Elijah, wid. Hannah... W 26729
   Frederick or Fredrick... S 15499
   Israel, wid. Ruth... W 20336
   Jedediah or Jedidiah.. S 15595
   Lemuel, wid. Love... W 21530
   Philip or Phillip... S 13640
   Philip W.. S 44480
      (Also given as KILBEY.)
KILBORNE, KILBOURN or KILBOURNE, or KILBORN.
   Araunah or Arannah... S 13649
   James, wid. Elizabeth... W 20340
   Samuel.. S 36679
   Simon, wid. Eunice.. W 20328
KILBY, Christopher A., Cont. (Conn.).. S 36678
   John.. S 31798
KIMBALL, Abraham T., wid. Sarah... W 26180
   Benjamin.. S 13631
   Charles, wid. Jerusha... W 21527

89

KIMBALL, Isaac.. S 32954
    Jared... S 41730
    Jedediah, wid. Eunice... W 26735
    Jesse.. R 5921
    Jesse, Conn. & Privateer.. S 13639
    John... S 42792
    Joseph, Conn. & Mass., wid. Ede.............................. W 10176
    Lebeus or Libbeus.. S 16179
    Richard... S 39814
    Samuel, Conn. & R. I.. S 21853
KIMBERLY, Ezra.. R 5924
    Robert, Hannah Foote, former wid. of......................... R 3638
        (Soldier never applied.)
KINCH, William, wid. Ruth.. W 21529
KINDAL or KINDALL. (See KENDALL.)
KINEY. (See KEENEY and KINNE.)
KING, Benjamin... S 4767
    Eli, Chloe Strong, former wid. of.............................. W 16746
    Eliphalet, Cont. (Conn.), wid. Silence....................... W 20338
    Esau.. S 23750
    Ichabod, Conn. & Cont... S 40901
    James.. S 13654
    John, wid. Jane.. W 20349
    Jonah, Conn. & Mass.. S 16908
    Joseph.. S 42786
    Joshua, Cont. service but Conn. residence................... S 13632
        BLWt, 1192-200, Lieut., was issued August 26, 1789. No papers.
    Lemuel, wid. Jane... W 26179
        Rozina, former wid. of Joseph CLARK.
    Samuel, wid. Betsey.. W 21531
    Theodore, wid. Lydia.. W 24854
KINGSBERY or KINGSBURY, Andrew, wid. Mary................... W 20327
    Asa... S 13644
    Daniel, wid. Martha.. W 20324
    Jabez.. S 17525
    Jacob, wid. Sally P... W 1881
        BLWt. 1190-150, Ensign, was issued Sept. 12, 1789. No papers.
    Joseph, priv. under Capt. Clark; Coventry, Conn., in 1832... S 17524
    Joseph, fifer, under Col. Chandler; Ellington, Conn., in 1818... S 36680
    Oliver, wid. Sally, BLWt. 6254-160-55......................... W 16038
    Sanford, Conn. & Vt.. S 2708
    Thomas, wid. Esther.. R 5967
        (Soldier was pensioned from Lawrence Co., N.Y., in 1832 as a priv. under Capt. Steadman.)
    Tilley, Conn. & Mass., Anne Seymour, former wid. of........ W 19342
KINGSLEY, Aaron, wid. Sarah.. W 1781
    Alpheus.. R 5968
    Asahel... R 5969
    Hezekiah, Cont. (Conn.), wid. Rhoda.......................... W 26181
    Jabez.. S 13651
    Jonathan... S 13461
    Rufus... S 13659
    Wareham, Conn. & War of 1812................................. R 5971
    William, wid. Deborah, BLWt. 24994-160-55.................. W 768
KINNE, KINEY, KINNEY or KINNY.
    Asa, Conn. & N. Y. & R. I., wid. Polly...................... W 26710
    Daniel, Cont. (Conn.)... S 42779
    Freelove, former wid. of George GALLUP.
    James, wid. Anne. (See KEENEY.)
    Jonas... R 5976
    Joseph.. S 22863
    Lawrence... S 42787
    Paley... S 29943
    Samuel, wid. Dorothy... W 1197
    Seth, Conn. & Cont. and Vt., wid. Hannah.................... W 20330
    Stephen, Conn. & R. I... S 2704
KIRCUM. (See KIRKHAM.)
KIRK, Thomas.. S 37130
KIRKHAM, KIRKUM, or KIRCUM.
    Philemon... S 2703
    Samuel.. S 42780
    William, Conn. & Cont., Deborah Buell, former wid. of....... W 20795
KIRKLAND, Jabez, wid. Eunice... W 14997
        (Given also as KIRTLAND.)
    Joshua, Conn. & Privateer...................................... R 5991
        Susanna, former wid. of John BUTTS.)
KIRTLAND, Charles.. S 13648
    Daniel, wid. Lovisa.. W 20348
    Elizur.. R 5994
    Jabez, wid. Eunice. (See KIRKLAND.)
    John.. S 23748
    Martin, priv. under Capt. Kirtland; Oneida Co., N.Y., in 1832... S 10947
    Martin, captain, BLWt. 1085-300.
    Nathan... S 17526
KNAP or KNAPP, Benjamin, wid. Hannah............................... W 1296
        BLWt. 14761-160-55.
        Hannah also claimed a pension as the former wid. of Zebulon MOSES, Vt., R 6009.
    Charles, Cont. (Conn.).. S 37141
    Ebenezer... S 37140
    Eleazar... S 40906
    Elijah.. S 27049

KNAP or KNAPP, Hezekiah, wid. Mary.. W 20364
    Isaac, Conn. & Cont.. S 13673
    Jacob, wid. Mary.. W 20362
    James, BLWt. 1513–100.
    Jared, wid. Catharine... W 1621
    John, priv. under Col. Waterbury; Fairfield Co., Conn., in 1832.................... S 10958
    John, priv. Capt. Brown, Col. Waterbury; Putnam Co., N. Y., in 1832............... S 13665
    John, priv. Col. Davenport; Stamford, Conn., in Revolution, died 1832; wid. Sally or Sarah,
        BLWt. 28593–160–55... W 26189
        (Widow was pensioned from Orange Co., Vt., in 1853.)
    Joshua, wid. Lodema.. W 5015
        BLWt. 1189–150, Ensign; was issued June 25, 1789.
    Lemuel... S 22865
    Nathan... S 10959
    Peter, wid. Sarah.. W 20366
    Samuel... S 42801
        Hannah, wid. of this soldier, was pensioned as the former wid. of John BURGER, Mass.,
        W. 16319.
    Solomon, wid. Rosanna... W 20355
    Titus.. S 16909
    Uzal... S 16182
        BLWt. 6066–100; Sergt., was issued June 27, 1789, to Uzal Knapp. No papers. And
        BLWt. 206–60–55.
    William.. S 16910
KNEELAND, Jesse.. S 42802
    Jonathan, Mary Wood, former wid. of... W 18360
    Samuel... S 42798
    Seth R., Cont. service, but Conn. residence and Agency; wid. Eunice.............. W 20369
KNICKERBACOR or KNICKERBACKER, Samuel, BLWt. 43504–160–55................. S 13662
KNIGHT, Artemas, Conn. & Mass... S 16438
    Charles.. R 6022
    Elijah... S 41732
    Jonathan, wid. Anna or Ann; BLWt. 56–300... W 3024
    Josiah... S 13664
    Phinehas... S 32959
KNOTT, Abraham. (See NOTT.)
KNOWLES, James, Conn. & Cont. priv. under Col. Baldwin (artificer); Ohio in 1818; wid. Martha W 4258
    James, Conn. & Navy; Serg't., Ensign, Lieut. & Midshipman; died in 1778; former wid. was
        pensioned from Berkshire Co., Mass., in 1832; Prudence Foot, former wid. of.............. W 14036
    John, Cont. (Conn.), wid. Heppy or Hepsibah....................................... W 20356
    Seth... S 42799
    Walker... S 23294
KNOWLTON, Frederick, Conn., Cont. & Mass... S 13670
    Nathaniel.. S 23291
    Stephen, wid. Deidamia; BLWt. 13426–160–55....................................... W 6261
    Thomas, BLWt. 1149–400; was issued to the heirs of Col. Thomas Knowlton, who was killed
        at the Battle of Harlem Heights.
    Thomas, priv., Corp. & Serg't. under Capt. and Col. Knowlton; Tolland Co., Conn., in 1832;
        BLWt. 3952–160–55... S 31803

L.

LACEY or LACY, Isaac L.. S 46501
    Zachariah, wid. Betty... W 20405
LAD or LADD, Amasa, Elizabeth Miller, former wid. of............................... W 26263
    Cyrus, wid. Amy.. W 20411
    Elisha... R 6076
    John, Esther Fish, former wid. of.. W 13162
    Oliver... S 21343
LAFLAN, LAFLEN or LAFLIN.
    Abraham.. S 40923
    Charles.. S 28785
    John... S 37601
    Samuel... S 42825
LAKE, Daniel, wid. Polly... W 12071
    David.. R 6088
    Reuben, BLWt. 546–100.. S 35515
    Roger.. S 42809
    William, wid. Mary, BLWt. 11177–160–55.. W 26191
LAM or LAMB, Asa, Conn. & Cont.. S 10970
    Benjamin... S 40915
    David, Conn. & Navy, wid. Anna.. W 20410
    Silas, Cont. (Conn.), wid. Jane... W 20399
LAMBERT, David, wid. Lois.. W 20377
LAMBERTON, Obed.. S 44493
LAMPHAER, LAMPHEAR, LAMBPHIER, LAMPHIER, LANPHERE, LANPHIR.
    Abel... S 16440
    Amos, Conn. & N. Y.. S 13698
    Fitch, wid. Jerusha... W 27145
        (Also given LANPHERE.)
    James, Conn. Sea Service & Navy, wid. Grace...................................... W 26197
    Jedediah, wid. Elizabeth or Betsey... W 20381
        (Also given LANPHERE.)
    Roswell, wid. Elizabeth... W 21544
        (See also LANFAIR.)
LAMPSON or LAMSON, Benjamin, wid. Mary... W 16323
    David, wid. Polly... W 7163
    Ebenezer, wid. Martha, BLWt. 38518–160–55... W 4262
LANDON, Ebenezer... S 13706
    James.. S 15505
    Rufus, Conn. & Cont... S 13682

LANE, Dan.. S 31808
    Jabez... S 31807
    John... S 38129
    Joseph.. R 6126
    Joseph, Conn. & N. Y... S 4495
    Nathaniel, wid. Melicent, BLWt. 3796–160–55............................ W 12060
LANFAIR, Roswell, Conn. & Conn., Sea service............................. S 30538
    (See also LAMPHAER.)
LANGDON, Philip, Cont. (Conn.)... S 35513
LANGTON, Daniel... S 32370
LAP, John... R 9200
    (Also given as SAP.)
LARABEE, LARABY, LARIBEE, LARRABEE.
    Lebbeus, wid. Mary... W 1882
    Seth, wid. Sally... W 20404
    Theophilus... S 40909
LARKIN, Joseph, Conn. & Vt., wid. Hannah................................. W 24497
    Joshua... S 16914
    Lorin, Conn., Mass. & Vt... S 13716
LARNED, Thomas, wid. Hannah, BLWt. 10219–160–55.......................... W 13608
LASELL, Josiah, wid. Lydia... W 20380
LASHBROOK or LASHBROOKS, William, wid. Zeruah, BLWt. 1376–100; & BLWt. 330–60–55.. W 24466
LATHAM, Amos.. S 36683
    Christopher, wid. Sabra, BLWt. 12564–160–55............................ W 8031
    Jesper... S 13707
    John... S 32967
    Joseph... S 16915
    William.. R 13688
LATHROP, Daniel.. R 13688
    David, wid. Anne... W 24509
    Dixwell.. S 17531
    Elias, wid. Dorcas, BLWt. 53753–160–55................................. R 6180
        (Soldier applied in 1832 from Orange Co., Vt., as teamster and also substitute in Militia
        for father ELIAS, but six months service was not proven.)
    Elisha... S 18925
    Job. (See also PRIMUS, Job.)
    Joshua, wid. Betsey.. W 15786
    Oliver... S 18484
LATHROP, Samuel, wid. Lois... W 16134
LATIMER, Charles, wid. Mary.. R 6177
    (Soldier never applied.)
    George, wid. Louisa L., BLWt. 30755–160–55............................. W 12061
        (Soldier was pensioned in Windsor, Conn., in 1832, as waggoner under Capt. Jones.)
    Solomon.. S 31806
    Witherell.. S 31809
LATTIMER or LATTIMORE, George, ensign under Capt. Chapman; New London Co. in 1832.. S 13701
    Jehiel... S 37600
LAW, John, wid. Lydia.. W 16324
    Joseph, Conn. & Cont., wid. Dulana..................................... W 21549
    Nathan, wid. Eunice.. W 20385
    Richard, Navy service, Conn. residence................................. S 13699
LAWRANCE, LAWRENCE or LORANCE.
    Abigail, former wid. of Edward Sutton.
    David, wid. Marven... W 26196
    James.. S 40921
    John, priv. under Col. Meigs; Franklin Co., Vt., in 1818: former wid. Hannah Dunham...... W 26662
    John, Conn. & Cont., priv. under Col. Webb; Berkshire Co., Mass., in 1818; wid. Sarah, BLWt.
      120–60–55.. W 5017
    Jonathan... S 10966
    Richard, Cont. (Conn.)... S 42807
    (Also given LORANCE.)
LAWSON, David, wid. Sarah, BLWt. 1906–160–55............................. W 233
    Ebenezer... S 15597
    Samuel... S 13708
LAY, Asa, wid. Sarah... W 20412
        BLWt. 1253–300, Capt., was issued July 7, 1792, to Jonas Prentice, Assigned. No papers.
    Edward, wid. Patty, BLWt. 27585–160–55................................. W 20383
    John... S 37149
LEACH, Hezekiah, Conn. & Cont.. S 49298
    James, priv. under Capt. Humphrey; New Haven Co. in 1818............... S 37606
    James, priv. under Col. Barton; Rutland Co., Vt., in 1832; wid. Sibbel.. W 24500
    Jedediah, Conn. & Cont., wid. Phebe.................................... W 20428
    Lewis.. S 38909
    (See also LEECH.)
LEAMING or LEMING, David, wid. Debby..................................... R 6223
    (Soldier was pensioned from N. Y. in 1818, as priv. under Col. Swift.)
LEASON, Jesse.. S 37608
    Job, BLWt. 1272–100.. S 37614
LEATHERS, Joseph... S 18077
LEAVENS, Hezekiah.. S 13740
    Jedediah, Conn. & Vt... S 16919
LEAVENWORTH, Edmund.. R 6232
    Eli, wid. Sarah.. BLWt. 641–400
LEBARON, Solomon, wid. Zada, BLWt. 27673–160–55.......................... W 9126
LEBRETT, Charles... S 32997
LEDYARD, Charles... S 21347
LEE, Abner, priv. in Third Conn. Reg't., Springfield, N. Y., in 1800.... BLWt. 42–100
    Abner, priv. under Col. Sherman; died in 1782, Pomfret, Conn.; Nancy Davis, former wid. of. W 16947
    Lived in Greene Co., N. Y., in 1841.
    Andrew... S 13748
    Dan, Conn. & Cont.. S 37157

LEE, David, priv. under Capt. Allen; Windham Co., Vt., in 1832 .... S 18940
    David, priv. under Capt. Betts, Col. Butler; Barkhamstead, Conn., in 1832; wid. Fanny;
      BLWt. 21816–160–55. .... W 2449
    Ebenezer .... S 42829
    Eber, BLWt. 26107–160–55 .... S 13729
    Elisha .... S 10977
    Ezra, Conn. & Cont .... S 37613
    Israel, Conn. & N. Y .... S 10981
    John, Conn. & 1812, wid. Bridget, BLWt. 6275–160–55. .... W 674
    Jonathan, wid. Mindwell, BLWt. 6454–160–55. .... W 20434
    Joseph .... S 18078
    Levi .... S 37167
    Matthew .... S 37605
    Miles, wid. Fanny .... R 6249
      (Both soldier and widow rejected.)
    Samuel, priv. under Capt. Mattox; Norwich, N. Y., in 1818 .... S 42837
    Samuel, wid. Betsey .... R 6242
      (Soldier never applied.)
    Samuel, Lieut., died in Litchfield, Conn., in 1829; wid. Eliza, BLWt. 19714–160–55 .... W 26203
    Thomas, wid. Theodocia .... W 20437
    Timothy .... S 15600
    William, priv. under Capt. Mason; Manchester, Conn., in 1832. .... S 31820
    William, Cont. (Conn.), Serg't. in Conn. Line; New Haven Co., in 1818; BLWt. 1748–100 ...... S 13735
    William H., wid. Phebe. .... W 20445
LEECH, Stephen .... R 6261
    William .... S 37616
    (See also LEACH.)
LEEDS, Abram .... S 15191
LEET, Allen, priv. under Col. Swift; Vt. in 1818; wid. Asenath .... R 6265
    Luther, wid. Sybil .... W 20467
    Miles .... R 6266
    Richard, Navy (Conn.) .... S 38908
LEMING. (See LEAMING.)
LEONARD, Asa, Conn. & Cont., wid. Olive. .... W 24518
    Benajah, wid. Mary. .... W 20436
    Patrick, Conn. & Penna. .... S 36038
    Silas, Conn. & Mass. .... S 31818
    Solomon, Conn., Cont. & Mass., wid. Sarah .... W 20466
LERAY or LEROY, John, wid. Bridget, BLWt. 27644–160–55. .... W 12104
LESTER or LESTOR, Asa .... S 16921
    Ebenezer .... S 37615
    Elihu, Conn. & Cont .... S 20041
    Jeremiah .... S 13743
    Joshua .... S 17535
    Nathan .... S 32991
LEWES or LEWIS, Abel, Serg't. under Capt. Burroughs; Danbury, Conn., in 1832. .... S 16920
    Abel, priv. & serg't. under Capt. Belcher; Rutland Co., Vt., in 1832. .... S 22358
    Abel, priv. in Conn. Line for six yrs. under Capt. Kimball; Hartford, Conn., in 1818 ...... S 37160
    Abel, Conn. Sea service. .... R 6306
    Abiah, former wid. of Reuben NICHOLS.
    Abijah .... S 37161
    Abraham .... S 29287
    Andrew, priv. under Capt. Curtis; Fairfield Co., Conn., in 1832. .... S 13724
    Andrew, priv. under Capt. Ely; Middlesex Co., Conn., in 1832. .... S 17536
    Augustus, priv. under Cols. Parsons & Ely; Haddam, Conn., in 1832 .... S 17541
    Augustus, priv. under Capt. Smith; Albany Co., N. Y., in 1832. .... S 28789
    Basil or Bazzel .... S 46230
    Benjamin, Conn. & Cont., wid. Polly, BLWt. 6291–160–55. .... W 675
    Chauncey, BLWt. 1278–100; BLWt. 13–60–55. .... S 37168
    Ebenezer, priv. Conn. Line; Oneida Co., N. Y., in 1818. (Papers withdrawn before 1870.)
    Ebenezer .... R 6310
    Ebenezer .... R 6311
    Eleazer, wid. Catharine .... W 20442
    Elijah, Conn. & Cont. .... S 13745
    Elisha, wid. Sarah .... W 24525
    Elizabeth, former wid. of Jesse CARRINGTON.
    Francis, wid. Sarah .... W 20435
    Isaac .... S 15922
    Jabez, priv. under Col. Swift; Lavonia, N. Y., in 1818 .... S 42838
    Jabez or Jabish, priv. under Col. Buell; Farmington, Conn., in 1818 .... S 37169
    Jacob, wid. Eunice. .... W 20453
    John, Conn. & Mass. .... S 10979
    Joseph, priv. under Col. Welch; Stratford, Conn., in 1832. .... S 13721
    Joseph, Conn. & Cont., priv. in Cavalry; died in 1825 in Berkahire Co., Mass.; wid. Esther. W 20455
    Justus, Cont. (Conn.), wid. Polly, BLWt. 14506–160–55. .... W 1298
    Martin .... S 28788
    Messenger .... S 31207
    Naboth, Cont. (Conn.), wid. Phebe. .... W 27810
    Nathan, Conn. & Cont .... S 13737
    Nathaniel, ensign under Col. Norton; Wolcott, Conn., in 1832. .... S 17540
    Nathaniel, disability pension in 1816; priv. Col. Pettibone .... S 20844
    Nathaniel, priv. under Col. Waterbury; N. Y., in 1832; wid. Abigail. .... W 15022
    Oliver .... S 4530
    Peter, Conn. & Cont.; Patience Peat, former wid. of. .... W 17463
    Philo, Conn. Sea service, wid. Charity. .... W 20469
    Robert, Sarah Curtis, former wid. of. .... W 20939
    Roger .... S 37611
    Ruth, former wid. of Aaron PHELPS.
    Samuel, priv. under Col. Lewis; Newton, N. J.; in 1832 .... S 1047
    Samuel, Quartermaster Serg't. in Conn. Line; Plymouth, Conn., in 1818. .... S 42839

LEWES or LEWIS, Sarah, former wid. of Stephen SEWARD.
  Seth, wid. Rhoda.. R 6327
      (Soldier never applied; said to have been major in Revolution, and member of Cincinnati.)
      Wid. applied in 1853.
  Stephen.. S 15506
  Valentine, priv. under Col. Bradley; New London Co., in 1818.............. S 37170
  Valentine, priv. under Capt. Stanton; died in 1819 in New London Co.; wid. Sally........... W 20431
  Wait... S 42858
  Walker, wid. Sarah.. R 6330
      Soldier never applied.
  William, priv. under Col. Webb; Poultney, Vt., in 1818.................... S 40926
  William, Conn. & Cont., priv. under Col. Lewis; Fairfield Co., Conn., in 1832........... S 13725
LIBERTY, Pomp... BLWt. 1761-100
  Sharp (colored), Lucy Mix, former wid. of............................... R 7286
      (Soldier never applied.)
LILLEY, LILLIE or LILLY.
  Abner, Sybil Upton, former wid. of..................................... W 15809
  Anna S., former wid. of Asa WATERMAN.
  Amariah... S 38914
  Benjamin, wid. Mary... W 20488
  Ebenezer, Conn. & Conn. Sea service, wid. Jerusha....................... W 20474
  Elijah.. S 22362
  Elisha.. S 15509
  John.. S 40092
  Jonathan.. R 6342
  Joseph.. S 42864
  Naomi, former wid. of Simeon CUMMINGS.
  Nathan, Conn. & Mass.. S 13759
  Reuben.. S 42873
LINCOLN, Elijah, Conn. & Cont... BLWt. 2077-100
  Elisha, wid. Rhuama... W 20475
  Nathan, wid. Eunice... W 20494
  Simeon, Cont. (Conn.)... S 37626
      (See also LINKON.)
LINDSEY, David.. BLWt. 854-100
      (Given also as LINDSLEY.)
  Felix... S 37627
  Solomon, wid. Lucy.. W 4266
      (Given also as LINSLEY and LINDSLEY.)
  Stephen... S 23771
LINDSLEY, LINDSLY, LINSLEY or LINSLY.
  Abiel, wid. Anna.. R 6366
      Soldier never applied.)
  Brainard.. S 13762
  Daniel, wid. Hannah... W 20486
  David. (See LINDSEY.)
  James, wid. Sarah... W 20479
  Obed, Conn. & Privateer... R 6358
  Simeon.. S 4553
  Solomon, wid. Lucy. (See LINDSEY.)
  Stephen, wid. Deborah, BLWt. 28571-160-55............................... W 677
LINES, Abel, wid. Arma.. W 12130
  Abraham, wid. Sarah... W 26214
  Benjamin.. S 13752
  Ebenezer, wid. Mercy.. W 2819
  John, priv. under Capt. Wilmot; Fairfield Co., Conn., in 1818........... S 37622
  John, private under Col. Sherman; Brookfield, Vt., in 1818; wid. Judith.............. W 26775
      (Also given as LYNDE.)
  Rufus, Conn. & Cont., wid. Tamer.. W 2820
      (See also LYNDE and LYNES.)
LINKON, John, priv. under Col. Ward; Chittenden Co., Vt., in 1832; wid. Weightstill......... W 24555
  Nathaniel... S 17546
  Samuel.. S 40941
      (See also LINCOLN.)
LINN, James, Conn. & Vt., wid. Abigail................................. R 6361
      (Soldier never applied.)
      (See also LYNN.)
LINUS, Robert... S 13750
LISCOMB, Darius, wid. Sarah, BLWt. 26607-160-55........................ W 774
  Nehemiah.. S 18942
  Thomas.. S 18943
LITCHFIELD, Eleazer... S 13753
  James, wid. Lucretia, BLWt. 48-100...................................... W 16329
LITTEL, Ebenezer.. S
  Hannah, wid. of this soldier was pensioned as the former wid. of Jonathan BADGELEY, N.J. W 8047
LITTLE, James, wid. Rosetta, BLWt. 49049-160-55........................ S 8256
  John, wid. Sarah.. W 26216
  Nancy, former wid. of Nathaniel ABBE.
  Samuel.. R 6386
  William... S 37179
LIVINGSTON, Isaac... S 37625
LOBDELL, Josiah... S 17552
LOCHARY, William. (See LAUGHREY.)
LOCKWOOD, Betsey, dau. of Joseph & Sarah MATHER.
  Charles, wid. Betsey or Elizabeth....................................... W 26225
  David, priv. under Capt. Granger; Stamford, Conn., in 1832.............. S 16453
  David, priv. under Col. Bradley; pensioned as David 2d in Stamford, Conn., in 1818........ S 37642
  David, priv. under Capt. Brown, Col. Waterbury; d. in 1825, in Fairfield Co., Conn.; wid.
      Hannah.. W 20491
  David, Cont. (Conn.) priv. under Col. Lamb; New Milford, Conn., in 1818; died in 1847 in
      Litchfield Co.; wid. Sarah.. W 26223

94

LOCKWOOD, Drake.. S 17548
    Ebenezer, wid. Ann, BLWt. 34926-160-55... W 8262
    Enos, wid. Sarah... W 20499
    George.. R 6403
    Gideon, wid. Lydia.. R 21786
      (Soldier never applied.)
    Henry... S 23302
    Isaac, priv. under Capt. Bell; Stamford, Conn., in 1832... S 17553
    Isaac, priv. under Capt. Billings, Col. Swift; Brookfield, Conn., in 1832; and died there in
      1838; wid. Ann.. W 20500
    James, priv. of infantry, and serg't. of cavalry; New Canaan, Conn., in 1832..................... S 17554
    James, wid. Anna.. R 6402
      (Soldier never applied.)
    Jared, Conn. & Cont., wid. Betsey or Elizabeth.. W 16639
    John, Eunice Joliff, former wid. of.. W 26166
    Lambert, wid. Elizabeth... W 20514
    Messenger, wid. Sarah... W 8062
    Nathan, wid. Mary, BLWt. 26141-160-55.. W 776
    Noah.. S 13778
    Reuben.. R 6405
    Reuben, wid. Mary.. W 21856
    William, wid. Jemima... W 20521
LODER, Jacob... S 31825
LOMBARD, Justin, wid. Elizabeth, BLWt. 26002-160-55.. W 2556
    Solomon... S 13769
LONG, Levi, wid. Martha, BLWt. 1965-160-55.. W 2138
    Stephen... S 22370
    William, Conn. Sea service & Mass., BLWt. 26296-160-55... S 29967
LONGWELL, Stephen, wid. Jane.. W 4268
LOOMIS LOOMISS or LUMIS.
    Abner, wid. Zilpha.. W 13637
    Amasa, Cont. (Conn.), wid. Ruth... W 24595
    Asa... S 4568
    Benjamin.. R 6441
    Benjamin, Cont. (Conn.), wid. Chloe... W 20511
    Dan., wid. Sarah.. S 20520
    Daniel.. R 6442
    Eleazer, wid. Mary.. W 15035
    Elijah, wid. Rachel... W 26221
    Epaphras.. S 13791
    Ezra.. S 23772
    Gamaliel.. R 6444
    George, wid. Deborah, BLWt. 26830-160-55.. W 3701
    Hannah, former wid. of Charles WEBSTER.
    Hezekiah, wid. Else... W 15042
    Isaiah, wid. Sarah, BWLt. 33745-160-55.. W 8054
    Israel, priv. under Col. Chapman; Coventry, Conn., in 1832....................................... S 23777
    Israel, Conn. & Cont., priv. under Col. Crane; Chataqua Co., N. Y., in 1818; wid. Hannah.. W 9141
    Jacob, priv. under Col. Durkee; Windham Co., Conn., in 1820...................................... S 46203
    Jacob, Hampden, Mass., in 1832; wid. Thankful.. W 15037
    Jerome, Conn., N. H. & Vt., wid. Elizabeth, BLWt. 17727-160-55.................................. W 1627
    John, priv. under Col. Israel Loomis; Lebanon, Conn., in 1832; wid. Mary; BLWt. 26892-
      160-55.. W 775
    John, Conn. & Mass., priv. under Col. Woodbridge; Erie Co., Penna., in 1832..................... S 23774
  X Joseph, Cont. (Conn.)... S 18947
      BLWt. 61312-100 was issued in 1790. No papers.
      BLWt. 76-60-55.
    Lebbeus or Libbeus, Conn. & Cont... S 28796
      BLWt. 1256-200, Lieut., was issued April 20, 1790. No papers.
    Martin.. R 6446
    Oliver, priv. under Col. Hoyt; Rutland Co., Vt., in 1832... S 13770
    Oliver, Conn. & Cont.. S 13781
      (Also given LUMIS.)
    Roswell... S 23775
    Samuel, wid. Betsey... W 20527
    Simon, priv. under Col. Ward; Tompkins Co., N. Y., in 1832, d. in 1842; wid. Molly........... W 20518
    Simon, Conn. & Cont., Corp. under Col. Ely; Hebron, Conn., in 1832.............................. S 17550
    Simon, Cont. (Conn.), priv. under Col. Sheldon; German Flats, N. Y., in 1818; wid. Martha... W 15925
    Thaddeus.. R 6447
    Thomas, Conn. & Cont.. S -17551
LORANCE. (See LAWRENCE.)
LORD, Abner.. S 37645
    Amey, former wid. of Edward MEAD.
    Asa, BLWt. 26412-160-55... S 29298
    Daniel, wid. Anna, BLWt. 537-160-55... W 26222
    David, wid. Hannah.. R 6452
      (Soldier never applied.)
    Elijah.. S 37188
    Eliphalet... S 42890
    Frederick... S 15599
    James, BLWt. 1257-200, Lieut., was issued April 23, 1800, to Damaris Lester and others. No
      papers.
    Jeremiah, priv. under Col. Webb; Saybrook, Conn., in 1818.. S 37644
    Jeremiah, priv. under Capt. Hezekiah Parsons as Jeremiah Jr.; died in 1812; wid. Tryphena.. W 20513
    John.. S 15510
    Joseph, priv. under Capt. Wolcott; East Windsor, Conn., in 1832.................................. S 18094
    Joseph, priv. under Col. Ely; Chenango Co., N. Y., in 1832; wid. Caroline; BLWt. 17872-160-55. W 20517
    Mercy, former wid. of Jonathan WHALEY.

LORD, Samuel, wid. **Mary**, BLWt. 15198-160-55... W 24572
    Theophilus.. S 37187
    Timothy.. S 42898
    William, priv. under Capt. Wadsworth; Oswego Co., N. Y., in 1832; died in 1849; wid. Anna.. W 20509
    William, wid. Chloe.. W 20501
        BLWt. 1255-200, Lieut., was issued Jan. 29, 1793, to Jonas Prentice, Assignee. No papers.
LOUDEN or LOWDEN or LOUDON, William, wid. Eunice............................. W 4270
LOUNDSBERRY, LOUNDSBURY, LOUNSBERRY or LOWNSBURY or LOUNSBURY.
    David.. S 33005
    Jacob.. R 6464
    Jarius or Jarlas, wid. Amelia... W 20495
    Linus, wid. Prudence... W 20492
    Nathan Munn, Conn. & Cont., wid. Sarah W., BLWt. 510-160-55......................... W 10204
    William... R 6465
LOVEJOY, John, wid. Anna... R 6471
    (Soldier never applied.)
    Nathan, Conn. & N. Y.. S 42885
LOVELAND, Abner.. S 45876
    Amos, wid. Jemima... W 8090
    Charles, wid. Mary.. W 9146
        BLWt. 1194-100; BLWt. 294-60-55.
    Daniel, wid. Mehitabel... W 20528
    Isaac, wid. Judah... W 8059
    James, wid. Mary... W 20496
    John.. S 13776
    Levi, wid. Esther... W 9145
    Nathan... S 42887
    Trueman, Navy service, Conn. residence... S 37189
LOVELL, Joshua.. R 6477
LOVERIDGE, William, wid. Lucinda, BLWt. 38841-160-55................................. R 6479
LOVETT, Joseph or Josephus, wid. Elizabeth.. W 21584
    Samuel... S 40099
LOWDEN. (See LOUDON.)
LOWNDSBURY or LOWNSBURY. (See LOUNDSBURY.)
LOWREY, James.. R 6494
LOYD, Samuel, Conn. & Cont.. S 13788
LUCAS, Amaziah... S 13798
    Ichabod.. S 44203
    Israel, Conn. & N. Y., wid. Mabel, BLWt. 56943-160-55............................... W 10205
    Samuel, wid. Abigail, BLWt. 1539-100.. R 6502
    (Soldier never applied for pension.)
    Thomas, wid. Abigail... W 26227
    William... S 28798
LUCE, Jonathan, wid. Parnel.. W 20544
    Lucy, former wid. of David McCLURE.
    Luke.. S 31827
    Nathaniel, wid. Hannah... W 26226
    Timothy.. S 37646
    Uriah... S 13802
LUCUS. (See LUCAS.)
LUDDINGTON or LUDINGTON, or LUDENTON.
    Eliphalet... S 31828
    Jesse... S 18098
    Lemuel... S 41785
    Stephen, wid. Betsey, BLWt. 26651-160-55.. W 1628
    William... S 22885
LUMIS. (See LOOMIS.)
LUNG, Joseph.. S 42902
LUTHER, Cromwell... S 42903
    Elisha,Conn.&Cont., wid.Lucy,BLWt.24903-160-55.................................... W 12164
    Ellis, Cont. (Conn.).. S 30555
    Levi, Conn. & Cont... S 11009
    Martin, Conn. & Cont... S 42900
LYMAN, Asa, Conn. & Conn. Sea service, wid. Mary..................................... W 26228
    Dan, wid. Hannah, BLWt. 24921-160-55... W 1792
    Elisha, wid. Abigail, BLWt. 17712-160-55.. S 8267
    Ezekiel, Conn. & Cont., wid. Mabel.. W 12169
    Francis... S 16456
    John, priv. under Col. Enos; Chittenden Co., Vt., in 1832.............................. S 13809
    John, priv. under Col. Butler; Pembroke, N. Y., in 1818............................... S 42904
    Jonathan, wid. Sarah... R 6545
    (Soldier never applied.)
    Richard, priv. under Col. Huntington; Salisbury, N. H., in 1818; died in 1838, at Washington
      Co., Vt., wid. Mehitable... W 2808
    Richard, priv. under Col. Starr; died in 1802 in Orange Co., Vt.; wid. Philomela........... W 24616
    Samuel... S 11012
    Simeon, wid. Joannah.. W 20548
LYNDE, Cornelius, Conn. Green Mt. Boys & Mass., wid. Rebecca........................ W 20489
    (See also LINES and LYNES.)
LYNE or LYNES, David... S 11013
    John. (See LINES.)
LYNN, David... S 32388
    John, Conn. & Cont.. S 11011
    Sarah, former wid. of John TURNER.
    William... BLWt. 1763-200
    (See also LINN.)
LYON, Asa... BLWt. 1869-200
    Ebenezer, wid. Chloe... W 24615
    Ephraim, Hannah Bradford, former wid. of.. W 17366
    Gideon... R 6555

LYON, Hezekiah .... R 6557
  Jesse. (See Jose.)
    Job .... S 17557
    Josse or Jesse, Lois Morris, former wid. of .... W 26273
    Joseph .... S 22306
    Joshua .... S 13811
    Nathan .... S 13816
    Nehemiah Web, BLWt. 26052-160-55 .... S 15928
    Noah, wid. Mary .... W 16640
    Stephen, wid. Abigail .... W 20547
    Thomas, wid. Eunice .... W 12172
    William, wid. Sarah .... W 21597
LYPORT, Jacob .... S 13813

M.

MAAR. (See MEARA.)
McCALL, John, wid. Loruhamah .... R 6599
  (Neither soldier nor widow applied.)
    (Also given CALL.)
McCARTY, Clark, wid. Mabel .... W 20248
  (Also given CARTY.)
    Daniel .... R 6612
McCLELLAN, Samuel, wid. Nancy .... W 2224
McCLURE, David, Lucy Luce, former wid. of .... W 12166
McCOY, Ephraim, wid. Sarah .... W 4024
    John, wid. Betsey, BLWt. 19731-160-55 .... W 2407
McCRACKIN, Philip, wid. Mary .... R 6666
  (Soldier never applied.)
McCUFF, Pomp .... S 36084
McCULLOUGH, Robert .... S 41833
McDONALD, Charles .... S 42963
    James, Abigail Russell, former wid. of .... R 9095
  (Neither soldier not widow applied.)
    James, Conn. & N. Y .... S 13902
    William, Conn., Md. & Privateer & Navy (1813) .... S 34978
McEWEN, John .... S 11056
  (Also given as CUNE.)
McFARLAND, Anna, former wid. of Asahel CHITTENDEN.
McGRAGORY or McGREGORY. (See MEGREGORY.)
McGREGOR, John, Conn. & Cont .... S 38937
  BLWt. 1377-300, Capt., was issued Feb. 20, 1800; certified July 17, 1815. No papers.
McGUIRE, Peter, wid. Ruth .... R 6830
  Also given as MAGIRA or MAGUIRA.
    (Under name of MAGUIRA, Peter was pensioned in 1818 at Chelsea Landing, Conn., as
      private under Col. Sherman, Conn. Line; died in 1827.)
McINTOSH, Timothy .... S 42936
McINTYRE or McINTIRE, Henry, wid. Jane Ann, BLWt. 1880-100 .... W 25684
MACK, Abner, wid. Anne or Anna .... W 16641
    Andrew .... S 17569
    Benjamin .... S 40958
    David .... S 40967
    Gurdon .... S 23782
    Hezekiah .... S 13843
    Jeremiah .... S 42923
    Joel, wid. Susanna .... W 20234
    Josiah, wid. Mary .... W 17103
    Nehemiah, wid. Caroline .... R 6572
  (Soldier never applied.)
    Ralph .... S 29313
    Richard, wid. Betty, BLWt. 1447-100 .... W 9910
    Zebulon, wid. Mary .... W 15691
McKEE, or MACKEE, Andrew, Conn. & Cont., wid. Diantha; BLWt. 38536-160-55 .... S 5364
    Robert, wid. Elizabeth .... W 20250
McKINLEY, John, Cont. (Conn. or N. H.), wid. Sarah .... W 16644
McKINSTERY or McKINSTRY, Paul .... S 42952
McKINZEY or McKINSEY, George, wid. Anna, BLWt. 1418-100 .... W 2226
McKNIGHT, Thomas .... S 15500
McLEAN, Jacob .... S 40903
    James .... S 31854
    John .... BLWt. 1942-100
McMANNERS, John, wid. Lucy, BLWt. 3963-160-55 .... W 306
McMURPHY, Rachel, former wid. of Benjamin COLE.
McNARY, or McNEARY, Martin .... S 42953
McNIEL, Henry, wid. Nancy .... W 2143
McNULTY, John .... S 28594
McQUEEN, William, Conn. & Conn. Sea service, Tryphena Palmer, former wid. of ...... W 17424
MAHAR. (See MEARA.)
MAIN or MAINE, David .... S 16937
    Ezekiel .... S 22893
    Henry, Hannah Wells, former wid. of .... W 22567
    Peres .... S 2720
    Rufus, Conn. & R. I .... S 17561
    Stephen .... S 13865
    William, Conn. & R. I., BLWt. 8021-160-55 .... S 9392
MAKER. (See MEEKER.)
MALARY. (See MALLERY.)
MALETT. (See MALLETT.)
MALLBIE, Benjamin .... S 2752
  (See also MALTBIE.)

MALLERY, MALLORY, MALARY, MALORY.

Aaron, wid. Huldah, BLWt. 26459–160–55.. W 305
Asa, Conn. & Conn. Sea service... S 15515
Benajah.. S 15930
Dan, wid. Alice, BLWt. 57646–160–55.. W 25678
David, Conn. & Conn. Sea service... R 6841
David.. R 6840
David, Cont. (Conn.), wid. Susannah, BLWt. 26375–160–55........................ W 4274
Gideon.. S 5727
Jacob, wid. Sarah, BLWt. 26623–160–55.. W 555
James, wid. Nancy.. W 18477
Lemuel, wid. Rebecca... W 6785
Levi, Cont. service but Conn. residence... R 6847
Nathaniel, Serg't. 3rd Conn. regiment; Erie Co., Penna., in 1828; wid. Sarah... W 2650
    BLWt. 1389–100 & BLWt. 126–60–55.
      (Also given MALLONY.)
Samuel.. R 6848
Samuel.. S 23312
Simeon.. R 6843
Truman, wid. Olive.. W 2824
MALLESON or MALLISON, Benjamin.. S 37209
Ezra.. S 19731
Roswell. (See MATTISON.)
MALLETT, MALET or MALLET, John... S 16936
Lewis, wid. Anne.. W 21760
    (Also given as MULLETT.)
Miles.. S 17560
MALLONY. (See MALLERY, Nathaniel.)
MALONE. (See MELONEY.)
MALORY. (See MALLERY.)
MALTBIE or MALTBY, Zacheus or Zaccheus, wid. Jerusha........................ W 27448
   (Soldier and widow died, and children received the pension alleged to be due.)
     (See also MALLBIE.)
MANLEY, Lucy, former wid. of John HITCHCOCK.
MANN, Andrew... S 16934
Elisha, Conn., Cont. & N. J., wid. Sarah.. W 4544
Jabez, wid. Ruhamah.. W 4540
Joseph.. S 16932
MANNING, Andrew... S 16935
Cyrus, wid. Mary.. W 17082
Dan, wid. Lydia... W 17099
Diah or Dyer, wid. Anna.. W 25673
Increase... S 13880
Joseph.. S 15518
Luther, wid. Sarah.. W 3573
Nathaniel, wid. Matilda.. W 19864
Rockwell, wid. Sarah.. W 25670
Samuel.. BLWt. 1050–100
Seabury.. S 13866
Thomas.. S 2742
William, priv. under Col. Webb; N. Y. in 1818, transferred to Vt................ S 40980
William, Serg't. under Col. Starr; Franklin Co., Ohio, in 1818................... S 41814
William.. R—
MANROSE. (See MONROSE.)
MANROW, Joseph, Conn. & N. Y.. S 11024
Noah... R 6881
MANSFIELD, Charles, BLWt. 43–100.. S 44539
Ebenezer, Cont. (Conn.), wid. Polly... W 18484
Hannah, former wid. of John DODD.
John... S 37217
    BLWt. 1382–200, Lieut., was issued May 17, 1790. No papers.
Jonathan, Conn. & Mass., wid. Martha.. W 18471
Joseph (Capt.).. S 37216
Joseph.. R 6883
Nathan, wid. Anna.. W 20240
Richard... S 37210
MANVIL or MANVILLE, David.. R 6888
Simeon.. R 6889
MAPLES, Joshua... S 13859
Josiah.. S 11014
William.. S 29317
MARBLE, Thomas.. R 6896
MARCHANT, Gurdon, Cont. (Conn.), wid. Hannah................................... W 20239
    (Given also as MERCHANT.)
Joel, wid. Molly, BLWt. 26724–160–55.. W 9928
John, Conn. & Cont., wid. Tabitha.. W 17088
Joseph, wid. Mary, BLWt. 29040–160–55.. W 25679
    (See also MERCHANT.)
MARCY, Alfred... S 13869
Alvan.. S 13860
MARK or MARKS, Joseph. (See claim of Silas BAILEY, R. I., R 390.)
MARKHAM, Dan... R 6904
Hannah, former wid. of Timothy ROGERS.
Isaac, wid. Cynthia... W 17073
Jeremiah.. S 20860
John... S 11034
Joseph.. S 44538
Nathaniel, wid. Hannah... R 6905
    (Soldier was priv. under Col. Wyllys; Chatham, Conn., in 1818.)

MARSH, Allen or Allyn, wid. Mabel... W 26245
  Ashbel.. R 6915
  David... R 6917
    (Also given as MASH.)
  Edmund... S 11019
  Jasper, Conn. & Mass... S 42912
  Job, wid. Salome... W 17096
  John, priv. under Col. Swift; Barkhamstead, Conn., in 1832..................................... S 11036
  John, priv. under Col. Talcott; Wethersfield, Conn., in 1832.................................. S 31836
  John L.. S 23309
  Roswell, wid. Huldah, BLWt. 6279–160–55... W 4273
  Silas, wid. Mary, BLWt. 26582–160–55.. W 1977
MARSHALL, Eliakim, wid. Anna.. W 17095
  Elijah... S 36053
  Elisha, wid. Mary.. W 17109
  Joel... R 6931
  Joseph, Conn. & R. I... S 13819
  Perez, wid. Dolly.. W 19857
  Preserved, wid. Ruth, BLWt. 34977–160–55.. W 2313
  Samuel B... S 36069
  Sylvanus... S 3853
  Thomas, Cont. (Conn.), wid. Freelove.. W 25734
MARTENUS, Goddard.. S 36062
MARTIN or MARTEN, Amasa, priv. under Col. Wyllys; Windham Co., Conn., in 1832.................. S 18494
  Amasa, Conn. & N. Y., priv. under Col. Wells; Rensselaer Co., N. Y. in 1832; wid. Sarah;
    BLWt. 14964–160–55... W 1630
  Andrew... S 18101
  Asa.. S 13858
  Ashbel... S 18499
  Charles, Conn., Privateer & R. I.; wid. Mary; BLWt. 26175–160–55.............................. W 1778
  David.. S 22382
  George... S 41794
  Isaac.. S 16186
  John... S 42910
  Joseph, priv. under Col. Hosford; Winfield, N. Y., in 1832.................................... S 13863
  Joseph, priv. under Col. A. Ward; Windham Co., Conn., in 1818................................. S 36061
  Joseph, priv. under Col. Coe; St. Lawrence Co., N. Y., in 1832; wid. Anna.................... W 17101
  Joseph, priv. under Col. Wyllys; died in 1829 in Wyoming Co., N. Y.; widow only pensioned;
    wid. Lovina.. W 20241
  Joseph, Cont. (Conn.), priv. under Col. Hazen; died in 1834 in Clinton Co., N. Y.; wid. May A. W 27971
    (Also known as POLLAND.)
  Joseph P., Conn. & Cont., wid. Lucy... W 1629
    BLWt. 13410–100 was issued April 20, 1797, & BLWt. 209–60–55.
  Joshua, wid. Elizabeth, BLWt. 6255–160–55.. W 18464
  Luther... S 42932
  Nathan, wid. Martha.. W 26239
  Nathaniel Ford, wid. Naomi, BLWt. 6028–160–55... W 2142
  Reuben, wid. Sally, BLWt. 21838–160–55... W 1906
  Samuel... S 22383
  Stephen, wid. Bethiah... W 16337
  Thomas... S 2730
MARVIN, Abraham, wid. Mary.. R 6985
    (Soldier never applied.)
  Benjamin, wid. Urania Pamela, BLWt. 26207–160–55... W 6786
  David.. S 15520
  David.. R 6984
  John C., Navy (Conn.), wid. Clarissa, BLWt. 26026–160–55..................................... W 18480
  Jonathan... S 15601
  Joseph... S 15516
  Matthew... BLWt. 1061–100
  Nathan, Rebecca Baker, former wid. of.. W 18558
  Ozias, wid. Althea, BLWt. 29054–160–55... W 1885
  Samuel, Conn. & N. Y... R 6986
MASH. (See MARSH.)
MASON, Ashbel, BLWt. 2251–100... S 42916
  Betsey, former wid. of Nathaniel HOVEY.
  Elisha, Cont. (Conn.), BLWt. 7202–160–55... S 13882
  Elnathan, wid. Mary.. W 15842
  Henry, wid. Anna... W 17097
  Isaac, wid. Sarah... W 17084
  James.. S 42919
  Jonathan, Conn., Cont., N. H. & Navy; wid. Deborah... W 21773
  Joseph... S 36079
  Luther, wid. Hepsibah or Hephsibeth.. W 9172
  Robert... R 7000
MASTERS, James, wid. Esther.. W 23907
MATHER, Eleazer.. S 2744
  Elihu, Polly Grosvenor or Grovenor, former wid. of.. R 4360
    (Soldier was pensioned in Madison Co., Ill., in 1831 for services as priv. under Col. Webb.)
  Increase... S 31831
  John, wid. Hepzibah... W 25674
  Joseph, priv. & Serg't. under Capt. Bray; Berlin, Conn., in 1832............................ S 15929
  Joseph, wid. Sarah.. W 29696
    (Soldier was priv., Serg't. & Ensign; Darien, Conn., in 1832. Betsey Lockwood, daughter,
      was pensioned by Special Act of Congress in August, 1888.)
  Joseph, Conn. & Navy; priv. under Col. Wolcott; Chenango Co., N. Y., in 1832................ S 13878
  Nathaniel.. S 13872
  Reuben... S 29306

99

MATHER, Samuel, Capt. & Surgeon in Conn. Militia; Lyme, Conn., in 1832................. S 33
    Samuel, priv. under Capt. Hooker; Hartford, Conn., in 1832....................... S 13871
    Samuel, priv. under Capt. Bell; Fairfield Co., Conn., in 1832.................... S 17568
    Silvanus or Sylvanus, wid. Caroline... W 21774
    Stephen, wid. Elizabeth.. W 16344
    Timothy.. BLWt. 1711-400
MATHEWS. (See MATTHEWS.)
MATHEWSON, Elisha, wid. Elizabeth... W 3437
MATSON, John... S 18963
MATTESON or MATTISON, David... S 40129
    Hezekiah, wid. Elizabeth... W 17090
    Roswell, wid. Elizabeth.. W 9913
    (Also given as MALLISON.)
    William, BLWt. 3990-160-55... S 9395
MATTHEWS or MATHEWS, Amos V., wid. Delila, BLWt. 75006-160-55...................... W 9537
    Gideon... R 7019
    James, Conn. Sea service, wid. Desire.. W 23909
    Jesse... S 36075
    John, Cont. (Conn.), BLWt. 321-100... S 36077
    Moses... S 17558
    Thomas.. S 13857
    William... S 33031
MAULEY. (See MORLEY.)
MAXAM, Adonijah, wid. Catherine.. W 5345
    Rejected BL.
MAXFIELD, Edward, wid. Mary.. W 17070
MAXON, Silas... S 11028
MAY, Joseph, wid. Rebecca.. W 21745
    Stephen... S 40976
    Thomas.. S 40969
MAYHEW, Elisha, Cont. (Conn.), wid. Eunice... W 8421
MAYNARD, Christopher, wid. Lucretia; also given MINARD.
    Ebenezer.. S 13874
    Jabez... S 36072
    James... S 17567
    John.. S 13829
    Lebbeus ori Libbeus... S 13821
    Zebediah, wid. Anna; also given MINARD.
    (See also MINARD and MYNARD.)
MAYO, Isaac, Conn. & Mass., wid. Hannah.. W 23900
MEACH. (See MEECH.)
MEACHAM or MEACHAM, Elijah, wid. Frances, BLWt. 518-160-55......................... W 2318
    Jeremiah, wid. Chloe (Conn. & Cont.)... W 23963
    (See also MEECHUM.)
MEAD or MEADE, Abraham, Captain, papers in case of WALL, John.
    Andrew, wid. Annah.. W 25700
    Calvin, Conn. & N. Y.. S 17580
    David, Conn. & N. Y., wid. Sarah.. W 19875
    Ebenezer, Conn. & N. Y.. S 13919
    Edward, Serg't.; died in Fairfield Co. Conn., in 1797; wid. Mary.............. W 25694
    Edward, Amy Lord, former wid. of.. R 6450
    (Soldier never applied; died 1820.)
    Eli... R 7073
    Enos, wid. Prudence... W 19874
    Israel.. S 13907
    Jasper.. R 7076
    Jasper, wid. Elizabeth.. W 9956
    Jeremiah.. S 36119
    John, wid. Elizabeth.. W 19872
    Joseph.. S 11066
    Jotham.. S 22903
    Levi, wid. Abigail.. W 9958
    Peter... S 15938
    Reuben.. S 16188
    Samuel, Conn. & Cont., wid. Lois.. W 17134
    Smith... S 22904
    Thaddeus.. S 17584
    Thomas, wid. Ellen, BLWt. 26458-160-55.. W 9952
    Uriah, wid. Betty, BLWt. 1775-100... W 1305
    Zaccheus, wid. Deborah.. W 25699
    (See also MEEDS.)
MEAKER. (See MEEKER.)
MEARA, MAAR or MAHAR, Patrick.. BLWt. 269-100
MEDCALF. (See METCALF.)
MEECH or MEACH, Elisha, Conn. & Mass., wid. Desire................................. W 23950
    Jacob, Conn., Privateer & R. I.. S 15524
    Thomas.. BLWt. 1712-100
MEECHUM, Philip.. S 21372
    (See also MEACHUM.)
MEEDS, Cato.. S 41866
MEEKER or MEAKER, Ephraim, wid. Comfort.. W 16643
    (Also given as MEAKER.)
    Ichabod, Conn. & N. Y... S 13912
    Joseph.. S 15517
    (Also given as MAKER.)
MEGREGORY, MAGREGORY, McGRAGORY or McGREGORY.
    Joel, BLWt. 6004-160-55... S 45009
    John, Conn. & Cont.. S 11027

MEIGS, Abel, wid. Deborah, BLWt. 9406-160-55... W 2410
    Abner, Conn. & N. H.. R 7102
    John, Conn. & Cont., wid. Elizabeth.. W 20255
      BLWt. 1383-200, Lieut., was issued Nov. 19, 1789. No papers.
    Nathan, wid. Mabel... W 17126
    Phineas or Phinehas.. S 42965
      Return Jonathan, BLWt. 1376-500, Colonel, was issued May 20, 1791. No papers.
    Simeon.. BLWt. 44-100
    Stephen.. S 36122
MELONEY, John, Cont. (Conn.), wid. Betsey... W 6820
    (Soldier also served in 1812.)
    (Also given as MALONE.)
MELROSS, William, wid. Cynthia... R 7111
    (Soldier never applied.)
MENTER or MENTOR, Naomi, former wid. of Nathaniel WILLIAMS.
    Thomas.. S 42973
MERCHANT, Gurdon. (See MARCHANT.)
    Thomas.. S 36126
    (See also MARCHANT.)
MERICK. (See MERRICK.)
MERIFIELD. (See MERRIFIELD.)
MERRELL. (See MERRILL.)
MERRIAM or MERRIAN, Aaron.. R 7122
    Amasa... S 23317
    Asaph... S 13911
    (Also given as MERRIMAN.)
    Christopher.. S 16959
    Ephraim... S 36121
    Ichabod, wid. Desire... W 15787
    Marshall.. S 2818
MERRICK or MERICK, Loly, former wid. of Reuben CARRINGTON.
    Luther.. S 31859
MERRIFIELD or MERIFIELD, Ithamar.. S 29324
MERRIL, MERRILL, MERRILS, MERRELL or MERRELLS.
    Aaron, priv. under Col. Swift; Ontario Co., N. Y., in 1818................................. S 42971
    Aaron, Conn. & Cont., priv. under Col. Webb; Litchfield Co., Conn., in 1818.............. S 36698
    Ashbel, Abigail Eaton, former wid. of... W 16970
    Daniel, Mercy Wilcox, former wid. of... W 18451
    Ephah... R 7134
    Ichabod, wid. Sarah.. W 17130
    James, Jane Dunmore, former wid. of... W 10769
    Jephtha... S 11059
    Jonathan.. S 23796
    Mead or Medad, BLWt. 665-100.. S 42969
    Nathaniel... S 36115
      BLWt. 6141-100, Private, was issued October 7, 1789, to Benjamin Tallmadge. No papers.
    Noah.. S 5759
    Noah, wid. Zulina... W 23964
    Phinehas, wid. Anna, BLWt. 3798-100-55.. W 18509
    Reuben.. S 34998
    Roger, Conn. & Cont... S 23318
    Samuel, wid. Artemetia.. W 20254
    Solomon, wid. Jerusha... R 7127
    Thomas.. R 7133
    William... S 11064
MERRIMAN, Asaph. (See MERRIAM.)
    Charles, wid. Anna.. W 18507
    Elisha, wid. Chloe... R 7135
    (Soldier died in 1814 in Wallingford, Conn. Never applied for a pension.)
    George, priv. under Col. Sheldon; Clinton Co., N. Y, in 1832.............................. S 13913
    George, priv. under Cols. Ward, Douglas & Enos; Wallingford, Conn., in 1832; wid. Catharine. W 17129
    Israel... S 11067
    (Also given as MERRIMON.)
    Josiah, Cont. (Conn.), wid. Lydia.. W 16647
    Marcus, Conn. & Privateer... S 13921
    Moses, wid. Lois.. W 18508
MERRIMON. (See MERRIMAN.)
MERRITT, Ebenezer, wid. Hannah... W 17127
    Reuben, wid. Mary... R 7139
    (Soldier never applied.)
MERRY, Cornelius... S 16479
MERWIN, Andrew, wid. Rhoda... W 6819
    Nathan, wid. Mary... W 4282
MESSENGER, Abner... S 9022
    Lemuel, wid. Abigail... W 9957
    Reuben.. S 36118
METCALF or MEDCALF, Dan, wid. Jedidah... W 3281
    Ebenezer, priv. under Col. Hosford; New London Co. in 1832.............................. S 18125
    Ebenezer, wid. Silence.. W 17128
    (Also given as MEDCALF.)
    Luke, wid. Nabby, BLWt. 520-160-55... W 25702
    Samuel.. S 16189
MEYERS. (See MYERS.)
MIDDILTOWN. (See MIDDLETOWN.)
MIDDLEBROOK, John, wid. Abigail.. W 804
    Oliver, Navy (Conn.)... R 7159
MIDDLETOWN, Peter, BLWt. 31-100... S 36140
    (Also given as MIDDILTOWN.)

MIEL, Charles.. S 28812
MIGATE. (See MYGATT.)
MILEHAM, William.. S 41878
MILES, Caleb... S 40157
  Daniel.. S 16962
  Isaac, wid. Martha, BLWt. 26500-160-55........................ W 19879
    (Soldier served under Col. Canfield as substitute for his father, Stephen Miles; Steuben
      Co., N. Y., in 1832.)
  Isaac, died in 1816 in Cortland Co., N. Y.; Serg't. under Col. Swift; never applied for pension;
    wid. Mary... W 9566
  Jesse... R 7167
  John, Cont. service, but Conn. residence...................... S 36128
    BLWt. 1402-200, Capt.-Lieut., was issued Oct. 23, 1790. No papers.
  Lucinda, former wid. of Darius HICKOK.
  Samuel, Conn. & Conn. Sea service............................. S 15526
  Simon or Timon, wid. Mercy.................................... W 17141
MILLAR. (See MILLER.)
MILLARD, Joseph, wid. Hannah.................................... W 25705
  Leavitt or Levitt, Cont. (Conn.).............................. S 13935
  London.. S 13926
  Sarah, former wid. of John WHITE.
MILLER or MILLAR, Abner, wid. Ruth............................. W 20259
  Benjamin.. S 36146
  Caleb, Conn. & Cont... S 18976
  Charles, Conn. & Cont... S 36132
    BLWt. 1381-200, Lieut., was issued June 3, 1791, to Isaac Bronson, Assignee. No papers.
  Daniel.. R 7181
  David B., wid. Adah... W 16651
  Ebenezer, wid. Sarah.. W 13006
  Edward.. S 13942
  Elizabeth, former wid. of Amasa LADD.
  John, Conn. & Privateer, born in 1756 in Lyme, Conn........... R 7209
  John, Cont. service, but Conn. residence of heir in 1830...... BLWt. 1621-100
  John Christine, wid. Roxalana................................. W 25708
  Jonathan, priv. under Col. Wyllys; Detroit, Mich., in 1829.... S 20477
  Jonathan, priv. under Col. Wyllys; died in Nov., 1811, in Vt.; Anner Bissell, former wid. of . W 23605
    Anner's other husband was also a pensioner. (See BISSELL, Ozias, Conn., S 37764.)
  Laura, former wid. of John REDINGTON.
  Martha, former wid. of Henry KEELER.
  Rebecca, former wid. of Joshua MINOR.
  Roswel or Roswell, wid. Betsey G., BLWt. 26613-160-55......... W 5375
  Sarah, former wid. of William BLAKE.
  William... S 23324
MILLETT, Andrew Jonathan.. R 7233
MILLINGTON, Samuel, wid. Christina............................. W 17145
MILLS, Aaron, Conn. & Mass..................................... S 13927
  Alexander... S 36147
  Amasa, Conn. & Cont... S 36148
  Ann, former wid. of Benjamin DYER.
  Constantine, wid. Philecta or Philcta......................... W 2151
  Elias... S 22399
  Elijah, wid. Huldah, BLWt. 9205-160-55........................ W 17147
  Gabriel... S 36131
  George.. S 43002
  Jedediah, wid. Sarah.. R 7249
  John, priv. under Col. Webb; New London Co. in 1818.......... S 36139
  John, priv. under Col. Webb; Tolland Co., Conn., in 1818..... S 36158
  John, priv. under Col. Webb; Suffolk Co., N. Y., in 1818..... S 42978
  Joseph.. S 36151
    Ann Beers, wid. of above soldier, was pensioned as former wid. of her first husband,
      PHILLIPS, Thomas, Conn., W 25233.
  Kanah... R 7246
  Samuel.. S 28107
  Samuel F., BLWt. 26016-160-55................................. S 13938
  Stephen... S 16201
MINARD, Amos... S 33106
  Christopher, Conn. & Cont., wid. Lucretia.................... W 21801
    (Also given as MAYNARD.)
  William, wid. Susannah, BLWt. 24327-160-55.................... W 9201
    (Also given as MINOR.)
  Zebediah, Conn. & Cont., wid. Anne............................ R 7062
    (Soldier was pensioned in New London Co., Conn., in 1818 for service under Col. Hunt-
      ingdon.)
    (Also given as MAYNARD.)
    (See also MYNARD and MAYNARD.)
MINER or MINOR, Aaron, wid. Hannah............................. R 7256
    (Soldier was pensioned from Washington Co., Vt., in 1832 for service under Col. Wooster.)
  Amos, wid. Mary... W 16346
  Anderson, Conn. & Mass.. S 21884
  Charles, wid. Rachel, BLWt. 19906-160-55...................... W 21808
  Christopher... S 42991
  Clement, Anna Joy, former wid. of............................. W 26682
  David, priv. under Col. Crane; Herkimer Co., N. Y., in 1832... S 11083
  David, priv. under Col. Smith; Tolland Co., Conn., in 1832; wid. Lydia.... W 7463
  Ebenezer, wid. Rhoda.. W 17143
  Elihu... S 36135
  Elnathan.. S 41871
  Ephraim, wid. Thankful, BLWt. 26238-160-55.................... W 24153
  Ichabod, BLWt. 31295-160-55................................... S 5765

102

MINER or MINOR, James, priv. under Col. Webb; New York City in 1818 .... S 23802
James, priv. under Capt. Starkweather; Stonington, Conn., in 1832 .... S 13932
James, priv. under Col. Silliman; Caledonia Co., Vt., in 1832; wid. Esther.., ... W 23977
John .... S 9414
Jonathan .... S 36157
Joseph, Conn. & Cont .... S 13934
Joshua, Rebecca Miller, former wid. of. .... W 15081
Philip .... R 7262
Richardson, wid. Sally, BLWt. 9482-160-55 .... W 2414
Seth, Cont. (Conn.) .... S 36152
Simeon, Conn. & R. I .... S 14857
Stephen or Steven, wid. Mary .... W 25710
   (Soldier was Gunner, and an Invalid pensioner; died in New London Co. in 1835.)
Stephen, Navy (Conn.), Mariner on ship *Alfred*. Lyme, Conn., in 1818; wid. Lydia received
   pay due him, but was never pensioned .... S 36134
Sylvester, BLWt. 652-100 .... S 42985
Timothy, wid. Mary or Polly .... BLWt. 34822-160-55
Titus .... S 36133
William, Conn. & Privateer .... S 13930
William. (See MINARD.)
MINTER, John .... S 9027
MINUET, Peter .... S 36159
MITCHEL or MITCHELL, Daniel, wid. Ruth .... R 7282
   (Soldier never applied.)
David, Cont. (Conn.) .... S 42981
Elisha, Cont. service, but Conn. residence; wid. Mary .... BLWt. 512-100
George, wid. Lucy, BLWt. 38534-160-55 .... W 21807
Ichabod .... S 41007
John Benjamin, wid. Jemima .... W 15693
Joseph, Conn. Sea service .... R 7278
Joseph, Conn. & N. Y .... R 20404
Margaret, former wid. of Samuel ABBEY.
Oliver, wid. Anna .... W 1632
William .... S 13928
Zephaniah, Conn. & Cont .... S 36155
MITTS, John. (See SMITH.)
MIX, Amos, wid. Clarinda .... W 7447
Benjamin, Conn. & Cont., wid. Esther .... W 19884
Eldad, wid. Mary .... W 20258
Elisha Corp. under Col. Swift; Northampton, N. Y., in 1818 .... S 42977
Elisha .... R 285
Elisha, Corp. under Col. Hinman; died in Hartford Co., Conn., in 1818; wid. Amna or Anna. W 21799
Enos .... S 36141
Jesse, wid. Polly .... W 20257
John .... S 13945
   BLWt. 1384-200, Lieut., was issued April 26, 1791. No papers.
Josiah .... S 2824
Levi, wid. Eunice .... W 19883
Lucy, former wid. of Sharp LIBERTY.
Rufus .... S 42982
Samuel, wid. Roxina .... W 23986
Timothy, priv. under Col. Wyllys; Bristol, Conn., in 1832 .... S 17587
Timothy, Continental service but Conn. residence in 1818, when he was pensioned from New
   Haven, Conn .... S 36154
   BLWt. 1386 200, Lieut., was issued Sept. 24, 1790 (no papers), to Peleg Sanford, assignee.
MIZE, William .... S 42983
MOFFATT, or MOFFITT, Matthew .... S 36160
MOGER, Joseph, Hulda Farlow, former wid. of .... W 25567
MOLTHROP or MOLTRUP. (See MOULTHROP.)
MONGOR, Jonathan, Conn. & Cont .... S 43018
   (See also MUNGER.)
MONRO or MONROE, John, priv. under Capt. Staples; Guilford, Conn. in 1832 .... S 31865
Joshua, Navy (Conn.) & Privateer .... S 9980
William .... S 11112
   (In the claim of his brother, Isaac MUNROE, S 43048, this man signs himself William
   Munroe.)
   (See also MUNRO and MUNROE.)
MONROSE or MONTROSE or MANROSE, Elijah, wid. Martha .... W 25735
MONSON. (See MUNSON.)
MONTAGUE or MONTIGUE, Jotham or Jonathan .... S 36171
Seth, Conn. & Cont .... S 33133
MONTGOMERY, Josiah, Conn., Mass. & R. I., wid. Ruth .... W 15097
MONTROSE. (See MONROSE.)
MOODY, Gideon W .... S 41014
MOON, Paul .... S 43028
MOOR, MOORE or MORE, Asa .... S 23817
Elisha, wid. Hannah .... W 20263
Grove .... S 18992
Hiram .... S 7326
James .... S 43032
Joel Forbus, Cont. (Conn.), wid. Rosanna .... W 17164
John .... S 41011
Joseph .... S 33118
Margaret, former wid. of Joseph B. CLINTON.
Peter, Conn. & Cont .... R 20408
   (Also given as MORE.)
Philander .... S 36162
Rodrick, wid. Mary .... W 9578
Simeon .... S 40181
William .... S 22913

103

MOREDOCK. (See MURDOCK.)
MOREHOUSE or MOORHOUSE, Aaron... S 13972
    Abraham.. S 13988
    David, wid. Rebecca... R 7365
       (Soldier was pensioned in 1832, in Sharon, Vt., as priv. and musician under Col. Pease.)
    David, priv. under Col. Canfield; Steuben Co., N. Y., in 1832, where he died in 1839; wid.
       Tryphena... W 20265
    Gershom, BLWt. 34851-160-55.. S 11116
    Grummon.. S 13955
    Peter, wid. Phebe... W 21812
    Samuel, wid. Anner... W 25723
       (Soldier never pensioned; died in 1830 in Fairfield Co., Conn.; was priv. under Col. St.
       John.)
    Samuel, wid. Mary.. W 25722
       (Soldier never pensioned; died in 1830 in Fairfield Co., Conn.; was priv. under Capt.
       Nash, Coast Guards.)
    Stephen, priv. under Capt. Marvin; Norwalk, Conn., in 1832................................ S 17593
    Stephen, priv. under Col. Waterbury, N. Y. in 1832...................................... S 29330
    Thaddeus or Thadeus, wid. Anne. BLWt. 7093-160-55.................................... W 5393
    Thomas.. S 17596
    William, wid. Ann... W 17172
MORELY. (See MORLEY.)
MOREY, Ephraim, Conn. & N. H... S 19402
    Jerusha, former wid. of Joseph GREEN.
    Robert.. S 17591
    Ruth, former wid. of Wait DEMING.
MORGAN, Asahel or Ashel.. S 9032
    Asher... S 13974
    Daniel.. S 36163
    David... S 16976
    Ebenezer, Conn. & Cont., wid. Olive... W 17178
    Ephraim, wid. Elizabeth. BLWt. 8468-160-55... W 2625
    James... S 20887
    Jesse, priv. under Col. Webb; Lorain, Ohio, in 1832...................................... S 5099
    Jesse, priv. under Col. Swift; Wayne Co., Penna., in 1832............................... S 5770
    John, Conn. & Privateer... S 17588
    Jonathan.. R 7380
    Jonathan, wid. Esther... R 7375
       (Soldier was not pensioned; died in 1828 in Litchfield Co., Conn.)
    Joseph, wid. Hannah.. W 26287
       BLWt. 6135-100, Serg't., was issued April 13, 1798. No papers.
    Joseph, priv. Col. Grosvenor, Conn. in 1832; died there in 1834; wid. Mabel.............. W 20266
    Joshua, wid. Wealthy or Welthy.. W 16658
    Lott, wid. Keziah... W 17174
    Lucy, former wid. of Jehiel GALPIN.
    Nathan, wid. Abigial.. W 17165
    Nicholas, wid. Phebe, BLWt. 6267-160-55... W 10532
    Seth, wid. Desire... W 17156
    Timothy... R 7390
    William, wid. Lucy.. S 13970
    William A., wid. Sarah, BLWt. 6437-160-55... W 1308
       Wid. was R. 7383.
MORISON. (See MORRISON.)
MORLEY, MAULEY or MORELY, Daniel.. S 40180
    Dimick.. S 13992
    Elijah... S 36078
       (Also given as MAULEY.)
    John, Cont. (Conn.)... S 40176
    Thomas.. S 18511
MORRIS or MORRISS, Andrew, Conn. Sea service, wid. Lucretia........................... W 1984
    Charles, wid. Sarah, BLWt. 26054-160-55... W 9207
    David, priv. under Col. Wells; died at Goshen, Conn. in 1833; pension paid his widow Dinah.. S 44542
    David, priv. and serg't. under Capt. Hepburn; died in 1810; wid. Mary.................... W 25728
    Edmund, Conn. Sea Service.. S 17590
    James, priv. under Col. Enos; Orange Co., Vt., in 1832.................................... S 16204
    James, Rhoda F. Wheeler, former wid. of... W 2035
       BLWt. 1378-300, Capt., was issued October 7, 1789. No papers.
    John, wid. Evia... S 13957
    Lois, former wid. of Jesse or Jose LYON.
    Robert, Conn. & Cont.. S 43019
MORRISON or MORISON, James.. S 13971
    Roderick.. S 16205
    William Cont. (Conn.) wid. Margaret, BLWt. 93-60-55.................................... W 1058
MORS or MORSE, Abiel, wid. Lucy, BLWt. 26114-160-55.................................. W 10217
    Charles, wid. Anna, BLWt. 26237-160-55.. W 23996
Darby. (See MOSS.)
    David, wid. Sarah, BLWt. 26775-160-55.. W 1982
       (Also given as MORSS.)
    Elihu... S 23812
    Isaac.. S 23813
    James, priv. under Col. Durkee; Canterbury, Conn., in 1818............................... S 43039
    James, Corp. under Greene; wid. in Providence, R. I., in 1836; wid. Bethiah.............. W 24156
    Jedediah.. R 7440
    John, Conn. & N. H., wid. Anna or Anne.. W 24019
    Moses... S 18510
    Rufus, wid. Rebecca.. W 20262
       (Also given as MORS.)
MORTON, Alexander, wid. Ruth... W 24157

MOSES, Ashbel, wid. Esther.. W 17170
 Enam, Cont. (Conn.), wid. Catharine... W 20267
 Ezekiel, wid. Eunice... W 4551
 Martin, wid. Lydia.. W 1633
 Seba.. S 13989
 Shubel, wid. Elizabeth.. W 17151
MOSHER, Joel.. S 36167
 John.. S 43024
 Stephen... S 36168
MOSS, Benoni, wid. Sarah.. W 25714
 Daniel, BLWt. 810–100.. S 40174
 Darby... R 7434
  (Also given as MORSE.)
 Elizabeth, former wid. of Reuben CARTER.
 Isaiah.. S 43738
 John, Conn. & Vt., wid. Mary, BLWt. 38538–160–55................................... W 25730
 Levi, wid. Martha.. W 17166
 Reuben, Esther Tyler, former wid. of, BLWt. 94–100................................ W 6329
 Thomas, wid. Lucy.. R 7459
  (Soldier never applied.)
MOTT, Eunice, former wid. of Henry WILLIAMS.
 Lent... R 7464
 Lyman, wid. Rebecca... W 15100
 Samuel... S 43011
MOTTHROP. (See MOULTHROP.)
MOULTHROP, MOULTHROUP, MOLTRUP, or MOTTHROP.
 John, Conn. & Cont.. S 36081
 Moses, wid. Mary, BLWt. 35837–160–55.. W 5383
 Reuben, wid. Hannah... W 17177
MOULTON, Gurdon.. S 43010
 Salmon... S 23810
 Stephen, BLWt. 3958–160–55.. S 49278
  (This soldier's widow, Nancy, was pensioned for service of her former husband, Henry
   KNEELAND, or KICKELAND, Mass., W 5681.)
 William, Conn., Cont. & N. Y... S 43026
  BLWt. 1380–300, Capt., was issued August 8, 1789 to John Doty, Assignee. No papers.
MOWREY or MOWRY, Reuben B., Conn. & Mass... S 2875
MOXLEY, Joseph. (See claim of Prudence, wid. of Benjamin DABOLL, who was first pen-
 sioned as the former wid. of Joseph MOXLEY.)
MOYER, George, Conn., Conn. Sea service & Mass. Sea service............................. S 18135
MUDGE, Abraham, wid. Phebe.. W 15694
MULKINS, Mary, former wid. of Joseph ROBINS.
MULLETT, Lewis. (See MALLETT.)
MUMFORD, Henry, Conn. & Mass.. S 11125
MUN. (See MUNN.)
MUNGER, Bela, Cont. (Conn.).. S 43047
 Billy, wid. Deborah.. W 15931
 Eber... S 15541
 Elias.. S 18996
 Jehiel... S 31875
 Lyman, wid. Eunice... W 18544
 Timothy, wid. Loraine.. W 16352
  (See also MONGOR.)
MUNN or MUN, Asa... S 11123
 David, wid. Lois... W 17191
 Gideon... R 7491
MUNRO or MUNROE, Daniel, BLWt. 2424–100.
 Isaac.. S 43048
 John, BLWt. 1219–100... S 43055
 John, wid. Susannah.. W 25738
 Joseph... S 36182
 Josiah... S 11105
 Leonard, Cont. (Conn.)... S 40188
 Willaim.. S 11112
MUNSELL or MONSELL or MUNSEL, Alpheus, wid. Eunice....................................... W 17187
 Benjamin... R 7497
 Calkins.. S 11124
 Hezekiah, wid. Irena... W 17184
 Levi, wid. Lucretia.. W 1917
MUNSON, Almond or Almun.. S 41909
 Elisha, wid. Mabel... W 17183
 Eneas, Conn. & Cont.. S 34
  BLWt. 1387–300, Surgeon's Mate, was issued May 31, 1791. No papers.
 Ephraim, wid. Deborah.. W 26260
 Isaac.. S 40187
 Jonathan, wid. Sally, BLWt. 26680–160–55... W 308
 Medad.. S 17601
 Moses.. S 47547
 Orange... S 43045
  BLWt. 6139–100 was issued in 1789. No papers. BLWt. 133–60–55.
 Samuel, Conn. & Penna., wid. Martha.. W 19902
 Stephen, wid. Elizabeth.. W 13749
 Theophilus, wid. Sarah, BLWt. 185–300.
  (Also given as MONSON.)
 Thomas E... S 36181
 William, "Hazen's Reg't. of Conn. Quota." BLWt. 1564–300, Capt., was issued Feb. 27,
  1797. No papers.
 Wait... S 13995
 Wilmot, Conn. & Privateer.. R 701

MURDOCK or MOREDOCK, Daniel, wid. Lurana.. W 18541
   Elisha.. R 7506
    (Also given as MOREDOCK.)
   Jonathan, wid, Lucretia... W 20269
MURRAY, MURREY, or MURRY, Amasa.. S 36184
   Benjamin, wid. Lucretia... W 24021
   Hannah, former wid. of Abel CLARK.
   Ichabod.. S 43049
   Jasper.. S 1400
   John... S 41022
   Solomon.. S 43058
   Stephen.. S 23329
MYERS or MEYERS, Henry, Conn. & N. Y.. R 7538
   Josiah, Conn. & N. Y., Lydia Granger, former wid. of................................ W 17032
MYGATT or MIGATE, Elisha, BLWt. 265–100... S 36185
   Jonathan, Conn. & Cont., wid. Prudence... W 17194
    (Also given MIGATE.)
   Zebulon, Bathsheba Hubbard, former wid. of... W 18078
MYNARD, Lemuel... ∞ 43060
   (See also MAYNARD and MINARD.)

N.

NAILS, John, wid. Sally.. W 20274
NASH, Daniel... S 11130
   Joel.. S 9983
   Jonathan, wid. Eunice... W 10778
   Joseph... S 29344
   Noah, wid. Ann, BLWt. 34976–160–55... W 26568
   Peter (colored), wid. Lydia... R 7558
    (Soldier never applied.)
   Silas, Hannah Tyre, former wid. of, BLWt. 28545–160–55............................. W 608
NEAL, William... S 4599
NEARING, Henry, wid. Jane.. W 6839
   John.. S 43071
   Joseph, wid. Julia, BLWt. 26205–160–55.. W 6840
NEDSON, James.. S 36188
NEEDAR, Toney, Conn. & Cont., wid. Phillis, BLWt. 19813–160–55................... W 7073
   (Also given as Anthony EDER.)
NEFF, Oliver... R 7573
NEGRO, Caesar, or SHELTON, Caesar or Cezer.
NEGRO, Caesar, or CLARK, Caesar, Negro.
NEGRO, Cato, or KENT, Cato.
NEGUS or NIGUS, John, Conn. Sea service, Desire Baldwin, former wid. of......... W 17228
NELSON, John, Conn. & N. Y., wid. Amy.. W 24340
NETTLETON, Benajah... R 7601
   Caleb, wid. Lois.. W 2659
   John.. S 14020
   Josiah.. S 36187
   Nathan... S 11133
   William, wid. Zillah... W 17399
NEVINS, David, Conn. & Cont... S 14010
NEWBERRY or NEWBURY, Amasa... S 11131
   Jeremiah... S 43072
   Stedman... S 14021
NEWCOMB, Azariah... R 7614
   Bethuel, wid. Mabel... W 26572
   Eleazer.. S 36186
   Luther, Conn., Mass. & Privateer... S 18527
   Thomas, Conn. & Navy, wid. Sylvia, BLWt. 8388–160–55............................. R 7615
    (Both soldier and widow were rejected as six months' service was not proven.)
NEWELL, Daniel, wid. Nancy.. W 24328
   Ebenezer.. S 43066
   Lydia, former wid. of Ezekiel WILLIAMS.
   Mark... S 36190
   Nathaniel... S 14011
   Norman, Cont. (Conn.).. S 40199
   Riverius or Reverius, wid. Abigail, BLWt. 34859–160–55............................. W 805
   Robert, Conn. & Cont., wid. Lydia, BLWT. 34915–160–55........................... W 19917
   Seth.. R 7618
   Theodore, wid. Hannah, BLWt. 14671–160–55... W 5417
NEWHALL, Joshua, Conn., Cont. & Navy.. S 36189
NEWMAN, Abraham, Conn. & N. Y., wid. Lucinda....................................... W 24332
   Jonathan, wid. Lucy, BLWt. 44507–160–55.. W 5418
   Rufus, wid. Polly.. W 1461
   Zadoc.. S 15544
NEWTON, Asahel, wid. Versalle or Versally.. W 15696
   David... R 7633
   Elias, wid. Alice... W 4298
   Israel, BLWt. 1963–160–55... S 19002
   James.. S 22919
   Joel.. S 23336
   John.. S 17602
NICHOL or NICHOLS or NICHOLLS, Daniel, priv. under Col. Waterbury; Kingston, N. Y., in
   1832.. S 11141
   Daniel, priv. under Col. Elmore; Stamford, Conn., in 1818........................... S 36191
   Daniel.. R 76413
   Daniel.. R 76453
   Daniel, pensioned as Daniel 1st in New Milford, Conn., in 1818 for service under Col. Webb;
    died there 1819; wid. Esther... W 17402
   Ebenezer, wid. Martha.. W 2231

NICHOL or NICHOLS or NICHOLLS, Eli, 58 in 1818 at Windsor, N. Y........................ S 14024
    Eli, priv. under Col. Swift; died in 1845, aged 84 yrs., in Trumbull, Conn.; his daughter, Mrs.
       Sally Smith, obtained a pension from 1832 to date of his death............................. S 43076
    Ely, Conn. & Cont.. S 22418
    Enos... S 14025
    Ephraim.. S 23340
    James.. R 7645
    James, Conn., Navy & R. I.. S 40206
    Jesse.. S 11142
    John, priv. under Capt. Miles; Oneida Co., N. Y., in 1832................................. S 23338
    John, priv. under Capt. Hoyt; Stamford, Conn., in 1832; wid. Mary......................... W 2685
    Jonathan... S 39829
    Joseph ,wid. Nancy... R 7655
       (Soldier never applied.)
    Mandfield, Cont. (Conn.)... S 41032
    Noah, wid. Abigail, Conn., Cont. & N. H.. W 21847
    Philip, wid. Abiah... W 17403
    Reuben, Abiah Lewis, former wid. of... W 21566
    Robert... S 40209
    Samuel, wid. Sibbel.. W 5419
    Silvanus... S 14027
    Stiles, wid. Phebe... W 2656
    William.. S 17607
NICHOLSON, Francis, Rachel Weston, former wid. of.. W 6454
NICKERSON, Jonathan... S 28824
NIGUS. (See NEGUS.)
NILES, Dan.. S 21397
    Elisha, wid. Naomi... W 26577
    Jehiel... S 43074
    Nathaniel.. S 36193
    Robert, Conn. Sea service & Privateer... S 36194
    William.. S 19006
NOBLE, Abigail, former wid. of Timothy HIBBARD.
    Elijah... S 36198
    Gideon, Lucy Hollister, former wid. of, BLWt. 38532-160-55............................... W 24445
    Goodman, wid. Sarah.. R 7681
       (Soldier was pensioned in 1818 at Cairo, N. Y., for service under Col. Swift; dropped on
         account of property; pensioned again in 1832 at Cairo.)
    Lyman, Conn. & Boat service on Lake Champlain, Elizabeth Whiting, former wid. of........ W 22613
    Nathan... S 43092
    William.. S 43093
NOBLES, Azer.. S 4620
    Roswell, wid. Anna... R 7682
       (Soldier was pensioned in 1832 at Simsbury, Conn., for service under Col. Ward.)
NOONEY, James, wid. Sarah... R 7687
    (Neither soldier nor widow applied.)
NORMAN, John, Conn., Conn. Sea service & R. I... S 30006
NORRIS, Henry, Navy (Conn.), wid. Desire.. W 17407
    John, wid. Ruth.. R 7705
       (Soldier was pensioned in 1832 at Ashtabula, Ohio, where he died in 1840, for service under
         Capt. Hatch.)
    Samuel, Conn. Sea service & Mass., wid. Lucy... W 13772
    Thomas, Conn. Sea service, wid. Sarah... W 3445
NORTH, Abi, former wid. of Justus FRANCIS.
    Abijah, Conn. & Cont., wid. Sarah, BLWt. 28632-160-55.................................... W 2232
    Levi, Conn. & Cont... S 14041
    Seth... S 36197
    Simeon... S 23342
NORTHAM or NORTHUM, Asa, Conn. & Mass... S 5834
    (Given as NORTHUM.)
    John... S 14040
    Jonathan, Conn. & Cont... S 14030
    Samuel, Conn. & Cont... S 14034
NORTHROP or NORTHRUP, Amos.. S 22424
    Andrew, wid. Clarissa.. W 17410
    Elijah... S 36199
    Gideon... S 22922
    Heth, wid. Ann, BLWt. 26723-160-55... W 17408
    Isaac.. S 36196
    Joseph, Conn. & Cont... S 23826
    Joshua, Phoebe Blackman, former wid. of... W 10419
    Lemuel... S 18530
    Lucy, former wid. of Dan HATCH.
    Stephen, Conn. & N. Y., wid. Rhoda... R 7715
       (Soldier was pensioned in 1832 in Madison Co., N. Y., for service as Serg't. and Q. M. Serg't.
         under Col. Waterbury.)
    Willson.. S 43082
NORTHWAY, George.. S 15548
    Ozias, wid. Sarah.. W 2419
NORTON, Abel, wid. Lucy... W 17404
    (Soldier died in 1803 at Guilford, Conn.; served under Col. Swift.)
    Abel, Conn. & N. Y., priv. under Col. Webb; Greene Co., N. Y., in 1832................... S 14042
    Abraham.. S 46429
    Ambrose, wid. Bethiah.. W 16356
    Benjamin, wid. Elsey... W 2234
       (Soldier pensioned in N. Y. in 1818.)
       BLWt. 1581-200, Lieut., was issued October 16, 1789, to Theodosius Fowler, Assignee.
         No papers.
    Benjamin, priv. serg't. and Ensign; died in 1812; never pensioned; wid. Azubah............ W 4299
    Charles.. S 28825

NORTON, David, wid. Lois... W 16663
    (Soldier died in 1829 in Oneida Co., N. Y., was never pensioned.)
    David, Conn. & N. Y... S 14036
    Eber... R 7717
    Elias.. S 4624
    Elijah, wid. Rebecca... W 20278
    Elnathan, wid. Ruth... W 19926
    Elon.. S 43090
    Giles, BLWt. 28524-160-55... S 29352
    Isaac... R 7719
    Jabez.. S 36195
    Jared, wid. Sarah.. W 26585
    John, wid. Lucretia.. W 15134
    Jonathan... S 14028
    Joseph... S 11146
    Levi.. R 7722
    Nathan, wid. Experience... W 17405
    Noah W.. S 17608
    Oliver, wid. Martha.. R 7724
    (Soldier was pensioned in Oneida Co., N Y., in 1832 for service under Capt. Bradley, Col. Strong.)
    Oliver, wid. Susanna... R 7726
    (Soldier was pensioned in 1832 in Washington Co., N. Y., for service under Capt. Skinner, Col. Stowers.)
    Ozias, priv. under Col. Mott; New Haven Co., Conn., in 1832................. S 16990
    Ozias, priv. under Col. Baldwin; Portage Co., Ohio, in 1832................. S 17609
    Samuel, wid. Phebe.. W 26582
    Seba, Conn. & N. Y., wid. Margaret.. W 19927
    Selah, wid. Anne or Anna.. W 17409
    William.. S 43083
    Zadock or Zadok, Conn. & Vt., wid. Anna................................... W 19928
NOTT, Abraham, wid. Abigail... W 10821
    (Also given as KNOTT.)
    Epaphras, Conn. & Cont.. S 14035
NOYES, John, BLWt. 1580-400, Surgeon, was issued May 29, 1789, to John Noyes. No papers.
NUGEN, John, BLWt. 2242-100; and S-.
NUGENT or NUGEON, John, wid. Elizabeth... W 26586
NYE, Daniel... S 21903
    David.. S 18532
    Elijah... R 7748
    Jonathan, wid. Deodama.. W 17412
    Solomon, wid. Mary, BLWt. 26345-160-55................................... W 9607
    (NOTE.—Mary received Bounty land also on account of the services of her former husband, Samuel WOODS, Mass. S 41367.)

O.

OAKLEY, Gilbert, wid. Eleanor.. W 26590
    John, wid. Catharine.. W 19934
    Miles.. S 18533
O'CAIN, Anthony F., or FRANCOIS, Anthony... R 7765
    Name also appears as Anthony FRANSWOI, FRANSEWAY or FRANSUAY.
ODELL, Isaac, wid. Grizel.. W 21863
    Nathan... S 17610
    William.. S 14048
OGDEN, David, wid. Sally... W 17414
    Edmond, Conn. & Navy, wid. Sibal.. R 7777
    (Soldier never applied and died in 1799; widow's claim rejected for insufficient proof of service.)
    Joseph... S 38277
    Sturges or Sturgess... S 14049
OLCOTT, Isaac.. S 31890
    Jared.. S 47577
    Jonathan... S 16996
OLDS, Aaron.. S 41035
    Daniel, wid. Lois.. W 4557
    Ebenezer, Cont. (Conn.)... S 43099
    Hannah, former wid. of Thomas STEPHENSON.
    John, Conn. & Cont.. S 43102
OLMSTEAD or OLMSTED, Ashbel... S 23346
    Benjamin, wid. Content.. W 20280
    Daniel, wid. Rosanna.. W 19936
    (Also given as OLLMSTED.)
    Ebenezer, wid. Esther... W 9611
    Francis, Conn. & Cont... S 40224
    Gamaliel, Conn. & Cont., wid. Elizabeth, BLWt. 30918-160-55.............. W 5435
    Gloriana, former wid. of Aarom Keeler.
    Isaac, wid. Sarah... W 26595
    James, BLWt. 1608-200, Lieut., was issued Sept. 1, 1790, to Theodosius Fowler, Assignee. No papers.
    James, wid. Mary.. R 7779
    (Soldier died in 1811; neither he nor wid. applied for pension, but son Henry.)
    James, priv. under Col. Swift; Onondaga Co., N. Y., in 1832................. S 5857
    John... R 7803
    John Bates, wid. Theodosha or Adosha..................................... R 7801
    (Neither soldier nor wid. applied.)
    Joseph... S 11157
    Matthew or Mathew.. S 14054
    Nehemiah... S 43739
    Oliver, Conn. & Cont., wid. Mercy... W 26594
    Roger.. S 5858
    Timothy... S 43740

OLNEY, Peter, wid. Tabitha... W 21864
ORCUTT, John.. S 15949
    Solomon, Conn. & Cont... S 41037
    Stephen, wid. Mary, BLWt. 8450–160–55.. W 26598
    William.. S 4632
ORMS, Jonathan, wid., Lura or Laura, BLWt. 18200–160–55....................... W 5632
ORMSBEE, ORMSBE or ORMSBEY, or ORMSBY.
    Ebenezer, Conn. & R. I wid. Experience, BLWt. 7076–160–55......................... W 21873
    Elijah.. S 14060
    Stephen... S 45039
ORR, Alexander, Conn. & Mass... S 34456
ORSBORN. (See OSBORN.)
ORTON, Azariah.. S 11161
    Darius... S 14055
    Eliada... S 41933
    Lemuel, Cont. (Conn.) wid. Sibbel... W 4753
ORVIS, David... S 14057
    Roger.. S 43751
    Samuel, wid. Caroline... W 25359
OSBON, OSBORN, OSBORNE, or ORSBORN.
    Abel, wid. Annah... W 20285
    Abijah.. R 7821
    Abraham, Conn., N. Y. & Privateer... S 14061
    Ebenezer.. S 15550
    Edward, wid. Elizabeth.. W 20282
    Eli... S 43743
    Eliada, wid. Abigail.. W 1639
    Ethan, BLWt. 34953–160–55... S 4635
    Ezekiel, wid. Lucretia, BLWt. 5205–160–55.. W 26600
    Ezra, wid. Abigail.. W 15147
    Isaac, Conn. & Mass., wid. Edna., BLWt. 28579–160–55........................... W 26602
        (Given as ORSBORN.)
    Jacob.. S 29355
    Jeremiah, priv. under Col. Denison; Fairfield Co., Conn., in 1832................ S 31894
    Jeremiah, Continental service but Conn. residence & Agency in 1818; Serg't.under Col. Lamb;
        Weston, Conn., in 1818... S 38278
    John... S 33408
        (Also given OSBON.)
        Pensioned as John 1st in Lanesboro, Mass., in 1818 for service under Col. Webb.
    John, priv. under Col. Waterbury; Fairfield Co., Conn., in 1832 and died there in 1843; wid.
        Jerusha.. W 21875
    John, Serg't., Ensign, and Lieut.,Litchfield Co., Conn., in 1832 and died there in 1833; wid.
        Rhoda... W 21877
    Joseph... S 23348
    Joshua, wid. Diana.. W 4559
    Josiah, Conn. & N. Y... S 4638
    Levi... S 14065
    Naboth, Conn. & Mass., wid. Susanna.. W 21878
    Nathan, teamster under Capt. Loomis, Greene Co., N. Y., in 1832................. S 11164
    Nathan, priv. under Col. Gould; Delaware Co., N. Y., in 1832..................... S 23347
    Nathaniel, wid. Elizabeth.. R 16862
        (Soldier never applied.)
    Samuel, priv. under Col. Evans; Adams Co., Penna., in 1832...................... S 7284
    Samuel, priv. under Col. Willet; Greene Co., N. Y., in 1832; BLWt. 28611–160–55; wid. Eliza-
        beth.. W 6862
        Widow later married Moses L. PENDELL, after whose death pension was renewed.
    Shadrach, Conn. & Cont., wid. Aletta or Alletta.................................. W 21879
    Stephen, Cont. (Conn.), wid. Apame, BLWt. 18380–160–55....................... W 9216
    Thomas, wid. Lovisa... W 17415
    White, Conn. & Cont.. S 14066
    William, Sarah H. Taylor, former, wid. of... R 10431
        (Neither soldier nor wid. applied. Sarah's other husband was pensioned on account of
        disability contracted in service in 1812. See case of TAYLOR, William B., S 6202.)
    Zebedee.. S 30012
OSGOOD or OZGOOD, Jeremiah, BLWt. 18014–160–55........................... S 7283
    Josiah... S 19415
OTIS, Barnabas, Conn. & Cont... S 9612
    Edward.. S 32425
    James, Navy service; Conn. Agency and residence................................ S 38276
    John T.. S 16998
    Joseph.. S 27276
        (In American State Papers, Vol. 9, p. 153, Joseph Otis, private, in Col. Zebulon Butler's
        regiment, afterwards transferred to Webb's reg't.; enlisted 1777 for the war. Wounded
        by musket ball Feb., 1781, at Morrisiana; res. Branford, Conn.)
    Richard, Cont. (Conn.)... S 45043
OVAITT, William, wid. Sarah.. W 24376
    (See also OVIATT.)
OVERTON, Seth, Conn. & Privateer.. R 7839
    Thomas... S 36201
OVIATT or OVIT, or OVIUTT, Ebenezer, wid. Eunice............................ W 21885
    Job.. S 38275
    (Given as OVIT.)
    Nathan.. S 14068
    (Also given as OVIUTT.)
    Samuel, Cont. (Conn.), wid. Mindwell or Murdwell.............................. W 10846
    (See also OVAITT.)
OWEN, Alvin or Alven... S 43733
    Alvan... R 7840
    Daniel, wid. Lydia.. W 18478
    Eleazer or Elezer... S 30628

OWEN, Elijah, Berkshire Co. Mass., in 1832; son of Lieut. Elijah (W 13787).................... S 30013
    Elijah, Lieut. of Guard at Newgate prison in 1776; wid. Lydia........................ W 13787
    Frederick...... S 43762
    Gideon, wid. Nancy.. W 20288
    John, wid. Lydia.. W 10221
    (Also given OWENS.)
    Samuel, Conn., Cont., Mass. & Vt... S 11168
    Thaddeus, Conn. & Cont. wid. Abigail.. R 1687
    (Soldier never applied.)

P.

OZGOOD. (See OSGOOD.)
PACKARD, Asahel, wid. Priscilla, BLWt. 26228–160–55.. W 1312
    Nehemiah... S 43787
PACKER, Eldredge, wid. Sabrina... W 21888
    John, Groton, Conn., in 1818, as John 2d; 65 in 1820, and had wife, named Esther........... S 38291
    John, wid. Hannah, b. 1735, d. 1835, New London Co., Conn.; Groton, Conn., in 1832....... W 26284
PAGE or PAIGE, Ann, former wid. of Thomas DOUGAL.
    Edmund, wid. Sarah.. R 7873
    (Soldier never pensioned.)
    Elias... S 23356
    Gad, wid. Abigail... W 17418
    Jared... R 7871½
    John.. S 41936
    Joseph, Conn., Conn. Sea service and Navy.. S 7866
    Luther.. S 46329
    Luther, wid. Rachel... R 7872
    (Soldier never pensioned.)
    Phinehas, wid. Jeruiah.. W 18725
    Timothy.. S 11186
    Titus... S 23836
PAINE or PAYNE, Edward.. S 3625
    Eleazer, wid. Aurel... R 8021
    Eli... S 14093
    Isaac... S 36208
    Thomas, wid. Elizabeth.. R 7876
    (Soldier never pensioned.)
    (See also PAYN and PAYNE.)
PAINTER, Deliverance.. S 15567
    Elisha...BLWt. 1603–400
    Thomas, Conn. Sea service & Privateer... S 18536
PALMER, Aaron, wid. Mary.. R 7895
    (Soldier never pensioned.)
    Abraham.. S 43768
    Benjamin, Branford, Conn., in 1832.. S 17616
    Benjamin, Voluntown, Conn., in 1832... S 31895
    Benjamin, wid. Sarah.. R 7907
    (Neither soldier nor widow, but daughter, Sally Jakway, of Ashtabula Co., Ohio, applied
    in 1851.)
    Chillon, Cont. (Conn.), wid. Lydia.. W 2629
    Chilleab, wid. Mary, BLWt. 11162–160–55... W 10365
    Daniel, Conn. & Privateer... S 7298
    David, wid. Anne.. W 18709
    Edward, wid. Delia.. W 18695
    Elijah, Conn. & Conn. Sea service, widow Polly, BLWt. 33533–160–55................... R 7885
    Elisha, wid. Eunice, BLWt. 36561–160–55... W 26287
    Ephraim, Conn. & N. Y... S 8940
    George, Chittenden Co., Vt., in 1832.. S 16221
    George, wid. Hannah, teamster, Otsego Co., N. Y., 1832, d. 1835...................... W 17419
    George, Conn. & Privateer... R 7887
    Henry, Conn. & N. Y... S 14102
    Humphrey, wid. Eunice, BLWt. 24151–160–55... W 4756
    Isaac, wid. Hannah.. W 21909
    James, Conn., Navy & Privateer, widow Pamela.. W 19969
    Jared, Conn. & Cont., BLWt. 164–60–55... S 23358
    Jesse, Conn. & N. Y., wid. Abigail.. W 18707
    Joel.. S 38979
    John, Chittenden Co., Vt., in 1832.. S 11189
    John, Greene Co., N. Y., in 1818.. S 43807
    Jonah... S 41049
    Joseph, wid. Eunice, BLWt. 6274–160–55.. W 13793
    Lazarus, wid. Rachel.. W 19952
    Levi, wid. Sarah.. W 16368
    Louisa, former wid. of Silas HOLMES.
    Marshall, Eunice Fox, former wid. of.. W 17918
    Milo.. R 7897
    Nathan.. S 43767
    Nathan.. S 20422
    Nehemiah, Conn. & Privateer, wid. Anna S., BLWt. 29012–160–55....................... W 9227
    Ozias or Osias, Conn. & Mass.. S 7294
    Param or Parrum... S 36204
    Reuben.. S 14091
    Samuel, Montville, Conn., in 1832... S 14108
    Samuel, N. Y. in 1818... S 43769
    Samuel, wid. Thankful... W 17420
    Soldier was pensioned in Stonington, Conn., in 1832, as private and serg't.
    Seth, wid. Deborah.. W 21911
    Smith... S 36205
    Stephen, Hannah Davis, former wid. of.. R 2721
    (Soldier never pensioned.)

PALMEK, Thomas, Hartford Co., Conn., in 1818.. S 36202
   Thomas or Thomas Kinne, wid. Margaret... W 27925
     (Soldier died 1827, Grafton, Vt.)
   Thomas, Conn., Cont. & N. Y... S 16217
     Soldier pensioned in Madison Co., N. Y., in 1832 as priv., corp. & serg't.
   Tryphena, former wid. of William McQUEEN.
   William... R 7911
   Wyatt.. S 23357
PALMES, Andrew, Conn. & Navy, wid. Sarah.. W 21887
   Samuel.. S 36206
PALMETER, PALMETTER, PALMITER or PALMITTER.
   Jesse, Conn. & Cont.. S 43775
   John, wid. Anna or Anne... W 5474
   Jonathan, Conn. & R. I.. S 11180
   Paul, Conn. & N. J... S 17624
   Phinehas, Conn. & R. I.. S 5870
   William, Conn. & R. I.. S 43765
PANGBURN, Adonijah... S 38290
   Zillah, former wid. of Asa PARKER.
PARDEE, Abijah, wid. Rosanna... W 21905
   Chandler... S 20905
   Charles... S 14087
   Daniel.. S 17615
   Eli... S 23365
   James, wid. Elizabeth.. R 7918
     (Soldier never pensioned.)
   Joseph, wid. Sarah... R 7921
     (Soldier was pensioned in New Haven Co., Conn., in 1832.)
   Lemuel.. S 43800
   Nathaniel... S 43795
   Thomas, Conn. & N. Y., wid. Susanna, BLWt. 26739–160–55.............................. W 3293
PARISH or PARRISH, Eliphas, Jerusha Cory, former wid. of, BLWt. 10313–160–55............ W 1563
   Jeremiah... S 11215
   Nehemiah, Conn. & Privateer.. S 12128
   Oliver.. S 9451
   Roswell, wid. Eunice, BLWt. 9428–160–55.. W 1918
PARK or PARKE, Amaziah, wid. Sabra or Sabry or Sabrey............................... W 2688
   Daniel.. S 7296
     (Also given as PARKE.)
   Ebenezer... S 14109
   Ezra, Cont. (Conn.), wid. Anna.. W 16362
   Isaac, wid. Mary... W 21895
     (Also given PARKE.)
   John.. S 43789
     (Given as PARKE.)
   John, BLWt. 7–100 was issued Aug. 29, 1866, for services as private.
   Jonas, Cont. & Conn. Sea service, wid. Rachel... W 19966
   Thomas... R 7932
PARKER. Abel, wid. Lydia, BLWt. 15165–160–55.. W 18706
   Abraham, Rosamon Ingersoll, former wid. of.. W 5002
   Amos, Oneida Co., N. Y., in 1818.. S 43766
   Amos, wid. Polly, Serg't. Hampshire Co., Mass., in 1832.............................. W 26848
   Asa... S 23354
   Asaph... S 7300
   Ashael.. R 7935
   Benjamin.. R 7937
   Benjamin, wid. Lorinda.. W 16360
   Edward.. S 14103
   Elijah, Conn. & Cont... R 7943
   Elisha, Hampden Co., Mass., in 1832.. S 5145
   Elisha, Boston, Mass., in 1832... S 31288
   Elisha, Conn., Cont. & N. C.. S 11354
     Pensioned from Morgan Co., Ala., in 1845.
   Gamaliel, Martha Hall, former wid. of.. W 17038
   Isaac, wid. Anna... W 16365
     Soldier was Serg't. and died in 1813; wid. was pensioned from Chataqua Co., N. Y., in 1838.
   Isaac, wid. Esther... W 19967
     Soldier died in 1821; widow resided in Windsor Co., Vt., in 1838.
   Isaac, wid. Susannah... R 7954
     Soldier was never pensioned.
   James, priv. & corp., Oneida Co., N. Y., in 1832....................................... S 14106
   James, Windsor Co., Vt., in 1832.. S 21409
   John, Saybrook, Conn., in 1818.. S 38982
   John, BLWt. 112–100; Chenango Co., N. Y., in 1818..................................... S 43792
   John, Conn. & Mass., wid. Elizabeth.. W 18722
     Soldier died in Tolland, Conn., in 1832.
   John, Conn., R. I. & Vt., Corp. Rupert, Vt., in 1832................................... S 14105
   Jonathan.. S 41039
   Joseph, wid. Hannah.. W 18704
     Soldier died in 1823 in Georgia, Vt.
   Joseph, Conn., Cont. & N. H., Windsor Co., Vt., in 1832.............................. S 14107
   Joseph, Conn. & Va., wid. Hannah... R 7952
     Soldier never pensioned.
   Jotham, wid. Sarah... W 19957
   Levi, Wallingford, Conn. in 1832.. S 14083
   Levi, wid. Eunice, BLWt. 34858–160–55... W 4754
     Soldier died in Orange Co., Vt., in 1835.
   Nathan, wid. Eunice, BLWt. 1661–100, BLWt. 146–60–55............................... W 24879

PARKER, Phineas .... S 9984
    Samuel, Ashtabula Co., Ohio, in 1832.. S 18541
    Samuel, Conn. & Mass., Genesee Co., N. Y., in 1832............................... S 11190
    Stephen... S 17625
    Timothy.. BLWt. 259-100
    William, wid. Ruth.. W 19954
    Wyman, Conn. & Cont., wid. Mercy or Marcy..................................... W 15793
PARKES. (See PARKS.)
PARKHURST, Abraham, Conn. & Cont... S 34465
    Azel.. S 21916
    David, Cont. (Conn.), wid. Susannah, BLWt. 155-60-55........................ W 24878
    Pierce, Conn., Conn. Sea service & Cont... S 15554
    Solomon.. S 34463
PARKS or PARKES, Aaron... S 43809
    David... S 43804
    Ebenezer, wid. Janette, BLWt. 16111-160-55..................................... W 2425
    (Also given PARKES.)
    Frederick.. BLWt. 755-100
    Robert, wid. Martha.. W 18710
    Rufus, wid. Lucy... W 26288
PARMALE, PARMALEE, PARMALIE, PARMELE, PARMELEE, PARMELY or
PARMLEE.
    Bani, wid. Charity, BLWt. 31565-160-55.. W 6852
    Charles, Conn. & Cont... S 11184
    Constant, wid. Hannah, BLWt. 6021-160-55..................................... W 5473
    Giles... S 14097
    Hiel.. S 14088
    James, Hartford Co., Conn., in 1832.. S 15950
    James, wid. Lydia, BLWt. 30701-160-55... W 5481
      Soldier was in Ontario Co., N. Y., in 1818.
    Jeremiah... S 41048
    Joel, wid. Sarah.. W 15172
    (Also given PARMELL.)
    Luther, Cont. (Conn.)... BLWt. 337-100
    Phinehas, wid. Rachel... W 18718
    Thomas.. S 28142
PARROTT, Esther, former wid. of Jonathan WAKELEY.
    John.. S 38284
    Mastin... S 18537
PARSONS, Abraham... S 14110
    Bartholomew.. S 33429
    Daniel.. S 11208
    David (private)... BLWt. 232-100
    David, BLWt. 1667-300, Capt., was issued Nov. 5, 1795. No papers.
    Eli, wid. Huldah... W 3111
    Jabez.. S 3644
    Jesse... S 38282
    John, Herkimer Co., N. Y., in 1832... S 31900
    John, wid. Sarah... W 18698
      Soldier was in Addison Co., Vt., in 1832.
    John, Conn., Cont. & Mass., Chataqua Co., N. Y., in 1832.................... S 11185
    Joseph... S 11207
    Mercy, former wid. of Ezra FOOT. (Also given as PARSON.)
    Osborn, BLWt. 1089-100.. S 40243
    Samuel, New York in 1818.. S 35024
    Samuel, Cont. (Conn.), New Haven County, Conn., in 1818.................. S 15552
    Samuel H., BLWt. 1665-1100, Major Gen., was issued August 23, 1790. No papers.
    Solomon.. S 4646
    William... S 14090
    (See also PEARSON.)
PARTRIDGE or PATRIDGE, Asa, wid. Anna....................................... W 16053
    James, wid. Amy.. W 16668
    Samuel, wid. Anna... W 15164
    Stephen, wid. Sarah... W 17423
PASCO, Jonathan... S 5140
PATCH, William... S 11196
PATCHEN or PATCHIN, Azor, wid. Abigail, BLWt. 1378-100, BLWt. 37-60-55.............. W 6854
    Daniel.. S 14089
    Ebenezer, wid. Sarah.. W 16672
    Elijah, Conn. & Cont.. S 36207
    Freegift, Conn. & N. Y., wid Molly... W 21910
    Isaac, wid. Rebekah... W 17425
    Jacob... S 38986
    Josiah, Eunice Keator, former wid. of.. W 21510
    William... R 7993
    Wolcott, Betty Bennett, former wid. of BLWt. 278-60-55.
      NOTE.—This woman's other husband was also a pensioner. (See Bennet or Bennett,
      Benjamin, Conn. S 38529.)
PATRICK, Abel.. R 7995
    Jacob, Conn. & Privateer, wid. Sarah, BLWt. 24992-160-55..................... W 19960
    James, Conn. & R. I., wid. Temperance... R 7998
      Soldier was pensioned in 1818 while living at Scipio, N. Y.
    Ralph.. S 2883
PATRIDGE. (See PARTRIDGE.)
PATTEN, Asa... S 19743
    John, BLWt. 7294-160-55... S 19745
    Thomas, wid. Mary.. W 13795
    William, Conn. & Cont., wid. Abigail... W 26293
    (See also PATTON.)

PATTENGELL, Jacob... S 43780
    (See also PETTINGALE and PETTINGILL.)
PATTERSON, Ansel, wid. Polly, BLWt. 10015-160-55............................... W 6855
    Sherman, wid. Huldah... W 19959
    William, Cont. (Conn.), wid. Lois... W 18691
PATTISON, Sunderland, Cont. (Conn.).. S 43786
PATTON, Christopher, Conn. & Mass... S 8662
    (See also PATTEN.)
PAUL, James, wid. Zeruah... W 26835
    Kiles, wid. Abigail, BLWt. 82541-160-55............................... W 572
PAULK, Ammi.. S 11199
    Ephraim, wid. Eunice.. W 18727
PAYN or PAYNE, Edward.. S 3625
    Eleazer, wid. Aurel.. R 8021
    Rufus, Chenange Co., N. Y., in 1832........................... S 28841
    Rufus, Litchfield Co., Conn., in 1818.............................. S 36203
    Solomon, wid. Mary.. W 2160
    Stephen, Conn. & Conn. Sea service......................... S 41040
    William.. S 11198
        (See also PAINE.)
PEAGAN, Joseph... S 33459
PEARCE, John... S 43826
    (See also PEARSE, PEIRCE and PIERCE.)
PEARL, Frederick.. S 36215
    Timothy, wid. Lois.. W 26292
PEARSE, Richard, Navy (Conn.), wid. Candace.................. W 4308
    (See also PEARCE, PEIRCE and PIERCE.)
PEARSON, Jesse, wid. Lydia.. W 16677
    Peter.. S 17635
    William E., wid. Hannah, BLWt. 31562-160-55............. W 3592
        (Given also PIERSON and PARSONS.)
        (See also PEIRSON and PIERSON.)
PEARSONS, Joseph Jabez, wid. Hannah.............................. R 26148
    (Soldier never pensioned.)
    (Given also as PARSONS.)
PEASE, Abner... S 30022
    Charles, wid. Elizabeth.. W 10869
    David, wid. Jerusha... W 19979
    Ebenezer... S 41054
    Edward, wid. Abigail... W 17431
        Soldier died in 1817, Hartford, Co., Conn.
    Edward, wid. Rhoda.. R 8049
        Soldier was pensioned while living in Chelsea, Vt., in 1832.
    Ephraim.. R 8045
    Gideon, wid. Prudence.. R 8048
        Soldier never pensioned.
    Isaac.. S 18545
    James... S 14124
    Joel.. S 40252
    Joel, Conn. & Mass... R 8046
    John, Cont. (Conn.)... S 18544
    Joseph... S 41065
    Joseph, wid. Elizabeth.. R 8044
        Soldier never pensioned.
    Moses... S 11225
    Peter, wid. Desire.. R 8043
        Soldier was pensioned in 1818 from Hadley, Mass.
    Phineas.. S 17630
    Robert, wid. Anna.. W 17432
    Samuel, wid. Lydia.. W 10873
        Soldier pensioned in 1832 from Luzerne Co., Penna., where he died in 1846.
    Samuel, wid. Sarah.. W 17430
        Soldier died in 1828 at Tolland, Conn.
    Silas, Conn. & Cont., wid. Rhoba...................................... W 6859
    Simeon.. S 14151
    Stone, wid. Mary.. W 26308
PEASELY or PEASLEY, Mary, former wid. of Martin TUBBS.
PECK, Aaron, wid. Hannah.. W 21956
    Abel, wid. Diadama, BLWt. 24436-160-55........................ W 2846
    Abijah, wid. Sarah, BLWt. 26993-160-55......................... W 6856
        Soldier pensioned in 1832 from New Haven Co., Conn.
    Abijah, Conn. & N. Y., Saratoga Co., N. Y., in 1832...... S 14153
    Abner, Conn. & Mass.. S 30650
    Asahel, wid. Anna or Anne... W 21957
    Azel.. S 11222
    Benjamin, wid. Mary, BLWt. 31557-160-55..................... W 3035
        Soldier pensioned in 1832 from Danbury, Conn.
    Benjamin, wid. Mary.. W 16370
        Soldier died in Greene Co., N. Y., in 1820.
    Benjamin, Cont. (Conn.).. S 15571
        Musician, Windham Co., Conn., in 1818; dropped on account of property; restored to
        rolls in 1852 from Providence, R. I.
    Bezaleel... S 14152
    Calvin, wid. Sarah, BLWt. 31593-160-55......................... W 1068
    Dan.. S 4644
    Daniel.. S 11228
    David, died 1834, Fairfield Co., Conn., pension paid wid. Althea.......... S 14128
    David, wid. Isabel.. R 8961
        Soldier never pensioned.

113

PECK, David, Sandlake, N. Y., in 1832... S 14156
 David, Sodus, N. Y., in 1818... S 43813
 Ebenezer... S 38300
 Eliphalet, wid. Abigail... W 21946
 Elisha, wid. Hulda... R 8054
  Soldier never pensioned.
 Elisha, wid. Lucretia.. W 15183
 Gad, wid. Mary, BLWt. 26885-160-55... W 8286
 George, wid. Ann.. W 19977
 Hiel, Conn. & Cont., wid. Hannah.. W 3294
  BLWt. 1687-200, Lieut., was issued Sept. 15, 1790, to Harry Williams. No papers.
 Isaac.. R 8059
 Isaac, wid. Elizabeth, BLWt. 26212-160-55.. W 9220
 Jacob, Conn. & Cont., wid. Elizabeth.. W 26869
 Jathleel, wid. Olive.. W 26873
 Jedediah or Jedidiah, Madison Co., N. Y., in 1832....................................... S 14114
 Jedediah, Cont. (Conn.), wid. Tabitha... W 16674
  Artificer, died in 1821, Otsego Co., N. Y.
 Jesse, wid. Sarah, BLWt. 31312-160-55... W 1922
 Jesse, Continental service but Conn. residence in 1818; Lieut., dropped in 1820 on account of
  property.. S 36213
 John, Brookfield, Conn., in 1832.. S 14158
 John, wid. Mary, BLWt. 300-60-55.. W 26301
  Soldier pensioned in 1818 from Litchfield Co., Conn.
 John, Conn. & Cont., wid. Lois, priv. and Lieut., died in 1825 in Conn................... W 21930
 Joseph, Hampden Co., Mass., in 1832... S 29373
 Joseph, Conn. & Cont., wid. Sarah... W 21939
  Soldier pensioned from New London Co., Conn., in 1818, and Lyme, Conn., in 1832.
 Josiah, wid. Helen.. W 17428
 Judson, wid. Mary... W 17429
 Lysias, Cont. (Conn.), wid. Phebe... W 26299
 Moses... S 14159
 Reuben, Cornwall, Vt., in 1832.. S 22432
 Reuben, Cayuga Co., N. Y., in 1818.. S 43812
 Samuel.. S 17012
 Simon, Cont. (Conn.).. S 7304
 Stephen... S 36214
 Thomas.. S 23841
 Ward, wid. Dorcas... W 26310
 William, wid. Elizabeth... W 26875
  Soldier was pensioned as Serg't. in Bethel, N. Y., in 1818 & 1832; died there in 1837.
 William, wid. Mary.. R 8066
  Soldier pensioned as priv. in Chenango Co., N. Y., in 1832.
  (See also PEEK and PIKE.)
PECKHAM, Benjamin, wid. Lucy.. W 21931
PEEK, Isaac.. R 8060
 (Also given as PECK.)
 Samuel.. S 41964
PEET, Elijah, wid. Anna.. W 18734
 John, Conn. & Cont., wid. Sally... W 17427
 Lemuel.. S 36218
 Thaddeus.. S 22434
PEIRCE, John, Penna. in 1832... S 3691
 (Also given as PIERCE.)
 Samuel, Conn. & Cont., wid. Hannah.. W 26901
  Addison Co., Vt., in 1818, where he died in March, 1832.
  (See also PEARCE, PEARSE, and PIERCE.)
PEIRSON, Amos, wid. Sarah.. W 4765
 (See also PEARSON and PIERSON.)
PELLON, Edward... S 36216
PELTON, Benjamin, wid. Hannah.. W 9921
 Daniel.. S 43827
 David... S 33468
 Freeman, wid. Prudence.. R 8083
  Soldier never pensioned.
 John.. S 28842
 Joseph, Conn., N. J. & Privateer, Oneida Co., N. Y., in 1832............................ S 11229
 Joseph, wid. Abigail, BLWt. 34904-160-55.. W 26303
  Soldier was pensioned from Lyme, N. H., in 1832. Abigail also applied for BL on account
  of her first husband, John Ayres or Ayers, Conn. BLRej.
 Moses, Dorothy Phillips, former wid. of... W 17441
PEMBER, Eli, wid. Clarissa, BLWt. 11417-160-55... W 2335
PEMBLETON, Jabez, wid. Lucy, BLWt. 26971-160-55.. W 2557
PENDELL, Elizabeth, former wid. of Samuel OSBORN.
PENDLETON, Daniel, Cont. (Conn.)... BLWt. 2152-300
 David... S 20910
PENFIELD, Abel... R 8089
 Daniel.. R 8090
 James, wid. Mary.. W 26298
 Jesse, Dorinda Shepard, former wid. of.. R 9477
  Soldier never pensioned.
 Jesse, Cont. (Conn.).. S 43834
 Nathaniel... S 23369
 Peter, wid. Hannah.. W 16679
 Phineas... S 15558
 Samuel.. S 5895
 Simeon.. S 18155
PENHALLOW, Richard, Conn. & Cont., wid. Huldah... W 18737
 (Also given HOLLOW, Richard P.)

PENNOYER, William... S 17631
    Served also in 1812.
PENOYER, Samuel.. S 15573
PENTLAND, Thomas, Conn. & Cont.. S 43840
PERCY, Joseph.. R 17029
PERIGO or PERRIGO, Ebenezer, wid. Mary.. W 17435
    William.. S 43818
PERKINS, Aaron, BLWt. 277-100... S 41053
    Abraham, Serg't.; pensioned in New London Co., Conn., in 1818; dropped on account of
      property in 1820; Cert. No. 3536.
    Charles, Cont. (Conn.).. BLWt. 340-100
    Daniel, Orange Co., Vt., in 1832... S 19026
    Daniel, Fairfield, Vt., in 1818... S 41063
    Ebenezer... S 36219
    Elias... S 14149
    Elisha... S 29379
    Francis, wid. Saloma, BLWt. 6438-160-55... W 6865
    Isaac.. S 33448
    Israel, wid. Lydia... W 18748
    Jason.. S 43816
    Leonard... S 23366
    Reuben.. S 14157
    Samuel.. S 9454
    William... S 14126
PERMELE or PERMELEE. (See PARMELEE.)
PERRIGO. (See PERIGO.)
PERRIT, Peter, BLWt. 1677-300, Capt., was issued January 8, 1790. No papers.
PERRY, Abijah.. S 40259
    Almon, wid. Elizabeth... W 18740
    Arthur.. S 14154
    Ebenezer, Dorcas Taylor, former wid. of (see papers in case of her first husband, Levi FAR-
      NAM or FARNHAM)... W 16572
    Eli.. S 14113
    Freeman, Conn. & N. Y... S 14121
    Hannah, former wid. of Nathaniel PETTINGALE.
    Ichabod or Jeremiah, Conn. & Navy, wid. Rebecca, BLWt. 31558-160-55................. W 17433
    John.. S 17628
    Jonathan, wid. Hannah.. W 26295
    Joseph, wid. Mary.. W 17434
    Nathaniel, wid. Eunice.. W 26864
    Ozias, Conn. & Cont.. S 43832
    Reuben, wid. Sally, BLWt. 54873-160-55.. W 2663
    Samuel, wid. Alice, Willington, Conn., in 1818, where he died in 1831...................... W 15189
    Samuel, wid. Tabitha, BLWt. 15438-160-55... W 26859
      Soldier never pensioned, died in 1821; widow lived in Maine in 1836.
    Sylvanus.. S 36212
      BLWt. 1670-200, Lieut., was issued June 30, 1789. No papers.
    Thomas, Conn. & Privateer.. S 14162
PETERS, Absalom.. S 14129
    Galloway, wid. Nancy.. W 18736
      BLWt. 6284-100, private, was issued June 14, 1790. No papers.
    Joseph.. S 11231
    Joseph P., wid. Lydia, BLWt. 38541-160-55.. W 2338
    Nathan, Conn., Cont. & Mass., wid. Lois... W 21937
    Peter... S 36210
    Samuel, wid. Hannah.. W 17437
PETTEBONE or PETTIBONE, Daniel, wid. Eunice, BLWt. 39492-160-55.................. W 26306
    Elijah... S 43837
    John, Susannah Pinney, former wid. of.. R 8262
      Soldier never pensioned. This woman's former husband, Jonathan Pinney, Conn., also
      served in the Revolution. (See papers within.)
    Stephen.. BL–
PETTINGALE, Nathaniel, Conn., Mass. & N. H., Hannah Perry, former wid. of........ W 21933
    Soldier also served in French and Indian War.
PETTINGILL, John, wid. Hannah, BLWt. 26017-160-55... W 10877
    (See also PATTENGELL.)
PETTIS, Joseph... S 14164
PEYATT. (See PIATT.)
PHELPS, Aaron, Ruth Lewis, former wid. of... W 20438
    Abel, Elizabeth Williams, former wid. of.. W 2630
    Abijah.. S 4648
    Alexander... S 11240
      Invalid pensioner, and Middlesex Co., Conn., in 1832.
    Alexander... S 22933
      Grafton Co., N. H., in 1832; transferred to Albany, N. Y., Agency.
    Amos.. S 18160
    Asahel, wid. Margaret, BLWt. 13718-160-55.. W 6866
      Soldier served in Conn. & Cont. Line.
    Austin, wid. Deborah.. W 17439
    Beriah.. S 23843
    Bissell, wid. Sarah, BLWt. 3822-160-55.. W 175
    Cornelius, wid. Philena, BLWt. 11284-160-55... W 5536
    Daniel... S 14143
    Darius, wid. Mary... R 8174
      Soldier never pensioned.
    David, Serg't., Enfield, Conn., in 1818 and 1832; died Nov. 3, 1834........................... S 11239
    David, Lieut. and Capt., died before 1832, Simsbury, Conn. (See papers of his son David,
      S 14141.)
    David, died Simsbury, Conn., in 1835... S 14141
    David, Vermont in 1818.. S 41069

PHELPS, Eli, wid. Rachel, Conn. & N. Y. service, BLWt. 27592–160–55........................ W 26314
    Elijah, wid. Mary.. W 15846
        Soldier died in Hartford, Conn., in 1823.
    Elijah, wid. Zeruiah, corp. Conn. Line in 1818; died in 1831 in Middlesex Co., Conn......... W 26313
    Elisha, Conn. & N. Y.. S 14135
    Erastus... S 14142
    Giles... S 9987
    Homer, wid. Adah, BLWt. 31564–160–55.. W 18754
    Ira... S 8952
    James, no definite service given, but Conn. residence.. R 8171
    Jared, wid. Rowena.. W 3113
    Joel, wid. Susannah, priv. dragoons: Warren Co., N. Y., in 1832, where he died in 1836...... W 18756
    Joel, Conn., Cont. & Mass., serg't; Bloomfield, N. Y., in 1818; transferred to Michigan....... S 35028
    John, private of infantry; Litchfield Co., Conn., in 1832.. S 14137
    John, wid. Catherine, Serg't and Lieut.; died in 1812 in Albany Co., N. Y.................... W 19986
    John, wid. Sarah, Litchfield Co., Conn., in 1832, where he died in 1837; priv. cavalry......... W 17447
    Jonathan, Conn. & Privateer, wid. Charity, BLWt. 26604–160–55............................. W 9594
    Joseph... S 15575
    Joshua, wid. Elizabeth... W 21970
    Judah, wid. Abigail.. W 17448
    Lancelot. (See PHILLIPS.)
    Mary, former wid. of Richard AUSTIN.
    Norman.. S 29384
    Obadiah, Cont. service, artificer; died in 1799; Arminda Hebard or Hibbard, former wid. of.. W 4985
        NOTE.—Arminda's last husband was also a pensioner. (See HIBBARD, William, Conn.,
        S 13400.)
    Oliver, St. Johnsbury, Vt., in 1832.. S 15574
    Oliver, Chenango Co., N. Y., in 1832.. S 22932
    Oliver, wid. Phebe.. W 5540
        Soldier was in Hartford Co., Conn., in 1832.
    Reuben, wid. Mary.. W 15214
    Roger.. S 14144
    Samuel, New London Co., Conn., in 1818... S 36224
    Samuel, Conn. & Privateer, Serg't & Seaman; Madison Co., N. Y., in 1832.................... S 5919
    Seth, BLWt. 1674–300, Capt., was issued July 5, 1796. No papers.
    Silas, Conn. & Cont., wid. Mary, BLWt. 284–60–55... W 26883
    Timothy, wid. Elizabeth.. W 26317
    William.. R 8178
PHILBROOK, Thomas, Conn., Mass. & Navy, wid. Abigail.. W 21964
PHILIPS. (See PHILLIPS.)
PHILLEY. (See FILLEY.)
PHILLIPS, PHILLIP or PHILLIPS.
    Asa, wid. Lois, BLWt. 38568–160–55.. W 9229
    Ayer.. R 8185
    Dorothy, former wid. of Moses PELTON.
    Elisha... S 21423
    Esquire.. S 14145
    Gideon... S 14138
    James, wid. Martha Sarah.. W 17443
    Jeruel, wid. Prudence.. W 17440
    Job, Athens Co., Ohio, in 1832.. S 16225
    Job, wid. Mary, Plainfield, Conn., in 1832 and died there in Dec., 1832....................... W 17442
    John... S 43846
    Lancelot, wid. Jerusha.. W 16372
        (Given as PHILIPS and PHELPS.)
    Michael.. S 36222
    Philip, wid. Elizabeth.. W 5532
    Samuel, wid. Lydia... W 21965
        Soldier died in 1815 in Litchfield Co., Conn.
    Samuel, wid. Millea, BLWt. 11068–160–55... W 5534
        Soldier pensioned in 1818 in Litchfield Co., Conn., and died in 1862 in Ashtabula Co., Ohio.
    Samuel H., Commissary Department (Conn.)... S 17018
    Thomas, Ann Beers, former wid. of, BLWt. 26391–160–55....................................... W 25233
        NOTE.—Ann's second and third husbands were also pensioners. (See MILLS, Joseph,
        Conn., S 36151, and BEERS, Samuel, Conn. & Mass., S 17267.)
PHILO or FILLOW, Adams.. R 8216
    Azor.. S 22931
PHINNEY, Asa.. S 14136
    John, BLWt. 808–100.. S 41066
        (Also given as FINNEY.)
    Joseph, wid. Mary.. W 16988
PHIPPENE, PHIPPNE or PIFFANY, Nehemiah.. S 14179
PHIPPS, Daniel Goffe, Conn., Conn. Sea service & Privateer.. S 15860
    Jason... S 14131
PIATT, Lewis, Conn. & N. Y.. R 8220
    (Also given as PEYATT.)
PICKET or PICKETT, Phinehas... S 23373
    Samuel.. S 30031
PICKSLEY. (See PIXLEY.)
PIDGE, Otis, wid. Jemima.. R 8229
    Soldier never pensioned.
PIER, Solomon... S 43856
PIERCE, Benjamin.. R 8232
    Daniel... S 36229
    (Also given PEARSE.)
    Job, Conn., Cont. & R. I.. S 14173
    Joseph.. R 8239
    Samuel, wid. Dorcas... W 5157
    (Also given PEARCE and PEIRCE.)
    William, wid. Catharine.. W 15847
    (See also PEIRCE, PEARCE and PEARSE.)

PIERPOINT, Thomas.. S 32444
PIERPONT, Eveline, wid. Rhoda.. W 17998
    John.. S 36227
PIERSON, Nathan... R 8248
    (See also PEARSON and PEIRSON.)
PIFFANY. (See PHIPPENE.)
PIKE, Abraham. (See PYKE.)
    Barnabas, wid. Hannah.. W 26904
        (Also given PECK.)
    James; wid., Sarah... W 4764
    John, wid. Betsey, BLWt. 18024–160–55....................................... W 26318
    Jonathan... S 40264
    Willard, Conn. & Cont., wid. Molly... W 18759
PILGRIM, Thomas.. S 36231
PINNEO, Joseph, wid. Azuba, BLWt. 26763–160–55............................ W 21978
PINNEY, Butler... R 8095
    Isaac, Serg't. Hartford Co., Conn., in 1832; died there in 1833............ S 14169
    Isaac, Conn. & Cont., wid. Mary, Serg't. Royalton, Vt., in 1818; died there in 1842........... W 26971
    Jonathan, wid. Martha... W 4760
    Jonathan, wid. Susannah.. R —
        (See case of Susannah's other husband, PETTIBONE, John, R. 8262.)
    Lemuel.. S 17020
    Nathaniel... S 36228
    Philaster.. S 43857
PINTO, Solomon, Clarissa Hall, former wid. of.................................... W 11263
    BLWt. 1673–150, Ensign, was issued June 3, 1795. No papers. Also BLWt. 1–10–55.
PITCHER, Abner... S 43858
PITKIN, John.. S 14165
    Stephen... S 3675
PITTS, Richard, Conn. & Md., wid. Sarah.. W 17452
PIXLEY or PICKSLEY, Elijah... S 40265
PLANT, Eli, BLWt. 26111–160–55.. S 14180
    Ethel... S 43870
PLATT, Daniel.. S 23374
    Ebenezer, wid. Anna, BLWt. 34528–160–55..................................... W 26323
        (Also given as PRATT.)
    Gideon... S 17026
    Isaac, Cont. service but Conn. residence... S 36232
    Jabez, wid., Jillin.. W 17462
    James, wid. Olive.. W 10903
    John, Litchfield, Conn., in 1818... S 36233
    John, wid. Sarah... W 5563
        Soldier died in Delaware Co., Ohio; not pensioned.
    Joseph, wid. Lydia... W 17459
        Died in 1792 in Fairfield Co., Conn.
    Joseph, wid. Mary, Fairfield Co. in 1832; died there in 1844................ W 9231
    Nathan, wid. Charlotte, BLWt. 90012–160–55.................................. R 8282
    Olive, former wid. of Eliphalet SMITH.
    Samuel, Cont. (Conn.), wid. Abigail... W 21980
    Truman... S 18549
PLATTS, Dan.. S 39018
PLUMB, Hannah, former wid. of Ichabod Talmadge.
    Isaac, wid, Catharine, BLWt. 28583–160–55.................................... W 6871
    Joseph, Middlesex Co., Conn., in 1832.. S 31910
    Joseph... R 8286
    Nathaniel, wid. Anna, BLWt. 2255–100... W 19994
    Samuel.. R 8237
PLUMBS, Daniel... S 38308
    George, wid. Eunice... W 26909
PLUMLEY, Ebenezer, wid. Dorothy.. R 8289
    Soldier was pensioned from N. Y. in 1818 and 1832.
POLK. (See PAULK.)
POLLEY or POLLY, Daniel... S 40285
    John, Cont. (Conn.), wid. Phebe, BLWt. 3133–160–55...................... W 10912
    Jonathan, wid. Mehitable or Mehetable, BLWt. 34903–160–55.......... W 6872
POLLOCK, Elijah... S 40286
    Mingo, wid. Molly... W 17469
POMEROY or POMROY, Amos.. S 14215
    Dan, Cont. (Conn.).. S 44251
    Daniel.. S 3721
        (Also given as POMERY.)
    Elisha, Conn. & Mass., wid. Lucy, BLWt. 36552–160–55.................. W 26335
    Medad... S 22940
        (Also given as POMROY.)
    Nathaniel, wid. Martha.. W 17482
        (Given as POMROY.)
    Phoebus... R 8310
    Ralph, BLWt. 100–200.. S 36237
POND, Barnabas, wid. Phebe P., BLWt. 31559–160–55......................... W 5573
    Bartholomew... S 23347
    Beriah, Cont. (Conn.), wid. Silvia or Silva....................................... W 18777
    Charles, wid. Catherine, Conn. & Sea service.................................. W 22005
    Dan... S 14218
    Elias.. S 36239
    Timothy, wid. Merina.. W 16374
POOL or POOLE, Chester, Conn. & Vt., wid. Bridget, BLWt. 14532–160–55.......... W 5569
    David, Navy service but paid at Conn. Agency................................. S 20923
    John, wid. Abigail... W 26332
    John, wid. Elizabeth.. R 8317
        Soldier never pensioned.

POOL or POOLE, Samuel, Serg't. in 1818 in New Haven Co., Conn............................. S 36234
Samuel, wid. Ruth... W 17466
   Died in 1827 in Windsor Co., Vt.
Thomas, Cont. service but Conn. residence, wid. Elizabeth................................ W 26922
POOLER or POOLLER, George, Conn. & Mass.. S 14198
POOR, Jonathan, Conn. & Cont.. S 38313
POPE, Ezra, wid. Mary... R 8329
   Soldier was pensioned in 1832 from Richland Co., Ohio.
PORTER, Abel, Cont. (Conn.)... S 14207
Abijah, wid. Sarah, BLWt. 26327-160-55.. W 1070
Alexander, wid. Zerviah.. W 15261
Amos... S 44254
Benjamin.. S 23376
   Clara, former wid. of Isaac RAYMOND or REYMOND.
Daniel.. S 36240
David, Weston, Conn., in 1832: transferred to N. Y................................... S 14216
David, wid. Sarah, BLWt. 26136-160-55.. W 13821
   Soldier was pensioned from Greene Co., N. Y., in 1832
Eldad.. S 44246
Eleazer... S 44258
Elijah, drummer, in Farmington, Conn., in 1818 and 1832.............................. S 14219
Elijah, Musician; Mass. in 1818, transferred to Ohio................................. S 40276
Elijah, Anna Harrington or Herrington, former wid. of............................... R 8337
   Soldier never pensioned.
Ephraim.. S 28846
Ezekiel... S 14199
Ezra... S 35568
Isaac... S 14188
Isaac... R 8342
John... R 8344
John, wid. Esther, BLWTt. 38839-160-55... R 8346
John, wid. Lucy... W 26336
   Soldier died in 1813, Fairfield Co., Conn.
John, Conn. & Cont., Grafton Co., N. H., in 1832.................................. S 14195
John, Cont. (Conn.)... R 17154
John, Cont. (Conn.), wid. Lydia... W 8526
   Artificer; Washington Co., N. Y., in 1818.
John, Cont. (Conn.), wid. Mary.. W 21988
   Artificer; died in 1806 in Hartford Co., Conn.
Joseph, Conn. & Cont.. S 35572
Martin... S 14213
Moses.. S 35029
Moses, wid. Sarah... R 8354
   Soldier never pensioned.
Nathaniel... S 44243
Samuel, Corp. Berlin, Conn., in 1832... S 14208
Samuel, Drummer; Coventry, N. Y., in 1832....................................... S 14191
Simeon, wid. Sarah.. W 17468
Thomas.. S 17640
Truman.. S 14220
Truman.. R 8355
William, Conn. & N. Y.. BLWt. 1519-100
William, wid. Hannah, BLWt. 3978-160-55... W 5557
   Soldier was in Lyme, N. H., in 1832.
POST, Ebenezer... S 36741
Ezra... S 14187
George, wid. Esther... W 17464
Jediah or Jedediah, wid. Isabella or Isobel.. R 8362
   Soldier pensioned in 1832 from N. J.
Jimmy... S 14206
   Patience, former wid. of Peter LEWIS.
Simeon... S 22447
Stephen.. S 31916
POTER. (See POTTER.)
POTTAGE, Jabez.. S 36241
POTTER, Alice or Allice, former wid. of Alvan GOODELL or Alvin GOODALL.
Benjamin, wid. Rachel... W 26326
Borden... W 3710
Caleb, Conn., Mass. & Vt.. S 19037
Daniel, wid. Martha, BLWt. 64-60-55.. W 2332
David, Conn. & R. I., Herkimer Co., N. Y., in 1832.............................. S 14189
David, wid. Hannah, BLWt. 19780-160-55... W 2242
   Artificer; Stratford, Conn., in 1832.
David, wid. Rebecca... R 8379
   Soldier was pensioned in 1818 from Chenango Co., N. Y.
Ebenezer, Conn., Mass. & N. H.. S 11255
Edward.. S 14209
Ezra, Cont. (Conn.).. S 35575
Israel..BLWt. 1703-200
Joel, wid. Thankful... W 26325
John... S 14203
Lemuel, wid. Lydia.. W 17472
Levi, Conn. & Cont.. S 11262
Medad... S 35564
Milton... S 21426
   (Also given POTER.)
Moses.. S 35569
Robert... S 40269
Sheldon, wid. Mary, BLWt. 45-100... W 18775

118

POTTER, Stephen, BLWt. 1668-300, Capt., was issued April 11, 1792. No papers.
Thaddeus.. S 23846
Timothy, wid. Martha.. W 17479
POTTS, Benjamin... S 44247
POTWINE, George.. S 14204
POWEL, Felix, Conn. & Cont.. S 44260
POWELL, Peter, wid. Eunice... R 8395
POWERS, Aaron... S 40282
James... S 35570
John, Conn. & Cont., wid. Anna, BLWt. 14763-160-55............................... W 26337
Nathan, wid. Sarah... W 17476
Timothy, wid. Elizabeth.. W 17473
PRATT, Abijah, wid. Mary... W 17483
Asa, Susanna Starkey, former wid. of, BLWt. 14955-160-55........................ W 11563
Augustus... S 14233
Benjamin, Conn. & Mass., wid. Sarah... R 8433
Soldier never pensioned.
Cary.. S 11265
Ebenezer. (See PLATT.)
Edmund, Conn. & Navy, wid. Sybil... R 8436
Soldier pensioned in 1832 in Niagara Co., N. Y.; later transferred to Michigan.
Edward... S 5950
Elias.. S 29392
Isaiah... S 33506
James... S 44262
Jasper or Jesper.. S 35581
Jonathan, Conn. & Cont.. S 14221
Lemuel, Conn. & Cont., wid. Mary, BLWt. 61095-160-55.............................. W 5577
Olive, former wid. of Caleb FOWLER.
Paul, Conn. & Mass... S 9990
Peabody, wid. Sarah.. W 26936
Phineas, Conn. & Cont.. S 40303
Russell... R 8429
Samuel, Conn. & Privateer.. R 8432
William, Granby, Conn., in 1832 as priv. and Serg't.................................. S 17029
William, Zuba or Zuby Byington, former wid. of....................................... R 1570
Soldier never pensioned.
Zadoc or Zadock, Conn. & Cont... S 44263
Zimri, Conn. & Vt.. S 19043
PRENTICE, PRENTIS, or PRENTISS, Elisha.. S 15563
Jesse, wid. Elizabeth... W 26608
Jonathan... R 8443
Nathaniel, Conn. & Privateer, wid. Margaret, BLWt. 31566-160-55................. W 6750
Samuel, wid. Lucretia.. R 8444
Soldier never pensioned.
Samuel.. S 5949
Thomas.. S 21931
William, Zephrah Kenyon, former wid. of... W 26709
PRESBREY, John, Conn. Sea service, Mass. and R. I................................... S 18555
PRESTON, Calvin, wid. Rachel, BLWt. 26884-160-55................................... W 2690
Daniel, New London Co., Conn., in 1818... S 35586
Daniel, wid. Esther, BLWt. 6106-160-55.. W 5581
Soldier was pensioned in 1832 in Otsego Co., N. Y.
David... S 40291
Hovey.. S 35578
Joseph.. S 36244
Noah, wid. Aner or Anor... W 20001
Shubael.. S 14230
Zephaniah, wid. Mary... BLWt. 73547-160-55
PRICE, David, wid. Susannah... W 17493
Eleazer, wid. Hannah... R 8466
Soldier never pensioned.
Elijah, Conn. & N. Y., wid. Beulah... R 8462
Jonathan, wid. Jemima... W 17497
Paul.. S 35579
Richard... S 36243
Rufus, wid. Ruth.. W 16685
PRICHARD or PRITCHARD, Benjamin.. S 40302
BLWt. 6280-100 was issued May 17, 1790. No papers.
Jared... S 8796
Nathaniel, wid. Comfort... W 5582
(See also PRITCHARD.)
PRIDE, Absalom, Conn. & Cont.. S 14232
Jonathan, wid. Anna.. W 15940
Reuben... S 44276
BLWt. 1671-200, Lieut., was issued Nov. 6, 1789, to Reuben Pride or Price. No papers.
PRIER. (See PRIOR.)
PRIEST, John, Cont. (Conn.), Lucy Cook, former wid. of, BLWt. 1227-100............ W 16539
PRIMUS, Job, Keturah Smith, former wid. of, BLWt. 61201-160-55................... W 10256
(Also given as LATHROP.)
PRINCE, Edward H.. S 14224
Philip.. S 35580
Timothy.. S 41079
PRINDLE, Abijah.. S 35588
Joel.. S 35585
Peter... S 31978
Samuel.. S 15577
Samuel.. R 8488
Zalmon, wid. Polly.. W 24920

119

PRIOR, Abner, wid. Abigail.. W 4311
    BLWt. 1666–400, Major, was issued May 20, 1791. No papers.
  Azariah, wid. Alice... W 17496
  Jesse.. S 44275
  Roswell, wid. Phebe... W 17495
  Simeon... S 4652
  William, Cont. (Conn.), wid. Elizabeth.. W 18783
    (Also given PRIER.)
PRITCHARD, George, wid. Abigail.. W 2342
  James... S 23852
    (See also PRICHARD.)
PROUT, Oliver.. S 14234
  William, wid. Naomi... W 22012
PROUTY, John Warner... S 8983
PROVEOST. (See PROVOST.)
PROVORSE. (See PROVOST.)
PROVOST, Daniel.. S 20296
  Samuel, wid. Anna, BLWt. 40696–160–55... W 26339
    (Also given as PROVEOST.)
  Thomas, Conn., N. Y. & Privateer... S 17028
    (Also given as PROVORSE.)
PUFFER, Daniel, Cont. (Conn.).. S 43875
  Simeon, Cont. (Conn.), wid. Fanny... W 20007
PULFORD, Elisha.. S 41088
  Joseph, wid. Phebe... W 22018
PULLMAN, John, Conn. Sea service & R. I., wid. Esther... R 8520
  Soldier never pensioned.
PURDY, Daniel, Conn. & N. Y.. S 9460
PUTNAM, Aaron, wid. Sally.. W 16146
  Daniel, wid. Catharine, Conn. & Cont.. W 17503
  Israel, Conn. & Cont., BLWt. 1664–1100, Major General, was issued Dec. 13, 1790.   No papers.
  Reuben.. S 43876
PYKE, Abraham... S 5168
  (See also PIKE.)

Q

QUACKINBUSH, Abraham... R 20426
QUI. (See QUY.)
QUIMBY, John... S 11273
QUINLEY, Thomas.. S 35592
QUINTARD, Evert, wid. Hannah.. W 20009
  Isaac, BLWt. 18011–160–55.. S 17033
  James... S 36248
QUY, Libbeus or Lebbeus... S 36249
  (Also given as QUI.)

R

RAINEY, Stephen, wid. Esther, BLWt. 1374–450; & BLWt. 9057–160–55........................ W 3040
RALPH, Jonathan.. S 36251
RAMSDELL, Ezra... S 35595
RANDAL, RANDALL, RANDEL or RANDELL.
  Amos, wid. Jemima... W 24725
  Charles.. S 4754
  Elijah, wid. Judith.. W 24727
  Jedediah, wid. Martha.. W 20010
  John, Conn. & N. Y... S 14245
  Jonas, Conn. & R. I... S 11279
  Joseph, Conn. & Cont.. S 22453
  Reuben, Cont. (Conn.).. S 35608
  Shubel or Shubal, wid. Sarah... W 22035
    (Given as RANDEL or RANDELL.)
  Timothy, wid. Eunice, BLWt. 40697–160–55.. W 26350
RANEY, RANNEY or RANNY.
  Amos, Conn. & Conn. Sea service.
  George, wid. Lucy.. W 16384
    BLWt. 6377–100, private, was issued July 14, 1789. No papers.
    (Also given as RANNY.)
  Seth, Conn. & N. Y.. S 11278
  Solomon... S 43903
  Stephen, wid. Elizabeth, BLWt. 1518–100... W 22036
  William... R 8593
  William, Conn. & Cont... S 15607
RANSOM, Abner, Conn. Sea service & Cont. (Conn.).. R 8596
  Amos.. S 15608
  Asahel.. S 14244
  David.. S 35597
    Pensioned in 1818 at New London Co.
  David, Conn. & Mass., wid. Anna.. W 20013
  Elijah.. S 35594
    BLWt. 1798–200, Lieut., was issued Feb. 23, 1799. No papers.
  Ezekiel, Conn. & Mass., wid. Lucinda.. W 5663
  George Palmer, wid. Elizabeth.. W 2694
  Israel, wid. Lois, BLWt. 80031–160–55.. W 9616
  James... S 15610
  Joseph, Azubah Blish, former wid. of, BLWt. 47614–160–55...................................... W 25255
    Soldier died in 1795 in Middlesex Co., Conn.
  Joseph, Conn. & Cont., Akron Co., Ohio in 1832... S 18559
  Samuel, killed in service July 3, 1778; BLWt. 408–300 was issued to his heirs.
  Samuel.   (Alive in 1808.)
RASAR. (See RAZAR.)

RASH, Jacob, Conn. & Cont., wid. Chloe.. W 5667
RATHBONE, RATHBUN, or RATHBURN.
    Asa, wid. Ruth.. W 17508
        (Given as RATHBURN.)
    Benjamin.. S 19438
    Ezra.. S 40314
    Jonathan, wid. Hannah.. W 11103
    Moses, wid. Olive.. W 22040
    Thomas, wid. Elizabeth.. W 3115
RAWDON, Ezra, wid. Sarah.. W 4772
RAWLS, Aaron, wid. Hannah... R 8608
    Soldier never pensioned.
RAXFORD, Denison. (See REXFORD.)
    Joseph. (See RIXFORD.)
RAY, Caleb, Conn. & Cont... S 15604
    Daniel... S 43891
    Gideon, wid. Zipporah.. W 17514
    John P.. S 31921
    Timothy.. S 14250
    Warwick.. S 35602
RAYMOND, Daniel, Conn. & Cont.. S 35601
    David, Hartford Co., Conn., in 1832... S 17037
    David, Fairfield Co., Conn., in 1832... S 35606
    Ebur.. S 36250
    George, Conn. & Navy, wid. Ann.. W 11111
    Isaac, Clara Porter, former wid. of.. W 26334
        (Also given as REYMOND.)
    James... S 35598
    Joshua, wid. Elizabeth... W 17512
    Lemuel... S 43890
    Miriam, former wid. of Benjamin DIMMICK.
    Moses... S 20928
    Napthali.. S 21436
    Nathaniel, wid. Dinah, BLWt. 36628–160–55... W 26356
    Nathaniel Lynde, Conn., Navy & Privateer, wid. Louisa..................................... W 26351
    Newcomb, wid. Lorinda, BLWt. 19804–160–55.. W 26360
    Stephen, wid. Mary... W 17513
    William... S 35596
    Zacheus, wid. Sarah.. W 3719
    Zadock or Zadok... S 16233
RAYNSFORD, Joseph.. S 40317
RAZAR or RASAR, Elisha, Conn. & Privateer.. R 8625
READ, Amos... S 14261
    (Also given as REED.)
    Bailey.. S 23865
    Elisha.. S 11286
    Zalmon, wid. Hannah, BLWt. 8458–160–55.. W 178
    (See also REED.)
REDFIELD, Ambrose... S 45100
    Constant.. S 17042
    Levi.. S 14276
    Martin.. S 17650
    Nathan.. S 31923
    Peleg... S 9464
    Roswell.. S 17647
    Samuel.. R 8640½
REDINGTON, John, Laura Miller, former wid. of, BLWt. 100371–160–55........................ W 10498
REDWAY, Comfort, wid. Roxana.. R 8646
    Soldier was pensioned in 1818 from Jefferson Co., N. Y.
    Joel.. S 30057
    Preserved, wid. Azubah... W 18796
REED or REID, Benjamin, Hartland, Conn., in 1818... S 35612
    Benjamin.. R 8651
    Daniel.. R 8653
        Indefinite service claimed, but Conn. residence.
    Diodama, former wid. of Benjamin ROWLAND.
    Ebenezer, Cattaraugus Co., N. Y., in 1832.. S 14275
    Ebenezer, wid. Polly, BLWt. 8185–160–55.. W 18795
        (Also given as REID.)
        Soldier died in 1827 in N. Y., was priv. & Serg't; wid. lived in Vt. in 1836.
    Eli, wid. Meliscent or Melison.. W 27235
    Enoch, BLWt. 1794–300, Capt. was issued May 29, 1789. No papers.
    Ithel... S 16235
    John.. R 8663
    Joseph.. S 36253
    Justus, wid. Lydia, BLWt. 34847–160–55.. W 814
    Kitchel... S 28851
    Richard... S 43908
    Samuel, Conn. & Privateer.. S 11285
    Stephan or Stephen... S 43916
    Tallcot... R 8677
    (See also READ.)
REEVE or REEVES, Daniel, Conn. & N. Y.. R 8842
    Luther, wid. Anna.. W 4570
    Puryer, Conn. & N. Y... S 28852
REID. (See REED.)
REMINGTON, Abijah, wid. Silence.. BLWt. 24601–160–55
    John.. S 21944
    Josiah, Conn. & N. Y... R 8700
    Simeon.. S 22948

RENELS or RENNELLS, Benjamin.. S 40327
RESSEGUE, RESSEGUÉ or RESSEQUIE.
    Abraham, Ellen Delanoy, former wid. of... W 24054
    Alexander, wid. Ruamy, BLWt. 26507–160–55.. W 1483
    John, Conn. & N. Y... S 14268
REW, Ephraim.. S 22946
    Memucan, wid. Hannah... W 26363
REXFORD or RAXFORD, Benjamin, wid. Mary Jane, BLWt. 34529–160–55............... W 5684
    Denison... R 8843
        (Also given as RAXFORD and ROXFORD.)
    Isaac.. S 41093
    Joseph, wid. Anna.. W 5708
        (Also given as RIXFORD.)
REYMOND. (See RAYMOND.)
REYNOLDS, Albrow... S 15963
    Charles, Cont. (Conn.), wid. Hannah.. W 17528
    David.. S 15964
        Pensioned as David 3d in 1832 in Washington, Conn.
    David, Plainfield, Conn., in 1832; moved to R. I.. S 21939
    David, wid. Margaret.. W 17523
        Soldier in Windham Co., Conn., in 1832; died in 1836.
    David, wid. Rebecca... W 24738
        Soldier in Washington Co., Me., in 1827; died in 1832.
    Eliphalet... S 37326
    Gamaliel, wid. Mary... W 24729
    Jacob.. S 7378
    James, wid. Mary... W 22057
    Jeremiah, Oneida Co., N. Y., in 1832.. S 14256
    Jeremiah, Bedford, N. Y., in 1832.. S 23385
    John, Broome Co., N. Y., in 1818; Pittsburgh in 1832.................................. S 4762
    John, Conn. & Privateer, BLWt. 26540–160–55; Susquehanna Co., Penna. in 1832.... S 22459
    Jonathan, wid. Mary... W 16692
        Died in 1809, York, N. Y.
    Jonathan, Cont. (Conn.), Vt. in 1818.. S 41972
        (See also RENNELLS.)
    Justus... S 40319
    Matthew.. R 8714
    Simeon, Mass. in 1818; transferred to Penna... S 41094
    Simeon, Philadelphia, Penna., in 1832... S 41095
REYNOLS or REYNOLDS, Solomon, wid. Elizabeth... W 17517
    (See also RENNELS.)
RHINEVAULT. (See RINEVAULT.)
RICE, Abigail, former wid. of Lemuel CARRINGTON.
    Abiram, wid. Lucy. (Also given as ROYCE.)
    Charles.. S 14292
    Chauncey, Northampton Co., Penna., in 1832... S 5990
    Chauncey, Conn. & Mass., Meriden, Conn., in 1832..................................... S 15616
    Daniel, Conn. & Cont., wid. Jemima... W 22086
    Elijah... S 36263
        (Also given ROYCE.)
    Isaac.. S 4087
    Jacob.. S 11298
    John... S 11301
    Moses, wid. Nancy, BLWt. 40687–160–55.. W 11153
    Nehemiah, BLWt. 1791–300, Capt., was issued June 18, 1790, to Nehemiah Rice. No papers.
    Samuel, Litchfield Co., Conn., in 1818... S 35631
    Wait.. S 35620
    William, Conn. & R. I... S 14313
RICH, Amos... S 43936
    Lemuel... S 5994
    Nathaniel, BLWt. 103–100.
    Samuel, BLWt. 6404–100... S 35626
    Thaddeus... S 14307
RICHARD, Silas.. S 43921
RICHARDS, Amos.. S 43925
    Edmond, wid. Ruth.. W 17539
        (Also given Edmund.)
    Gershom, wid. Elizabeth... W 22069
    Hezekiah, wid. Jerusha... R 8760
    Isaac.. S 27383
    Israel... S 8759
    Jacob, wid. Mary... W 2346
    Jesse, wid. Clarissa... R 8758
        Soldier pensioned in 1832 from New Canaan, Conn.
    Luther.. R 8761
    Mark.. S 23389
    Nathaniel, Navy service but Conn. residence.. S 35624
    Peter.. S 35625
    Samuel, Vt. in 1818... S 41985
    Samuel, Conn. & Cont., Lieut. in Hartford Co., Conn., in 1818....................... S 17652
    William, Conn. & Cont.. S 35623
        BLWt. 1796–300, Capt., was issued Jan. 28, 1790. No papers.
RICHARDSON, Asa or Fidelio... S 41097
    David, wid. Sarah.. W 5711
    Fidelio. (See Asa.)
    Gershom.. S 16237
    Jesse.. S 4775
    John, St. Lawrence Co., N. Y., in 1832... S 23871
    John, wid. Judith, BLWt. 88525–160–55.
    Rufus, wid. Ruth... W 18816

RICHARDSON, Russel or Rossel.. S 43932
 Samuel, wid. Susannah... W 17533
 Sanford, wid. Roxy... W 17531
 Stanton, Conn. & Vt., wid. Anna.. R 8764
 Stephen, wid. Hannah.. W 26386
 William, Conn. & Cont.. S 11291
RICHMOND, Abner, Conn. & Mass., wid. Eunice................................... W 17534
 Vail or Viall, Conn. & Navy, wid. Clarissa, BLWt. 38544-100-55.............. W 1935
RIDER, Daniel, wid. Elizabeth.. W 5705
 Jeremiah... S 14296
RIGGS, James... R 17439
 Laban, Conn. & Cont., wid. Dorcas.. W 4780
 Moses.. S 35629
RILEY, John, BLWt. 1792-300, Capt., was issued April 22, 1796. No papers.
 John, Delaware Co., N. Y., in 1832; Lieut....................................... S 14304
 Joseph... S 4105
 Roger, wid. Sarah.. W 22084
RINDGE or RING. (See RINGE.)
RINEVAULT, William, wid. Mary.. R 8830
 (Also given as RHINEVAULT.)
 (Soldier was pensioned in 1818 in Conn. and transferred to N. Y.)
RINGE, RINDGE or RING, Thomas, wid. Anna, BLWt. 3522-160-55............. W 26187
RIPLEY, Abraham.. S 33565
 Charles, Conn. & N. H.. S 43931
 Epaphras, Conn. & Vt... R 8833
 Hezekiah or Hezekiel, Conn. & Cont... S 11305
 Jabez, wid. Mary... R 8836
  Soldier never pensioned.
 Jeremiah, wid. Mary.. R 8835
  Soldier never pensioned.
 John A., Conn. & Privateer... R 8834
 Nehemiah, wid. Lucy, BLWt. 15196-160-55...................................... W 1489
 Pirum, Conn., Sea service & Navy & N. Y....................................... S 23388
RISDON, John... S 18569
RISING, Ben.. S 9086
 Josiah, Cont. (Conn.), wid. Huldah... W 18818
RISLEY, Allen.. S 21449
 Asa.. S 12226
 Asahel or Asahael, Cont. (Conn.).
  BLWt. 6410-100, private, was issued in 1790.
 David, wid. Cynthia.. W 24768
 Eli, wid. Mindwell.. W 10236
 Elijah... S 23391
 Levi... S 35619
 Moses, Conn. & Mass... R 8839
 Richard... S 23390
 Samuel, wid. Stacy O., BLWt. 27587-160-55..................................... W 26369
 Stephen... S 43930
  (Also given RISLY.)
 William... S 14305
RIX, Nathan, Conn. & R. I.. S 14306
ROACH, Thomas, BLWt. 26121-160-55... S 14373
ROATH. (See ROTH.)
ROBARTS. (See ROBERTS.)
ROBBARTS. (See ROBERTS.)
ROBBINS, Brintnal, wid. Mary, BLWt. 26760-160-55................................. W 7150
 Daniel, wid. Ruth, Conn., Conn. Sea service & N. Y., BLWt. 8184-160-55..... W 18826
  (Also given as ROBINS.)
 Ebenezer, wid. Zeruah, BLWt. 27588-160-55..................................... W 9636
 Ephraim.. S 17052
 Frederick, wid. Abigail, BLWt. 47767-160-55.................................... W 26426
 John, Cont. & Conn. Sea service, wid. Alice..................................... W 17558
 Joshua... R 8856
 Josiah.. S 35633
 Lorin or Lorrin, Conn., Cont. & R. I.. S 14372
 Samuel, Conn. & R. I... S 14374
 Silas, wid. Hannah... W 17565
  (See also ROBINS.)
ROBERTS, ROBARTS or ROBBARTS.
 Amos... S 6024
 Ashbel... S 18580
 Benjamin. (See SIMMONS.)
 Clark, wid. Sarah.. W 17550
 Daniel, Hartford Co., Conn., in 1832... S 31942
 Daniel, wid. Asenath.. W 16391
  Soldier died in 1827, Genesee Co., N. Y.
 David, Cont. (Conn.).. S 36256
 Elijah, Montgomery Co., N. Y., in 1832.. S 14314
 Elijah, Middletown, Conn., in 1832.. S 14377
 Elisha, Cont. (Conn.).. S 43939
 Freelove, Cont. (Conn.)... S 41995
  (Also given as ROBBARTS.)
 Gideon, wid. Jerusha.. W 2006
  (Also given as ROBARTS.)
 Isaac, wid. Sally... W 26399
  Canaan, N. Y., in 1818; d. in 1836, BLWt. 29026-160-55.
 Isaac, Conn. & Mass., wid. Sarah.. W 10243
  Washington Co., Vt., in 1832; died in 1835.
 James.. S 28862

ROBERTS, ROBARTS, or ROBBARTS—Continued.

John, Hartford Co., Conn., in 1832.. S 31939
John. Served also in French and Indian War; applied in 1809 for pension.
John, Berlin, Conn., in 1832... S 11329
John, Conn. & Cont... S 36259
    Invalid pensioner & 1818 from Litchfield Co., Conn.
Judah... S 15622
Lucretia, former wid. of Jeduthan ABBE.
Luke, wid. Catharine or Catherine, BLWt. 41–60–55... W 4326
    (Also given ROBARTS.)
Nathan.. S 43969
Nathaniel, Cont. (Conn.).. S 14346
Noah.. S 43974
Pearly, wid. Submit... W 22127
Rufus... S 44232
Samuel.. S 43961
Stephen, wid. Rebecca... W 2860
Timothy... S 14337
William, West Springfield, Mass., in 1818; corporal... S 33611
William, wid. Abigail... W 20033
    Soldier died in 1797 in Hartford Co., Conn.
William, Conn., Mass. & Vt., wid. Margaret, Trumbull Co., Conn., in 1832..................... W 4784
Ziba, Mary Chase, former wid. of... W 22759
ROBERTSON, Daniel, wid. Esther.. W 16704
Ephraim, wid. Priscilla... W 17547
Peter.. BLWt. 1795–300
    (Also given as ROBINSON.)
Seth, wid. Hannah... W 17553
Simeon. (See ROBINSON.)
ROBIN or ROBINS, Brintnall. (See ROBBINS.)
Daniel. (See ROBBINS.)
Joseph, Conn. & Cont., wid. Elizabeth... W 17567
Joseph, Mary Mulkins, former wid. of.. W 17181
Lorin or Lorrin. (See ROBBINS.)
Samuel, Conn., Cont. & R. I., wid. Zeruviah... W 17566
    (See also ROBBINS.)
ROBINSON, Abel.. S 44235
Amasa, wid. Marcia, BLWt. 1966–160–55... W 9268
Andrew, wid. Bethiah or Bethia, BLWt. 26912–160–55.. W 2348
Asher, wid. Sarah... W 22121
Benjamin, wid. Ruth... R 8915
    Soldier never pensioned.
Benjamin, Conn. & Cont.. S 43980
Chandler.. S 22957
Charles, wid. Chloe D... W 26409
Daniel, Conn. & Cont.. S 11316
Eber, wid. Lucinda, BLWt. 10257–160–55.. W 5745
Eleazer, wid. Mary, BLWt. 851–100... W 24793
Elias, wid. Amy or Amie... R 8893
    Soldier received BLWt. 1799–200, Lieut., April 6, 1796. No papers.
Elias, wid. Betsey, BLWt. 31578–160–55.. W 11163
    Soldier pensioned in 1818 & 1832 in New London Co., Conn.
Ephraim... S 22474
James, Conn., Md., N. J. & Penna.. S 7432
Jared, BLWT. 1785–200... S 43982
Jason, BLWt. 6003–160–55.. R 8904
John, Jefferson Co., N. Y., in 1819... S 43979
John, wid. Esther... W 24791
    Soldier died in Jefferson Co., N. Y., in 1818.
John, wid. Lucy... W 26407
    Soldier in Branford, Conn., in 1832.
John, wid. Sarah.. W 17573
    Fairfield Co., Conn., in 1832 where he died in 1834.
Jonathan.. S 18182
Joseph, wid. Abbey.. W 17555
Joshua, wid. Chloe, BLWt. 13020–160–55.. W 2440
Levi, BLWt. 1291–100.. S 33595
Moses, Conn. & R. I., wid. Hannah... R 8897
Nathaniel, wid. Susanna... W 16706
Noah, Conn. & N. Y.. S 23884
Peter, BLWt. 1795–300, Capt., was issued Sept. 14, 1789. No papers.
Reuben, Tolland Co., Conn., in 1818... S 36269
Reuben, wid. Rosannah... W 7152
    Soldier was in Killingly, Conn., in 1832; BLWt. 7217–160–55.
Reuben, Conn., Mass. & Vt., Windsor Co., Vt., in 1832....................................... S 16238
Reuben, Stonington, Conn., in 1832.. S 29421
Richard... S 22473
Robert.. R 8914
Simeon.. S 43949
    (Also given as ROBERTSON.)
Susan, former wid. of Alva WEST.
William... S 14315
Ziba.. S 14332
Zophar, wid. Charity.. W 17564
ROCKWELL, Amasa, Conn. & Mass., wid. Prudence, BLWt. 12702–160–55............................ W 1086
Clapp... S 17660
Grove... S 36268
Jabez, wid. Betsey B., BLWt. 26759–160–55... W 3722
    Soldier pensioned in 1832 in Pike Co., Penna., as private & fifer.
Jabez, wid. Deborah... W 22122
    Soldier died in 1818 in Grand Isle, Vt.

124

ROCKWELL, John, N. Y. in 1818.. S 44237
   John, wid. Abigail... W 18838
      Soldier died in 1823 in Mass.
   Joseph, wid. Esther, BLWt. 31583-160-55... W 11155
   Noadiah.. S 18181
   Oswald, wid. Sarah... W 17562
   Samuel, Sharon, Conn., in 1832.. S 23375
   Samuel, Oneida Co., N. Y., in 1832... S 14356
   Silas.. S 28856
   William, Conn. & N. Y., wid. Sarah... R 8923
      Soldier pensioned in 1828 in Fairfield, Conn.
RODGERS or ROGERS, Abel... S 14322
   Abijah, wid. Lydia.. W 11160
   Bela, wid. Rebecca.. W 18823
   Bixbee.. S 40357
   Chester, Eunice Boynton, former wid. of... W 20744
   Daniel.. S 11336
   David.. S 36274
   Ebenezer, Norwich, Conn., in 1832.. S 31941
   Ebenezer, wid. Ruth.. W 17571
      Northfield, Conn., in 1832; died there in 1833.
   Howard, wid. Hannah.. W 22118
      (Soldier was Captain.)
   Edward, Conn. Sea service, Medina Co., in 1832... S 4795
   Elisha, wid. Anna, BLWt. 6426-160-55.. W 22116
   Elnathan.. S 14376
   Ephraim, wid. Martha... W 17561
   Ethan... S 4139
   Gideon, wid. Lucy... W 27479
   Gurdon... S 31940
   Heman, wid. Hannah, BLWt. 316-60-55... W 815
   Hezekiah.. BLWt. 1793-300
      Capt. was issued July 21, 1789, to Hezekiah Rogers. No. papers.
   Isaac, wid. Mary... W 11168
   Israel.. S 14383
   Jabez, wid. Sarah.. R 8959
      Soldier never pensioned.
   Jedekiah, Cont. (Conn.), wid. Sarah.. W 17570
      BLWt. 1802-300, Capt. of Col. Sheldon's Regiment of Cavalry, was issued October 2, 1789.
      No papers.
   Jeduthan, wid. Elizabeth... R 8940
      Soldier was pensioned in Windsor Co., Vt., in 1832.
   John, Conn. & Privateer, Broome Co., N. Y., in 1832.................................... S 14380
   Jonah.. R 8948
   Joseph (N. Y. in 1818).. S 43978
      BLWt. 1801-150, Ensign, was issued July 21, 1789. No papers.
   Joseph, Claremont, N. H., in 1832... S 45858
   Josiah, Serg't. in Litchfield Co., Conn., in 1818.. S 36272
   Josiah (Clarkson, N. Y., in 1832), Alice Rogers Hewett, former wid. of (wid. pensioned from
      O. in 1848)... W 10099
      BLWt. 92107-160-55.
   Josiah, or Josias, wid. Ruth... W 3605
      Soldier in Luzerne Co., Penna., in 1832; died there in 1841.
   Josiah, Conn. & N. H., wid. Hannah... R 8943
      Soldier never pensioned.
   Leonard... S 31937
   Levi, wid. Abigail, BLWt. 26618-160-55... W 8292
   Nathaniel... S 23877
   Noadiah, wid. Rebecca, BLWt. 26942-160-55.. W 2641
   Oliver, Navy (Conn.)... S 36275
   Perley, wid. Esther.. W 57303
   Peter, Bernardstown, Mass., in 1818.. S 33582
   Peter, wid. Nancy... W 5731
      Monroe Co., Ill., in 1834, where he died in 1849.
   Richard.. S 4784
   Samuel, Wayne Co., Pa., in 1832... S 22482
   Samuel, Conn., Privateer & Vt... R 8954
      Soldier never pensioned; wid. Mehitable.
   Simeon, wid. Mary.. W 27807
   Steven or Stephen, Abigail Byrne, former wid. of, BLWt. 2185-160-55............. W 25319
   Thankful, former wid. of Elihu AVERY.
   Thomas (given also as RODGERS) .... S 36270
   Thomas, Rutland, Vt., in 1832... S 22480
   Thomas, Conn., Navy, Privateer & R. I., New London Co., Conn., in 1832....... S 14343
   Timothy, Hannah Markham, former wid. of... W 25677
   Zephaniah, wid. Elizabeth... W 3192
ROLF, Henry, wid. Patty... W 104
ROLLO, Zachariah, BLWt. 1448-100... S 36267
ROLO, Joseph, wid. Polly, BLWt. 31577-160-55... W 26405
ROLOO, Daniel.. S 4315
   (Also given as ROLO and ROOLO.)
ROOD or ROODE, Briggs.. R 8979
   (Given as ROODE.)
   David, wid. Lucretia... R 8981
   (Soldier never pensioned.)
   Jeremiah.. S 44231
   John.. S 20940
   Joseph... R 8980
   Roger... R 8982

ROOD or ROODE, Rozzel .... S 23403
   Simeon .... S 43964
     (See also RUDE.)
ROOLO. (See ROLOO.)
ROOT, Amos .... S 14317
   Billa, wid. Polly .... R 8991
     Soldier was pensioned in 1832 in Allegany Co., N. Y.
   Daniel .... S 11321
   Eleazer, wid. Lucinda .... R 8987
   Elijah, Farmington, Conn., in 1832 .... S 14386
   Elijah, Conn. & Mass., Genesee Co., N. Y., in 1832 .... S 23399
   Erastus, wid. Lucy, BLWt. 9207-160-55 .... W 1650
   Ezekiel N., Cynthia Cowles, former wid. of .... W 4927
   Israel, Conn. & Mass .... S 15627
   Joel, Cont. (Conn.) .... S 33589
   John, wid. Polly .... W 26404
   Joseph, Albion, N. Y., in 1832 .... S 14324
   Joseph, wid. Mary .... W 4323
     Soldier died in 1816.
   Joshua .... S 11314
   Josiah, Cont. (Conn.) & Sea serv .... S 14328
   Lydia, former wid. of Joseph WATERS.
   Moses, wid. Esther .... W 24809
   Nathan .... S 47751
   Nathaniel, Onondaga Co., N. Y., in 1832 .... S 14368
   Nathaniel, Coventry, Conn., in 1832 .... S 18574
   Nathaniel, Canaan, Conn., in 1818 .... S 36277
   Nathaniel H .... S 18573
   Salmon or Solomon, wid. Bulah .... W 1084
   Samuel, wid. Dinah .... W 24779
   Seth .... S 36273
   Solomon. (See SALMON.)
   Thomas .... S 43984
ROOTS, Daniel, wid. Lucy .... W 22098
ROSE, John, Cont. (Conn.), BLWt. 1584-150 .... S 43967
     John BLWt. 1804-400, Surgeon, was issued Feb. 24, 1797. No papers.
   Jonathan, wid. Hannah, BLWt. 12565-160-55 .... W 26395
   Levi, wid. Mary .... W 22114
   Peleg, wid. Mary .... W 22120
   Peter, Conn. & Cont., Esther Edmonds or Edmunds, former wid. of .... R 3244
     Soldier never pensioned.
   Prosper .... S 35
   Samuel .... R 9011
   William .... S 11324
   Winthrop .... S 43968
ROSETTER. (See ROSSITER.)
ROSS, Perin .... BL
ROSSETER, ROSSETTER, ROSSITER or ROSETTER.
   Benjamin .... S 23595
   Bryan, wid. Sarah, BLWt. 435-100 .... W 24782
     (Given as ROSSETTER.)
   Noah, Conn. & Mass., wid. Amanda, BLWt. 26230-160-55 .... W 7156
   Timothy, New Haven Co., Conn., in 1832 .... S 17062
   Timothy, Conn. & Cont., BLWt. 1604-100; N. Y. in 1818 .... S 44233
     (Given as ROSSETER.)
ROTH or ROATH, Daniel, wid. Hannah .... W 17559
   Silas .... S 36260
     (Given as ROATH.)
ROUNDY, Uriah, wid. Lucretia .... R 9034
     Soldier never pensioned.
ROWE, David .... S 42214
   Ezra, Conn. & Cont .... S 15970
   Isaiah, wid. Mary .... R 9043
     Soldier never pensioned.
   John, Conn. & Cont .... S 14358
ROWEL, Philander. (See ROWLEY.)
ROWLAND, Benjamin, Conn. & Cont., Diodama Reed, former wid. of .... W 24741
   Daniel .... S 36271
   David .... S 14379
   Hezekiah, wid. Grace .... W 4328
   Jack .... S 17058
     (Also given FREEMAN.)
   Jesse .... S 36264
   Luke, wid. Elizabeth .... W 9271
   Sherman .... S 36262
ROWLANDSON or ROWLINSON, Joseph .... S 42218
   Rubn, wid. Eunice .... W 9272
ROWLEY, Abijah, Conn. & Cont .... S 32493
   Eli Smith .... S 11312
   Joseph L., Conn., Conn. Sea service & N. Y .... S 7408
   Philander .... S 14327
     (Given also as ROWEL.)
   Seth, Conn., Cont. & N. Y., wid. Innocent, BLWt. 5110-160-55 .... W 24777
   Silas .... S 14326
   Thomas, wid. Mary .... W 15277
ROWLINSON. (See ROWLANDSON.)
ROYCE, Aaron .... S 45126
   Abiram. (See RICE.)
   Asa .... S 31936
   Elijah, Woodstock, Vt., in 1818 and 1832 .... S 23397

ROYCE, Elijah, New Haven Co. in 1818. (Also given as RICE.)
Isaac, wid. Abigail .... R 9056
    Soldier never pensioned.
Samuel, Conn. & Cont .... S 12256
ROZELL, Jeremiah, Conn. & Cont .... S 42219
    BLWt. 6391-100, Private, was issued March 1, 1797. No papers.
RUDD, Andrew, Conn. & Cont. .... S 30077
Daniel, Conn. & Navy, wid. Abigail, BLWt. 7209-160-55 .... W 22137
William, wid. Eunice .... W 22138
RUDE, Ezekiel, wid. Phebe .... W 26417
Isaac .... S 17066
    (See also ROODE & ROOD.)
RUGGLES, Benjamin A., wid. Betty .... W 26418
Bostwick, wid. Lucy .... W 17576
Joseph .... S 14392
RUICK, Owen .... S 36034
RULAND, Thomas W., Mary Deforest, former wid. of, BLWt. 12834-160-55 .. W 2663
RUMSAY or RUMSEY, David .... S 42225
Jeremiah, wid. Asenath .... W 3461
John .... S 41970
William .... S 41970
RUNDEL, RUNDELL or RUNDLE, Henry .... R 9073
John, wid. Rachel, BLWt. 2170-100 .... W 11194
    (Also given RUNDLE.)
Joseph .... R 8582
Phinehas .... S 18191
Reuben, Conn. & N. Y .... S 9298
RUSCO or RUSCOE, David .... S 41115
RUSS, Asa .... R 9093
Epaphras .... S 42224
Jonathan .... S 42210
RUSSEL or RUSSELL, Abigail, former wid. of James McDONALD.
Asher or Ashur, Conn. & Cont., BLWt. 1195-100 .... S 40368
Cornelius, BLWt. 248-200 .... S 41112
David, Burlington, Vt., in 1832 .... S 15972
David, wid. Eunice .... W 26419
    New Haven Co., Conn., in 1832: where he died in 1836.
Ebenezer .... S 14387
Eleazer .... S 42223
Elmore, Cont. (Conn.) .... S 14391
Gideon .... S 7434
Ichabod, wid. Hannah .... R 9101
    Soldier never pensioned.
John, Warwick, R. I., in 1818 .... S 39836
John, wid. Lovice .... W 17578
    Soldier died in 1826 in Tolland Co., Conn.
Jonathan .... S 10000
Josiah, Conn. & Cont .... S 42226
Riverius or Riverus, Conn. & Cont., wid. Charity; both sold. & wid. Rej . R 9105
Timothy, wid. Elizabeth .... R 9100
    Soldier pensioned in Chatham Co., Conn., in 1832.
William, Chloe Folker, former wid. of .... W 7313
    Soldier pensioned in Cornwall, Conn., in 1818 as drummer.
William, Otsego Co., N. Y., in 1818 .... S 42221
RUST, Abel .... S 42231
RUSTIN, William .... S 36278
RUTTY, Jonah, wid. Mary .... R 9116
    Soldier never pensioned.
RYAN, Jeremiah, Conn. & Cont., wid. Mary .... R 9122
    Soldier pensioned while living in Conn. in 1824, and N. Y. in 1832.
RYON, John .... S 40377
    BLWt. 6364-100, private, was issued Sept. 8, 1790. No papers.

S.

SABEN or SABIN, Billings .... S 42247
Eldad .... S 14395
Elihu, wid. Hannah (Conn. & Cont.) .... W 17769
Hezekiah, wid. Sarah .... W 13870
Israel .... S 11340
    (Given as SABEN.)
Jonathan .... S 31950
Nathaniel, wid. Deborah .... W 26428
Timothy .... R 9133
SACKET or SACKETT, Benjamin, wid. Mercy, BLWt. 31317-160-55 .... W 1940
Buel or Buell .... S 14396
Daniel, Conn. & N. Y., wid. Martha .... W 17770
Samuel, Conn. & Penna .... S 4811
Skeen or Skeene Douglass, wid. Lorrilla, BLWt. 18019-160-55 .... W 4619
    (Given also as DOUGLASS, Skeen.)
William, wid. Parthena, BLWt. 11282-160-55 .... W 26956
SAFFORD, David .... R 9137
Gideon .... R 6081
Rufus, wid. Mary .... R 9138
    (Soldier never pensioned.)
SAGE, Abraham, wid. Candace .... W 24887
Daniel, Conn., Mass. & N. Y .... S 17069
Epaphras, wid. Elizabeth .... W 26430
Harlehigh, wid. Lucinda, BLWt. 35724-160-55 .... W 5972
    NOTE.—Lucinda's first husband, William PRATT, also served in the Revolution.

SAGE, Nathaniel, Cont. (Conn.).. S 33624
    Stephen... S 30080
    Zadoc.. R 9142
ST. GEORGE, George, Conn. & Ga.. S 39090
ST. JOHN, Adonijah, Cont. (Conn.)... S 36802
    David, wid. Mary, BLWt. 38542-160-55..................................... W 25104
    Enoch, wid. Maria, BLWt. 9076-160-55...................................... W 11566
    Jesse, Wilton, Conn., in 1818.. S 36804
    Jesse, Williamsburgh, N. Y., in 1828....................................... S 42418
    John, wid. Hannah.. W 19125
    Matthias.. S 18200
    Samuel... R 9147
SALMON, Asahel... S 36292
    Gershom.. S 14411
SALTONSTALL, Gurdon Flanders, Conn. & Navy.. R 9159
SAMPSON or SAMSON, Zephaniah, Conn. & Cont., wid. Tamar................................ R 9164
    Soldier was pensioned in 1818, as resident of Windham Co., Conn.
SANDERS, Thomas.. S 17661
    William... S 41128
    (See also SAUNDERS.)
SANDERSON, Reuben.. S 45142
    BLWT. 1961-200, Lieut., was issued April 19, 1791, to Asa Worthington, Assignee. No
    papers.
    Silvanus or Sylvanus, Conn. & Mass., wid. Charlotte...................... W 24882
SANDFORD, SANDIFORD or SANFORD, Archibald.. S 14412
    (Given also as SANDFORD.)
    Daniel W., Conn. & Conn. Sea Service..................................... S 29435
    (Given as SANDIFORD.)
    David, wid. Abiah.. W 22151
    David, wid. Hannah, BLWt. 45718-160-55.................................... R 9195
    Soldier never pensioned; widow could not prove six months' service.
    Ebenezer, wid. Mary.. W 11382
    Elihu, wid. Nancy.. W 5974
    Elisha, wid. Rhoda... W 17772
    Ezekiel.. S 43103
    Holsey, wid. Miriam, BLWt. 31714-160-55.................................. W 586
    Jairus... S 15207
    James, Saratoga Co., N. Y., in 1818....................................... S 43104
    James, Conn. & Cont., Fairfield Co., Conn., in 1832...................... S 14410
    Jesse, wid. Eleanor.. W 17774
    Jonathan... S 46068
    Joseph... S 29434
    Kingsbury, Cont. (Conn.) & Privateer...................................... S 14398
    Liffe, wid. Huldah... W 17773
    Moses, wid. Elizabeth.. R 9196
    Both soldier and widow were rejected.
    Samuel, BLWt. 1947-300, Capt., was issued Oct. 30, 1789. No papers.
    Samuel... S 4810
    BLWt. 26242-160-55; Portage Co., Ohio, in 1832.
    Samuel, wid. Ruhamah.. W 19313
    Fairfield Co., Conn., in 1832; died there in 1834; widow in Chemung Co., N. Y., in 1836.
    Strong... S 36289
    Zacheus or Zaccheus, or Zacheous, wid. Eunice............................. W 22154
SANGER, Daniel... S 30081
    Pearley.. R 9199
SAP. (See LAP.)
SARDAM, Henry, wid. Sylvia.. W 17775
SARGEANT, Jacob, Conn. & Cont.. S 15208
    Sarah, former wid. of Elijah CARPENTER.
    (See also SERGEANT.)
SATTERLEE or SATTERLEY or SATTERLY.
    Elisha, wid. Cynthia... W 2967
    James, wid. Desire, BLWt. 405-100... W 4508
    John, Conn. & R. I., wid. Hannah.. W 18996
    Samuel, Conn. Sea service.. R 9212
SAUNDERS, Cuff, former widow, Phillis Tatton.. W 18103
    (Also given as WELLS, Cuff.)
    Peter.. S 36288
    Robert, Navy (Conn.)... S 36286
    Samuel... S 36287
    (See also SANDERS.)
SAVAGE, Abijah, Conn. & Cont... S 36281
    BLWt. 1954-300, Capt., was issued Jan. 28, 1790. No papers.
    Gideon, Cont. (Conn.), wid. Sarah.. W 16064
    John... S 11337
    Luther... R 9225
    Selah.. S 17071
    Seth, Conn. & Cont... S 15211
    Solomon, wid. Lydia.. R 9227
    Neither soldier nor widow applied.
    Thomas, Conn. & Vt... S 14402
SAVY, Stephen, Conn. & Cont., N. H. & Vt.. R 17664
SAWYER, Asa.. S 36283
    Asahel... S 15210
    Azariah, wid. Esther... W 26429
    Conant... S 41129
    Cornelius, wid. Sarah, BLWt. 18023-160-55................................ W 8704
    Ephraim.. S 36284

SAWYER, John, Ridgeway, N. Y., in 1818 & 1832.. S 9472
   John, BLWt. 1771-100, private, Continental service; died 1804 at sea; heirs resided in Conn.
     in 1830.
   Samuel, wid. Mary... R 9236
     Soldier was invalid pensioner.
   William... S 13709
SAXTON, John.. S 42252
   Zephaniah, Conn., Green Mt. Boys & Vt.. S 14405
SCARBOROUGH, Elisha, wid. Prudence.. W 26962
   John... S 17079
SCARRITT, James, wid. Eliza, BLWt. 19913-160-55...................................... W 1942
   Nathan.. S 45144
SCHELLENGER, SCHELLENEX or SCHELLENX, Abraham, wid. Jane............... W 16724
   (See also SKELLENGER.)
SCHOFIELD or SCHOLFIELD, Jesse... S 31349
   (See also SCO FIELD.)
SCHOOLCRAFT, Samuel, wid. Mary, BLWt. 1108-100.................................. W 5999
SCHOVIL, Jacob, Conn. & Green Mt. Boys.. S 36294
   (See also SCOVILL.)
SCOFIELD, Asahel.. S 23891
   Elisha, Conn. & N. Y., wid. Abigail, BLWt. 15425-160-55............................ W 11399
   Else, former wid. of Samuel COMSTOCK.
   Enos, wid. Amy.. W 17786
     Poundridge, N. Y., in 1818; died there in 1830; widow in Fairfield Co., Conn., in 1837.
   Enos, Conn. & N. Y., Chataqua Co., N. Y., in 1832................................ S 15219
   Ezra, wid. Milly.. W 1896
   Gershom, wid. Lydia... W 22166
   Gideon, Abigail Garret. former wid. of... R 3922
     Soldier never pensioned.
   Hart, Conn. & Cont... S 17665
   Israel, Conn. & N. Y.. S 6052
   Jacob, wid. Abigail... W 17779
   Jared... S 16242
   Josiah Weed.. S 17662
   Neazer... S 23892
   Reuben.. S 11355
   Seely or Selah... S 10004
   Stephen.. S 42266
   Sylvanus, wid. Sarah.. W 17781
   William.. S 28871
   (See also SCHOFIELD.)
SCOTT, Amasa.. S 42258
   Caleb.. S 42267
   Daniel, wid. Esther, BLWt. 3762-160-55.. W 9511
   Eleazer.. S 27450
   Elisha... R 9293
   Ethiel... S 41132
     Franklin Co., Vt., in 1832; served in 8th. reg't. Conn. Line.
   Ethiel... ELWt. 46-100
     3d reg't. Conn. Line; Addison Co., Vt., in 1800.
   Ezekiel.. S 15220
   John... S 42254
   Joseph, Tolland Co., Conn., in 1832.. S 15644
   Joseph, Glastonbury, Conn., in 1818... S 36295
   Justus... R 9305
   Lucy, former wid. of John FENTON.
   Moses, wid. Eunice... W 15313
     Soldier died in 1817; wid. resident of Franklin Co., Mass., in 1837.
   Moses, wid. Matilda... W 2176
     BLWt. 6475-100, private, was issued Aug. 3, 1790. No papers.
     Soldier was in Waterford, N. Y., in 1818; died 1853.
   Oliver, Indiana Co., Penna., in 1818; died in Ohio in 1845........................ S 41143
   Oliver, wid. Ruth.. W 19327
     Soldier died in 1830 in Tolland Co., Conn.
   Stephen.. S 23895
   Thomas, wid. Ruth... W 17780
   Uri.. S 15217
   William, wid. Susannah.. R 17700
     Soldier was pensioned in 1830 while resident of Fairfield Co., Conn.
SCOVEL, SCOVELL, SCOVIL, SCOVILL, or SCOVILLE.
   Abijah, wid. Rebecca.. W 2628
   Abijah, Conn. & Mass.. R 9319
   Amasa, Cont. (Conn.).. R 9322
   Amasa... S 18592
     Pensioned in Trumbull Co., Ohio, in 1832 as private and musician.
   Benjamin, wid. Eunice... R 9320
     Soldier was pensioned in Galway, N. Y., in 1818.
   Ebenezer.. S 42259
   John... S 14420
   Jonah, wid. Sarah... R 9318
     Soldier was Invalid pensioner; wounded in 1777.
   Joseph... S 23412
   Matthew, Conn. & Conn. Sea service.. S 14414
   Michael.. R 9321
   Michael.. S 30691
   Moses, wid. Rachel.. W 4796
   Samuel, Litchfield Co., Conn., in 1818; Broome Co., N. Y., in 1832............... S 11360
   Samuel, wid. Lydia.. W 16714
     Pensioned as Samuel, Jr., and sergeant in N. Y. in 1818.

129

SCOVEL, SCOVELL, SCOVIL, SCOVILL, or SCOVILLE—Continued.
```
Solomon.............................................................................. S  15214
Stephen, N. Y., in 1818............................................................. S  42265
Timothy, wid. Chloe................................................................. W 19006
Westol or Westole................................................................... S  23897
  (See also SCHOVIL.)
SCRANTOM or SCRANTON, Abraham, Durham, Conn., in 1832................................ S  49288
Abraham, wid. Lucy.................................................................. W 17787
  Soldier was pensioned as private & Sergeant in 1832, at Guilford, Conn.
John, Conn. & Sea Service........................................................... S  17664
Thomas.............................................................................. S  15222
Timothy, wid. Sally, BLWt. 56-60-55................................................. W 8707
Torey or Torry...................................................................... S  15230
SCRIBNER, Ezra, wid. Nancy, BLWt. 40686-160-55...................................... W 26433
Jared............................................................................... R 9324
Jonathan, Conn. & N. Y.............................................................. S  15215
Levi, wid. Esther................................................................... W 26961
SCRIPTER or SCRIPTURE, John......................................................... S  42264
SCRIVEN, James, Conn. & R. I........................................................ S  14417
SEAGER, Darius...................................................................... S  13713
SEALEY or SEALY, George, wid. Lois.................................................. W 19339
  (See also SEELY & SEELYE.)
SEAMAN, Andrew...................................................................... S  28872
SEAMAN, S., James, Conn. & R. I..................................................... S  15229
SEARS, David, Middlesex Co., Conn., in 1832......................................... S  17539
David, Conn., Sea service & Mass., widow Martha..................................... W 17795
  Soldier was pensioned in Windham Co., Conn., in 1832 as private & serg't.; died 1841.
  Hannah. (See Obadiah.)
Isaac, Cont. (Conn.), wid. Grace.................................................... W 16401
Obadiah............................................................................. S  43121
  Hannah Sears, widow of above soldier, was pensioned as former widow of Elias WILCOX,
    Cont. (Conn.), W 17792.
Willard............................................................................. S  17667
SEDGEWICK or SEDGWICK, Asher or Ashur, wid. Temperance, Conn. & Cont. service....... W 15026
Ebenezer, wid. Martha............................................................... W 17799
John, wid. Sally.................................................................... W 2007
Samuel.............................................................................. S  43120
Timothy, wid. Lucy, BLWt. 38547-160-55.............................................. W 26440
William............................................................................. S  36298
SEELEY, SEELY or SEELYE, or SELEY.
Abraham............................................................................. S  2944
Benjamin, Cont. (Conn.), wid. Sarah................................................. W 2358
  Pensioned as Benjamin 2d in Salem, N. Y., in 1818; died in Warsaw, Wyoming Co., N.
    Y., in 1842.
Benjamin, wid. Sarah................................................................ W 3463
  Soldier was pensioned as private in Steuben Co., N. Y., in 1818; moved to Tioga Co.,
    Penna., where he died in 1828.
David............................................................................... R 9363
Denton.............................................................................. S  17081
Ebenezer, wid. Betsey, BLWt. 7077-160-55............................................ W 6013
  Soldier was in Weston, Conn., in 1832.
Ebenezer............................................................................ S  13734
  Pensioned in 1832 as fifer, Tompkins Co., N. Y.
Ebenezer, Conn. & Cont., wid. Mabel................................................. W 3308
  Soldier pensioned in Tioga Co., Penna., in 1818 as private in Sheldon's Dragoons; died
    there in 1837.
Isaac............................................................................... S  11369
John, wid. Abigail.................................................................. W 22173
  Soldier pensioned in Goshen, Conn., in 1818, where he died in 1833.
John, Betsey Campbell, former wid. of.............................................. W 4419
  Soldier died in 1813; widow in Tioga Co., Penna., when pensioned.
Joseph.............................................................................. S  36296
Seth, Cont. (Conn.)................................................................. S  43109
  (See also SEALEY.)
SEGER, Elijah....................................................................... S  21962
Joseph, Conn. & Cont................................................................ S  15228
SELBY, David Melville, wid. Hannah, BLWt. 61196-160-55.............................. W 10249
SELDEN, Benjamin.................................................................... R 9371
Elijah.............................................................................. S  36297
Ezra, Conn. & Cont.................................................................. BLWt. 687-300
SELEY. (See SEELY.)
SELKRIG, Jeremiah................................................................... S  29443
SELLACK, SELLECK or SELLICK, Henry.................................................. S  41149
James, wid. Chloe.  BLWt. 26231-160-55; BLWt. 57783-160-55.......................... W 2256
  Soldier was in Vermont in 1832; died in 1851 in Silver Creek, Mich.
James, wid. Phebe................................................................... W 19331
  Soldier died in 1803 in Saratoga Co., N. Y.
  (Also given as SILLICK.)
Jesse............................................................................... R 9379
Joseph, wid. Phebe.................................................................. W 17796
Peter, Conn. & Cont................................................................. S  15226
Stephen, wid. Ann................................................................... W 7170
  (See also SILLICK.)
SERGEANT, Isaac, Elizabeth Taylor, former wid. of.................................. R 104141/2
  Soldier was never pensioned.  Widow was pensioned as widow of her other husband,
    Josiah TAYLOR, Conn., W 824.
  (See also SARGEANT.)
SESSIONS, Abijah, wid. Hannah....................................................... W 26434
Robert, wid. Anna................................................................... W 24925
```

SEWARD, Jedediah, wid. Susan... W 1943
    Job, wid. Lois... W 16716
    Nathan, wid. Martha... W 9283
    Silas... S 43118
    Stephen, Sarah Lewis, former wid. of... R 6329
      Soldier never pensioned.
    Timothy, Albany Co., N. Y., in 1818.. S 43111
    Timothy, widow Rebecca, BLWt. 38558-160-55... W 11416
      Soldier was in Guilford, Conn., in 1832; and died there in 1849.
SEXTON, Elijah, wid. Thankful, BLWt. 26879-160-55.. W 2444
    Ezra... S 3879
SEYMOUR, Anne, former wid. of Kingsbury TILLEY.
    Asa.. S 6072
      Granville, Mass., in 1832. (Given as Mass. service in report of 1834.)
    Asa, wid. Elizabeth.. W 17798
      Soldier died in 1810 in Hartford, Conn.
    Eli... R 9403
    George, Conn. & Cont., wid. Mabel.. W 17800
    Henry.. R 9404
    James, wid. Hannah... W 11415
      Soldier died in 1814; was priv. & Corp.; widow died in 1837.
    James, wid. Rebecca... W 22172
      Soldier pensioned at Norwalk, Conn., as Quartermaster Serg't. in 1832.
    John, wid. Sally, BLWt. 26124-160-55... W 24923
    Joseph... S 43116
    Nathaniel.. S 15225
    Noah, wid. Miriam... W 22171
    Samuel, private of Cavalry, in N. Y. City, and died there in 1834....................... S 28873
    Samuel, wid. Rebecca.. W 17797
      Pensioned as private & serg't. died in Litchfield, Conn., in 1837.
    Seth, wid. Sally, BLWt. 36536-160-55.. W 26438
    Stephen.. S 43107
      (Also given as SEYMOR.)
    Stephen.. R 9406
    Thomas Young, Cont. (Conn.), wid. Susan.. W 19008
    William.. S 20951
      Invalid pensioner; living in 1824, when pension was changed to "18."
    William, Conn. & N. Y., wid. Sarah... W 19012
      Saratoga Co., N. Y., in 1832.
    Zachariah, Conn. & Cont., wid. Elizabeth... W 26441
    Zadock.. S 29440
SHAILER, Hezekiah, Conn., Cont. & Navy... S 17675
    (See also SHAYLOR.)
SHALLIESS or SHALLEISS, Francis, wid. Anna.. W 24943
SHANDLER, Robert. (See CHANDLER.)
SHARP or SHARPE, Caleb, Conn. & Cont.. S 11380
    Daniel, wid. Jemima... W 26465
    Isaac, Conn., Cont. & Green Mt. Boys, wid. Amey....................................... W 19358
    Reuben, Conn. & Cont... S 14450
SHATTOCK or SHATTUCK, David.. S 36308
    William.. S 17670
SHAW, Benjamin... S 36305
    Ichabod, Conn. & N. Y... S 40398
    Richard, Albany Co., N. Y., in 1832... S 22986
    Richard, Conn. & Cont... S 40402
      Addison Co., Vt., in 1818; transferred to Ohio in 1836.
    William.. S 42284
SHAY, Timothy, wid. Hannah.. R 9447
    Soldier pensioned in 1828 in Westchester Co., N. Y.
SHAYLOR, Joseph, BLWt. 1960-200, Lieut. was issued Sept. 16, 1791. No papers.
    (See also SHAILER.)
SHEFFIELD, Joseph.. S 42272
    Samuel, Navy (Conn.) & R. I.. S 39842
SHELDON, Caleb... S 19087
    Ebenezer, wid. Love... R 9466
      Soldier never pensioned
    Elisha, BLWt. 1936-500, Colonel, was issued Dec. 12, 17—(no papers) to Theodosius Fowler,
      assignee.
    Ephraim... S 14442
    James, wid. Abigail... W 22184
    Moses, Cont. (Conn.).. S 15639
    Remembrance wid. Phoebe... W 24955
    Roger, wid. Elizabeth.. W 22189
    Samuel... BLWt. 36654-160-55
SHELLENX. (See SCHELLENGER.)
SHELLEY or SHELLY, Abraham, Cont. (Conn.), wid. Hannah.............................. W 26463
    Ebenezer.. S 11391
    Medad... R 9469
    Samuel, Jefferson Co., N. Y., in 1828; living in 1832.................................... S 42271
    Samuel, New London Co., Conn., in 1818; BLWt. 1287 .... S 36306
SHELP, William... S 17672
SHELTON, Caesar or Cezer... S 19764
    (Given also as NEGRO, Caesar.)
SHEPARD, SHEPEARD, SHEPHARD, SHEPHERD, SHEPPARD or SHEPPERD.
    Amos.. S 33647
      Pensioned as corporal in Conn. in 1818; transferred to Mass.
    Amos, wid. Laminta, Chatham, Conn., in 1832.. W 22193
    Asa.. S 14435
    Daniel... S 17671

SHEPARD, SHEPEARD, SHEPHARD, SHEPHERD, SHEPPARD, or SHEPPERD—Con.
Dorinda, former wid. of Jesse PENFIELD.

Edward Sears..	R	9481
Henry...	S	14448
James, Cont. (Conn.)...	S	33646
Jesse...	S	36307
(Given as SHEPPERD.)		
John. Cont. (Conn.), wid. Sarah, BLWt. 74-60-55....................	W	11452
Jonathan...	S	41154
(Given as SHEPPARD.)		
Joseph. Cont. (Conn.)...	S	33659
Phineas, Conn. & Cont..	S	3895
Samuel, Canterbury, Conn., in 1832..................................	S	17674
Samuel, wid. Sabra...	W	19351
Soldier was pensioned in Orange Co., Vt., in 1832.		
Stephen..	S	30700
Thomas..	S	36311
(Given as SHEPHERD.)		
Whitman...	S	17087
(Given as SHEPHARD.)		
William..	S	22505
SHERMAN, Benjamin, wid. Lydia.....................................	W	17806
Elijah, wid. Betty...	R	9494
Soldier not pensioned.		
Enoch, wid. Catharine..	W	15321
Isaac, Conn., Cont. & Mass..	S	33662
BLWT. 1938–500, Colonel, was issued Aug. 7, 1789, to Richard Platt, Assignee. No papers.		
John, wid. Nancy..	W	8721
BLWt. 1962–200, Lieut, as issued March 7, 1792 to Jonas Prentice, Assignee. No papers.		
Nathaniel...	S	14456
SHERWIN, Ahemaaz or Ahimaas, Conn. & Mass.....................	S	40424
SHERWOOD, Abel, wid. Mary..	W	26458
Asa, wid. Molly..	W	26468
Daniel, wid. Polly...	W	17812
Eliphalet, wid. Abigail..	W	22187
Jane, former wid. of David BURR.		
Jedediah or Jeddidiah...	S	41156
Jonathan...	R	9503
Lemuel...BLWt.	1739–100	
Nehemiah, Steuben Co., N. Y., in 1832..............................	S	11374
Nehemiah, Ridgefield, Conn., in 1818................................	S	36309
Nehemiah...	S	40426
Venango Co., Penna., in 1820; suspended later for lack of identity with soldier.		
Reuben...	S	14455
Seth..	S	14431
Seymour or Seymore, Conn. & Navy..................................	S	42289
Thomas, Conn., Cont. & N. Y...	S	15637
Zachariah, Conn. & Cont., BLWt. 467–100...........................	S	36313
SHETHAR, John, Cont. (Conn.)..	S	11385
SHIPMAN, Benoni...	S	36310
BLWt. 1955–200, Capt. Lieut., was issued June 28, 1790. No papers.		
George, wid. Mary..	W	24946
James..	S	33645
John, wid. Mercy or Marcy..	W	17808
Samuel, wid. Sarah, BLWt. 9523–160–55.............................	W	2670
Silas, wid. Sarah..	W	17807
SHIPPEY, William, Conn.. N. Y. & Penna............................	S	1103
SHIRLIFF or SHIRTLIFF, John..	S	21966
Noah, Conn. & N. Y..	S	7478
SHOLES, Carey Wheeler..	S	36314
Jabez or Jabish..	S	11378
Miner...	S	14457
SHOPP, Peter...BLWt.	1210–100	
SHORT, Samuel, wid. Mary, BLWt. 35731–160–55...................	W	26454
Seth..	S	17673
Siloam..	S	11384
SHUMWAY, John, Conn. & Cont......................................	S	41157
BLWt. 1946–300, Capt., was issued Dec. 19, 1799, to Israel Harris, Assignee. No papers.		
SIBLEY, Ezra, wid. Ann or Anna......................................	W	15337
Moses..	S	29456
SIKES, David, wid. Nancy, BLWt. 24442–160–55.....................	W	11425
Gideon, wid. Mercy, BLWt. 26482–160–55...........................	W	6066
Jacob, wid. Sarah...	W	6217
(Also given as SYKES.)		
John, Conn. & Vt., wid. Lucy, BLWt. 26020–160–55................	W	19133
(Also given as SYKES.)		
(See also SYKES.)		
SILL, Andrew, Conn. & Cont...	S	10014
David F., BLWt. 1940–450, Lieut. Colonel, was issued Jan. 28, 1790. No papers.		
Elisha N., wid. Chloe...	W	6057
Isaac, Sarah Brockway, former wid. of...............................	W	17358
Jabez..		9570
Richard, BLWt. 1950–300, Capt., was issued Dec. 15, 1790, to Eliza Sill & others. No papers.		
Samuel, Cont. (Conn.)...	S	36344
SILLICK, Benjamin...BLWt.	436–100	
(See also SELLECK.)		

SILLIMAN, Issac, wid. Mary, BLWt. 35722-160-55... W 19033
    James, wid. Huldah... W 17818
    Samuel, Conn. & Navy, wid. Roxillana, BLWt. 27687-160-55... W 1266
SIMMONS, Benjamin. wid. Patty... W 24974
    (Also given as BLACK or ROBERTS.)
    Benoni, Conn., Cont., Navy & R. I., widow Nancy, BLWt. 18376-160-55.................... W 13899
    Chapman, Conn. Sea service, widow Elizabeth... W 19362
    John, wid. Rachel.. W 24965
    Peleg, wid. Amy, BLWt. 26549-160-55.. W 11428
    Samuel, Jay, Maine, in 1818, as corporal... S 37394
    Samuel, wid. Sarah... W 24967
        Grafton Co., N. H., in 1818; died in 1841. BLWt. 341-60-55, BLWt. 2155-100.
    Stephen.. S 32521
        (See also SIMONDS & SIMONS & SYMONDS.)
SIMON, Cummy... S 36315
SIMONDS or SIMONS, Aaron. wid. Mehitable... W 17816
    Andrew... S 42300
    Arad. Conn.. Conn. Sea service & Cont., wid. Bridget............................... W 15339
    Asa, Conn. & Mass... S 7519
    Eli... S 33668
    Elijah, Greenwich, Conn., in 1832... S 15647
    Elijah, wid. Lucy... W 17813
        Soldier died in 1831; widow died in 1837, in Windham Co., Conn.
    Isaac... R 9583
    Isham, Conn. & Cont., wid. Deborah, BLWt. 5102-160-55............................. W 1898
    Jeduthan, wid. Mary, BLWt. 56917-160-55.. R 9582
        Soldier rejected; did not serve six months.
    John, wid. Ann.. W 16406
        Soldier served as serg't.; died in Cayuga Co.. N. Y., in 1814.
    John, Navy.. S 15203
        Enlisted on frigate *Confederacy* in 1779, in Columbia Co., N. Y., in 1820.
    Joseph, Delaware Co., N. Y., in 1818.. S 42305
    Joseph, wid. Prudence.. W 17814
        (Also given as SYMONS.)
        Soldier pensioned in Hartford Co., Conn., in 1818; died in 1830.
    Joseph, Conn.. Cont. & Mass., Chemung Co., N. Y., in 1832........................ S 14460
    Joshua, wid. Elizabeth... W 24960
    Lycus, wid. Julia.. R 9584
        Soldier pensioned in 1818 in New London Co., Conn.
    Nathan... S 17094
    Paul G... R 9585
    Sarah, former wid. of David VIBBARD or VIBBIRD.
    Thomas, Rebecca BARBER, former wid. of.. W 20679
    William, wid. Beulah... W 17817
        (Also given as SEMONS.)
        (See also SYMONDS.)
SIMPSON, John, BLWt. 1942-400, Surgeon, was issued Sept. 2, 1789. No papers.
SINNOTT, Partick, wid. Mary... W 4585
SIP, Jesse, Navy (Conn.).. S 36316
SIZER, Anthony, wid. Lucretia... W 24550
    Daniel... S 36317
    Jonathan... S 14459
    Lemuel, wid. Elizabeth... W 22215
    William, Cont. (Conn.)... S 33672
SKEEL or SKEELE, Amos, wid. Lucy.. W 6070
    Phebe, former wid. of Robert HUBBARD.
SKEELS, Simeon, Cont. (Conn.), Asenath Amedon, former wid. of........................ W 20605
SKELLENGER, Daniel.. S 4844
    (See also SCHELLENGER.)
SKIFF, Stephen, wid. Abah... W 19039
SKINER or SKINNER, Adonijah, wid. Abigail... R 9631
    NOTE.—Adonijah was son of Capt. John Skinner, and John's commission is on file in the
    Department.
SKINNER, Ashbel, wid. Rhoda... W 17819
    Benjamin, Conn. & Vt., wid. Sarah.. W 17820
    Beriah... S 42306
    Daniel, Conn. & N. H., wid. Hannah... W 24976
    David, wid. Ruth, BLWt. 6422-160-55.. W 2448
        (Given as SKINER.)
    Elisha, wid. Achsa... W 17822
    Ira, wid. Hepsibah... R 9633
        Their son Riley B. Skinner, of Trumbull Co., Ohio, applied for pension in 1855.
    Isaac, wid. Lucy... W 24975a
        Soldier in Windsor Co., Vt., in 1820; died there in 1843.
    Isaac, wid. Mabel.. W 22220
    Soldier died in Hartford Co., Conn., in 1816; widow living there in 1836.
    Israel, wid. Lovisa.. W 17821
    John... S 42310
        Pensioned as Lieut. in Ballston, N. Y., in 1818.
    John, Catharine Emerson, former wid. of, BLWt. 7097-160-55....................... W 24120
        Soldier served as artificer and died in 1801; widow living in Cortland, N. Y., in 1836.
    John, wid. Cleopatra... W 24980
        Soldier pensioned in 1832 in Hartford Co., Conn., where he died in 1833.
    Jonathan, wid. Judith.. W 22222
    Luther, wid. Sarah... W 22219
        Washington Co., N. Y., in 1818; died there in 1827; widow in Franklin Co., Vt., in 1842
    Luther, wid. Temperance.. W 24978
        Soldier pensioned in Windsor Co., Vt., in 1832; died there in 1838.

SKINNER, Richard... S 14471
    Samuel, wid. Elizabeth.. W 22221
    Stephen.. S 31965
    Thomas, BLWt. 1943–400, Surgeon, was issued Dec. 3, 1789 to Daniel Watrous, Assignee. No.
      papers.
    Thomas.. S 42307
    Timothy, BLWt.. 946–100
    Uriah... S 22991
    Zenas... S 14468
SLADE, Abner, Conn. & Cont.. S 16248
    Jacob... R 9644
    William, BLWt. 15418: 160–55... S 23921
SLASON, Jonathan.. S 22513
    Nathanial, wid. Hannah.. W 24982
      (Soldier died May 1, 1835.)
SLASSON, Deliverance... S 29461
SLATE, Thomas... R 17896
SLATER, Amos, wid. Rachel... R 9651
    Neither soldier nor widow applied; daughter, Martha Spies, of Livingston Co., N. Y., in
      1850 was rejected.
    James, wid. Esther... W 17825
SLAUSON, Ezra... S 17701
    (See also SLAWSON.)
SLAUTER, Ephraim, wid. Ruth.. W 6079
SLAWSON, Eleazer, Conn. & N Y.. S 23420
    Nathan, wid. Hannah, BLWt. 8017–160–55....................................... W 22226
      Soldier died in Oct., 1844.
      (See also SLAUSON.)
SLEAD, John... S 36331
SMALLIN or SMALLING, Jacob, Conn. & N. Y., wid. Mary...................... R 9671
    Soldier was pensioned from Windham, Greene Co., N. Y., in 1832.
SMITH, Aaron.. S 20966
    Invalid pensioner; died 1824, Haddam, Conn., aged 87 yrs.
    Aaron.. R 20435
      Was of N. Y. City in 1830 and Litchfield Co., Conn., in 1831.
    Aaron, Conn. & Cont... S 42346
      (Also given as Aron.)
      Enlisted from Washington, Conn.; was in Middlefield, Otsego Co., N. Y., in 1818, aged 63
      years.
    Abel, wid. Sarah.. W 11479
      Soldier born in Brookfield, Litchfield Co., Conn., May 20, 1757; enlisted there, and died
      there Apr. 27, 1849.
    Abel, Conn., Cont. & Mass.. S 43156
      Soldier born Oct. 18, 1750; enlisted from Mass. and resided in 1818 in Windham, N. Y.
    Abel, Conn. & R. I... S 43154
      In N. Y. City in 1820, aged 56 yrs.
    Abijah, wid. Judith.. R 9783
      Soldier never pensioned.
    Abisha, Conn. & Cont.. S 18226
    Abner... S 18232
    Abraham... S 18225
    Allen.. S 43161
      Enlisted from New Haven Co., Conn., was in Plattsburgh, N. Y., in 1820, aged 63 yrs.
    Allen, Conn, & Privateer... S 17686
      Born East Haven, Conn., 1750; died 1834, Branford, New Haven Co., Conn.
    Amos... S 22518
      Born Lyme, Conn., & enlisted there; in 1832 was in Greensboro, Vt., aged 75 yrs.
    Amos... R 9685
    Amos, wid. Lydia... W 24989
      Soldier born New London Co., Conn., May 8, 1757; enlisted there, and died Mch. 17, 1836,
      at Schoharie, N. Y.
    Andrew... S 17097
    Anthony, wid. Esther... W 17844
    Asa, Conn. & Cont... S 32528
    Asaph, Cont. (Conn.).. S 36323
    Asher, wid. Sarah.. W 17834
    Austin.. S 23426
    Azariah, wid. Alathea.. W 17843
    Benjamin.. S 14530
      Born Dec. 31, 1761, at Canterbury, Conn.; enlisted there and was living there in 1832.
    Benjamin.. S 17099
      Born Apr. 20, 1747, in Fairfield Co., Conn.; enlisted there and was living there in 1833.
    Benjamin, wid. Amelia... R 9684
      Soldier died in Windham Co., Conn., in 1834, not pensioned.
    Benjamin, Conn. & Cont.. S 41175
      Enlisted from Pomfret, Conn., in 1818; was in Bethel, Vt., aged 64 yrs.
    Benjamin, Cont. (Conn.), widow Lydia... R 9792
      Soldier was born in East Haven, Conn., and died in 1794; never pensioned. Lydia was
      84 in 1838, at East Haven, Conn.
    Bill, Conn. & N. Y... S 14528
      Born New London Co., Conn., Feb., 1753; enlisted from Middletown, Conn., & New Leb-
      anon, N. Y.; in 1832 was in Rome, N. Y.
      (See also SMITH, William.)
    Caleb, Conn. & Conn. Sea service, wid. Sarah................................ W 17837
    Calvin, wid. Anna.. R 9688
      Soldier never pensioned; died in Hampshire Co., Mass., in 1832.
    Charles... S 15983
    Cuff.. S 36321
    Dan, wid. Betsey.. W 5174
      Soldier enlisted at Sharon, Conn., & in 1818 was in Rutland, Vt., aged 60 yrs.; died Feb.
      15, 1833; widow died Sept. 23, 1845.

SMITH, Daniel.. S 17681
    Born East Haven, Conn., Sept. 23, 1762; enlisted there & in 1832 was in New Haven, Conn.
Daniel.. S 36319
    In 1820 was in Preston, Conn., aged 74 yrs.
Daniel, wid. Mary, BLWt. 26754–160–55.. W 19070
    Resided Stamford, Conn., & died in North Castle, Westchester Co., N. Y., Dec. 15, 1831.
Daniel, Conn. & Cont... S 45154
    In 1818 was in Marcellus, Onondaga Co., N. Y., aged 62 yrs.
Daniel, Conn. & R. I.. S 11416
    Born Stonington, Conn., Oct. 7, 1753; & in 1832 was in Columbia, Herkimer Co., N. Y
David.. S 17683
    David, BLWt. 1941–400, Major, was issued Sept. 16, 1789. No papers.
    Born Feb. 16, 1763, at Stamford, Conn.; lived there until after 1832.
David.. S 31968
    Born Mch. 26, 1764, Vernon, Conn.; there in 1832.
David.. S 40468
    In 1818 was in Washington Co., Ohio, aged 72 yrs.
David.. R 21792
    In 1829 was in Wayne Co., Ohio, aged 75 yrs. & had a wife, Mary.
David, wid. Hannah... W 6123
    Soldier enlisted from Derby, Conn., & in 1832 was in Auburn, Geauga Co., Ohio, aged 69
    yrs.; died there Nov. 19, 1852.
David, wid. Lois... W 25016
    Soldier born in Fairfield Co., Conn., June 16, 1757, & enlisted there; died May 31, 1835,
    at Patakill, Ulster Co., N. Y.
David, wid. Mary.. R 9797
    Soldier born in 1758, Canterbury, Conn.; enlisted there, & in 1832, when pensioned, was
    in Braintree, Vt.; died Mch. 23, 1840; widow died Oct. 23, 1843.
David, wid. Mary.. R 9798
    Soldier born Nov. 20, 1756, at Milford, Conn., & enlisted there & lived there when pen-
    sioned in 1832; died Nov. 7, 1841; widow died Dec. 7, 1843.
Dow... S 14519
Ebenezer.. S 17108
    Born July 27, 1762, at Stamford, Conn., living there in 1832.
Ebenezer, wid. Elizabeth... R 9722
    Soldier born Ridgefield, Conn., Oct. 3, 1761, & enlisted there; in 1832, when pensioned, in
    Elmira, N. Y., died Apr., 1844.
Ebenezer, Conn. & Cont. & N. Y... S 42343
    In 1818 in Onondaga Co., N. Y., & in 1820 in Cortland Co., N. Y., aged 66 yrs.
Ebenezer, Conn. & Cont., wid. Naomi.. W 11471
    Fairfield Co., Conn., where he died Aug. 14, 1832.
Edmund... S 20964
Eli, wid. Deborah.. W 17833
    Soldier died May 29, 1824, Litchfield Co., Conn.
Eli, Phebe Gouge, former wid. of... W 19520
    Soldier was born Oct. 8, 1760; enlisted from Brookfield, Conn., & died in Bridgeport,
    Conn., July 17, 1819.
Elijah... R 9717
    Died Scipio, N. Y., in 1848, aged 88 yrs.
Elijah, wid. Betsy, BLWt. 33755–160–55... W 17835
    Soldier was born Sept., 1763, in Norwich, Conn., & in 1832 was in Lebanon, Conn.; died
    Mch. 24, 1848.
Elijah, wid. Prudence... W 17829
    Soldier was pensioned in 1818, at Granby, Conn., aged 61 yrs., and died there Nov. 21, 1824.
Elijah, Conn. & Mass., wid. Hannah.. R 9740
    Soldier died Oct. 2, 1824, in Sempronius, N. Y., not pensioned; widow applied in 1844
    & said soldier enlisted in 1775 from Stafford, Conn., & in 1778 from South Brimfield, Mass.
Elijah, Conn. & N. Y.. S 14493
    In 1832 in Saratoga Co., N. Y., aged 74 yrs.
Eliphalet, Olive Platt, former wid. of, BLWt. 26996–160–55.. W 2241
    Soldier was born Feb. 25, 1761, at Fairfield Co., Conn.; in 1832 was in Norwalk, Conn.,
    & died Apr. 26, 1836.
Eliphalet, Conn., Cont. & Green Mt. Boys... S 40457
    Was pensioned from Bedford Co., Penna., in 1820, aged 69 yrs., and died Dec. 31, 1839.
Elkanah.. S 36320
Elnathan, Cont. (Conn.), wid. Mary.. W 24984
    BLWt. 6518–100, Serg't., was issued April 7, 1790. No papers.
Enoch, Conn. & Conn., Sea service, wid. Hannah, BLWt. 28542–160–55.. W 17842
    Soldier born Dec. 29, 1759; d. 1824, N. Y. City.
Enoch... S 17106
    Born 1753, Chatham, Conn.; died there Mch. 19, 1833, leaving no widow.
Enos... R 9729
Ephraim... S 23423
    Born Aug. 28, 1759, Cheshire, Conn., & enlisted there; in 1832 was in Mendon, N. Y.
Ephraim, wid. Deborah.. R 9711
    Soldier was born Sept. 5, 1762, in Lyme, Conn., & enlisted there; in 1833, when pensioned,
    was in LeRay, Jefferson Co., N. Y., & died Aug. 21, 1837.
Ethan, wid. Hannah... W 17845
Ezekiel.. S 18599
Ezra, BLWt. 1959–200, Lieut., was issued Dec. 18, 1789, to Joshua Henshaw, Assignee. No
    papers.
Ezra, Cont. (Conn.)... S 42319
    Enlisted in Conn., & in 1820 was in Stamford, Conn., aged 67 yrs.
Francis, Conn. & N. H... R 9733
Frederic or Frederick.. S 23428
    Born in 1762 in Norwich, Conn., & in 1832 was in Colchester, Conn.
Frederick... S 19470
    Born Jan. 10, 1765, at Middletown, Conn., & enlisted there; in 1834 was in Manchester, Vt.

SMITH, Frederick, Conn. & Privateer... S 11410
    Born Mch. 1, 1760, Haddam, Conn., & enlisted there; pensioned in 1832 in Jefferson,
    Schoharie Co., N. Y.
Gabriel... S 16251
Gideon, Conn., N. H. & Vt... S 11409
Gregory, Cont. (Conn.), wid. Hannah... W 16408
Heman.. S 23427
Henry, wid. Huldah... R 18007
    Soldier never pensioned. Was married in Fairfield Co., Conn., & died Jan. 9, 1828. Chil-
    dren resided in Conn. & N. Y.
Henry, Cont. (Conn.)... S 43155
    Born in 1758; enlisted from Middletown, Conn., in 1818; was in Lee, Mass., & in 1820 in
    Tioga Co., N. Y.
Ira.. S 11417
    Born in 1763, East Haven, Conn., & enlisted there; in 1832 was in Ulysses, Tompkins Co.,
    N. Y., and died in 1837.
Ira, wid. Chloe.. R 9704
    Born Sept. 7, 1757, in Wallingford, Conn., & enlisted there; in 1832 it was called Prospect;
    died April 22, 1835.
Isaac.. S 14517
    In 1818 was at Greenville, Greene Co., N. Y., aged 56 years., and in 1820 at New Canaan,
    Conn.
Isaac.. S 34516
    In 1820 was in West Boylston, Mass., aged 65 yrs.
Isaac.. S 42340
    Born in 1758; in 1818 was in Chittenden Co., Vt., & in 1831 in Penna., & in 1834 in N. Y.
    state.
Isaac, wid. Mary, BLWt. 75106–160–55... W 11485
    Soldier was 63 yrs. in 1820 at Greenwich, Conn., where he died July, 1829.
Isaac, wid. Sarah.. R 9853
    Soldier never applied for pension; died Oct. 6, 1828.
Isaac, Conn. & N. Y., Abigail Finch, former wid. of... W 3537
    Soldier died Feb. 15, 1805, at Stamford, Conn.
Isaac Sheldon, Conn. & Mass... R 9745
Isaiah, Conn. & Cont., wid. Nancy or Ann.. W 17826
Israel... S 16531
    Born in 1759, Lyme, Conn.; enlisted there & in 1832 was in Dempster, Sullivan Co., N. Y.
Israel, wid. Eleanor, BLWt. 69–60–55.. W 502
    In 1818 soldier was in Cazenovia, N. Y., aged 54 yrs., & died Dec. 6, 1836, in Chataqua
    Co., N. Y.
Israel, Conn. & R. I... S 14534
    Born Sept. 22, 1754, at Gloucester, R. I.; enlisted there & at Thompson, Conn.; in 1833
    was in Brookfield, Mass.
Ithamar, Conn. & Cont., wid. Deborah.. W 19068
Jabez.. S 14506
Jacob, Conn. & Cont., wid. Hannah, BLWt. 26335–160–55... W 22240
    Soldier enlisted from Stamford, Conn., where he was born, & died in N. Y. City Sept., 1811.
Jacob, Conn. Sea service, Cont. & Mass.. S 34503
    Born in Dedham, Mass., in 1752; in 1818 in Orrington, Maine, & died May 11, 1834.
Jairus, wid. Sarah... W 25032
James.. S 11426
    Born 1762 at Old Haddam, Conn.; enlisted there; in 1832 at Harpersfield, Delaware Co.,
    N. Y.
James, wid. Marcy, BLWt. 28582-160-45... W 19372
    Soldier was born July 18, 1765, & died in Otsego Co., N. Y., Aug. 2, 1827.
James, wid. Phebe.. W 27567
    Soldier was born in 1762 in New London Co., Conn.; enlisted there; in 1834 in Westmore-
    land, Oneida Co., N. Y., & died Jan. 16, 1836.
James, Conn. & Cont... S 42349
    Enlisted from Lyme, Conn., in 1820 in Kent, Putnam Co., N. Y., aged 62 yrs.; had wife,
    Mary.
James, Conn. & N. Y., wid. Ruth Ann... W 26488
    Soldier was born in 1757, White Plains, N. Y.; enlisted in Wyoming Co., Penna., & in
    1832 was in Hector, Tompkins Co., N. Y.
James, Cont. (Conn.), wid. Sarah H., BLWt. 26502–160–55... W 11482
    Soldier enlisted from Southington, Conn., where he died Mch. 3, 1819.
James A.. R 9750
    Born Mch. 16, 1763, in Groton, Conn., & in 1840 was in West Stockbridge, Mass.
Jedediah, wid. Esther, BLWt. 125–60–55.. W 22233
Jeffery.. S 16250
Jehiel, wid. Rachel.. W 22246
Jeremiah... S-
    Born Dec. 24, 1746, at West Haven, Conn.; enlisted there & in 1832 & died July 19, 1835,
    there (then called Orange).
Jeremiah, wid. Anna.. W 26481
    Soldier born June 30, 1762, at Norwalk, Conn.; enlisted there; in 1832 at Nevisink, Sullivan
    Co., N. Y., & died there July 25, 1851.
Jeremiah, wid. Temperance... W 22268
    Soldier born July 29, 1758; in 1818 at East Haddam, Conn., & died there Dec. 20, 1837.
Jesse.. S 36768
    In 1820, aged 63 yrs., was at Woodbridge, Conn.; died Aug. 15, 1831.
Jesse.. R-
    Born, lived, & died in Stamford, Conn.; died in 1801, 1802, or 1803.
Jesse, wid. Susanna.. R 9861
    Pensioned as Jesse 2nd in 1819, Great Barrington, Mass., aged 62 yrs.; enlisted at Strat-
    ford, Conn.; died May 24, 1841, Mexico, N. Y., where widow died in 1846. Neither
    soldier nor widow rejected, but children.
Job, wid. Esther... W 17831
Joel... BLWt. 198–150
    In 1802 was resident of Owego, Tioga Co., N. Y.

SMITH, Joel, wid. Sarah... W 19066
    Soldier was born Nov. 10, 1756, at Redding, Conn.; enlisted there; in 1832 was at Butter-
    nuts, Otsego Co., N. Y., where he died May 19, 1837.
John.. S 29468
    Born June 11, 1757, at Springfield, Mass.; enlisted at Suffield, Conn., & in 1832 was at
    Granville, Hampden Co., Mass.; died Sept. 3, 1835.
John.. S 34493
    Enlisted from East Haddam, Conn.; in 1818 at Middlefield, Hampshire Co., Mass.
John.. S 42352
    Born 1742; enlisted at Stamford, Conn.; in 1818 at Locke, Cayuga Co., N. Y., & in 1820
    had wife, Tamer.
John, wid. Anne... W 17830
    Born in 1744; died Aug. 5, 1827, at New Milford, Litchfield Co., Conn.
John, wid. Betsey... W 22244
    Born 1741; enlisted at Conn., & died in 1835 at Lewis, Essex Co., N. Y.
John, wid. Lydia... W 3724
    Born Apr. 27, 1760; Montville, Conn.; enlisted there and died in 1852 at Montville.
John, wid. Mary, BLWt. 26722-160-55... W 26965
    Born June 14, 1756, at New Haven, Conn.; enlisted at North Haven; in 1832 at the latter
    place & died there Nov. 3, 1847.
John, Nancy Ann Wilbur, former wid. of... R 11510
    Invalid pensioner, who died in 1813 at New Lisbon, N. Y.
John, Conn. Sea service, wid. Tabitha.. W 13915
    Soldier was born in 1750 and died at sea Sept. 20, 1783; widow at Providence, R. I., in
    1836.
John, BLWt. 1990-200, Lieut., in Col. Lamb's reg't. Artillery was issued May 18, 1790, to
    Isaac Guion, Assignee. No paper.
John, Cont. (Conn.)... S 14497
    Born Mch. 19, 1756, at Farmington, Conn., where he enlisted; in 1818 was at Bristol,
    Conn., with wife, Chloe.
John, Cont. (Conn.)... S 36772
    In 1820 was at Haddam, Conn., aged 64 years, with wife, Anna; died May, 1834, at
    Haddam.
    BLWt. 13776-100, private in Artillery Artificers, was issued Dec. 6, 1799. No papers.
John, Cont. (Conn.)... S 36774
    Enlisted from Stratford, Conn., where he was living in 1818, when pensioned.
    (Also given SMITTS & MITTS.)
Jonathan.. R 9776
    Born Groton, Conn., in 1746; in 1833, at Geneva, Cayuga Co., N. Y.
Jonathan, wid. Polly or Molly, BLWt. 7436-160-55... W 19373
    Soldier enlisted at Ashford, Conn., & died May 2, 1824.
Jonathan, wid. Rebecca, BLWt. 6107-160-55... W 24990
    Enlisted from Haddam, Conn., where he died Aug. 16, 1812.
Jonathan, Conn. & Navy... S 34497
    Enlisted in New Haven Co., Conn.; in 1818 at Sheffield, Mass.
Jonathan, Jr., wid. Rebecca... R 9835
    Soldier never applied; widow claimed that he performed sea service, applying while a
    resident of Rock Co., Wis.; in Feb., 1850; in May, 1850, she had died.
Joseph.. S 14 11
    Born in 1756 in New London Co., Conn.; enlisted there & was pensioned there in 1832.
Joseph, Elizabeth Chapman, former wid. of.. R 1865
    Soldier was born, Hebron, Conn., 1760; in 1821 was in Ontario Co., N. Y.
Joseph, wid. Eunice... W 6121
    Soldier enlisted from Derby, Conn., & in 1820 lived there, aged 65 yrs.; died there Apr.
    28, 1834.
Joseph, wid. Rebecca.. W 17827
    Soldier born, lived & died at Stamford, Conn.; died Aug. 6, 1828.
Joshua.. S 42329
Josiah.. S 14533
    Born Dec. 20, 1747, Windham Co., Conn.; enlisted there & pensioned in 1832 there.
Josiah.. S 42330
    Born & enlisted in New London Co., Conn.; in 1833 at Tamworth, N. H., aged 83 yrs.;
    died Mch., 1838.
Josiah.. S 47992
    In 1787 at Cheshire, Conn., aged 28 yrs., living there in 1824; in 1830 in Geauga Co.,
    Ohio; died Nov. 7, 1833.
Josiah, wid. Sarah.. W 25023
    Soldier born July 12, 1750; in 1788 at Poundridge, Westchester Co., N. Y., & died Nov.
    29, 1830, at Stamford, Conn.
Josiah, Conn. & Privateer, wid. Anna... W 25012
    Born Aug. 3, 1759, & enlisted in New London Co., Conn., & in 1818 was in Philipstown,
    Putnam Co., N. Y.; died Jan. 8, 1842, in Richmond Co., N. Y.
Josiah, Continental service.. S 36759
    In 1818 in Berlin, Conn., aged 62 years.
Keturah, former wid. of Job PRIMUS or LATHROP.
Laban, Conn. & Privateer.. S 14525
Lemuel.. S 14502
Lewis, wid. Ann, Conn. & Navy Service... W 19509
Lucy, former wid. of William FRENCH.
Lue or Lewee.. S 36722
Luther, wid. Ruth... W 26486
Martin.. S 18598
Matthew or Mathew... S 31379
    Born May 12, 1753, at East Haddam, Conn., & enlisted there; in 1832 at Middlefield,
    Hampshire Co., Mass.
Matthew, wid. Susan... R 9860
    Soldier died at Vernon, Oneida Co., N. Y., Nov., 1815. Never pensioned.
Matthew, Conn. & Vt., wid. Emma, BLWt. 27585-160-55... W 2010
    Soldier was born Jan. 13, 1760, at Pomfret, Conn., where he enlisted; his third enlistment
    was at Hartland, Vt., & in 1832 he was at Chaplin, Conn., where he died Dec. 25, 1841.

SMITH, Michael, wid. Mary... W 17846
    Miner, wid. Submit, BLWt. 3612-160-55... W 25010
    Nathan.. S 17680
        Born Feb., 1735, at Lyme, Conn.; enlisted at Montville, Conn., & in 1832 was at He-
        bron, Conn.
    Nathan, wid. Rachel.. W 26477
        Soldier was born at Holden, Mass., & lived there in 1818, aged 55 yrs.; died there Aug.
        23, 1824; enlisted "in Susquehanna River in N. Y."
    Nathaniel... S 36764
        In 1820, aged 59 yrs., was at Lyme, Conn., with wife, Lucinda.
    Nathaniel, wid. Lucy... W 17832
        Born Aug. 11, 1761, at Canterbury, Conn., & died there July 21, 1835.
    Nathaniel, Conn. & Cont... S 36761
        In 1820, aged 66 yrs., was in Litchfield Co., Conn.
    Noah, wid. Hannah... R 9819
        Both soldier & widow rejected.
    Oliver... S 21980
    Peter.. S 36767
    Philemon, Conn. & N. Y... S 14503
    Phineas, Conn. & Vt.. S 19471
        Grand Isle, Vt., in 1832.
    Phinehas, wid. Abiah... W 26487
        Soldier died in 1812 at Fairfield Co., Conn.
    Phinehas, wid. Deborah Ann.. W 11480
        Litchfield Co., Conn., in 1832; died in 1839.
    Ralph, wid. Anne... W 17841
        New Milford, Conn., in 1818; died there in 1825.
    Ralph, wid. Hannah.. W 15945
        Died in 1807 in Albany Co., N. Y.
    Ralph, wid. Mary... W 819
        Middlesex Co., Conn., in 1832.
    Richard... S 14520
    Robert, Conn. & Cont... BLWt. 1267-100
    Robert, Cont. (Conn.).. S 11421
        Meriden, Conn., in 1832.
    Roger... S 14529
    Roswell... S 17684
    Samuel.. S 31971
        Private, corporal & Serg't.; in 1832 was in Savannah, Ga.
    Samuel, wid. Anna.. W 22265
        New Haven Co., Conn., in 1832.
    Samuel, Conn. & Cont.. S 14494
        Southington, Conn., in 1832.
    Samuel, Cont. (Conn.).. S 17107
        Norwalk, Conn., in 1832.
    Samuel B.. S 17104
    Sarah, former wid. of Robert STOGDILL.
    Seth... .•... S 14507
    Sherman, wid. Amarillas.. W 25005
    Silas.. S 18597
    Simon... S 11411
    Sparrow, wid. Eunice... W 26489
    Stephen... S 17100
        Haddam, Conn., in 1832.
    Stephen, Conn. & Conn. Sea service... S 14523
        Branford, Conn., in 1832.
    Stephen, Conn. & Cont.. S 42337
        Butternuts, N. Y., in 1818.
    Sylvanus.. S 40469
    Sylvester, wid. Hannah... W 24983
    Theophilus M.. S 14532
    Thomas, wid. Thankful.. W 26474
    Timothy... S 42314
        Pensioned as Timothy 3rd. in 1829, at Collins, Erie Co., N. Y.
    Timothy... S 41164
        Tinmouth, Vt., in 1818.
    Wells, wid. Elizabeth... W 17848
    William, BLWt. 1956-200, Lieut., was issued Aug. 5, 1789. No papers.
    William, wid. Esther.. W 25018
        Captain; died in 1816 in Windham Co., Conn.
    William, Conn. & Cont.. S 14508
        Bozrah, Conn., aged 67 yrs., in 1823.
    William, wid. Hannah... W 17839
        Born in North Kingston, R. I., in 1758; Voluntown, Conn., when he died July 4, 1839.
           (See also Bill SMITH.)
    Zachariah... S 41177
    Zebina, wid. Martha.. W 19047
SMITTS, John. (See SMITH.)
SNELL, Joseph.. S 36776
SNOW, Abraham, wid. Lavina, BLWt. 26727-160-55.. W 504
    Amaziah, wid. Sarah.. R 9916
        Soldier not pensioned.
    Ezra, wid. Lavina.. W 25036
    Isaac, Conn. Sea service & Mass... S 19098
    Ivory, Conn. & Mass.. S 11434
    John.. R 9913
    Jonathan.. S 16256
        Tolland Co., Conn., in 1832.
    Jonathan, wid. Mercy... W 25038
        Norwich, Vt., in 1818; died in 1833.

SNOW, Joseph.. S 14536
 Levi.. S 17688
 Nathan, Conn. & Mass.. S 21495
 Nathaniel, wid. Mehitable.. R 9915
  Soldier pensioned from Chatham, Mass., in 1818, & Barnstable, Mass., in 1829.
 Robert, wid. Anna, BLWt. 2180–160–55.. W 25041
 Shubeal, wid. Rachel, BLWt. 45717–160–55.. W 26492
 Silas.. S 14544
 Thomas, wid. Lucy.. W 17849
SOLLACE, Eliza Whitney, former wid. of David WHITNEY.
SOLLEY, Thomas, Cont. (Conn.), wid. Eunice.. W 17853
SOPER, Jesse, Conn. & N. Y... R 9935
 Prince, Conn., Cont. & Green Mt. Boys, wid. Elizabeth................................. W 25044
 Timothy.. S 17691
SOUTHMAYD, Daniel... S 14547
SOUTHWARD, Andrew... S 36778
SOUTHWELL, Asahel, wid. Hannah.. W 3363
SOUTHWORTH, Elijah.. S 10022
 Isaac... S 22525
  (Also given as SUTHARD.)
 Joseph, Cont. (Conn.).. S 33693
 Lemuel.. S 41180
 Samuel Wells, wid. Marcy.. W 15802
 William... S 40479
SOWL, David... S 14546
SPALDING, Barzillai or Brazillai, Conn. & N. H.. S 19101
 Darius, wid. Mary, BLWt. 27684–160–55... W 1879
 John, wid. Wealthy Ann.. W 3312
 Joseph.. R 9952
 Joseph, Conn. & Vt.. S 22529
 Josiah.. BLWt. 75115–160–55
  Soldier was son of Josiah, a soldier who had a disability pension.
 Philip.. S 14567
 Reuben.. S 17695
 Silas... S 22530
 Simon, BLWt. 1948–300, Capt., was issued Dec. 15, 1791. No papers.
 Wright.. S 43168
  (See also SPAULDING.)
SPARKS or SPARKES, Ebenezer, wid. Margaret.. W 19395
 Joseph, wid. Eleanor.. W 20063
SPARROW, Stephen, wid. Lydia, BLWt. 10247–160–55.. W 2366
SPAULDING, Oliver, Conn. & N. H... S 14558
 (See also SPALDING.)
SPEAR, Elijah... R 20436
 Joshua.. S 4875
SPELMAN, Jemima, former wid. of Joseph CLARK.
SPENCE. (See SPENCER.)
SPENCER, Aaron, wid. Mindwell or Mindel... R 9980
  Soldier not pensioned.
 Ancel or Ansel, wid. Loly, BLWt. 26048–160–55....................................... W 11522
 Daniel.. R 9976
 Daniel.. S 3961
  In 1832 was living in Penna.
 Daniel, Cont. (Conn.), BLWt. 53–100... S 29475
 David, BLWt. 334–200.. S 14563
  Pensioned as 2nd Lieut. in East Haddam, Conn., in 1818 and 1832.
 David... S 36780
  Pensioned as private in Windham Co., Conn.
 Elam.. S 23938
 Elihu, wid. Ruth, BLWt. 11396–160–55.. W 26496
 Elijah.. S 11453
  Saratoga Co., N. Y., in 1832.
 Elijah, Conn. & Conn. Sea service, wid. Hannah...................................... W 25062
  Soldier was in Canterbury, Conn., in 1832 and died there in 1838.
 Emmons.. S 14561
 Ephraim... S 36779
 Gardner, wid. Mary.. W 17856
 Ichabod, wid. Hannah.. W 22283
 Isaac... S 15653
 Israel, wid. Temma.. W 6154
 Jabez, Conn., N. Y. & Vt., wid. Patience.. W 22295
 James, Conn. & Cont., wid. Elizabeth, BLWt. 50889–160–55............................ W 1328
  (Also given SPENCE.)
 James, wid. Thankful.. W 4811
  Soldier died in 1802 in Ashtabula Co., Ohio.
 James, Cont. (Conn.), wid. Rachel, BLWt. 19621–160–55............................... W 27667
  Soldier was pensioned in Somers, Conn., in 1832 & died there in 1845; widow was living
  there in 1853.
 Jared Wilson, wid. Margaret... W 16419
 Jehiel, wid. Anne P... R 9975
  Soldier never pensioned.
 Jehiel, wid. Naomi.. R 9981
  Soldier never pensioned.
 Joel, BLWt. 13898–160–55.. S 36781
 John, wid. Mary... R 9979
  Soldier never pensioned.
 John, Conn. & Cont., wid. Eunice.. W 6157
  Rej. BL.
 Noah.. S 28892
 Peter, wid. Jerusha, BLWt. 31584–160–55... W 7198

SPENCER, Reuben, **wid.** Mehitable.. W 17857
    Samuel, wid. Eunice... W 22286
        Soldier was in Worcester, N. Y., in 1832 & died there in 1838.
    Samuel, Cont. (Conn.), wid. Sarah... W 22288
        Soldier was in Windham Co., Conn., in 1818; and died in 1826 in R. I.
    Samuel B., Conn. Sea service.. S 23935
    Seth.. S 23004
    Theodore, Cont. (Conn.), wid. Nabby... W 26497
    Thomas, wid. Huldah, BLWt. 49–100.. W 2186
    Walter... S 16533
    William.. S 6143
        Chenango Co., N. Y., in 1832.
    William, wid. Phebe... W 17859
        Soldier died in 1804 in Middlesex Co., Conn.
    Zaccheus... R 9989
SPERRY, Army.. S 42367
    Benjamin.. R 9991
    Ebenezer.. S 15652
    Elijah, Conn. & Cont., wid. Polly... W 3885
    Jacob.. S 17693
    Job, wid. Rebecca... W 17862
    Jonathan, Conn. & Cont.. S 11443
    Joseph, wid. Abigail.. W 16734
SPICER, Abel, wid. Sarah, BLWt. 15420–160–55.. R 9995
        Soldier never pensioned as he did not serve six months.
    Asher, wid. Rebecca.. W 16418
    John, wid. Mary.. W 22284
SPOONER, Nathaniel, wid. Ruth... W 2015
    William, Cont. (Conn.), wid. Jerusha, BLWt. 28591–160–55................................ W 25071
SPRAGUE, Dan... S 14553
    Dyer, wid. Faith.. W 15365
    Ebenezer, Conn. & N. Y.. R 10010
    Frederick, Conn. & Mass., wid. Rebecca.. R 10012
        Soldier was pensioned in 1818 from Washington Co., Ohio.
    James, Conn. & Cont.. S 40482
    Samuel H., Conn., Cont. & Mass.. R 10013
SQUARES. (See SQUIRE.)
SQUIER, SQUIRE or SQUYER, Abner.. S 17718
    Asa.. S 42024
        (Given as SQUYER.)
    Calvin, wid. Mabel, BLWt. 26204–160–55.. W 6160
        (Given also as SQUARES & SQUIRES.)
    Daniel... S 42376
        (Given also SQUIRES.) BLWt. 26463–160–55. Washington Co., N. Y., in 1818.
    Daniel... S 22531
        (Given also as SQUIRE.) Rutland Co., Vt., in 1832; priv. & drummer.
    Edward Adam, wid. Mary.. R 10025
        Soldier never pensioned.
    Ebenezer, wid. Lucy.. W 17864
    Elisha, Cont. (Conn.), wid. Huldah... W 4342
    Ephraim, Conn. & Mass., wid. Priscilla... R 10026
        Soldier pensioned in 1832 from Windham Co., Conn.
    Isaac, Conn. & Conn. Sea service, wid. Susanna... W 17863
    Philip.. S 36785
    Thomas.. S 11454
    William, wid. Esther, BLWt. 26555–160–55.. W 26966
SQUIRES, Abiathar, wid. Mary... W 4591
    Ezra, Conn. & Vt., wid. Betsey.. W 4812
    Justus, wid. Polly.. W 17865
    Phinehas.. S 46401
    Samuel, Ellen Turney, former wid. of... W 22458
        NOTE.—This woman's second husband, James CHAPMAN, Conn. S 37831, was a pensioner; and her third husband, Aaron TURNEY, Conn. S 18633, was also a pensioner.
    Selah or Seley, wid. Hannah.. W 17866
SQUYER. (See SQUIER.)
STAFFORD, Thomas, BLWt. 469–100.
STALKER, Peter, wid. Achsah, BLWt. 1381–100.. W 19098
STANARD, William, wid. Hannah.. W 19120
    (See also STANNARD.)
STANBROUGH, or STANBRAUGH, Lemuel, wid. Jane, BLWt. 9543–160–55................ W 2453
STANCLIFT, Comfort... S 23949
    John, Conn. & Cont... S 14612
    Lemuel, wid. Mehitabel or Mehitable, BLWt. 2086–160–55................................ W 3733
STANDISH, Amasa, Conn. & Mass.. S 14600
STANDLY. (See STANLEY.)
STANLEY, Elisha... S 29481
    Frederick... S 7610
    Jesse. (See STANLY.)
    Noadiah, wid. Hannah.. W 19413
        (Also given STANDLY.)
    Noah, wid. Naomi... W 25143
    Salmon.. R 10055
    Timothy... S 11475
STANLY, Jesse.. R 10052
STANNARD, Abel, wid. Phebe.. W 19114
    David, wid. Ruth, BLWt. 36530–160–55.. W 25142
    Eliakim, Conn. & Cont... S 7596
    Elijah... S 17709
    Ezra... S 7606

STANNARD, Jasper.. S 31981
    Job.. S 17700
    John.. S 17702
        Middlesex Co., Conn., in 1832.
    Joseph.. S 41199
    Libbeus, Conn. & Green Mt. Boys & Vt.. S 14619
    Samuel, wid. Elizabeth... W 19119
        (See also STANARD.)
STANTON, Daniel.. S 20978
    Ebenezer, Cont. (Conn.) & Privateer, wid. Mary... W 25105
    Edward, wid. Martha.. W 2481
    Elijah, Conn., Cont. & Mass.. S 14623
    Jason, wid. Sally, BLWt. 8152–160–55... W 505
    Joseph, wid. Priscilla... W 22302
    Nathan.. R 10061
    Samuel, wid. Hannah... W 23305
STAPLES, Abel.. S 14595
    Asa... S 21997
    Ebenezer.. S 17710
    John, wid. Lydia.. W 6212
STARK, Abraham... S 42407
    John, Conn. & N. H., wid. Tryphena, BLWt. 26308–160–55..................................... W 15405
        (Also given STARKS.)
STARKE, Aaron.. R 10073
    (Also given STARK.)
STARKEY, Susannah, former wid. of Asa PRATT.
STARKS, Ebenezer... R 10074
    Nathan, Cont. (Conn.)... S 33723
    Samuel.. S 23959
STARKWEATHER, Elijah... S 46072
    Ephraim, Conn. & R. I., wid. Rachel... W 22308
        (Also given STARKWATHER.)
    John, wid. Hannah... R 10075
        Soldier pensioned from Conn. in 1832.
    Prince, wid. Marcy.. R 10076
        Soldier never pensioned.
        (Also given as WILLIAMS, Prince.)
    Thomas.. S 17126
STARLING, Jacob.. S 36797
STARNES. (See STEARNS.)
STARR, David, BLWt. 1949–300, Capt., was issued Nov. 19, 1789. No papers.
    Dumill, Navy service but Conn. residence.. R 1418
    Eli... R 10078
    Jehosaphat, wid. Mary... W 22298
    Jesse, Cont. (Conn.), wid. Polly.. W 19415
    Jonathan.. R 10081
    Joshua.. S 14609
    Josiah, BLWt. 1935–500, Capt., was issued Oct. 7, 1789. No papers.
    Josiah.. R 10082
    Robin... S 36810
    Samuel Moor, wid. Abigail... W 6209
    Thaddeus.. S 14606
    Thomas, wid. Lois... W 17887
        Soldier died in 1801 in Fairfield Co., Conn. BLWt. 1957–200, Lieut., was issued May 29,
        1792. No papers.
    Thomas, Conn. & Mass.. R 10083
    William, Deerfield, Mass., in 1819... S 33711
    William, wid. Eunice.. W 8756
        Soldier was pensioned as Lieut. in Baltimore, Md., in 1818.
STAUGHTON. (See STOUGHTON.)
STAUNTON. (See STANTON.)
STEARNS, Charles, wid. Sarah.. W 6176
    (Also given as STARNS.)
    Levi.. S 30716
    Roswell... S 23439
STEBBINS, Ebenezer... S 41203
    Joseph.. R 18144
    Samuel, wid. Ruth... W 25135
STEDMAN, Isaac, wid. Lucretia.. W 2264
    James... S 28898
    Levi, Conn. & Cont., wid. Anna, BLWt. 20–160–55... W 19108
    Lucy, former wid. of Adriel HUNTLEY.
    Nathan, Conn. & Privateer... R 10093
    Philemon.. S 33742
    Selah... S 11491
    Thomas.. S 17121
        St. Lawrence Co., N. Y., in 1834
    Thomas.. S 36809
        Hartford Co., in 1818.
STEEL, Elijah, wid. Hannah... W 25124
    John.. R 10095
    Joseph, wid. Olive.. W 19105
    Josiah.. S 36791
    Perez, wid. Hannah.. W 28035
        NOTE.—Lucy Steele also applied for pension as widow of above soldier and was rejected
        (R. 10096). See papers in this case.
STEELE, Ashbell, wid. Eunice.. W 25162
    Bradford, wid. Ruth, BLWt. 7085–160–55.. W 17869
    David, wid. Hannah.. W 25102

STEELE, Isaac, wid. Lavinia .... W 17888
James, wid. Jemima.. W 26448
John.. S 36790
    Hartford Co., Conn., in 1818.
John, Sarah Hillard, former wid. of... W 21331
    Soldier died in service.
Josiah, wid. Phebe.. W 871
Lucy. (See note to STEEL, Perez.)
Moses, wid. Amanda.. W 15372
Samuel, wid. Sarah, BLWt. 57524-160-55.
    Soldier not pensioned; died at Sharon, Vt., in 1849.
Samuel.. S 17129
    Pensioned as drummer and sergeant in New Haven Co., Conn., in 1832.
William, wid. Rebecca Renea... W 22056
Zadock or Zadok, Conn. & Vt.. S 14571
STEEVENS, William. (See STEPHENS.)
STENT, Eleazer, wid. Rhoda... R 10110
    Soldier never pensioned.
Othniel... S 18221
STEPHENS, James, Conn. & Vt.. S 23951
William, Conn. & Cont.. S 11470
    (Also given STEEVENS.)
    (See also STEVENS.)
STEPHENSON, Thomas, Hannah Olds, former wid. of... W 15143
STERLING, Seth.. S 15994
Thaddeus... S 17714
STERRY, Silas, wid. Olive.. W 22342
STEUBEN, Jonathan, Conn. & Cont., wid. Lucy... W 22344
STEVENS, Aaron, BLWt. 1945-300, Capt., was issued Apr. 10, 1795. No papers.
Abel.. S 11476
Adams or Adam, Conn. & R. I., wid. Rena, BLWt. 9439-160-55................................. W 5185
STEVENS, Amos... S 31986
    Fairfield Co. Conn. in 1832.
Amos, wid. Rachel, BLWt. 38543-160-55... W 11556
    Soldier died in New Haven Co., Conn., in 1831.
Asa, wid. Lois.. R 10132
    Soldier never pensioned.
Benjamin, Conn. & Cont.. S 15665
Caleb, wid. Mary... S 19102
Daniel, wid. Pollyphena or Polyphena... W 11562
Ebenezer, Cont. (Conn.).. BLWt. 625–150
Elias, wid. Lucretia... W 9314
    Killingworth, Conn. in 1818 & 1832; BLWt. 6022-160-55.
Elias, Conn., N. H. & Vt.. S 14621
    Pensioned as Lieut. in Royalton, Vt., in 1832.
Elkanah, Conn. & N. Y.. S 15664
Elnathan.. S 9486
Ephriam... S 41198
Forward, wid. Mary.. W 6185
Henry.. S 36805
    Plymouth, Conn., in 1818.
Henry, wid. Polly, BLWt. 5104-160-55.. W 821
    Windsor Co., Vt., in 1832.
Hubbel.. S 42404
Israel, wid. Love... R 10134
    Oneida Co., N. Y., in 1832.
James, Cont. (Conn.), wid. Esther, BLWt. 9442-160-55... W 6187
    BLWt. 13775-100, private, was issued Jan. 25, 1796. No papers.
    (Also given as STEPHENS.)
Jeremiah.. S 17698
John, BLWt. 1944-300, Capt., was issued June 18, 1791. No papers.
John, Chloe Smith, former wid. of, BLWt. 3609-160-55.. W 28034
    Soldier died in 1822; widow was in Watertown, Conn., in 1851.
John, Conn. & Mass... S 42431
    Dutchess Co., N. Y., in 1818.
Jonathan, wid. Elizabeth, BLWt. 6277-160-55.. W 2674
Lemuel, Conn. & Cont... S 18217
Moses.. S 6148
    (Also given STEPHENS.)
    Otsego Co., N. Y., in 1832.
Moses, Conn. & N. Y.. S 11474
    Cayuga Co., N. Y., in 1832.
Nathaniel, wid. Amy... W 17883
    Cont. service, but Conn. residence & Agency of widow.
Oliver, wid. Nancy... R 10137
    Soldier never pensioned.
Peter.. S 41186
    Wells, Vt., in 1818.
Peter, Conn. & Vt.. S 19109
    Pawlet; Vt., in 1832.
Phinehas or Phineas... S 42411
Reuben, wid. Jerusha.. W 17870
    Litchfield Co., Conn., in 1818; died in 1822.
Reuben, Conn. & N. Y., wid. Molly.. W 19409
    Greene Co., N. Y., in 1832; died there in 1842.
Safford, Conn. & N. H... S 41209
Silvanus, wid. Sarah.. W 19096
Solomon, wid. Abelinah... R 10121
    Soldier pensioned in 1832 in Greensville, N. Y.

142

STEVENS, Thomas... S 11492
    Litchfield Co., Conn., in 1832.
  Thomas.. S 36792
    Grandy, Conn., in 1818.
  Thomas, wid. Lucy.. W 3471
    Huntingdon, Penna., in 1818; died in 1841.
  Timothy, wid. Prudence.. W 17882
    Soldier died in 1823 in Litchfield Co., Conn.
  Timothy, Conn. & Cont., BLWt. 1286-100.................................... S 36796
    (Also given STEPHENS.)
    New Haven Co., Conn., in 1818.
STEWARD, Albert, wid. Reuana.. W 19100
  Eliphalet, Conn., N. Y., & R. I.. S 6156
  Elisha... S 11488
  William... S 4890
    (Also given STEWART.)
STEWART, Andrew, Conn. & N. Y., wid. Lucretia, BLWt. 27683-160-55..... W 19099
  Charles, BLWt. 1922-150, Ensign, was issued Mch. 1, 1797; also recorded as BLWt. 2677. No
    papers.
  Charles... S 41196
    (Also given STUART.)
  Daniel, wid. Lovisa, BLWt. 26253-160-55.. W 9673
  Henry... S 23950
  James, Conn., N. J. & Penna.. S 40520
  John... S 28902
  Joseph.. S 11484
    Steuben Co., N. Y., in 1832.
  Joseph, Anna Harvey, former wid. of.. W 13348
    East Haddam, Conn., in 1818; died 1823.
  Oliver, wid. Rebecca, BLWt. 27657-160-55... W 26444
  Samuel.. R 10168
  William... S 42398
    Greene Co., N. Y., in 1830
  William, wid. Amanda or Manda.. W 8760
    Voluntown, Conn., in 1832.
STILES, Asa, Conn. & War of 1812, wid. Olive....................................... R 10182
  Asahel.. S 31987
  Beriah.. S 14610
  Gould... S 19108
  Jeff. (See BRACE, Jeffery.)
  Joseph.. BLWt. 1043-100
  Lewis... S 28894
  Martin, wid. Candace or Candice... W 25079
  Reuben, Cont. (Conn.), wid. Submit... W 22301
  Robert.. S 42392
    Sarah, former wid. of Isaac COFFIN or COFFING.
STILLMAN, Joseph... S 31988
  Nathaniel... S 14603
  Roger, Conn. & Cont... S 14588
STILLWELL, STILWELL, STILLWILL, Elias.. S 36806
  BLWt. 1952-300, Capt., was issued Sept. 29, 1790 to Elias Stillwell. No papers.
STILSON, Ebenezer... S 1114
STIMSON, David.. S 14627
  Joel, wid. Susanna.. W 19095
STOCKER, Thaddeus... S 15992
STOCKING, Amasa... S 30137
  Eber, BLWt., 581-100.. S 36793
  Moses, Navy (Conn.), wid. Elizabeth.. W 15384
STOCUM, Reuben... S 11456
STODDARD, Clement, Conn. & War of 1812, Esther Carpenter, former wid. of.... R 10202
    Soldier never pensioned.
    (Also given STODDART.)
  Cyrenius or Cyrenus... S 42383
  Daniel, wid. Lucretia.. R 10204
    Soldier pensioned in 1832 in New London Co., Conn.
  David, wid. Elizabeth.. R 10201
    Soldier never pensioned.
  Frederick... S 36800
  James... S 14591
  Nathan... BLWt. 106-300
  Philo, wid. Polly, BLWt. 14952-160-55.. W 2676
  Robert.. S 14577
  Samuel.. S 42377
  Simeon C. or Simon C.. S 43176
  Wells.. S 18212
  William... S 17716
STOEL, Asa, wid. Judith... W 11535
  (See also STOWELL & STOYELL.)
STOGDILL, Robert, Sarah Smith, former wid of................................... W 22245
STOKES, Jonathan, Conn., Conn. Sea service, Navy & Privateer; wid Sally..... W 25123
  Richard, wid. Jerusha, BLWt. 6020-160-55... W 11541
STONE, Albernarle, Conn. & Navy, wid. Sally or Sarah, BLWt. 6117-160-55..... W 2483
  Andrew L. Mary Hoit, former wid. of.. W 18056
    Betsey, former wid. of Andrew DEWY.
  Bille, wid. Rachel.. W 2879
  Daniel.. S 36813
  John Evarts.. S 18614
  Levi... S 31989
    Thompson, Conn. in 1832.

STONE, Levi, wid. Mary... W 17875
    Kent, Conn., in 1832: died 1836, Artificer.
Samuel... S 17708
    Tolland Co., Conn., in 1832.
Samuel... S 42401
    Onondaga Co., N. Y., in 1818.
Thomas, Conn. & Cont.. S 36795
    BLWt. 6482- was issued Oct. 7, 1789, to Benj. Tallmadge, Assignee.   No. papers.
William.. S 42429
STORER, Nehemiah, Navy (Conn.).. S 36801
STORES.   (See STORRS.)
STOREY, James.. S 15658
    (See also STORY.)
STORRS, Augustus, wid. Anna.. W 16152
    Chipman, Conn., R. I. & War of 1812.. R 10231
    (Also given STORES.)
    Ebenezer... S 15995
    Justus, BLWt. 1925–300, Surgeon's Mate, was issued July 14, 1797; also recorded as above under
      Wt. 2692.   No papers.
    Lemuel, Conn. & Cont., wid. Elizabeth.. W 25136
    Prentiss, Conn. & Cont... S 11468
STORY, John, Conn. & Cont.. S 15657
    Oliver, Conn. & Cont., wid. Lois... W 25082
    Solomon... S 36812
    (See also STOREY.)
STOUGHTON, Alexander... S 14596
    (Also given STAUGHTON.)
    Augustus, wid. Cylinda or Celinda... W 3315
    Jonathan, wid. Hitta.. W 17874
    Russell... S 14622
    Shem, wid. Flora... W 17878
    William, wid. Eleanor.. W 17885
STOVER, William... S 17705
STOW, Elihu, Cont. (Conn.), wid. Mary.. W 20071
    Jedediah.. S 14593
    John.. S 11480
    Joshua, wid. Ruth... W 26447
    Samuel, Conn. & Cont.. S 36819
      New Haven Co., Conn., in 1827; died in 1831.
    Samuel, Cont. (Conn.).. S 48632
      Serg't., Windsor, N. Y., in 1818.
    Stephen, wid. Mary.. W 22311
    Zacheus.. S 36811
STOWELL, Nathaniel, Aurelia Fisk, former wid. of, BLWt. 45666–160–55.... W 7266
    Samuel.. S 42432
    (Also spelled STOEL & STOWEL.)
STOYELL, Stephen... S 11465
    (Also spelled STOELL.)
STRATTON, Samuel.. S 23013
    Stephen.. S 23435
    Thomas.. S 17131
STRAWBRIDGE.   (See STROWBRIDGE.)
STREET, John.. S 17712
STRICKLAND, David.. S 35084
    (Also spelled STRICTLAND.)
    Jonah.. R 10263
    Seth, wid. Anna, BLWt. 9469–160–55.. W 17889
    Simeon, wid. Mary... W 17880
    Stephen.. R 10265
STRONG, Anthony... S 36814
    Barnabas or Barnabus... S 40498
    Chloe, former wid. of Eli KING.
    David, BLWt. 1951–300, Capt., was issued Oct. 17, 1789.   No papers.
    David, BLWt. 26346–160–55.. S 14573
    Elnathan, wid. Margaret, BLWt. 29060–160–55.. W 8753
    Ephraim.. S 18613
    Israel.. S 11467
    Jacob, wid. Elizabeth, BLWt. 3139–160–55.. W 25146
    Joel, Conn., Cont. & N. Y., BLWt. 26526–160–55..................................... S 11466
    John.. S 15659
      Norfolk, Conn. in 1832.
    John.. S 31984
      Pensioned as John 2nd. in Woodbury, Conn., in 1818 & 1832.
    John.. S 36818
      Pensioned as Serg't. in Middletown, Conn., in 1818.
    John, wid. Martha... R 10274
      Soldier never pensioned.
    John, Cont. (Conn.).. S 14587
      Pensioned as musician in 1832, at Oneida Co., N. Y.
    Joseph, wid. Hannah... R 10272
      Soldier never pensioned.
    Joseph, Conn. & Cont.. S 7598
      Pensioned in Copiah Co., Miss., in 1832.
    Josiah.. S 42428
    Nathaniel, Conn. & Privateer... S 15993
    Phinehas.. S 41187
    Roger, Conn. & Cont.. S 14575
    Selah... S 29483
    Seth, wid. Rachel.. W 17879
    Solomon... S 41213
    Stephen.. S 18216

STROWBRIDGE or STRAWBRIDGE, George, wid. Bethsheba (see claim of widow, as former
    widow of Jason CRAWFORD, Conn.)... W 19110
STUART, Joseph... S 3974
    Samuel, Conn. & Mass... S 17713
    (See also STEWART.)
STUDWELL, Henry... S 14617
STUDEVANT, Caleb.. S 35645
    James.. S 46076
    (See also STURTEVANT.)
STURGES, Aquilla... R 10288
    Augustus, wid. Mercy... W 17884
    Benjamin, wid. Thankful.. W 25073
    David... R 10289
    Hezekiah.. S 14601
    Lewis... S 17704
    Moris Simmons, wid. Lois... R 10290
    Soldier never pensioned.
    Moses... S 36815
STURGIS, Aaron... S 31389
    Abram, wid. Anna, BLWt. 38561–160–55.. W 19407
STURTEVANT, Zebedee.. S 14615
    (See also STURDEVANT.)
SUMMERS, David, wid. Mary.. W 2877
    Neram or Nirum.. R 20186
    Sylvester.. S 16263
SUMNER, Ebenezer, Cont. (Conn.) & Sea service, wid. Jemima..................................... W 19418
    George.. R 10311
    John, BLWt. 1939–450, Lieut. Colonel, was issued April 9, 1790, to Elizabeth Sumner, Admin-
    istrator. No papers.
    Robert. wid. Jemima.. W 22350
    Shubell or Shubill... S 42436
    William... S 36820
SUNDERLAND or SUNDERLIN, Daniel, Conn. & R. I... S 17718
    (Given as SUNDERLIN.)
    Samuel.. S 41221
SUTHARD, Isaac. (See SOUTHWORTH.)
SUTLIEF, Gad.. S 23961
    Janner or Jonner or Jonah, Conn. & War of 1812, Hepsibah Joiner, former wid. of............ R 5682
    Soldier never pensioned.
SUTLIFF, David... R 10319
SUTLIFFE, Benjamin, BLWt. 1681–200.
SUTTON, Benjamin, Cont. (Conn.) & Green Mt. Boys.. S 42434
    Edward, Abigail Lawrence, former wid. of... W 2897
SWADDLE or SWADLE, John... S 36822
SWAN, Adin... S 28903
    Elias, Conn., Navy & R. I., wid. Anne... R 10331
    Soldier never pensioned.
    John, wid. Sarah.. W 19422
SWANEY, John, wid. Abigail... W 22352
SWEATLAND. (See SWETLAND.)
SWEET, James... S 21518
    John, wid. Anna... W 19131
    Jonathan... S 14635
SWEETLAND or SWETLAND, Aaron, Conn. & Cont. wid. Lois...................................... W 19423
    Ebenezer Leach.. S 15235
    (Given also as SWEATLAND.)
    Luke, BLWt. 477–100.. S 40546
SWIFT, Charles, Conn. & Vt., wid. Johannah... W 16431
    Haman, BLWt. 1937–500, Colonel, was issued Oct. 7, 1789. No papers.
    John, wid. Anna... W 22353
    Soldier died March 12, 1838; was pensioned in 1832 in Onondaga Co., N. Y.
    John, Conn. & War of 1812 from N. Y., Hepzibeth T. Buck, former wid. of, BLWt. 2505–100. W 872
    Widow was pensioned in 1858 while a resident of Detroit, Mich.
    Nathaniel... S 36823
    Philetus, Conn. & War of 1812, wid. Fawnia.. W 501
    Roland or Rowland... S 42437
    William... R 10363
    William, wid. Eunice.. W 19420
SYKES, Ashbel, Conn., Mass. & Vt... S 18618
    (See also SIKES.)
SYMONDS, Ashna or Ashney... S 17679
    (Also given as SIMONDS.)
    (See also SIMONDS and SIMONS.)

T.

TABER, William, wid. Lucinda... W 16749
TAFT, Abel, Conn. & Vt.. S 19117
TALBUT, Ebenezer.. S 17723
TALCOTT, Aaron.. S 36332
    Abraham... S 23452
    (Given as TALLCOTT.)
    Daniel.. R 10379
    (Given as TALLCOTT.)
    Elizur, wid. Dorothy.. W 18108
    Soldier was son of Col. Elizur Talcott, and served as priv. & Serg't. in Revolution, dying
    in 1831 in Tioga Co., N. Y., where his widow died in 1838; pension issued to date of her
    death in 1846 to George Talcott, heir.
    Elizur or Eleazer, Sally Frisby, former wid. of... W 27522
    Soldier was pensioned in 1832 in Trumbull Co., Ohio, as private, and died there in 1835.
    NOTE.—Sally's other husband, was also a pensioner.
    (See FRISBIE, FRISBEE or FRISBY, Luther, Cont. (Conn.), S 42731.)

TALCOTT, Joseph, wid. Rebecca... W 22377
    Justus, wid. Lydia, BLWt. 28574-160-55.. W 6247
    Phineas.. S 16001
TALLMADGE, TALMADGE or TALMAGE.
    Benjamin, Conn. & Cont.. S 46412
        BLWt. 2171-400, Major, was issued Oct. 7, 1789. No papers.
    Daniel, wid. Rebecca, BLWt. 26647-160-55... W 3737
    Ichabod, Hannah Plumb, former wid. of.. W 17460
    John.. S 11523
    Nathaniel.. S 18624
    Samuel... S 14653
    Seymour... S 16268
    Solomon... S 11524
TALLMAN, Peleg, Navy (Conn.), wid. Eleanor, BLWt. 35689-160-55................................ W 26509
    Peter, Conn. & Mass., wid. Margaret.. R 10382
        Soldier was pensioned in 1832 from Onondaga Co., N. Y.
TAMBLIN, Timothy, Conn., Cont. & Mass., wid. Susanna... W 19428
TANNER, Ebenezer, wid. Lydia... W 22372
        BLWt. 2174-200, Lieut., was issued Dec. 14, 1795. No papers.
    Tryal... S 6189
TARBOX, Temperance, former wid. of John ABBOTT.
TATTON, Phillis, former wid. of Cuff WELLS (colored.)
TAYLER & TAYLOR, Abraham... S 7689
    Absalom, wid. Sabra... W 18118
    Augustine, Conn. & War of 1812, wid. Huldah.. W 26502
    Azariah.. S 14050
    Chiles, wid. Rhoda... W 4597
    David, Conn. & Cont... S 15675
        Canton, Conn. in 1832.
    David, wid. Ester or Esther, BLWt. 520-160-55.. W 4827
        Cont, service, but resided in Berlin, Conn., in 1818; transferred to Mass.; widow pensioned
        from N. Y.
    Dorcas. (See Thomas.)
    Eleazer or Eleazar.. S 14639
    Eli.. S 14646
    Elias... S 14642
        Jefferson Co., N. Y., in 1832.
    Elias... S 17725
        Warren, Conn., in 1832.
    Elijah, Conn. & Cont., BLWt. 1485-100.. S 36335
    Elisha... S 17722
        Litchfield, Conn., in 1832.
    Elisha... S 17726
        Portage Co., Ohio, in 1832.
    Eliud... S 14644
    Elnathan, wid. Lydia... R 10419½
        Soldier never pensioned.
    Gad, wid. Abigail.. W 6227
    George... R 10415½
    Isaac... S 11516
    Jesse... S 36336
    Jesup, wid. Sarah, BLWt. 26675-160-55.. W 1509
    Job, wid. Mercy.. W 26969
    John.. S 14652
        Tolland Co., Conn., in 1832; pensioned as private and sergeant.
    John.. S 29496
        Otsego Co., N. Y., in 1818 & 1832.
    John.. R 10419
    John, BLWt... 533-100
        Westchester Co., N. Y., in 1810.
    John, wid. Hannah.. W 18102
        Ellington, Conn., in 1832 & died there in Oct. 13, 1832.
    John, wid. Elizabeth.. W 22384
        Elizabeth was in Onondaga Co., N. Y., in 1845 & died in 1849 in McHenry Co., Ill. Pen-
        sion given her four children in 1850 to date of her death.
    Jonathan... S 23448
        Westchester Co., N. Y., in 1832.
    Jonathan, Conn. & Cont., wid. Hannah.. W 18107
        Middlesex Co., Conn., in 1818; died there in 1821.
    Jonathan, wid. Nancy... W 18105
        Fairfield Co., Conn., in 1832; died there in 1834.
    Joshua, wid. Eunice... W 22375
    Josiah, wid. Elizabeth.. W 824
        NOTE.—Elizabeth also applied on account of service of her first husband, Isaac Sergeant
        or SARGEANT, R 10414½.
    Lemuel, wid. Ada.. W 11604
    Levi.. S 17724
    Martin.. R 10420
        (Given also TAYLER.)
    Nathan, wid. Mehitable, BLWt. 98565-160-55.. W 11596
    Niles... S 42447
    Noah... S 46513
    Obadiah, Cont. (Conn.), wid. Rhoda, BLWt. 1476-100.. W 3373
    Phineas.. S 14655
    Reuben, Conn. & Cont., wid. Anna... W 16433
    Russel... S 11509
    Samuel... S 11521
        Hampden Co., Mass., in 1832.

TAYLER & TAYLOR, Samuel... S 14649
    Danbury, Conn., in 1832.
    Sarah H., former wid. of William OSBORN.
    Simeon, wid. Olive... W 22385
        Litchfield Co., Conn., in 1832; died 1840.
    Simeon, wid. Sibilla.. W 16753
        Batavia, N. Y., in 1818; died in 1820.
    Solomon, wid. Abigail.. W 26513
    Stephen, wid. Prudence... W 22365
    Theodore.. S 36333
    Thomas.. S 46202
        Dorcas, widow of the above soldier. was pensioned as the former wid. of Levi FARNAM
          or FARNHAM, Conn. W 16752.
    Timothy, BLWt. 2172-300, Capt., was issued May 21, 1789. No papers.
    William.. S 36334
        BLWt. 6569-100, Serg't, was issued Sept. 4, 1789, to Ezekiel Case, Assignee. No papers.
    Zalmon, wid. Hannah.. W 25470
TEAL, Joseph, wid, Hannah... W 18119
    Died in 1795 in Hartford Co.. Conn.
    Nathan, wid. Polly, BLWt. 18221-160-55.. W 19438
        (Also given TEALL & TEEL.)
TEALL, Joseph... S 46473
    Herkimer Co., N. Y., in 1828; died in 1837.
    Oliver... S 11529
TENEYCK, Henry, BLWt. 2173-300, Capt., was issued March 7, 1792. No papers.
TENNANT, John... R 10453
TERREL, Elihu.. S 3773
    Jared.. S 18625
TERRELL, Asahel, Conn. & N. Y., Hannah Blackman, former wid. of......................... W 17311
    (See also TERRILL and TURRELL and TIRRELL.)
TERRILL, Ephraim... S 11528
    (Also given TERRIL.)
    Hezekiah, wid. Betsey, BLWt. 36668-160-55... W 22393
    (Also given TYRELL.)
    Joel, wid. Eunice.. W 4353
    Nathan, wid. Dorothy.. W 4083
    Stephen... S 41234
TERRY, Asaph, wid. Nancy, BLWt. 26938-160-55... W 6249
    Ebenezer.. S 11525
        Hartford Co., Conn., in 1832.
    Ebenezer, Conn. & N. H... S 10661
        Chenango Co., N. Y., in 1832.
    Gamaliel, wid. Susannah.. W 16755
    Josiah, wid. Deborah.. W 19437
    Julius... R 10466
    Martin.. S 14661
    Solomon... S 14662
    Stephen... S 17140
    William N. or William, wid. Eleanor... R 10461
        Soldier pensioned at Pontiac, Mich., in 1832.
    Zeno, wid. Tabitha.. W 22392
THACHER, Benjamin, Phebe Buel or Buell, former wid. of, BLWt. 26736-160-55............. W 2521
    Eliakim, Cont. (Conn.).. S 23970
    (See also THATCHER.)
THARP, Abel, Hannah Austin, former wid. of.. W 20641
    Earle or Earles, Conn. & Cont., wid. Lydia.. W 19444
    (See also THORP.)
THATCHER, Asa, Cont. (Conn.)... S 41242
    John... R 1439
    Josiah... S 14670
    Samuel, Conn. & N. Y.. S 11542
    (See also THACHER.)
THAYER, Asa... S 43199
    David, Cont. (Conn.).. S 36338
    Jerijah, Conn. & Cont., BLWt. 3768-160-55... S 41252
    Joseph, Conn. & Cont., wid. Abigail.. W 18133
THOMAS, Aaron, Cont. (Conn.)... S 35098
    Caleb.. S 35353
        New Haven Co., Conn., in 1818.
    Caleb, wid. Polly, BLWt. 28573-160-55... W 6273
        Ashtabula Co., Ohio, in 1832; enlisted from Tolland, Conn.
    Daniel... S 11536
        Groton, Conn., in 1818 and 1832.
    Daniel, wid. Eunice... R 10495
        Soldier died in 1825, not pensioned.
    Elijah... S 42485
    Enoch, wid. Anne.. W 16756
    James... S 18245
    Jesse.. S 23454
    John, BLWt. 6371, issued 1790.
        NOTE.—This may be identical with the following, W 18136, but the data is so meager it is
          impossible to tell.
    John, Conn. & Cont., wid. Mary.. W 18136
        Priv. & corp. in Woodbridge, Conn., in 1818; died in 1843.
    Joseph, wid. Esther, BLWt. 71188-160-55... W 19452
    Noah, wid. Mary... W 18121
    Simeon, wid. Lucretia... W 18139
    Stephen, wid. Ann... W 25479

THOMPSON, Abraham.. S 36341
    Conn. in 1818.
Abraham, wid. Dorcas B., BLWt. 34599-160-55.............................. R 10521
    Both soldier and widow rejected for pension.
Amos.. S 22016
Asa, Conn. & Cont... S 11541
    (Also given THOMSON.)
David... S 35351
David... R 10527
Epaphras, Cont. (Conn.)... S 40566
    (Also given THOMSON.)
Henry.. S 17727
Hugh... S 23021
James.. S 14681
    N. Y. in 1818. Also given as THOMSON.
James, Conn. & N. H.. S 42487
    Sullivan Co., N. Y., in 1818.
John.. S 11534
    East Haven, Conn., in 1832.
John, wid. Ellis, BLWt. 26720-160-55.. W 25480
    Stratford, Conn., in 1832; died in 1836.
John, wid. Mabel.. W 3317
    New Paltz, N. Y., in 1818.
John, wid. Mary, BLWt. 100290-160-55... W 503
    (Also given Jonathan TOMPSON.)
    Saratoga Co., N. Y., in 1833; Washtenaw Co., Mich., in 1842.
Jonathan. (See John.)
Joseph, BLWt. 1705-100.. S 42491
    N. Y. in 1818.
Joseph, wid. Ruby, BLWt. 26862-160-55.. W 2488
    Coventry, Conn., in 1818; died in 1829.
    (Also given TOMPSON.)
Joshua, wid. Hannah.. W 22400
Matthew, Conn. & Navy, wid. Betsey, BLWt. 3140-160-55............... W 25478
Nathan, Betty Warner, former wid. of.. W 22519
Nathaniel... S 41241
Nehemiah, wid. Esther, BLWt. 33531-160-55................................. W 827
Samuel... S 11537
    Bath, N. Y., in 1832.
Samuel... S 43998
    Newport, N. H., in 1818 & 1832.
Samuel, Hannah Waldo, former wid. of... W 18298
    Captain, died in Tolland Co., Conn., in 1793.
Stephen... S 42478
    Onondaga Co., N. Y., in 1818.
Stephen, wid. Abigail.. R 10519
    Soldier never applied.
Thomas, wid. Lydia.. W 19453
    Oneida Co., N. Y., in 1832; died there in 1840.
Thomas, wid. Lucy... R 10547
    Soldier died in 1831, not pensioned.
William, wid. Thankful B., BLWt. 1530-100.................................. W 2275
Zebulon, wid. Lucy... W 18134
    (Also given THOMSON.)
THOMSON, Edward... S 14683
James.. S 17731
John, Cont. (Conn.), wid. Parmelia... W 26472
Joseph... S 23022
Moses.. S 11177
Nathaniel... S 14695
Rufus, wid. Sally.. W 3621
Samuel... S 35352
THORNTON, Elisha... S 14676
THORP, Amos.. BLWt. 382-100
Amos, wid. Naomi... R 10573
    Soldier pensioned in New London Co., Conn., in 1818; died in 1820.
    (Also given as THARP.)
Daniel.. S 23023
David, wid. Elizabeth.. W 15427
Ezekiel.. S 36339
Ezra, Conn. & Cont.. S 11545
James, wid. Lydia... W 26525
Joseph... S 6237
    Livingston Co., N. Y., in 1832.
Joseph, wid. Loly, BLWt. 26419-160-55... W 15423
    (Also given THARP.)
    Bennington, Vt., in 1832; died in 1842.
Nathan, wid. Huldah... W 6259
Peter... S 11535
Thaddeus... S 15673
THRALL, Lemmy.. R 10575
William.. S 43198
THRASHER, Bezaleel or Bazaleel, wid. Elizabeth, BLWt. 26224-160-55.... W 2372
THRESHER, Ebenezer, wid. Hannah... W 18124
THROOP, Benjamin... S 42492
    BLWt. 2170-400, Major, was issued Jan. 28, 1790. Name spelled THROPP. No papers.
Dan, wid. Mary.. W 20088
THROPP, Benjamin. (See THROOP.)
THURBER, Samuel, Conn. & R. I... S 22018

148

THWING, James... S 22553
TIBBALS, Samuel, wid. Miriam.. W 6285
  Stephen, Conn. & Cont... S 11559
  Thomas, wid. Elue... W 25482
  (Also given TIBBLES.)
TIBBITTS, Abner, Cont. (Conn.).. S 14698
TIBBLES. (See TIBBALS.)
TIFF, Major.. S 35354
TIFFANY, Amasa, wid. Sarah, BLWt. 26603–160–55................................... W 15433
  Asa.. S 17733
    Isaiah, BLWt. 2175–200, Lieut., was issued August 22, 1789. No papers.
  Nathaniel.. S 16005
  Philemon... S 42498
  Simon, Conn. & Cont.. S 11554
  Timothy.. S 17149
  Walter, Cont. (Conn.), wid. Osee, BLWt. 78–60–55................................... W 2976
    Soldier enlisted under Col. Sheldon; was in Williamson Co., Tenn., in 1832; wid. pen-
    sioned from Kentucky.
  Walter, Sally or Sarah Durkee, former wid. of, Cont. (Conn.), BLWt. 2169–100........... W 19205
    Soldier died in 1791 in Lee, Mass.; served also under Sheldon.
  William... S 7728
TIFT, John.. S 23455
  Solomon.. S 14703
TILDEN, Daniel, Conn. & Cont... S 4683
  Ebenezer, wid. Elizabeth, BLWt. 15415–160–55...................................... W 25486
  Elisha.. S 33202
  Joshua.. S 36342
  Stephen, wid. Dorothy... W 26537
TILLETSON, TILLISON, TILLOTSON or TILOTSON.
  Abraham, Cont. & Conn., wid. Abigail... W 22424
  Asahel.. S 43999
  Ashbel.. S 11558
  Daniel.. S 14705
  Elias, Cont. (Conn.), wid. Experience.. W 18142
  George, wid. Sila, BLWt. 31729–160–55.. W 25489
  Isaac, wid. Sarah, BLWt. 40929–160–55.. W 1002
  Jacob, wid. Lovena or Lovina.. W 25490
  Simeon.. S 36343
TINKER, Absalom, wid. Mary... W 18139
  Amos, wid. Hannah.. W 3624
    Waterbury, Conn., in 1818.
  Amos, wid. Mary... W 26535
    Soldier died 1808 in New London Co., Conn.
  Benjamin, wid. Lucy.. W 25483
  Ezekiel, Elizabeth Gardiner, former wid. of... R 3902
    Soldier was pensioned from Waterford, Conn., in 1832.
  John... S 6245
  Nathan, Conn. & Privateer... S 17413
    Polly, former wid. of Samuel BECKWITH.
  Samuel, wid. Sally, BLWt. 33762–160–55.. W 4606
  Silas.. R 10615
  William, wid. Elizabeth... W 25488
TIRRELL, Samuel.. S 17148
  (See also TERRELL, TERRILL, and TURRELL.)
TITUS, John, Conn., Vt. & War of 1812, wid. Mehetable............................ W 25484
  Joseph.. S 14706
TODD, Benjamin, wid, Phebe.. W 26540
  Eli.. R 10627
  Jehiel... S 14708
  Jonathan, wid. Sally., BLWt. 8160–160–55.. W 2197
  Samuel, wid. Jane, BLWt. 19507–160–55... W 2276
  Thaddeus... S 36346
  Timothy, wid. Phebe.. W 25495
  Yale, Cont. (Conn.), Phebe Davenport, former wid. of.............................. W 17710
TOHN. (See TOME.)
TOLLES, Jared... S 11565
TOLMAN, Lyman, BLWt. 26348–160–55.. S 22020
  (See also TALLMAN.)
TOMLINSON, Agur.. S 14713
  Benjamin, Cont. (Conn.).. S 36347
  Curtis or Curtiss, wid. Lucy, BLWt. 26315–160–55.................................. W 25494
  David...BLWt. 1314–150
  Eliphalet, wid. Polly, BLWt. 89–60–55... W 18152
  Henry... R 10638
  Jabez H., wid. Phebe.. W 6305
  Joseph, wid. Bathsheba, BLWt. 13419–160–55.. W 11638
  William Agur, wid. Phebe.. W 18151
TOMPKINS, Solomon, wid. Deborah.. W 19462
TONE, John F... S 43986
  (Also given as TOHN.)
TOOCKER, James.. S 36349
  Phillip.. S 36348
  (See also TUCKER.)
TOPLIFF, Calvin... S 23028
  James... S 16275
TOPPING, William... S 13766
TORRANCE, Joseph, wid. Sarah.. W 26547
TORRENCE, Thomas... S 23457

```
TORREY or TORRY, Amos, wid. Sarah, BLWt. 38344-160-55.............................. W 22437
    Asa................................................................................. S 42501
    Bill................................................................................. S 14710
    Jesse............................................................................... S 42509
    John, wid. Abigail.................................................................. W 26542
TOTTENDEN, John......................................................................... S 35355
TOURTELLOT or TOURTELOTT, Joseph, wid. Abigail.......................................... W 25491
TOUSLEY, William, Conn. & Cont., wid. Sally............................................. W 22433
    (See also TOWSLEY.)
TOWER, Gideon, Conn., R. I. & Vt........................................................ S 17735
TOWLES. (See TOLLES.)
TOWN, William........................................................................... S 32020
    Thompson, Conn., in 1832.
    William, Cont. (Conn.), wid. Mary.................................................... W 31
    Stamford, Conn., in 1818; died in 1828; widow in N. Y. in 1836 & Tenn. in 1843.
TOWNER, Elijah.......................................................................... S 11570
    Greene Co., N. Y., in 1832.
    Elijah.............................................................................. S 22558
    Bradford, Penna., in 1832.
    Samuel, Conn. & Mass., BLWt. 3389-160-55............................................ S 28913
TOWNSEND, John.......................................................................... S 11563
    John................................................................................ R 10659
    Jonathan, wid. Miriam............................................................... W 18149
TOWNSLEY. (See TOWSLEY.)
TOWSLEE, Nathaniel, Conn. & N. Y........................................................ S 22022
TOWSLEY, Moses, wid. Abigail............................................................ W 6301
    (Given also TOWNSLEY.)
    (See also TOUSLEY.)
TOZER, Jared, Conn. & Cont.............................................................. S 42506
    John................................................................................ S 42513
    Julius, wid. Elizabeth J., BLWt. 26986-160-55....................................... W 25493
    Richard, Conn. & Privateer.......................................................... R 10664
TRACY, Calvin, wid. Elizabeth........................................................... W 19465
    Cyrus............................................................................... S 19130
    Daniel, Conn. & Cont................................................................ S 19823
    Dudley, Cont. (Conn.), wid. Sarah................................................... R 10667
    (Given also TRACEY.)
    Soldier pensioned in Franklin, Conn., in 1818.
    Eleazer, wid. Hannah, BLWt. 31724-160-55............................................ W 11652
    Elias............................................................................... S 6269
    Elijah, Conn. & Vt., wid. Deidamia, BLWt. 26805-160-55.............................. W 829
    Elisha, wid. Hannah................................................................. W 18163
    Ezekiel, wid. Patience.............................................................. W 18161
    Gamaliel R., wid. Sarah............................................................. W 11660
    Gilbert, wid. Deborah............................................................... W 4088
    Giles............................................................................... S 30748
    Hezekiah.......................................................................BLWt. 547-200
    Jedediah.......................................................................BLWt. 1535-100
    Jeremiah............................................................................ R 10668
    John, wid. Esther................................................................... W 16448
    Levi................................................................................ S 28915
    Moses, wid. Mary.................................................................... W 26555
    Philemon, Cont. (Conn.), wid. Abigail............................................... W 3625
    Solomon, Conn. & Mass............................................................... S 32025
    Jefferson Co., N. Y., in 1832.
    Solomon, Conn. & Conn. Sea Service, wid. Phebe...................................... W 20097
    Pensioned as Serg't. in Rutland Co., Vt., in 1818; died there in 1819.
    William............................................................................. S 35362
TRAVIS, Philip, Conn. & N. Y............................................................ S 42525
TREADWAY, Alpheus....................................................................... S 15680
    David............................................................................... S 11578
    (Given also TREADAWAY.)
    Elijah.............................................................................. S 16007
    Jonathan............................................................................ S 41265
    Josiah, wid., Rana.................................................................. W 18158
TREADWELL, Abel......................................................................... S 23458
    Benjamin, wid. Rachel, BLWt. 21832-160-55........................................... W 2376
    Cato. (See TREDWELL.)
    Daniel, wid. Sarah.................................................................. W —
    NOTE.—This woman was also pensioned as former wid. of Daniel HOYT, W 18155.
TREAT or TREET.
    James, wid. Anna, BLWt. 26621-160-55................................................ W 606
    John, Cont. (Conn.), wid. Elizabeth................................................. W 18156
    Jonathan, wid. Caturah or Katurah................................................... W 14051
    Joseph.............................................................................. S 35360
    Philo............................................................................... S 35361
    Robert, wid. Content................................................................ R 10691
    Soldier never pensioned.
    Russell............................................................................. S 35359
    (Also given as TREET.)
    Samuel P............................................................................ S 42526
    Theodore, Cont. (Conn.), wid. Zippora, BLWts. 486 & 2275-100; also 48-60-55......... W 2460
    Thomas, wid. Rachel, BLWt. 29007-160-55............................................. W 25502
TREDWELL, Cato.......................................................................... S 35358
    (Also given as TREADWELL.)
TREMAIL, Nathaniel, Conn. & Mass........................................................ S 30168
TRIM, Ezra, Conn., Cont. & N. Y......................................................... S 14729
TROBRIDGE or TROWBRIDGE, Benjamin....................................................... S 42530
    Benjamin H.......................................................................... S 40592
    (Given as TROBRIDGE.)
    Billy, Rhoda James, former wid. of................................................. W 20173
```

150

TROBRIDGE or TROWBRIDGE, Ebenezer, wid. Parnel .... W 4607
   (Given as TROBRIDGE.)
   Elihu... S 36350
   John, BLWt. 2176-200, Lieut., was issued Sept. 13, 1790, to John Trowbridge. No papers.
   John, Conn. & Cont... S 36352
   Philemon, Cont. (Conn.), wid. Eunice.. W 18162
   Samuel, wid. Lydia.. W 18154
   Stephen... S 14721
      Washington Co., N. Y., in 1832.
   Stephen, Conn. & Cont., wid. Isabel... S 46494
      Soldier pensioned as Serg't. in Vt. in 1818.
   Thomas.. S 17738
   William, wid. Dorcus... BLWt. 36549-160-55
TRUAIR, Manuel, Conn., Cont. & R. I.. S 42533
TRUEMAN or TRUMAN, Shem... S 42524
TRUMBULL, David, Cont. (Conn.), wid. Sarah... W 14052
   Ezekiel... S 36353
   John.. S 14178
   Jonathan, BLWt. 2169-450, Lieut. Col., was issued Aug. 7, 1789. No papers.
   Robert.. S 21543
   William, wid. Rachel.. W 22456
TRYON, Elizabeth, former wid. of William BROWN.
   Ezra.. S 40586
   Isaac, Cont. (Conn.), wid. Elizabeth... W 25500
   Salmon.. R 10724
   Thomas.. S 14716
      Glastonbury, Conn., in 1832.
   Thomas.. S 32023
      Oneida Co., N. Y., in 1832.
   William... S 36351
TUBBS, Cyrus... S 38448
   Enos, wid. Sarah, BLWt. 24981-160-55.. W 25506
   (Also given as TUBS.)
   Isaac, Eunice Cross, former wid. of... W 16937
   John.. S 14370
   Lemuel.. S 15687
   Martin, Mary Peasley or Peasly, former wid. of...................................... W 19978
   Samuel, BLWt. 378-100... S 40603
   Simon, Conn. & Cont... S 41272
   Thomas.. R 10729
TUCKER, Benjamin, wid. Polly, BLWt. 31329-160-55....................................... W 6317
      Orange Co., Vt., in 1832.
   Benjamin, Conn., Cont. & Mass... S 42549
      Schenectady Co., N. Y., in 1818.
   Elisha, wid. Elizabeth.. S 17159
   John.. S 42550
   Joseph, Conn. & R. I., BLWt. 1101-100... S 42542
   Reuben.. R 10740
   Wait, Conn. & Vt.. S 15681
   Zepheniah, wid. Huldah.. W 18166
   Zoeth, wid. Mary.. W 11677
TUELL or TUELLS, Benjamin.. S 22026
TUFTS, John.. S 18635
TULLER, Augusta, daughter of WAY, Isaac.
   Elijah, wid. Polly... W 18167
   Israel.. S 35959
   Jacob... S 35960
TULLY. Elias... S 32028
TUPPER, William.. S 36356
TURNER, Andrew, Conn. & Md... R 10750
   Asa... S 23975
   Asenath, former wid. of Samuel DUNHAM.
   Bates... S 41275
   Enoch... S 48697
   Henry, Conn. & Cont., wid. Esther, BLWt. 34992-160-55............................... W 25504
   Jabez... S 31440
   John, wid. Hannah... W 3626
      Norwich, Conn., in 1832; died there in 1837.
   John, Conn. & N. Y., Sarah Lynn, former wid. of..................................... R 6550
      Soldier never pensioned.
   Moses... S 41270
   Nathaniel, Conn. & Cont... S 42544
   Selah, wid. Rebecca... W 18173
   Seth.. S 35365
   Stephen... R 10765
   Thomas.. R 10766
   Thomas, Conn. & Privateer... S 11586
   William... S 35104
      Steuben Co., N. Y., in 1818; transferred to Michigan.
   William... S 35104
      Killingworth, Conn., in 1818; transferred to Chataqua Co., N. Y.
   Zebedee or Zebade... S 11590
TURNEY, Aaron.. S 18633
   Ellen, wid. of Aaron, was pensioned as former wid. of her first husband, Samuel SQUIRES, Conn., W 224458.
   Abel, Conn. & Navy.. S 15682
   Asa... S—
      No papers.
   Clarissa, former wid. of Burr GILBERT.
   Ellen. (See Aaron.)

TURREL or TURRELL, Amos... S 14735
TURRIL or TURRILL, Isaac.. S 14736
   John, wid. Polly... R 10770
     Soldier never pensioned.
TUTHILL, Daniel, Conn. & N. Y... S 14738
   David... S 42554
   Olive or Olivet, former wid. of Joseph CRUMB.
TUTTLE, Aaron.. S 6284
     Hamden, Conn., in 1816; invalid pensioner.
   Aaron, BLWt. 1496-100.. S 46519
     In 1828 a resident of Southbury, Conn., and died in 1841; member of "Congress' Own"
     regiment.
   Abel.. S 33838
   Abner, wid. Elizabeth.. W 18169
   Abraham.. S 41268
   Andrew, wid. Betsey.. W 22464
   Asahel... S 17160
   Benjamin, Conn. & Mass.. R 10775
   Caleb.. S 33844
   Charles, War of 1812.
     Lucy Hitchcock, former wid. of, was pensioned for his services in the War of 1812, and also
     as the wid. of Ichabod HITCHCOCK, Conn., W 11293.
   Clement.. S 16276
   Edmund... S 17741
   Enos... S 17740
   Hezekiah... S 35366
   Jared, wid. Roxana... W 22461
   Joel... S 42555
   Joseph, wid. Sally... W 3627
   Joseph... R 10778
   Josiah... S 11589
   Lemuel, Cont. (Conn.).. S 14734
   Levi... S 36355
   Lucius... S 14731
   Moses.. S 11588
   Peletiah, wid. Elizabeth... W 15805
   Solomon.. S 42539
   Thaddeus, Conn. & Cont... S 19488
TWICHEL or TWICHELL, Benoni.. S 33848
TWISS, Joseph, Cont. (Conn.), wid. Lois.. W 26566
TYLAR or TYLEE. (See TYLER.)
TYLER, TYLAR or TYLEE, Abel.. S 16009
   Amos, Cont. (Conn.).. BLWt. 1371-100
   Bishop... S 17162
   Daniel, wid. Sarah... W 18177
     Capt.; died in April, 1832, in Windham Co., Conn.
   Daniel, Conn. & N. H... R 10789
   David.. R 10787
     (Also given TYLEE.)
   Esther, former wid. of Reuben MOSS.
   Jacob, wid. Abi or Abigail, BLWt. 26939-160-55....................................... W 4839
     Schoharie Co., N. Y., in 1832; transferred to Ohio, where he died.
   Jacob, wid. Julia.. W 18176
     Fife major; died July, 1832, at Southington, Conn.
   James.. R 10792
   James, wid. Sarah.. W 19479
   John, wid. Anna.. W 18178
     Branford, Conn., in 1832; died there in 1837; also given TAYLAR.
   John, wid. Ruth. (See FYLER.)
   John, wid. Waity... W 3890
     Lenox, Mass., in 1818; died in 1840; widow moved to Lee Co., Va., to be with son Henry &
     was pensioned from there.
   John, Cont. (Conn.), wid. Mabel.. W 18175
     New Haven Co., Conn., in 1818; died in 1829.
   Major, wid. Hannah, Conn. & N. Y... W 20102
   Nathaniel.. S 42563
     N. Y. in 1818.
   Nathaniel, Conn. & Cont.. W 24450
     Mabel Hotchkiss, former wid. of, BLWt. 12571-160-55. Mabel was also pensioned as wid.
     of her last husband, Jeremiah HOTCHKISS (q. v.).
   Nehemiah, wid. Prudence.. W 25508
   Oliver... S 19137
   Peter.. S 23460
   Reuben... S 14740
   Stephen, wid. Polly.. W 18181
TYRELL. (See TERRILL.)
TYRER, Hannah, former wid. of Silas NASH.

U.

UFFORD, Samuel M.. S 17163
UNCAS or UNCOS, John, wid. Martha, BLWt. 1288-100; BLWt. 509-160-55.................... W 26610
UNDERWOOD, Betsey, former wid. of John WHITE.
   Josiah, wid. Lucy.. W 20101
   Shadrach, BLWt. 1223-100... S 33849
   Timothy.. S 35371
UPHAM, Chester.. S 35372
UPSON, Asa, wid. Ruth... R 10809
     Soldier never pensioned.
   Ashbell, Conn. & Cont.. W 18084
     Mary Hungerford, former wid. of, BLWt. 3994-160-55.

UPSON, Ezekiel... S 42566
James, wid. Mary.. R 10808
   Soldier never pensioned.
Jesse... S 768
Joseph, Conn. & Mass... S 9493
Noah, wid. Rachel.. W 18222
Simeon, Conn. & Privateer... S 19139
UPTON, Sybil, former wid. of Abner LILLY.
USHER, Robert, wid. Anna.. W 3628
UTLEY, Samuel, Conn. & Cont., wid. Sally... W 20100
   Thomas, wid. Abigail.. W 19565
UTTER, James... S 14747
Jesse, Conn. & N. Y., wid. Sarah... R 10815
   Soldier pensioned as fifer in 1832 from Otsego Co., N. Y.

V.

VAGHAN, William.. S 14751
   (Also given VAUGHN.)
VAIL or VAILL, Peter, Conn. & Privateer, widow Nancy... R 10817
   Soldier was pensioned in 1832 while a resident of Suffolk Co., N. Y.
VAILS, Nathaniel, Conn. & N. Y.. R 10819
VAN DUERSEN, William, widow Martha... W 22480
VANORMAN, Isaac, Conn. & N. Y... R 10886
VAN WOMER or WURMER, Peter.. S 23464
VARGISON, Elijah, wid. Margery M. M.. W 19576
   (Also given VERGASON.)
VAUGHAN, Benjamin, Conn., Cont. & Vt... S 14755
   Frederick... S 32565
   (Also given VAUGHN.)
   John... S 42570
VAUGHN, William. (See VAGHN.)
VERGASON. (See VARGISON.)
VERGESON, Daniel, wid. Phebe... R 10929
   Soldier was pensioned in 1818 in Bradford Co., Penna., then transferred to N. Y. State; then
   to Lycoming Co., Penna., where he died.
VERY, or VERRY, Jonathan... S 35373
VIBBARD or VIBBIRD.
   David, Cont. (Conn.), Sarah Simons former wid. of.. W 22214
   Jesse. (See VIBBERT.)
   John, Conn. & Cont., wid. Hannah... W 18223
VIBBART, VIBBERT or VIBBARD, Jesse, Cont. service but Conn. residence...................... S 35374
VICKERY, Timothy... R 10944
VINTON, Seth, widow, Polly... W 611
VOGUE, Publius V... S 46024
VORS or VORSE, Jesse.. S 35375
VOSE, Charles, wid. Elizabeth.. W 6375
   BLWt. 6598 was issued in 1791. No papers. BLWt. 132-60-55.
   William... S 35376

W.

WACK, Frederick William.. S 40647
WADE, Timothy, widow Sabra... W 19585
   (See also WAID.)
WADHAM, Abigail, former widow of Heman ALLEN.
WADSWORTH, Epaphras... S 22567
   Hezekiah... S 6335
   Israel.. S 19146
   John, widow Nela.. W 18273
   Joseph, Conn. & Mass., widow Chloe, BLWt. 39489-160-55..................................... W 9155
   Reuben... S 32042
   Roger, widow Ann.. W 22529
   Thomas, BLWt. 11080-160-55.. S 11645
WAGGONER, Michael or Michal.. S 40636
WAID, Abraham.. S 35381
   Henry.. S 35705
   Increase, widow Freelove... W 18293
   John.. S 35378
   (See also WADE.)
WAINWRIGHT, Thomas.. S 36361
WAIR, Elias.. S 33226
   (See also WARE, WEARE, WIER and WIRE.)
WAKELAND, James, Conn. & Cont., widow Mercy.. W 25845
   (Also given WAKELEE and WAKELEY.)
   BLWt. 13877-100, private, in Hazen's regiment, was issued April 15, 1796, to Nathl. Ruggles,
   Assignee. No papers.
WAKELEE, David, widow Mary... W 6422
   (Also given WAKELEY.)
WAKELEE, John, widow Elizabeth.
   (See WAKLEE.)
WAKELEY, James, widow Mercy.
   (See WAKELAND.)
   Jonathan, Esther Parrott, former wid. of.. W 26286
   (Also given WAKELEE.)
WAKELIN. (See WAKELY.)
WAKELY, Abel.. BLWt. 1337-100
   Henry, Cont. (Conn.), wid. Deborah... W 20113
   (Also given WAKELIN.)

153

WAKEMAN, Gershom, widow Lucy Ann, BLWt. 27590-160-55.................................. W 2282
    Gideon... S 14774
    Jabez... S 11681
    Joseph, widow Rachel.. R 11009
        Fairfield Co., Conn., in 1832; soldier was pensioned.
    Lyman... S 14777
    Seth, widow Mary... W 18232
    Stephen.. S 11683
WAKLE, Thomas.. S 40633
WAKLEE, Benjamin.. S 44004
    John, widow Elizabeth, BLWt. 29030-160-55... W 3479
        (Also given WAKELEE or WAKLY.)
    Joseph, Conn. & Cont.. S 35377
WAKLY. (See WAKLEE.)
WALBRIDGE, Ames, BLWt. 2338-400, Major, was issued Oct. 16, 1789, to Theodosius Fowler,
Assignee. No papers.
    Joshua, Conn. & Mass., widow Priscilla, BLWt. 19515-160-55...................................... W 3318
    Porter.. S 36367
WALDEN, David, Conn. residence... R 11013
    Mary, former wid. of Andrew BAKER.
    Robert, widow Lucretia, BLWt. 16123-160-55... W 8981
WALDIN, Ichabod. (See WILLIAMS, John.)
WALDO, Daniel, BLWt. 28501-160-55... S 14782
    Hannah, former wid. of Samuel THOMPSON.
    Jesse, widow Martha... W 25891
    Joseph, Conn. & Cont... S 11649
    Nathan, widow Deborah.. W 22522
    Zaccheus or Zacheus.. S 16013
    Zachariah, widow Abigail, BLWt. 3805-160-55.. W 25890
WALER. (See WALLER.)
WALES, Ebenezer... BLWt. 1895-200
    Eleazer... S 11653
    Eliel.. S 40650
WALKER, James... S 43231
    Joanna, former widow of Cordilla FITCH.
    Joseph, BLWt. 1218-300, Captain, was issued to his duaghter Catherine & two other heirs
      (grandchildren) for his services as Captain.
    Joseph.. S 11672
        Private, pensioned in 1832, while a resident of Canada.
    Joseph, Eunice Eaton, former widow of... W 17740
        Soldier died in 1798. Eunice was in Hartford Co., Conn., in 1836.
    Joseph, widow Sela... W 3368
        Soldier was in Erie Co., Penna., in 1818, and died there in 1843.
    Nathaniel... S 6328
        Mill Creek, Erie Co., Penna., in 1832.
    Nathaniel... S 35380
        Stafford, Conn., in 1818.
    Obadiah... S 36384
        BLWt. 6631-100 was issued Oct. 6, 1797. No papers.
    Peter... S 23473
    Phineas, widow Susan... W 22534
    Samuel.. S 21556
    Simeon.. S 23993
    Simons.. S 17763
    William, widow Hannah.. W 22518
    Zebulon, widow Hannah.. R 11057
        Soldier never pensioned.
WALL, John, Conn. & N. Y.. S 29529
WALLACE, John... S 22031
    London, Phoebe Freeman, former widow of.. W 18290
        (Also given WALLIS.)
    Richard, Conn. & Vt.. S 46659
    William, Cont. (Conn.), widow Sarah.. W 18277
        (See also WALLIS.)
WALLER, Ashbel or Asbel, widow Jane, BLWt. 49744-160-55................................... W 25861
    (Also given WALER.)
WALLIS, Hammond, Conn. & N. Y., widow Rebecca... R 11086
        Soldier never pensioned.
    Zebulon, widow Eleanor... R 11083
        Soldier never pensioned.
        (See also WALLACE.)
WALMSLEY, William, Conn. & Cont.. S 36368
    BLWt. 2355-150, Ensign, was issued June 27, 1789, to William Walmesley. No papers.
WALTER, Charles... S 36840
    Elijah.. R 11098
    John.. S 11673
        Caledonia Co., Vt., in 1832.
    John, widow Rhoda.. W 2381
        Onondaga Co., N. Y., in 1818; BLWt. 11259-160-55.
WALTON, George, widow Mary.. W 15971
    John, Conn. & Privateer, widow Mary... R 1107
        Soldier not pensioned.
    Silas... S 44017
WARD, Aaron.. BLWt. 1311-100
    Benjamin.. S 7810
    Ichabod... S 40646
        Susquehanna Co., Penna., in 1818.
    Ichabod, Conn. & R. I.. S 14775
        New London Co., Conn., in 1832.

WARD, Jacob .... S 35111
James .... S 22568
Jedediah .... S 22566
John, wid. Abigail .... W 22516
Joshua, wid. Mary, BLWt. 34535-160-55 .... W 18276
Moses, Cont. (Conn.) .... S 36838
Nathan, Conn. & Mass .... S 40629
Samuel, widow Anna .... W 4843
   St. Lawrence Co., N. Y., in 1832; died 1835.
Samuel, Conn. & Mass .... S 17754
   Hampshire Co., Mass., in 1832.
Thomas .... S 35379
   Urial. (See BASCOM, Urial.)
William, widow Martha .... W 25848
WARDELL, Samuel .... S 44010
   (See also WARDWELL.)
WARDEN, Benjamin. (See WORDEN.)
Ichabod, widow Margaret .... R 11132
   (Also given WORDEN.)
   Soldier was pensioned in 1818 in Jefferson Co., N. Y.
James, Conn. & N. Y .... R 11131
   John. (See WORDEN.)
WARDWELL, Jacob .... S 36837
Nathan .... S 29523
William, widow Catharine .... W 2030
   (See also WARDELL.)
WARE. (See WAIR.)
WARIN. (See WARREN.)
WARING, Anthony, Conn. & Cont. widow Mahittable .... W 11735
Henry .... S 36372
James .... S 17757
Jonathan .... S 3460
Joseph .... S 11689
Schuder, BLWt. 36526-160-55 .... S 11692
   (Also given WARRING, Schudder.)
Solomon .... S 14787
   (Also given WARRING.)
Thaddeus, widow Deborah .... W 18280
WARNER, Amasa .... S 44209
Amos .... S 36371
Benjamin, Conn. & Cont .... S 14798
   Ticonderoga, N. Y., in 1832.
Benjamin, Conn., Cont. & N. Y .... S 11644
   Broome Co., N. Y., in 1832.
Betty, former widow of Nathan THOMPSON.
Charles, widow Sarah .... W 20111
Daniel .... S 14791
   Pensioned as private & sergeant in Canandaigua, N. Y., in 1832.
Daniel .... S 11680
   Wethersfield, Conn., in 1832.
Daniel, widow Sarah .... W 25869
   Soldier pensioned as private & corporal in 1832 at Rupert, Vt., died in 1843.
Deliverance, widow Esther .... W 18278
Demas, widow Rhoda .... W 18283
Eleazar or Eleazer, Conn. & N. Y .... S 28934
George, widow Nabby G .... W 25855
Jabez I., widow Mary .... W 10272
Jesse, Conn. & Mass .... R 11145
John .... S 6329
   Conn. Militia; disability pension for wounds in 1777; Litchfield Co., Conn., in 1821.
John .... S 7842
   Hartwick, N. Y., in 1832.
John .... S 14786
   Suffield, Conn., in 1832.
John, widow Abigail .... W 11736
   New Milford, Conn., in 1832; died in 1850.
John, widow Hepsibah .... W 18243
   Continental service, but resided in Norfolk, Conn., in 1818 & 1832; serg't.
Loomis or Loome, widow Eunice .... W 18297
Moses, widow Rachel .... W 3742
Nathaniel .... S 23990
   Chataqua Co., N. Y., in 1832.
Nathaniel, widow Ruth, BLWt. 26232-160-55 .... W 10271
   Washington Co., N. Y., in 1832; died in 1843.
Richard, widow Merab, BLWt. 18025-160-55 .... W 2829
Robert, widow Mary .... W 18237
   Soldier died in 1813 in Hartford Co., Conn.
Robert, Conn. & Cont .... S 36362
   Soldier was in Middlesex Co., Conn., in 1818; BLWt. 2340-400, Major, was issued April 8,
   1796. No papers.
Samuel .... S 32041
   Granby, Conn., in 1832.
Samuel, widow Deborah .... W 18288
   Soldier was in Vt. in 1818 & 1832; and died at Pownal, Vt., in 1834.
Samuel, Conn. & Cont .... S 11679
   New Haven Co., Conn., in 1832.
Saul .... S 17747
Selden, Conn. & Privateer .... S 16014
Solomon .... S 11687

WARNEK, Thomas, Cont. (Conn.), wid. Belinda... W 19584
    Soldier was in N. Y. in 1818; transferred to Penna. & died in 1840; widow applied from
    N. Y. BLWt. 299-60-55.
Thomas, widow Huldah... W 20110
    Soldier died in 1818 in Madison Co., N. Y.
Timothy.. R 11151
    (See also WORNER.)
WARREN, Abraham.. S 44007
    Abijah or Elijah.. R 11153
    Ashbel, widow Penelope.. W 25894
    David.. S 43230
    Edward, wid. Mary... W 25878
    Elijah. (See Abijah.)
    Enoch.. R 11155
    Ezra.. S 30774
    James. (See WORREN.)
    John.. S 36370
        Tolland Co., Conn., in 1818.
    John, wid. Rachel.. W 18241
        Soldier pensioned as sergeant in Hartford Co., Conn., in 1818; died at Hartford in 1827.
    John, widow Sally.. W 25884
        (Given also as WARRIN.)
        Soldier was in Saratoga Co., N. Y., in 1832; died there in 1838.
    John, Conn. & N. Y., BLWt. 1341-100.. S 44012
        Kortright, N. Y., in 1818.
    Jonathan, Conn. Sea service... R 11159
    Joseph, widow Hannah, BLWt. 24622-160-55... W 4378
        Soldier served from Conn. & Mass.
    Jotham... R 11162
        Connecticut residence in 1851.
    Moses, wid. Mary.. W 25876
    Nathan... S 17175
    Nathaniel... S 14773
    (See also WORREN.)
WARRIN, Jesse... S 17749
    John. (See WARREN.)
WARRING. (See WARING.)
WASHBURN, Bazaliel, Conn., Mass. & R. I., widow Meribah........................... R 11171
    Soldier was pensioned from Bristol Co., Mass., in 1832.
    Eli, Cont. (Conn.), widow Mary.. W 2031
    Lemuel... S 44210
    Nathan, widow Anna or Annah.. W 25877
    Samuel.. S 43235
WASSON, John, Cont. (Conn.), widow Amea, BLWt. 152-60-55......................... W 18268
    (Also given James WATSON.)
    Robert, Conn. sea service & Privateer.. S 17748
WATERBERRY, Nathaniel... S 14796
WATERBURY, Daniel, Conn. & N. Y... S 28933
    (Also given WATERBERY.)
    Deodate, widow Mary.. W 18227
    Enos, widow Amy... W 2280
    John, widow Hannah, BLWt. 51762-160-55.. W 6432
    Jonathan, widow Sally.. W 18282
    Joseph.. S 17174
    Nathaniel. (See WATERBERRY.)
    Samuel.. R 11177
    Thomas... R 11178
    William, Darien, Conn., in 1832.. S 17177
    William, Greenwich, Conn., in 1832... S 35697
    William, widow Sally... R 11179
        Soldier never pensioned.
WATERHOUSE, Jonathan, Conn. & Conn. Sea service................................... S 18258
    (See also WATROUS and WATEROUS.)
WATERMAN, Abram or Abraham, widow Hepsibah or Hepzibah, BLWt. 9405-160-55........ W 2287
    Asa, Anna S. Lilley, former widow of.. W 21577
    Calvin, widow Priscilla, BLWt. 26934-160-55.. W 8985
    Charles, widow Sarah... W 4611
    Chester... S 43221
    Darius, Conn., Conn. sea service & Cont. & Privateer, widow Rhoda, BLWt. 7207-160-55.... W 1336
    Elijah... S 7825
    Glading, Conn. & Conn. sea service, widow Charlotte.................................... W 15814
    Ignatius.. S 40644
    John.. S 43218
    John O. Faith Foster, former widow of... R 3684
        Soldier never pensioned.
    Joseph.. S 23054
    Luther, Conn. & Cont., widow Phebe... W 4379
    William... S 19838
    Zebedee.. S 17555
WATEROUS, Benjamin, widow Elizabeth.. W 22527
    (Also given WATROUS.)
    Josiah, Conn. & Cont... S 3483
    Samuel, Conn. & Cont., Sarah Eddy, former widow of.................................. W 21045
    (See also WATROUS.)
WATERS, Benjamin... S 18642
    Bigelow... S 11667
    Daniel, widow Sarah, BLWt. 27568-160-5... W 23542
    (Also given WATTERS.)
    John, widow Mindwell.. W 15464
    Joseph, Conn. & Cont., Lydia Root, former widow of................................... W 17543

WATERS, Oliver.. R 11184
    Phebe, widow of above soldier, applied for pension as the former widow of her first husband,
      Samuel JUDD, Conn.
    Richard. (See WATROUS.)
    Theodore.. R 11185
WATKINS, Boadwell, Boadewell or Badwell... S 41294
    Ephraim.. S 43220
    Jedediah, Conn. & French and Indian War, widow Abigail.................................... R 11188
      Soldier never pensioned.
    Nathan... S 41304
    Robert.. S 43226
      (Also given WATKIN.)
    William, widow Lois... R 11193
      Soldier never pensioned.
WATROUS, Allen.. S 4715
    Ambrose... S 32043
    Benjamin. (See WATEROUS.)
    John R., Conn. & Cont., Lucretia W. Hubbard, former widow of........................... W 3018
      BLWt. 2343-400, Surgeon, was issued Jan. 28, 1790. No papers.
    Richard.. S 36364
      (Also given WATRUS and WATERS.)
    William.. S 41292
      (See also WATERHOUSE and WATEROUS.)
WATSON, Amariah... S 4717
    Caleb... S 44009
    James. (See WASSON, John.)
    John... S 32037
    Levi... S 32039
    Sipeo, widow Juda or Judah... W 18240
    Thomas.. S 11685
      Tolland Co., Conn., in 1832.
    Thomas, widow Sarah, BLWt. 10221-160-55.. W 22505
      Soldier was pensioned from Washington Co., R. I., in 1818; died in 1822.
    Timothy, widow Anne... R 11201
      Soldier never pensioned.
    Titus, widow Mercy.. W 18271
WATTERS. (See WATERS.)
WATTLES, Charles... S 14799
    Dan, widow Cynthia.. S 3743
    David.. S 44028
    Joshua, widow Sarah Ann, BLWt. 3797-160-55... W 26618
    William, Conn. & N. Y... S 14795
WAUGH, Joseph, widow Mary, BLWt. 26478-160-55.. W 3745
    Samuel, Conn. & N. Y., widow Elizabeth.. W 25866
    Thaddeus, widow Ruth... W 22514
WAY, Abner, widow Eunice.. W 25899
    Asa, Cont. (Conn.), widow Susannah.. W 22504
    Durien or Duren, widow Sarah... W 4612
    Elisha, widow Hannah, BLWt. 27578-160-55... W 1006
    George, widow Mary.. W 18286
    Isaac, Conn. & Cont., Augusta Fuller, daughter of... W 29943
    John, widow Mary.. R 11223
      Soldier was pensioned in 1832 in Allegany Co., N. Y,. as priv. of Dragoons.
    Peter, widow Lucy... W 18228
    Reynold, widow Irene.. W 15462
    Selah, widow Lucy, BLWt. 28570-160-55... W 1675
WAYLAND, Edward, widow Molly.. W 18242
    James... S 6330
WAYLEY or WHALEY, Aaron, widow Hannah.. W 19895
WEARE, William.. S 36376
    (See also WAIR and WIER, and WIRE.)
WEAVER, Lodowick, Conn. & R. I., widow Polly... W 8323
    Samuel.. BLWt. 266-100
      Hartford Co., Conn., in 1788.
    Samuel, Conn. & Cont., widow Hannah, BLWt. 13746-160-55.................................. W 1111
      Salisbury, Conn., in 1832; died in 1835.
    Thomas.. S 35717
WEBB, Abner.. S 14821
    Benjamin.. S 11704
    Christopher, Conn. & Cont... S 11705
    Constant.. S 6349
    Daniel, widow Luranda, BLWt. 27689-160-55... W 2291
    David, widow Sarah... W 6443
    Ebenezer, widow Hannah, BLWt. 12836-160-55.. W 18233
      Soldier was pensioned in 1818 from Conn.; transferred to N. Y. and died in Delaware Co.,
      N. Y., in 1835.
    Ebenezer.. S 14824
      Malone, N. Y., in 1832.
    Ebenezer, widow Phebe... W 25921
      Stamford, Conn., in 1832; died in 1834.
    Isaac, widow Mary.. W 4851
    Jared, widow Prudence.. W 18300
    John... R 11253
    John, Cont. (Conn.)... S 36374
      BLWt. 2356-300, Capt., was issued Nov. 13, 1792. No papers.
    Libbeus or Libbius... R 11250
    Moses, widow Abigail... W 25920
    Nathaniel, BLWt. 2344-300, Capt., was issued May 18, 1790, to Theodosius Fowler, Assignee.
    No papers.

WEBB, Reynolds, Conn. & Cont., widow Catherine... W 25919
  Samuel, widow Abigail... W 16781
    Lieut. & Brigade Major; died in 1825 in Dutchess Co., N. Y.
  Samuel, Conn., Cont. & N. Y.. R 11255
  Samuel B., BLWt. 2337-500, Colonel, was issued Jan. 29, 1790. No papers.
  Seth, widow Ann, BLWt. 77513-160-55.. W 25922
WEBSTER, Aaron... S 14815
  Abijah, widow Olive, BLWt. 36559-160-55.. R 11266
    Soldier never pensioned.
  Abraham.. S 43272
  Allen, widow Rebecca... W 25963
  Amos, Conn. & N. Y... R 11259
  Ashbell or Ashbil, widow Mercy... W 18313
  Benjamin, widow Eve.. W 2288
    Schaghticoke, N. Y., in 1828; BLWt. 143-60-55.
  Benjamin, Conn. & Navy, widow Lydia.. W 22562
    Soldier was pensioned in Allegany Co., N. Y., in 1832, and died in 1840.
  Charles, Hannah Loomis, former widow of.. W 20503
  Daniel... S 43273
  Eleazer.. S 33890
  Elizabeth, former widow of Isaac GOODSELL.
  Isaac, Conn., Cont. & Green Mt. Boys, widow Anna................................... W 20122
  Israel, Conn. & Cont., widow Mary Sophia... W 18307
  James.. R 11262
  John... S 11728
  Joshua... S 43277
  Michael.. S 3521
  Nathan... S 14817
    Soldier was in Geauga Co., Ohio, in 1832, aged 79 years; transferred to N. Y.
  Nathan... S 26888
    Soldier was born 1760; was in Chatauqua Co., N. Y., in 1825; transferred to Ohio and back
    to N. Y.
  Obed, widow Lucy, BLWt. 26921-160-55... W 613
  Samuel, widow Margaret... W 18318
  Simeon... S 35715
  Timothy, widow Sarah... R 11267
    Soldier never pensioned.
  William, widow Anna, BLWt. 31773-160-55.. W 4848
WEED, Abishai.. S 17191
  Alexander.. S 11717
  Benjamin, Conn. & Cont., widow Hannah, BLWt. 11398-160-55.......................... W 8986
  Charles, widow Mary.. W 2501
    (Also given as WEEDS.)
  Daniel... S 17768
  Daniel, widow Elizabeth.. R 11271
    Soldier never pensioned.
  David.. S 14825
  Eleazer, Conn. & Cont., widow Anna......................................BLWt.W 18302
  Elnathan... S 23998
  Frederick.. R 11272
  Gilbert, widow Margaret, BLWt. 27659-160-55.. W 18326
  Hannah, former widow of Joseph HOYT.
  Henry, widow Rebecca, BLWt. 51763-160-55... W 2289
  Hezekiah, widow Rebecca.. W 18299
  Isaac, widow Hannah.. W 22575
  Ithamar or Ithamer, widow Delight.. W 22558
  Jabez, widow Hannah.. W 22551
  James, widow Sarah... W 19606
  Jared, Conn. & Conn. Sea service... R 11275
  Jesse, widow Martha.. W 18327
  John... S 23999
    Delaware Co., N. Y., in 1832.
  John, Conn. & Conn... S 11724
    Soldier was pensioned from Stamford, Conn., in 1818; and Darien, Conn., in 1832.
  Jonas, Abigail Daskam, former widow of, BLWt. 32239-160-55......................... W 22896
    Abigail's other husband, William DASKAM, was also a Rev. pensioner. (See Conn.
    S 36495.)
  Jonathan, Conn. & N. Y... S 11682
    Fairfield Co., Conn., in 1832.
  Jonathan, Conn. & N. Y., widow Susannah.. W 20119
    Soldier was in Delaware Co., N. Y., in 1832, and died there in 1837.
  Nathan, widow Mary... W 18314
  Reuben... S 11720
  Seth... S 6346
  Smith, widow Sarah, BLWt. 13734-160-55... W 2290
  Stephen, widow Elizabeth... W 25947
    Thadeus, BLWt. 2345-300, Capt., was issued June 27, 1789. No papers.
WEEKS, Micajah, widow Bersheba, BLWt. 1592-100... R 11278
    Soldier was pensioned in Hancock, N. Y., in 1818.
WELCH, Amos, Cont. (Conn.)... S 44032
  Barney. (See WELTS.)
  Daniel, BLWt. 919-100.. S 36841
    (Also given WELSH.)
  David, widow Lurene.. W 22571
  Ebenezer... S 40665
    Delaware Co., Ohio, in 1818, as fifer.
  Ebenezer...BLWt. 1196-100
    Amity Coats, wife of Obediah Coats, of Sherman, Fairfield Co., Conn., obtained Bounty
    land in 1826, as daughter and only heir of Ebenezer WELCH. No date of his death
    given.

WELCH, Hopestill.. S 36382
John, widow Jemima... W 8987
   Soldier was pensioned from Erie Co., N. Y., in 1832; BLWt. 34579-160-55.
John, Cont. (Conn.).. S 14804
   Warren, Conn., in 1818; died there in 1845.
Robert... S 43282
Samuel, Conn. & Cont... S 43263
Solomon, Orpha Dygert, former widow of.. W 14664
William... R 11299
WELD, John.. S 22578
WELDEN, Abraham... S 35713
Isaac... S 43258
   (Also given WELDIN.)
WELLER, Amos, Conn. & N. Y., widow Dimis.. W 25952
WELLES, Benjamin. (See WELLS.)
Noah... S 23063
   (See also WELLS.)
WELLMAN, Barnabas, Conn. & Cont.. S 29534
John, widow Phebe... W 18325
Jonathan, Conn. & Vt., BLWt. 26108-160-55.. S 15700
   (Also given John.)
Paul.. S 43264
William... S 17774
Zadock, Conn. & Vt.. R 11306
WELLS, Abner.. S 14805
Ashbel.. R 11309
Austin... S 32054
Bayze or Bazze, Conn. & boat service on Lake Champlain, widow Ruth............... W 18311
   (Also given WELLES.)
Benjamin, Conn. & Mass., widow Sarah.. W 6435
   BLWt. 23502-300, Surgeon's Mate, was issued Jan. 17, 1793. No papers.
   Also recorded as above under BLWt. 2622.
   (Also given WELLES.)
Cuff (colored), Phillis Tatton, former widow of.. W 18103
   (Also given as Cuff SAUNDERS.)
Daniel, Conn. & N. Y.. S 6354
Elisha... S 14813
   Trenton, N. Y., in 1832.
Elisha... S 36377
   Hartford Co., Conn., in 1818.
Gideon.. S 18273
Hannah, former widow of Henry MAIN.
Hezekiah, widow Sarah... W 25967
   (Also given WILLES.)
Israel.. S 40664
James.. S 17764
Jedediah F., widow Hannah... W 22576
Jonathan... S 16018
Josiah.. S 28938
Noah. (See WELLES.)
Robert... S 16188
Roger, BLWt. 2349-300, Capt., was issued April 22, 1796, to Jemima Wells, Adx. No papers.
Samuel, widow Isabel Catharine.. W 6439
Simon, Conn. & Cont.. S 14809
Thomas.. S 11721
Timothy... S 40651
WELSH. (See WELCH.)
WELTON, David, widow Sarah... W 18250
Eben... S 16577
George... S 18282
   (Also given WILTON.)
Joel... S 35714
Josiah.. R 11319
   (Also given WETTON.)
Shubael... S 43283
Solomon... S 36380
WELTS, Barney, Cont. (Conn.) & Penna... S 40670
   (Also given WELCH.)
WENTWORTH, Alpheus, Conn. & Cont., widow Polly... W 22582
   (Also given WINTWORTH.)
Amos, Conn. & Conn. Sea service, widow Lydia.. R 11325
   Soldier never pensioned.
   NOTE.—A list of men sent on by Lieut. GOODELL, from Norwich, Conn., July 6, 1780,
      giving place of abode, date of enlistment, number of regiment, and term for which
      enlisted, was forwarded the War Department from this case, Jan. 16, 1913.
Daniel... S 30776
Elijah... S 41311
Ezekiel.. R 11323
Gibbens... R 11324
Josiah W.. S 23062
Levi W., BLWt. 55-100.. S 37511
WERDEN, Jesse, Conn. & R. I., widow Ruth... W 19655
   (Also given WORDEN. See also WORDEN.)
WESCOAT, Joseph.. S 43281
WESCOTT, Daniel... S 17767
   (See also WESTCOTT.)
WEST, Aaron, widow Susanna.. W 19607
Alva, Cont. (Conn.), Susan Robinson, former widow of..................................... W 17557
Amos, widow Helen, BLWt. 31762-160-55... W 11772

159

WEST, Anthony... S 44034
    Benjamin... S 29537
    Caleb.. S 11723
    David.. S 43275
    Ichabod, widow Lovina... W 1113
    Ira.. S 32052
    Joseph, widow Sally, BLWt. 47836-160-55... W 9157
    Moses, Mary Wright, former widow of.. W 18387
    Richard.. S 11709
    Samuel... S 17773
WESTBROOK, James, Conn. & N. J... R 11350
WESTCOT or WESTCOTT, Amos, Conn. & R. I., widow Abigail............................... W 18330
    (See also WESCOAT & WESCOTT.)
WESTLAND, Joseph...BLWt. 2311-100
    Robert... S 36378
WESTON, Abraham, widow Naomi... W 19597
    Benjamin, widow Mary... W 18320
    John, widow Margaret, BLWt. 31769-160-55.. W 4852
    Rachel, former widow of Francis NICHOLSON.
    Zachariah.. S 43257
WETHERLY. (See WITHERILL.)
WETHY, Henry, widow Esther... W 22574
    Jeduthan, Conn. & N. Y.. R 11752
    (Also given WITHEY.)
WETTON. (See WELTON.)
WHALEY, Aaron. (See WAYLEY.)
    Hezekiah... S 36387
    Jonathan, Mercy Lord, former widow of, BLWt. 13744-160-55............................. W 2739
    Theophilus, widow Lois... W 2038
WHAPLES, Samuel, widow Huldah.. W 19613
WHEADON. (See WHEEDON.)
WHEATLEY, Andrew, widow Rubie, BLWt. 7059-160-55...................................... W 19614
WHEATON, Andrew, widow Avis... R 11372
    Soldier never pensioned.
    Jeremiah... S 23486
    (Also given WHEATEN.)
    Jonathan... S 40687
    Roswell, Conn. & N. H... S 36383
    Rufus.. S 35721
    (Also WHEDON and WHEEDON.)
WHEDON, Abraham, widow Lydia, BLWt. 12719-160-55..................................... W 11802
    (Also given WHEADON & WHEEDON.)
    Rufus. (See WHEATON.)
WHEELER, Aaron... S 28941
    Volney, N. Y., in 1832.
    Aaron.. S 11748
    Schoharie, N. Y., in 1832.
    Benjamin, widow Loly or Loby, BLWt. 39-100.. W 6483
    Beriah, Conn. & Conn. Sea service, widow Eunice.. W 25968
    Chauncey, Conn. Sea service & Navy, widow Caroline Matilda............................ W 25998
    Comfort, Conn., N. Y. & War of 1812, widow Parmelia or Amelia......................... R 11385
    Soldier was pensioned in 1832 in Caledonia Co., Vt.; BLWt. 105622-160-55.
    Daniel, widow Amy.. W 18390
    David.. S 44046
    Dimond.. S 24006
    Edward, Conn., Mass. & N. Y.. S 16292
    Hezekiah, Conn. & Cont., widow Meribah, BLWt. 95-60-55............................... W 6486
    James, widow Elizabeth, BLWt. 31776-160-55.. W 2295
    Job... R 11381
    John.. S 40672
    Genesee Co., N. Y., in 1818.
    John, widow Almira... W 25997
    Windham Co., Conn., in 1818; BLWt. 36820-160-55.
    John T.. R 11382
    Jonathan... S 15245
    Joshua... R 11383
    Josiah... S 36388
    Stafford, Conn., in 1818.
    Josiah, widow Hannah.. W 19628
    Washington Co., Vt., in 1818; died in 1828; enlisted from Plainfield, Conn.
    Nathaniel, widow Ellen... W 18408
    Prosper, widow Sarah... W 22604
    Rhoda F., former widow of James MORRIS.
    Rufus, Conn., Mass. & N. Y., Sarah Wood, former widow of, BLWt. 99516-160-55......... W 11881
    Sally, former widow of Jabez BREED.
    Samuel, widow Julia, BLWt. 26531-160-55.. W 26002
    Simeon... S 17776
    Thomas.. S 33903
    William, widow Anna.. R 11376
    Soldier never pensioned.
    Zadock, widow Martha.. W 19620
WHELPLEY, Ebenezer... S 29541
    James.. S 41332
WHIPPLE, Benjamin... S 11766
    Caleb, Conn. & War of 1812, widow Polly.. W 1965
    Elijah, Conn. & Cont.. S 3552
    Joseph, widow Mary... R 11389
    Soldier never pensioned.
    Zebulon, widow Lydia, BLWt. 31778-160-55... W 6491

WHISTON, Joseph, widow Elizabeth... W 16469
WHITAKER, Abraham... S 6375
   Catharine, former widow of Silas BEARDSLEY.
   Ephraim, BLWt. 1902–300.. S 9526
    (Also given WHITTAKER.)
   Nell... S 32588
   Philip.. S 15255
   Stephen.. S 34527
WHITCOMB, Hiram, widow Sarah W.. W 19896
   John or John Skinner, Conn., Cont. & N. Y., widow Sarah.................................... W 3371
WHITE, Abijah.. S 20943
   Adonijah, widow Hannah.. W 22601
   Anna, former widow of William JOHNSTON.
   Caleb, Conn. & Privateer.. S 11758
   Charles... S 11745
   Consider, widow Sarah T., BLWt. 13196–160–55.. W 320
   Daniel.. S 15238
    Hebron, Conn., in 1832.
   Daniel, widow Sally... R 11443
    Soldier pensioned in 1821 for disability, while resident of N. Y.
   David... S 43302
    Pompey, N. Y., in 1818.
   David, widow Hannah, BLWt. 26577–160–55... W 18403
    Soldier in N. Y. in 1832; died in Otsego Co., N. Y., in 1837.
   David, Hannah Wilcox, former widow of... R 11521
    Soldier never pensioned.
   Ebenezer... R 11407
   Elisha, widow Abigail, BLWt. 18370–160–55... R 11408
    Both soldier and widow rejected as service was not six months.
   Elisha, Conn. & Cont.. S 18279
   Ephraim, BLWt. 1765–100.. S 40676
    Penna. in 1818.
   Ephraim, Conn., Cont. & Mass., widow Hope.. W 1680
    Soldier was pensioned in 1832 in Hartford Co., Conn., as Corporal.
   Ezra, widow Lucy.. W 22605
   Israel.. S 6382
   Jacob, widow Esther.. W 18407
   Jedidiah or Jedediah.. S 36386
   Joel... S 11775
   John, BLWt. 2353–200, Lieut., was issued July 6, 1795, to Eneas Munson, Jr., assignee of Sam
    GOULD, Admr. No papers.
   John... S 32589
    Wabash Co., Ill., in 1832.
   John, Betsey Underwood, former widow of.. W 3739
    Soldier died in 1802; widow applied from Colchester, Conn., in 1853.
    NOTE.—Travel roll of Capt. John Isham's Co., Col. Chester, dated N. Y. Aug. 10, 1776,
     was sent the War Department from this case.
   John, Sarah Millard, former widow of.. R 7172
    Neither soldier nor widow applied; but Josiah WHITE, son of Sarah by her first marriage.
   John, Conn. & Continental.. S 3532
    Athens Co., Ohio, in 1832 as private and sergeant.
   John, Cont. (Conn.), widow Martha.. W 16786
    Soldier died in 1812; widow in Cortland Co., N. Y., in 1837.
   Joseph, widow Mary... W 18392
   Lawrence, Cont. (Conn.), widow Eunice.. R 11411
    Soldier was pensioned in 1818 & 1832 while residing in Cincinnatus, N. Y., as member of
    Sheldon's Dragoons.
   Lemuel... S 10045
   Matthew, widow Esther... W 18409
   Nathaniel.. S 44040
    Niagara Co., N. Y., in 1818.
   Nathaniel, Cont. (Conn.), widow Abigail.. W 4532
    Erie Co., N. Y., in 1826; died in 1830.
   Obadiah.. S 15243
   Oliver.. S 24004
   Peregrine.. R 11434
   Philip, widow Olive, BLWt. 119–60–55... W 25969
   Samuel, widow Betsy.. W 25976
   Solomon, Conn. & N. Y.. S 15250
   Thomas.. S 15244
   William.. R 11450
   William.. S 36384
    Chatham, Middlesex Co., Conn., in 1818.
   William.. S 40684
    Killingworth, Conn. (Middlesex Co.), in 1818.
   William, widow Zilpha.. W 22596
    Soldier died in Tolland Co., Conn., in 1837; widow was pensioned by special act of Congress
    in 1848.
WHITEHEAD, David, widow Judith, BLWt. 26405–160–55.. W 10278
WHITELEY, John, Cont. (Conn.), widow Rebecca... W 25978
   William.. S 43308
    (See also WHITLEY.)
WHITING, Elihu... S 11176
   Elijah, Cont. (Conn.), widow Anna, BLWt. 245–60–55....................................... W 18412
   Elizabeth, former widow of Lyman NOBLE.
   Francis, BLWt. 2440–200, Lieut. of First Regiment Light Dragoons, was issued August 25,
    1789. No papers.
   Frederick J., BLWt. 2358–200, Lieut. Sheldon's Regiment of Horse, was issued August 23,
    1790. No papers.

WHITING, Harvey, widow Olive .... W 11801
John... S 15241
 New Hartford, Conn., in 1832.
John, widow Alida.. W 19618
 Madison Co., N. Y., in 1818; died there in 1823.
 (Also given WHITTING.)
Joseph... S 35724
Joseph... R 11462
Nathan, Conn., Navy & R. I., widow Sarah....................................... W 22595
Nathan H., BLWt. 2351-200, Lieut., was issued Feb. 22, 1790, to Theodosius Fowler, Assignee.
 No papers.
Samuel, Conn. & Mass.. S 17777
William.. S 11746
WHITLEY, Joseph... S 44039
 (See also WHITELEY.)
WHITLOCK, Abel, widow Phebe... W 18413
Hezekiah.. S 15706
Justus, Conn. & Privateer.. S 18648
Nathan.. S 6368
WHITMAN, John.. S 35719
Lemuel.. S 43319
Samuel, widow Abigail... W 18402
WHITMORE, Hezekiah.. S 32056
Jabez, BLWt... 1537-100
WHITNEY, Cornelius, widow Hannah... W 14136
Daniel, widow Hannah... W 25995
David, Eliza Whitney Sollace, former widow of, BLWt., 105237-160-55........... W 2013
 Soldier was in Addison Co., Vt., in 1832; died in 1850.
David, widow Nancy, BLWt., 38341-160-55,...................................... W 3636
 Soldier was in Delaware Co., N. Y., in 1834, and died there Sept. 7, 1834; widow was in
  Cortland Co., N. Y., in 1854.
Ebenezer, widow Ruth.. W 22609
Enos.. S 22580
Ezekiel.. S 44036
 Saugerties, Ulster Co., N. Y., in 1818.
Ezekiel, widow Phebe.. W 19626
 Saratoga Co., N. Y., in 1818; died in 1835.
Hezekiah, widow Olive... W 18406
James R., Conn.& Navy... S 44037
John... S 17192
Joshua, Conn. & Green Mt. Boys.. S 41326
 BLWt., 2354-200, Lieut., was issued May 31, 1790, to Theodosius Fowler, Assignee. No
 papers.
Josiah, widow Sally, BLWt., 51764-160-55....................................... W 2297
Peter.. S 41330
Samuel.. S 35723
Walter.. S 11737
William.. S 35720
 (Also WHITNY.)
WHITON, Joseph, widow Amanda... W 14145
Thomas... S 44049
WHITTAKER. (See WHITAKER.)
WHITTING. (See WHITING.)
WHITTLESEY, Charles H... S 17197
WIARD, Darius... S 28946
WICKES, Alexander... S 44090
 (Also WICKS.)
WICKHAM, William, widow Sarah.. W 26026
WICKS. (See WICKES.)
WICKWIRE, Grant.. S 11785
James, Conn. & Cont., widow Sarah... W 22629
WIDGER, Andrew.. S 36390
Eli, Conn., Cont., Navy & Privateer, widow Lucy, BLWt. 3618-160-55............ W 18425
Samuel.. R 11497
WIER, James R... S 30802
 (See also WIRE, WEARE and WAIR.)
WIGHT, Jacob.. S 33934
William.. S 15711
WILBUR, Josiah.. S 44220
 Nancy Ann, former widow of John SMITH.
WILBY. (See WILLEY.)
WILCOX, Abraham, Conn. & Cont., widow Lucretia, BLWt. 26255-160-55........ W 27505
Billy, widow Rebecca... W 18423
 Chloe, former widow of Isaac ISAACS.
Eleazer.. S 16023
Elias, Cont. (Conn.), Hannah Sears, former widow of............................ W 17792
 NOTE.—Hannah's other husband, Obadiah SEARS, was also a Rev. pensioner. See
  Conn. S. 43121.
Elijah, widow Lois... W 18419
Elisha, Conn. & R. I... S 24011
Ezekiel. (See WILLCOX.)
Ezra, widow Rebecca... W 18420
 Hannah, former widow of David WHITE.
Hosea... S 40709
Jacob, widow Rachel... W 18442
 (Also given WILLCOX.)
James. (See WILLCOX.)
James, Conn., Green Mt. Boys, Mass. & Vt...................................... S 19162
Jehiel, widow Catharine... W 2211
 Delaware Co., Ohio, in 1832.

162

WILCOX, Jehiel, widow Thankful... W 6542
    New Haven Co., Conn., in 1818 & 1823.
    (Also given WILLCOX.)
    Joel.. S 40695
    John.. S 32068
    Jonathan... S 11844
    Joseph... S 32073
    Josiah, widow Rosannah.. W 26051
    (Also given WILLCOX.)
    Lemuel, widow Anate... W 22663
    Mercy, former widow of Daniel MERRELL or MERRILL.
    Nathan... S 36391
    (Also given WILLCOX.)
    Rebecca, former widow of Richard DOUD.
    Reuben... S 11859
    Stephen.. R 11528
    Timothy. (See WILLCOX. See also WILLCOX.)
WILCOXEN, David... S 36389
WILCOXSON, WILCOXON or WILLCOXSON & WILLCOXON.
    Finathan... S 15715
    Ephraim J., widow Mary, BLWt. 27694-160-55.................................... W 2392
WILDER, Aaron... S 18655
    Elijah.. S 11779
    Jonathan... S 11793
    Thomas, widow Taphnes or Zaphenes... W 22642
WILDMAN, Matthew, widow Polly.. W 18452
WILEY, Eleanor, former widow of David CROUCH.
    James. (See WYLIE.)
WILKESON or WILKINSON, Abel, Conn. & R. I... S 14842
    Edward M. or Mott, BLWt. 26349-160-55... S 24015
    Ichabod.. S 40710
    Butler Co., Ohio, in 1819.
    Ichabod. widow Anna Taylor.. W 3202
    Soldier died in 1817 at Erie Co., Penna.
    John.. S 11830
    Joseph... R 11550
    Levi, Conn., Cont. & Mass.. S 7913
    Malachi, widow Sally... W 4866
    (Also given as WILKESON.)
    Mott. (See Edward M.)
    Peter... R 11551
    Reuben or Reubin... S 44214
WILLARD, Elisa, widow Lois... W 4715
    Joseph... S 6432
    Lizur.. S 14850
WILLCOX, Benjamin, BLWt. 31770-160-55... S 14852
    Ezekiel... S 34556
    (Also given WILCOX.)
    James, widow Elizabeth.. W 18417
    Soldier was in Middlesex Co., Conn., in 1832; died in 1838.
    (Also given WILCOX.)
    James, Conn. & Cont., widow Lucretia... W 9019
    Soldier pensioned in N. Y. in 1818; widow pensioned in Mich, in 1852; BLWt. 3192-160-55.
    John, widow Lois... W 10283
    Joseph, BLWt. 2350-200, Lieut., was issued Jan. 28, 1790. No papers.
    Nathan... S 19167
    Roger, widow Elizabeth.. W 18453
    Stephen, Conn. & R. I.. S 6412
    Madison Co., N. Y., in 1832.
    Stephen, Conn. & R. I., widow Sabra.. W 18454
    Serg't, Chataqua Co., N. Y., in 1828.
    Timothy.. S 41336
WILLES, Hezekiah. (See WELLS.)
    John.. S 36848
    Silvanus, Conn. & N. H., widow Eunice... W 22619
    (See also WILLIS.)
WILLEY, Abraham.. S 24016
    Ahimaaz or Ahimaas or Ahimaz... S 34560
    Barzillai... S 16299
    Ephraim, widow Bethia.. R 11559
    Sold. in Washington Co., Vt., in 1832.
    Jonathan... S 35734
    New Hartford, Litchfield Co., Conn., in 1818; son of Jonathan WILLEY, a Rev. soldier
    for three years.
    Jonathan, Conn. & N. Y., widow Irene or Irena, BLWt. 517-160-55.............. W 6827
    Torrington, Conn. in 1832; moved to Ohio.
WILLFORD, Joseph.. R 11537
WILLIAMS, Alexander.. S 35740
    Andrew... S 44213
    Anna, former widow of Isaac GALLUP.
    Asa... S 14846
    East Hartford, Conn., in 1832.
    Asa, widow Prudence, BLWt. 26182-160-55... W 2040
    Soldier in Mass. in 1818; died in 1834; widow in Hampshire Co., Mass., in 1855.
    Asahel.. S 6411
    Otsego Co., N. Y., in 1832.
    Asahel, widow Hannah... W 26053
    Rutland Co., Vt., in 1832; died in 1841.
    Asher, widow Elizabeth.. W 18445
    Soldier died in 1812; widow was in Orange Co., Vt., in 1836.

WILLIAMS, Asher, Conn. & N. Y., widow Elizabeth.. W 2216
    Soldier in St. Lawrence Co., N. Y., in 1832.
Bartholomew, Cont. (Conn.) widow Mary, BLWt. 3754-160-55........................ W 2627
Benjamin... S 11855
Caleb, Conn. & Cont., widow Eunice, BLWt. 38337-160-55............................ W 9165
Daniel.. S 23077
    Schoharie Co., N. Y., in 1832.
Daniel.. S 32074
    New London Co., Conn., in 1832.
Daniel, widow Hannah.. W 6512
    Trumbull Co., Ohio, in 1832; died in 1835.
Davenport... S 11813
David.. S 11781
    East Hartford, Conn., in 1832.
David, Conn. & Cont., widow Lucy... W 22632
    Rome, N. Y., in 1832; died in 1837.
Durell... S 14838
Ebenezer... S 35729
    Saybrook, Conn., in 1818; died in 1819
Ebenezer... S 28950
    Albany, N. Y., in 1832.
Ebenezer... S 32072
    Canandaigua, N. Y., in 1832; private & Serg't.
Edward, Conn. Sea service, widow Mary .... W 22633
Elisha... S 14839
Elisha S.. S 30796
Elizabeth, former widow of Abel PHELPS.
Ezekiel, Lydia Newell, former widow of, BLWt. 4681-160-55..................... W 5409
Henry, widow Electa.. W 2889
    Oswego Co., N. Y., in 1832; transferred to Penna.
Henry, Conn. & Cont., Eunice Mott, former widow of............................... W 24163
    Soldier died in 1781; widow in Onondaga Co., N. Y., in 1837.
Hiel, widow Abigail, BLWt. 26176-160-55.. W 6513
Isaac... S 44224
    Athol, N. Y., in 1818.
Isaac, widow Nancy, BLWt. 26371-160-55.. W 6500
    Soldier in Stonington, Conn., in 1832.
Isaac, Conn. & Cont.. S 15719
    Soldier in Norwich, Conn., in 1832.
Jacob, widow Frances... R 11580
    Soldier never pensioned.
Jacob, widow Mary... W 18422
James, widow Grace.. W 19640
John.. S 11809
    Paris, N. Y., in 1832.
    (Also given as Ichabod WALDIN.)
John.. S 11851
    Pensioned as serg't. in Chataqua Co., N. Y., in 1832.
John, widow Polly... W 26067
    Delaware Co., N. Y., in 1832; BLWt. 29008-160-55.
John, Conn. & Cont... S 14873
    Pensioned as private & corp. in Rome, N. Y., in 1832.
John, Conn. & Navy.. S 23072
    Pensioned as private & teamster in Darien, N. Y., in 1832.
Joseph.. S 40704
    Waterford, Penna., in 1818.
Joseph, Conn. & Navy.. S 14868
    New London Co., Conn., in 1832.
Nathan.. S 49269
Nathaniel, Naomi Menter, former widow of... R 19136
    Soldier never pensioned.
Obed... S 35741
Peter... S 11829
    Saratoga Co., N. Y., in 1832.
Peter, widow Mary... W 18435
Prince. (See STARKWEATHER.)
Robert, Hannah Fitch, former widow of.. W 10990
    New London Co., Conn., in 1818; died there in 1822.
Robert, Conn. & Cont.. S 17200
    Groton, Conn., in 1832.
Robinson... S 23493
Samuel William, Conn. & Cont., widow Emily... W 26071
    BLWt. 2347-300, Capt., was issued May 14, 1796.   No papers.
Silas, Conn. & Vt.. R 11620
Simeon, widow Prudence.. R 11609
    Soldier never pensioned.
Solomon.. S 14862
    New London Co., Conn., in 1832.
Solomon, widow Lucy... W 20133
    Soldier served as serg't. and died in 1807; widow in Broome Co., N. Y., in 1847.
Solomon, Conn. & Cont... S 14867
    Oneida Co., N. Y., in 1832.
Sophia, former widow of Enos CRANE.
Thomas... S 6428
    Soldier served between six and seven yrs. in Revolution, and received wounds for which
    in 1806, while resident of East Haddam, Conn., he rec'd pension of $20,00 per annum.
Thomas... S 6421
    Lorain Co., Ohio, in 1832.
Thomas, BLWt. 1275-100.
    Wilkes-Barre, Penna., in 1828.

WILLIAMS, Thomas, widow Content.. W 19645
    Soldier died at Hartford, Conn., in 1817.
    Uriah, Cont. service but Conn. residence in 1818, widow Johannah or Jehannah............ W 22665
    Veach... S 17789
    Warham or Wareham, widow Anna... W 11856
    Weeks or Wilks, widow Tamer... W 26059
    William, BLWt. 26352-160-55... S 14832
        Fairfield Co. ,Conn., in 1832.
    William or William R... R 11624
WILLIAMSON, Nathan... S 11789
WILLIS, Daniel, Cont. (Conn.).. S 44064
    Silvanus. (See WILLES.)
    (See also WYLLIS and WYLLYS.)
WILLISTON, Payson, BLWt. 23118-160-55.. S 17787
WILLMOT, Timothy, Conn. & Cont., widow Polly.. W 26036
    (See also WILMOT and WILMOTT.)
WILLOUGHBY, Bliss.. S 7914
    Salmon, widow Ruby, BLWt. 28598-160-55... W 2634
    Samuel, Conn. & Privateer.. S 11807
WILLS, Joel.. S 19166
    Jonathan, Conn. & Cont., widow Lydia... W 19644
WILLSON, John... S 15713
    Born 1764; Fairfield Co., Conn., in 1832.
    John.. R 11668
        (Also given WILSON.)
    Joseph, widow Eleanor.. W 18443
        (Also WILSON.)
    Sarah, former widow of Samuel DIX.
    Thomas.. S 44091
        (Also WILSON.)
WILLYS, Thomas, Conn. & Cont.. S 17784
    (See also WILLIS & WYLLIS.)
WILMOT, Timothy. (See WILLMOTT.)
    Walter... S 35736
        (Also WILLMOTT.)
WILMOTT, Elijah... R 11648
WILSON, Abiel... S 35739
        (Also given Abial WILLSON.)
    Asa, widow Joanna... W 26037
    Calvin, widow Submit... W 18424
    Daniel S... S 14837
    Elnathan... S 24014
    George... S 23079
    Jacob, Conn. & Cont., widow Ruth.. W 22621
    James, Cont. (Conn.).. R 11658
    Javin... S 35738
    Joab... S 17783
    John, widow Sally, BLWt. 13736-160-55... W 2679
        (Also given WILLSON.)
        Soldier was born in 1762; in Thompson, Conn., in 1818, and died there in 1838.
    John.. S 16296
        Born in 1760; in Clinton Co., N. Y., in 1832.
    John, Conn. & N. Y... S 32075
        Born in 1762; in Sharon, Conn., in 1832.
    John, Conn., Cont. & Penna.. S 44069
        Born in 1755; in Cayuga Co., N. Y., in 1820.
    John, Conn. & Privateer.. S 14847
        Born in 1749; in Thompson, Conn., in 1818 & 1832. (Also given WILLSON.)
    Jonathan.. S 17791
    Lewis.. R 11673
    Moses.. S 17792
    Nathaniel, Conn. & Navy, widow Ruth.. W 26062
    Nehemiah, widow Rachel.. W 18437
    Peter... R 11681
    Samuel... S 15709
        Hartford, Conn., in 1832.
    Samuel, widow Eleanor.. W 18438
        Fairfield Co., Conn., in 1832; died in 1842.
    Thomas, Conn. & N. Y., widow Sarah, BLWt. 61162-160-55............................. W 10280
        (See also WILLSON.)
WILTON. (See WELTON.)
WINCHEL, John... S 17790
    William, widow Elviry... W 19651
        (Also given WINCHELL.)
WINCHESTER, Jabez.. S 14871
    Richard, widow Lydia... W 9027
WINDHAM, Thomas, widow Sarah... W 9020
WINSHIP, Jabez, widow Hannah... R 11725
    Soldier never pensioned.
WINSLOW, Hannah, former widow of Oliver BROWN.
WINTER, Abner, widow Anna... R 11733
    Soldier never pensioned.
    Asa, widow Lydia... W 14158
    Jonathan W... S 17202
    Nicholas... S 11797
WINTERS, Juvenil, widow Amelia, BLWt. 3818-160-55... W 2217
    (Also given Juvenal WINTER.)
WINTON, Joseph, Conn., Cont. & Privateer.. S 11814
    Nathan... S 39899
WINTWORTH. (See WENTWORTH.)

WIRE, Samuel, Cont. (Conn.), widow Eunice... W 18441
    (See also WAIR, WARE, WEARE, WIER.)
WISE, William, Cont. (Conn.)... S 11791
WITHERILL, David.. R 11750
    (Also given WETHERLY.)
WITHY. (See WETHY.)
WITTER, Ebenezer, Conn. & Mass.. S 11802
  Jonah... S 17793
  Josiah, Conn. & Mass... S 41359
  William.. R 11757
WOLCATT, Solomon. (See WOLCOTT.)
WOLCOTT, Abiel... R 11761
  Benajah.. S 40729
    (Also given WOLCOT.)
  Elijah, widow Mary.. W 22678
    Erastus, BLWt. 2346-300, Capt., was issued Feb. 23, 1799, to Chloe Wolcott, guardian to
    Erastus, Chloe Jr., Edward, Julius, otherwise called Julah, and Helen Wolcott (minors),
    the only surviving heirs. No papers.
  John, Conn. & Boat service on Lake Champlain, widow Martha............................... W 20137
    (Also given WOOLCOTT.)
  Joseph, Sarah Hixon, former widow of.. W 21336
    (Also given WOLCUTT.)
    NOTE.—Sarah's last husband, Elkanah HIXSON, was also pensioned. (See Mass.
    S 39694.)
  Josiah, widow Elizabeth, BLWt. 17733-160-55.. W 9034
  Oliver.. R 11763
  Samuel, widow Jerusha.. W 22535
    Soldier died in 1813 at Hatford, Conn.
  Samuel, Conn. & R. I., widow Sarah.. R 11765
    Soldier was pensioned from Lexington. N. Y., in 1818.
  Solomon, widow Cornelia, BLWt. 26527-160-55.. W 26096
    (Also given WOOLCOTT & WOLCATT.)
  William, widow Huldah, BLWt. 11070-160-55.. W 26090
WOLCUTT. (See WOLCOTT.)
WOLF, Levi. (See De WOLF, Levy.)
  Seth. (See D'WOLF.)
WOOD, Abner, widow Betsey.. W 18377
  Asa... S 17798
  Benjamin... R 11779
  Benjamin... S 40732
  Charles... S 39916
  Daniel, Conn. & Vt... S 14898
  David, widow Electa, BLWt. 12848-160-55.. W 6564
  Eli, Conn. & N. Y., widow Rhoda.. W 16480
    (Also given WOODS.)
  Elisha, Conn. & R. I... S 14902
  Jacob... S 44095
    Putnam Co., N. Y., in 1818.
  Jacob... S 44102
    Pensioned as Jacob, Sen., in Orange Co., N. Y., in 1818.
  Jared, Conn. & N. Y... S 11882
  Joel, Conn. & Cont.. S 17206
  John, widow Nabby or Nebby.. W 26110
    Serg't. died in 1832 in New London Co., Conn.
  John.. S 18663
    Lyme, Conn.. in 1832.
    (Also WOODS.)
  John, Conn., Cont. & Privateer... S 11868
    Serg't in East Windsor, Conn., in 1832.
  John, Conn. & N. H.. R 11790
  John, Conn. & Vt., widow Abigail... R 11774
    Soldier never pensioned.
  Joseph... S 23084
  Lemuel, widow Elizabeth or Elizebeth.. W 4106
  Levi, Conn. & Vt.. S 6446
    Mary, former widow of Jonathan KNEELAND.
  Nathan... S 11870
  Nathaniel, Conn., Green Mt. Boys & Vt., Lois Collins, former widow of.................... W 16928
  Samuel... S 35748
    Fairfield Co., Conn., in 1819.
  Samuel... S 44101
    Camden, N. Y., in 1818.
    Sarah, former widow of Rufus WHEELER.
  Silas... S 35747
  Solomon, Cont. (Conn.), widow Christiana, BLWt. 31764-160-55............................. W 2427
  Thomas, widow Abigail.. W 27506
    Soldier pensioned from Springfield, Mass., in 1818; widow pensioned in 1836.
  Thomas, Conn. & Mass.. S 14879
    Schuyler, N. Y., in 1832.
    (See also WOODS.)
WOODARD, James. (See Josiah.)
  Jesse, Conn. & Vt.. S 14967½
  Josiah or James, widow Jane.. W 26100
    (See also WOODWARD.)
WOODBRIDGE, George, Conn. & Privateer.. S 11877
    Theodore, BLWt. 2339-400, Major, was issued April 14, 1790, to William Wells, Assignee. No
    papers.
WOODBURN, Moses.. S 22605
WOODCOCK, John.. R 11812
  Samuel, widow Rhoda... W 9169

WOODDIN. (See WOODIN.)
WOODEN. Charles... S 15722
  Jeremiah. (See WOODIN.)
WOODETH, Benjamin, Cont. (Conn.)... S 16025
WOODFORD, Bissel.. S 11873
  Joseph... S 29561
  Timothy... S 41370
WOODHOUSE, Samuel, widow Abigail.. W 26108
WOODIN, Aner, Cont. (Conn.), widow Ruth.. W 18365
  Jeremiah.. BLWt. 1891–100
    (Also given WOODEN and WOODDIN.)
  Philo.. S 45161
WOODRUFF, Amos... S 14901
  Baldwin, Cont. (Conn.), Bede Hough, former widow of.. W 14926
    (Also given Nathaniel Baldwin.)
  Gedor, widow Sarah.. W 26102
  Jason.. R 11819
  John, widow Sarah... W 16483
    Berkshire Co., Mass., in 1832; died in 1834; widow in Columbia Co., N. Y., in 1836.
  John, Conn. & Privateer.. S 15721
    Torrington, Conn., in 1832.
  Joseph, Cont. (Conn.).. S 14889
  Lambert... R 11821
  Nathaniel Baldwin. (See Baldwin.)
  Noadiah, widow Dorcas... W 18366
  Oliver, Conn. & Privateer.. S 14885
  Philo.. S 15720
  Samuel.. S 7964
    Bradford Co., Penna., in 1832.
  Samuel.. S 14875
    Litchfield Co., Conn., in 1832.
  Samuel.. S 39915
    Chenango Co., N. Y., in 1818; transferred to Penna.
  Samuel, widow Chloe, BLWt. 36545–160–55.. W 4406
    Soldier in Windsor Co., Conn., in 1832.
  Selah, widow Caroline.. W 11882
  Solomon, widow Chestinah or Christina... W 18367
  William, widow Ruth... W 20136
WOODS, Justus.. S 35746
  (See also WOOD.)
WOODWARD, Aaron.. R 11836
  Abner... S 11866
  Asa.. S 41371
    Fairlee, Vt., in 1818.
  Asa, Conn., Mass. & Vt., widow Ruth.. W 6579
    Licking Co., Ohio, in 1832.
  Asa, Conn., Conn. Sea service & Cont., widow Sally... W 26129
    Lyme, Conn., in 1832; died in 1840.
  Ebenezer.. S 41372
  Frederick... R 11838
  Gideon.. S 11897
  Hezekiah, widow Aseneth... W 3640
  James. (See WOODARD, Josiah.)
  John, Conn. & Vt... S 14877
  Joshua.. S 11879
  Noah.. S 11874
  Oliver... S 40727
  Reuben.. S 11864
    (See also WOODARD.)
WOODWORTH, Abel, Navy (Conn.).. S 23496
  Benjamin.. S 11881
  Darius.. S 36851
  Dyer, Conn. & N. Y... S 17799
  Ezra... S 4733
  Ichabod... S 32080
  Jedediah, widow Adah.. W 18362
  Joseph, Cont. (Conn.), widow Wayty... W 6584
  Josiah, Cont. (Conn.)... S 14890
  Roger... S 41373
  Roswell, Conn. & N. H., widow Phebe.. W 18369
  Samuel, widow Sally, BLWt. 26922–160–55... W 26095
  Swift.. S 29560
  Timothy, widow Lydia, BLWt. 6290–160–55.. W 2475
  William... S 29559
  Ziba, widow Lucy... R 11848
    Soldier was an Invalid pensioner.
WOOLBRIDGE. (See WOOLDRIDGE.)
WOOLCOTT. (See WOLCOTT.)
WOOLDRIDGE, William, Conn. & War of 1812; Catharine Austin, former widow of.......... W 10359
  (Also given WOOLBRIDGE.)
WOOLSEY, Gilbert... S 14884
  John... S 10047
WOOLWORTH, Ebenezer.. BLWt. 1023–100
  Levi... S 45456
WOOSTER, Benjamin, widow Sally.. W 2396
  David, BLWt. 2285–850, Brigadier General, was issued July 27, 1789, to Thomas WOOSTER,
    Admr.
  Ephraim... S 14883

WOOSTER, Lemuel .... S 14887
    Moses, Conn. & Cont., BLWt. 1806–100 .... S 46333
    Thomas, BLWt. 2360–300, Capt., was issued July 27, 1789. No papers.
    Walter, widow Ursula .... W 26106
WORDEN, Benjamin .... S 40724
    (Also given WARDEN.)
    Billings .... S 14886
    Elizabeth, former widow of Obed HOLCOMB.
    (Also given WORDIN.)
    Ichabod, James and Jesse. (See WARDEN.)
    Joseph .... S 35749
    Roger, Conn. & N. Y .... S. 14891
    Sylvester or Silvester .... S 45463
    Thomas, widow Jemima .... W 4407
    Wait, widow Diannah .... R 11864
        Soldier pensioned in 1832 from Remsen, N. Y.
    William. (See WORDIN.)
WORDIN, Elizabeth. (See WORDEN.)
    John, Conn. & N. Y .... S 14776
    (Also WARDEN.)
    William, widow Dorcas .... W 22679
    (Also WORDEN.)
WORNER, Abner .... S 34569
    (See also WARNER.)
WORREN, James, Conn. & Cont .... S 45452
    (Given also WARREN.)
WRIGHT, Abijah, widow Sally, BLWt. 26876–160–55 .... W 2477
    Abraham, Conn. & Conn. Sea service, widow Rebecca .... W 22699
    Asher, widow Bulah .... W 22700
        Killingworth, Conn., in 1832; died in 1833.
    Asher, Cont. (Conn.) .... S 36854
        Coventry, Conn., in 1818.
    Benjamin .... S 36852
        Killingworth, Conn., in 1818.
    Benjamin, Cont. (Conn.), widow Susanna .... W 19662
        Genesee Co., N. Y., in 1818 & 1832.
    Charles, widow Betsey, BLWt. 6391–160–55 .... W 3486
    Cornelius .... S 45467
    Daniel .... S 32086
        Wethersfield, Conn., in 1832.
    Daniel, widow Mabel .... W 26133
        Hartford Co., Conn., in 1818; died in 1831.
    Deborah, former widow of Samuel BATES.
    Ebenezer .... —
        Wethersfield, Conn., and died in 1808.
    Elijah, widow Jane .... W 26135
    Ephraim .... S 19515
    Francis .... BLWt. 1118–100
    George, widow Elizabeth, BLWt. 7062–160–55 .... W 22702
    James, widow Elizabeth .... W 9038
        Soldier died in 1813 in Ashtabula Co., Ohio.
    James, Conn. & Navy .... S 36857
        Killingworth, Conn., in 1818.
    Jeremiah .... S 36856
    Joab, widow Peninah .... W 6598
    John .... S 36858
        Saybrook, Conn., in 1818.
    John .... S 45464
        Unadilla, N. Y., in 1818.
    John .... S 45466
        Greene Co., N. Y., in 1818.
    Jonathan .... S 11908
        Litchfield Co., Conn., in 1832.
    Jonathan, widow Margaret or Pegga .... W 11895
        Granville, Mass., in 1832; died in 1837.
    Joseph Allyn, Conn. & Cont .... S 36855
        BLWt. 2342–400, Major, was issued October 30, 1789. No papers.
    Mary, former widow of Moses WEST.
    Moses, widow Abigail .... W 18385
    Reuben .... S 17212
    Roswell, widow Abigail .... W 26134
    Roxavene, former widow of Martin DENSLOW.
    Samuel .... S 14904
        Oneida Co., N. Y., in 1832.
    Samuel, Conn. & Mass., widow Jemima .... R 11890
        Soldier never pensioned.
    Simeon, widow Sarah .... W 16797
WRISLE, George .... S 17800
WRISLEY, Samuel .... S 32085
WYLIE, James .... S 11816
    (Also WILEY.)
    Peter .... S 41392
WYLLIS, John Palsgrave, BLWt. 2336–400, Major, was issued July 27, 1789. No papers.
WYLLYS, Samuel, BLWt. 2341–500, Colonel, was issued October 12, 1789. No papers.
    (See also WILLIS, WILLES and WILLYS.)

Y.

YALE, Daniel.. S 11912
    James... S 11914
    Waitstill or Wate.. S 36860
YARINGTON, Daniel... S 45478
    (Also given YARRINGTON.)
YEOMANS, Edward, wid. Gratiss, BLWt 8181-160-55........................... W 11902
    (Also given YOMANS.)
    Joshua, wid. Elizabeth.. W 20145
    Samuel... S 22612
YOMANS. (See YEOMANS.)
YONG. (See YOUNG.)
YORK, Allen... S 17217
    Elisha, wid. Sarah, BLWt. 1959-160-55.. W 18246
    James.. S 17218
    Jeremiah, widow Thankful, BLWt. 27662-160-55............................ W 2045
    Sawney... S 36862
    (See also CROSBY, Sawney.)
YOUNG, Ebenezer, widow Elizabeth.. W 22713
    (Also given YONG.)
    Eli.. S 11920
    Isaac... S 22615
    John, Conn. & N. Y... S 14912
    Joseph. (See YOUNGS.)
    Joseph, Conn. & Mass... S 11926
    Robert, Conn. & N. Y., wid. Abigail.. W 20150
    Solomon.. S 14911
    (Also given YOUNGS.)
    Stephen, Conn., Cont. & R. I.. S 22072
    William, Conn., Navy & Privateer, widow Mary............................ W 20148
YOUNGLOVE, John, Conn. & Cont.. S 45486
    Moses, Conn. & N. Y., widow Polly.. W 4410
YOUNGS, Benjamin... S 36863
    Joseph... S 24032
    (Also given YOUNG.)

Z.

ZIBBERE, Bristo, wid. Silvia... R 11986
    NOTE.—Soldier never applied for a pension. Widow was a resident of Norwich, Conn., when she applied and stated that they were married in 1781 in that town, where they had lived as boy and girl.